Staffing the New Workplace

Also available from ASQC Quality Press

The Reward and Recognition Process in Total Quality Management
Stephen B. Knouse

Making Training Work: How to Achieve Bottom-Line Results and Lasting Success
Berton H. Gunter

Integrating Reengineering with Total Quality
Joseph N. Kelada

Avoiding the Pitfalls of Total Quality
Charles C. Poirier and Steven J. Tokarz

The Change Agents' Handbook: A Survival Guide for Quality Improvement Champions
David W. Hutton

Reinventing Communication: A Guide to Using Visual Language for Planning, Problem Solving, and Reengineering
Larry Raymond

Managing the Four Stages of TQM: How to Achieve World-Class Performance
Charles N. Weaver

TQM: Quality Training Practices
Richard S. Johnson

To request a complimentary catalog of ASQC Quality Press publications, call 800-248-1946.

For a CCH Incorporated book catalog, call 800-TELL-CCH, priority code 9402.

STAFFING THE NEW WORKPLACE

Selecting and Promoting for Quality Improvement

Ronald B. Morgan and Jack E. Smith

ASQC Quality Press
Milwaukee, Wisconsin

CCH Incorporated
Chicago, Illinois

Staffing the New Workplace: Selecting and Promoting for Quality Improvement
Ronald B. Morgan and Jack E. Smith

Library of Congress Cataloging-in-Publication Data

Morgan, Ronald B., 1952–
    Staffing the new workplace: selecting and promoting for quality
improvement / Ronald B. Morgan, Jack E. Smith.
        p.   cm.
    Includes bibliographical references and index.
    ISBN 0-87389-361-1
    1. Employee selection. 2. Employees—Recruiting. 3. Manpower
planning.   I. Smith, Jack E., 1942–   .   II. Title.
HF5549.5.S38M67   1996
658.3'11—dc20   95-4512
                                                                          CIP

ISBN 0-87389-361-1

Acquisitions Editor: Susan Westergard
Project Editor: Kelley Cardinal

ASQC Mission: To facilitate continuous improvement and increase customer satisfaction by identifying, communicating, and promoting the use of quality principles,
concepts, and technologies; and thereby be recognized throughout the world as the
leading authority on, and champion for, quality.

Attention: Schools and Corporations
ASQC Quality Press books, audiotapes, videotapes, and software are available at
quantity discounts with bulk purchases for business, educational, or instructional
use. For information, please contact ASQC Quality Press at 800-248-1946, or write
to ASQC Quality Press, P.O. Box 3005, Milwaukee, WI 53201-3005.

For a free copy of the ASQC Quality Press Publications Catalog, including ASQC
membership information, call 800-248-1946.

For a CCH Incorporated book catalog, call 800-TELL-CCH, priority code 9402.

Printed in the United States of America

 Printed on acid-free paper

ASQC
Quality Press
611 East Wisconsin Avenue
Milwaukee, Wisconsin 53202

CCH INCORPORATED
4025 W. Peterson Avenue
Chicago, IL 60646-6085
1 800 TELL CCH

To Joann Lynch Petrie, my high school English teacher,
and my parents, Robert and Nancy Morgan.

—RBM

To my sons Jake and Casey
and a special group of friends at White Lake.

—JES

I am myself reminded that we are not all alike;
there are diversities of natures among us
which are adapted to different occupations.

—Plato's *Republic*

Contents

Preface

It is a fact that the world of work is rapidly changing. And much of that change can be directly or indirectly attributed to the strategic decision many organizations have made to focus on providing quality goods and services. To be effective in the quality-oriented organization, employees must possess a higher degree of technical and problem-solving skills and be able to work well in a more participative and team-oriented environment. For example, the plant worker of the past was hired and trained to perform "a" job. Today, in a total quality organization, that same worker will likely be required to perform a wide variety of duties and jobs and be expected to collect and interpret quality data, systematically apply problem-solving techniques, operate in a team environment, and continually learn and develop.

Similarly, the role of management is substantially changing. Traditional management functions of planning, directing, and controlling are rapidly giving way to a new set of quality-related skills. Managers are now expected to involve and empower their employees, assume the role of coach and facilitator, and continually improve their work processes. And if it hopes to survive, the entire organization must adopt a customer focus and become lean and adaptable. Finally, and most importantly, the firm and all of its employees must be flexible and prepared to embrace the changes that will continue to occur in the modern workplace.

Clearly, this new work environment has created the need for individuals who can both manage and adapt to these changes. The knowledge and skills once required to perform effectively on the job are no longer adequate for today's workplace. A new set of attributes (for example, W. Edwards Deming's "profound knowledge") is needed for the quality environment to flourish. This book is about how to recruit, select, and promote for that new set of attributes.

In particular, we hope to strengthen the link between the firm's strategic quality initiative and its entire staffing process. As such, we attempt to convince those individuals spearheading the quality initiative that the staffing process should be an integral part of their change strategy. Similarly, we hope to persuade human resource (HR) professionals that they should more closely align their staffing activities with the strategic quality initiative of the organization.

We have attempted to demonstrate wherever possible the contributions that staffing can make to quality. In doing so, we've taken a page from quality theory and practice by assuming that staffing, like any process, can be systematically described, studied, measured, analyzed, and improved—and then improved again. We also argue that the staffing process, in many ways, may be the organization's most important process because it becomes the building block for all other activities. People determine the strategic direction of the firm. People make suggestions and improve processes. And people provide the goods and services that meet the customers' needs and expectations. Thus, paying careful attention to who is hired, promoted, and retained makes good business sense in today's competitive environment.

In an effort to make the book relevant, we have attempted to illustrate the various staffing concepts and issues using the experiences of several benchmark organizations. While little has been written concerning staffing the new workforce, our research has uncovered many organizations that have, in fact, attempted to modify their staffing processes to address those changes.

We also attempt to elevate the status of staffing in the new work environment. Implicit in most efforts at introducing quality is the notion that it can be simply introduced and then trained. But the fact is that many of the attributes associated with quality are not available in the present workforce and are not easily trained for in practice. Willingness to work as part of a team, being a self-starter, openness to learning, and many other quality-related attributes should become important considerations when making staffing decisions.

Finally, we contend that staffing decisions will become more frequent and critical in the organization of the future. Historically, staffing decisions were made at the onset of employment and then possibly later for promotion. The new quality-focused organization will require constant staffing decisions as workers move from one location or project to another and in and out of the firm.

The purpose of this book is to provide practicing managers, teams, quality professionals, and HR professionals with a comprehensive guide to the issues and techniques involved in staffing the contemporary quality-oriented organization.

It is our intent that the resources we have assembled here will provide guidance in designing, implementating, and improving your staffing process.

Acknowledgments

While it is impossible to thank all those who contributed to this effort, several individuals and groups warrant special recognition. Those individuals include Ann Reilly, who provided clerical, editorial, and (most importantly) emotional support; Brenda MacDonald, who conducted literature research, analyzed survey results, and developed examples of interview questions for the leadership chapter; and Nicole White, who provided clerical support and assembled the quality recruiting sources. We also thank Paul and Susan ("the comma lady") Nielsen for their reviews of early manuscript drafts, and Roy Richardson for his multiple reviews and insightful comments and recommendations.

Our efforts to make this book practitioner-oriented required extensive input from several benchmark organizations and consulting firms. In particular, we are thoroughly impressed with the time and support given by representatives from the "big three" consulting firms that specialize in the staffing and development of the new workforce: Pam Owens of Developmental Dimensions International, Bridgeville, Pennsylvania; John Arnold of HRStrategies, Grosse Pointe, Michigan; and Tim Hansen of Personnel Decisions, Inc., Minneapolis, Minnesota. They all contributed examples and case studies to the book. Each of these three firms consistently apply the concepts we preach here. We also want to sincerely thank Kimberly Rath and the many quality-focused organizations that contributed their examples of "best staffing practices" for inclusion in the book. We especially thank Jim McSheffrey of 3M Canada.

Our final words of acknowledgment go to the staff members at ASQC Quality Press for their encouragement and support during the writing and production of the book. ASQC practices what it preaches in terms of quality and service. In particular, we want to thank acquisitions editor Susan Westergard for her belief in and support for the project from the very beginning. Thanks also to project editor Kelley Cardinal for guiding our efforts throughout development. Kelley demonstrated a great deal of patience as she praised us when we needed encouragement, pushed us when we needed nudging, and provided the support we needed to complete the project. Finally, thanks to production editor Annette Wall for her flexibility, cheerful nature, and professionalism in guiding the book through production.

While the input of those listed was invaluable, we take complete responsibility for the content of this book. The concepts presented throughout the text delineate good theory and practice, yet they represent the viewpoint of the authors and not necessarily those of the various contributors.

Ronald B. Morgan
Jack E. Smith

Introduction to Staffing the New Workplace

Overview

First, we begin this chapter by describing the impact effective, systematic staffing can have on an organization. Second, we present a process model of staffing and use the model to review the content of this book. Third, we introduce and describe a benchmark organization that appears at various points throughout the book. Fourth, we present an overview of a recent survey of staffing practices in quality-oriented settings. Finally, we end the chapter with a primer on the application of process improvement tools to the staffing process.

The Challenge and Opportunity of Effective Staffing

Organizations are undergoing profound changes as they implement quality improvement concepts and techniques. A variety of tools and processes (such as benchmarking, process improvement, reengineering, problem-solving teams, self-managed teams), either used individually or packaged in total quality initiatives, are remaking organizations. The staffing challenges experienced within organizations as they implement quality improvement processes can be summarized in the following observations.

A New Workforce. First, a quality-oriented organization requires employees with a greater variety and complexity of skills than those that typified traditional organizations. For example, group problem solving, data analysis, design of experiments, and interpersonal skills needed in team and customer interactions are valued attributes. Furthermore, these new settings place greater value on personality and temperament factors such as flexibility/adaptability; openness to learning, development, and retraining; and initiative. Some have characterized the new workplace as requiring "the whole person."[1] It is clear that the availability and development of these diverse attributes will be critical to the competitiveness of organizations and, in fact, to the competitiveness of nations, throughout the coming decade.[2]

Individual Differences. A second important observation is that individuals differ in the degree to which they possess the attributes needed to successfully contribute within the quality-oriented organization. They differ in both the level at which they have mastered relevant knowledge and skills, and in their capacity and willingness to accept and apply these principles. Organizations have discovered this as they've installed quality processes. Some individuals easily adapt to the challenge of quality, while others struggle, and some even resist. Because individuals vary in these important, complex attributes, organizations must employ staffing practices capable of accurately identifying these individual differences.

Impending Scarcity of Critical Attributes. Related to our observation that individuals vary in the extent to which they possess the attributes needed in the new workplace is the observation of a growing skills shortage. It is suggested that large segments of the workforce are deficient, not only in basic skills, but in the attributes needed to succeed in the new organization. For example, Nynex Corporation recently reported that only 4 percent of 57,000 entry-level applicants performed adequately on its entry-level tests.[3] The fact that individuals differ, combined with the relative scarcity of some attributes, will place greater importance on the organization's staffing effort.

The Role of Staffing in "Making the Organization." A fourth observation is that staffing activities serve a defining, critical role in the overall effectiveness of the organization's workforce. As The Ritz-Carlton Hotel®, L.L.C. president, Horst Schulze, notes, "The company's success at quality begins with the right selection of employees."[4]

Many organizations contend that "our people are our most important asset." If that is true of your organization, then you will want to make effective decisions in the selection and promotion of these resources. As we demonstrate in this book, the investment made in staffing can pay great dividends in organizational competitiveness and profitability.

Building Quality into the Staffing Process Saves Resources. A fifth observation is that ineffective staffing is very costly to the organization. It is an adage in the quality profession that investment in quality actually saves resources and increases profitability. This is because the consumption of resources attributable to poorly designed processes (for example, inspection, waste, and rework) is costly. Improving the process reduces these costs. Similarly, it follows that there are clear costs associated with poorly conceived and poorly executed staffing efforts. First, training efforts and resources are diverted to remedial training (or rework), as new employees enter without the underlying attributes needed to function in total quality settings. Consequently, training costs soar. Second, individual and organizational strain results from the failure associated with poor selection decisions, as individuals are placed in employee and management roles for which they are poorly prepared. The strain associated with demotion or termination is disruptive in any setting. It is particularly counterproductive in the quality-oriented setting because those settings typically espouse a value for development, support, and fair treatment. The process of termination is particularly costly to the development of these cultural values. Third, the credibility of total quality processes is jeopardized as ill-prepared employees struggle with the philosophy and practices of quality improvement. For example, consider the application of process improvement tools. Clearly, these tools have merit. However, if employees are ill-prepared to master these tools (for example, they are lacking basic math or analytical skills) and their initial application fails, then the philosophy and practices of quality become stigmatized. Fourth, poorly designed staffing processes create competitive disadvantages as critical talent is lost to competitors. Simply put, you would prefer to employ that segment of the workforce that is most able and willing to prosper in your quality setting—the bright, flexible, customer-oriented workers—while your competitors rely on the remainder of the workforce.

There is research evidence to support the relationship between effective staffing practices and overall organization performance. A recent study investigated the relationship between five specific staffing practices (use of recruiting studies, validated selection tools, structured interviews, cognitive ability tests, and biographical predictors) and measures of organization performance. Overall, the use of these staffing practices was significantly related to annual profit ($r = .25, p < .05$), profit growth ($r = .15, p < .05$), and overall performance ($r = .20, p < .05$).

The magnitude of the relationship was even stronger in specific industries. For example, in the service industry, effective staffing practices were directly related to annual profit ($r = .72, p < .05$), to profit growth ($r = .86, p < .05$), to sales growth ($r = .86, p < .05$), and to overall performance ($r = .86, p < .05$). A similarly strong relationship was found in the financial industry where the use of effective staffing practices was directly related to annual profit ($r = .73, p < .05$), profit growth ($r = .71, p < .05$), sales growth ($r = .72, p < .05$), and overall performance ($r = .77, p < .05$).

We'll examine these five effective staffing practices in detail in later sections of this book. For now, the conclusion is clear: effective staffing practices do make a difference in organization performance.[5]

In summary, while training will always play a role in preparing a staff for any complex organization change, including a move toward quality improvement, it is the staffing practices that determine the extent to which the organization possesses the fundamental skills on which training efforts can build. A strategy that neglects staffing and relies solely on training will be costly and ineffective.

The Current State of Staffing for Quality. A study of the human resource (HR) practices of eight early Malcolm Baldrige National Quality Award winners found that those firms had made significant adjustments in virtually all of their HR practices, with the glaring exception of staffing. That study, published in 1993, found little change in the staffing practices in seven of the eight initial Baldrige Award winners.[6] Only Federal Express had, at that time, revised its staffing practices by establishing its now well-documented peer-based recruitment and selection centers. At the time, the authors of that study called for more attention to staffing in quality settings.

In an effort to determine how much progress had been made, we developed a survey. American Society for Quality Control (ASQC) sustaining member organizations were surveyed to address the question: To what extent has the quality improvement effort led organizations to revise their staffing practices? That survey revealed some interesting trends in the effort to staff for quality.[7] On the one hand, organizations appear to be incorporating quality attributes into their selection process. Furthermore, they appear to be doing so to a much greater extent for technical and managerial staff, and less so for hourly workers. The data in Table 1.1 summarize the extent to which that sample of ASQC sustaining member organizations are evaluating quality-related attributes in their staffing process.

While organizations appear to be more attentive to quality-related attributes, they do not, on the other hand, appear to be doing so in a systematic fashion. To investigate this question, we asked the sample of ASQC sustaining member organizations to identify specific assessment procedures used to evaluate quality attributes. Only 21 percent of the sustaining member organizations report that they use specific assessment tools to assess quality-relevant knowledge, skills, ability, and temperament in their hiring or promotion process. Presumably, the remaining organizations reporting that they evaluate quality attributes do so on an informal, subjective basis. What is the consequence of this neglect? Only 8.9 percent of those organizations report that their hourly hires are proficient in quality attributes; 39.8 percent report that their technical hires are proficient in quality attributes; and, 45.3 percent report that their managerial hires are proficient in quality attributes. Their response to date, as predicted, is to train. For example, 88 percent of the firms report that they must train their hourly hires in quality; 84 percent report that they must train their technical employees in quality; and 78.9 percent report that they must train their managerial hires in quality.[8]

Finally, there is mounting evidence to suggest those firms that made the greatest strides in revision of their staffing practices report greater success with their total quality effort. For example, in the study of ASQC sustaining member organizations, the greater the ex-

Table 1.1. Evaluating quality-related attributes in selection and promotion.

Survey question:	To what extent are quality-related attributes evaluated when making selection and promotion decisions?		
	Very little/ little	Some	Much/ extensive
Hourly	29.6%	41.3%	29.1%
Technical	19.1%	32%	48.9%
First-level management	19.5%	31.5%	49%
Middle management	17.5%	31.2%	51.3%
Senior management	22.3%	26.9%	50.8%

N = 206

tent to which the organization has incorporated the philosophy and practices of a total quality management (TQM) organization in how it does business, the more likely it is to include specific quality attributes in the staffing process.[9] Furthermore, a recent survey of 245 HR managers found that respondents from firms that had implemented more of these newer selection, promotion, and career development approaches described their TQM outcomes more positively in terms of commitment and effectiveness.[10]

To Train or Select?   Clearly, there is an optimum balance between staffing and training efforts. Furthermore, this balance changes as the organization gains greater experience with its quality tools and processes. Historically, as organizations initially installed quality processes, they stressed training of the existing workforce. However, as the typical quality initiative matures, and the organization strives to institutionalize these practices into its culture, it can turn increased attention to recruiting, screening, selecting, and promoting employees who will move comfortably into the total quality environment. They can select individuals who are more able and willing to learn and implement quality philosophy and practices. You will see as you read this book that many premier organizations are rethinking, revising, and even remaking their staffing process to make it more supportive of their quality initiative, and, in doing so, they can focus their training efforts in ways that are far more cost-effective. Staffing, therefore, can lay the basis for effective training.

Use Staffing to Reinforce the Quality Culture.   A final argument for stressing quality improvement in the staffing process is based on the fact that the selection and promotion process serves as an important means by which the organization strengthens and reinforces a culture supportive of the quality initiative. These principles are reinforced as applicants are selected, and as they are considered for subsequent promotions. It becomes clear to each employee that the principles and techniques of quality are central to how the organization functions, and it is in the best interest of each employee to master the underlying philosophy and skills. Conversely, imagine the message sent to the applicant when the organization promotes itself as a quality-oriented setting but then neglects to evaluate an applicant's quality-relevant knowledge, skills, and temperament, or neglects to promote those individuals who are willing and able to embrace the quality paradigm. Under these circumstances, both applicants and current employees are likely to view quality as mere rhetoric rather than as a central organization value.

Proactive Staffing. Because total quality organizations are now more dependent on such a diverse mix of attributes, and these attributes are variably distributed in the population of both internal and external applicants, it follows that they must be more proactive and systematic in the practices they use to identify, recruit, assess, select, and promote. Quality-oriented organizations can no longer assume that any individual can, through training and experience, develop the knowledge, skills, and temperament necessary to effective participation in the organization. Instead, organizations recognize that they must identify, select, and promote those individuals who will prosper within the total quality environment.

The complexity and variability in total quality attributes present both challenge and opportunity. The challenge requires that organizations adopt effective staffing practices; in particular, practices sophisticated enough to accurately identify, assess, select, and promote quality-oriented employees. The opportunity lies in the fact that there are systematic methods on which the organization can depend. The competitive advantage will go to the proactive organization that takes the necessary steps to systematically find, hire, and promote those individuals. That is the overall purpose of this book: to guide you in the sourcing, assessment, selection, and promotion of quality-ready employees.

Staffing as a Systematic Process

Consistent with the quality paradigm, effective staffing is conceived, planned, and executed as a process. This perspective has several important implications.

First, steps in the process are generally viewed as sequential. For example, a thorough understanding of the organization's strategic quality initiative and an analysis of the target position(s) is necessary before subsequent recruiting and selection activities can be conducted.

Second, a change in any one component is likely to influence other activities in the process. For example, an organization's efforts at downsizing some or all of its operations will directly impact its ability to attract and recruit qualified individuals for those openings that do occur.

Third, just like any other process, staffing can be systematically improved. Each component can be measured, systematically analyzed, and refined through the application of process improvement tools. We will take a closer look at the application of reengineering and process improvement to the staffing process later in this chapter.

The fourth implication of a systems view of staffing is that improvements made at the beginning of the process will have the most impact on the effectiveness of the overall system. The quality literature advises that the biggest payoff occurs when improvement efforts are focused upstream in a process. In terms of the human element, that means organization entry. We agree with one of W. Edwards Deming's suggestions for improving the organization system—"more careful selection of people in the first place."[11] Downstream efforts at training and developing employees will be much more effective if employees with the necessary attributes have been hired in the first place.

Fifth, viewing staffing as a process illustrates the fluid, dynamic nature of the contemporary system. Approximately 20 years ago staffing meant selecting from a group of individuals those most likely to perform effectively on "a" job, typically an entry-level position. Today, the movement into and out of organizations occurs at many points. Figure 1.1 depicts the flow of the contemporary staffing process. A review of that diagram shows the complex patterns of movement in and out of today's organization. Clearly, movement into, through, and out of organizations is far more dynamic than in past eras.

Design of the Staffing Process. The staffing process can be expressed in terms of a sequence of design questions.

- What is quality readiness? What specific attributes (knowledge, skills, aptitudes, and personal characteristics) must employees possess in a total quality setting? Which of these attributes are most relevant in your specific organization? Which of these attributes must new employees bring into your organization? Which attributes can and should be developed through training?

- By what legal, professional, and technical standards is the staffing process measured and evaluated? How are these standards designed into the staffing process?

- What role does the staffing function play in the strategic plan of the organization? How can systematic staffing contribute to the quality initiative?

- What recruiting strategies and sources will generate quality-oriented applicants?

- What tools (interviews, written tests, performance tests, reference checks) will yield useful information about applicants?

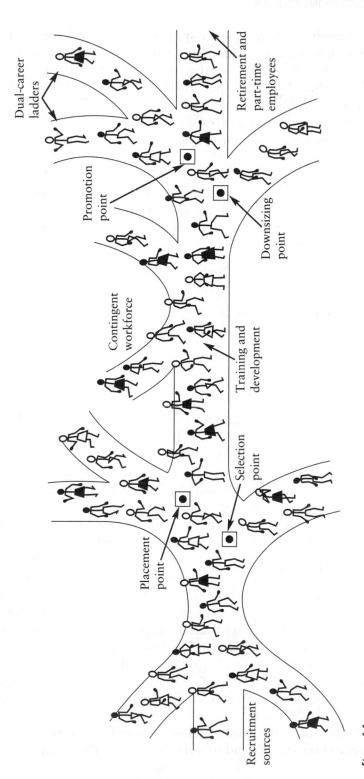

Figure 1.1. Staffing as a process.

9

What are benchmark companies doing now to build a staff for the challenges of the future?

- What should the organization do to foster continual development of its workforce?

- How can quality-oriented leaders be identified, selected, and developed?

- What factors should be considered when staffing teams?

- What effect will the issues of downsizing and the use of contingent workers have on the quality effort?

- How should the staffing process be evaluated and improved?

This book provides guidance on answering these questions and, by doing so, constructing an effective TQ-based employee selection and promotion process. Figure 1.2 presents the major components of that process. The next section outlines the content of the book and how it addresses these fundamental issues.

Organization of the Book

The following overview addresses the content of the book. We've organized this overview in terms of the fundamental questions of systematic staffing.

The Total Quality Success Profile: What Attributes Are Needed in Your Organization?   Chapters 2 and 4 address the first, fundamental question: What individual attributes (knowledge, skills, abilities, and personal characteristics) are required in the total quality organization, or, more generally speaking, in any organization intent on surviving in today's dynamic environment? To begin to address that question, we must first deal with the question of how quality-oriented organizations differ from traditional organizations. In chapter 2 we examine the changes in structure, culture, and work associated with successful quality initiatives. It is these changes—structure, culture, and work—that generate the need for new workforce attributes. We present profiles of these attributes in chapter 2 and build on them in chapter 4. The profiles we provide will serve as a valuable reference for the design of an organization-specific total quality skills profile. Toward that goal, chapter 4 presents a systematic process for building a company-specific quality success profile. In particular, the process we outline can be used to adapt the total

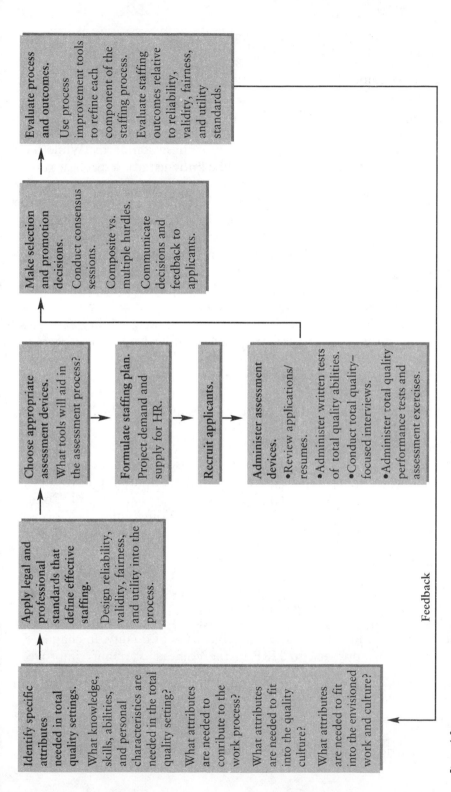

Identify specific attributes needed in total quality settings.

What knowledge, skills, abilities, and personal characteristics are needed in the total quality setting?

What attributes are needed to conribute to the work process?

What attributes are needed to fit into the quality culture?

What attributes are needed to fit into the envisioned work and culture?

Apply legal and professional standards that define effective staffing.

Design reliability, validity, fairness, and utility into the process.

Choose appropriate assessment devices.

What tools will aid in the assessment process?

Formulate staffing plan.

Project demand and supply for HR.

Recruit applicants.

Administer assessment devices.

• Review applications/resumes.

• Administer written tests of total quality abilities.

• Conduct total quality–focused interviews.

• Administer total quality performance tests and assessment exercises.

Make selection and promotion decisions.

Conduct consensus sessions.

Composite vs. multiple hurdles.

Communicate decisions and feedback to applicants.

Evaluate process and outcomes.

Use process improvement tools to refine each component of the staffing process.

Evaluate staffing outcomes relative to reliability, validity, fairness, and utility standards.

Feedback

Figure 1.2. An overview of the staffing process.

11

quality attribute profile to your organization. This attribute profile can then serve as the framework around which the entire staffing process is organized.

What Legal, Professional, and Technical Standards Must the Staffing Process Meet? There are technical and legal standards by which the staffing process is evaluated. Chapter 3 presents an overview of these standards. While the experienced staffing professional may be knowledgeable of these standards, work team members, quality professionals, and other practitioners will find this primer very useful. We believe that mastery of the content of that chapter will help you design, evaluate, and improve staffing practices. Knowledge of these standards will help you understand the basis for many of the recommendations we make in subsequent chapters. Also, abiding by the standards will help you avoid unnecessary, costly legal challenges, and will yield a greater return on the investment made in the staffing process.

We detail four traditional standards: reliability, validity, fairness, and utility (return on investment). These standards have been formulated by testing and staffing specialists and adopted by the courts and by administrative agencies such as the Equal Employment Opportunity Commission (EEOC). Together, these standards define effective staffing. Inattention to these standards results in wasted resources, poor hiring and promotion decisions, and even costly litigation. Consequently, these standards should be considered as we design the staffing process, choose assessment tools, assess applicants, make selection and promotion decisions, and evaluate staffing effectiveness. Chapter 3 also presents guidelines for the standardization and administration of employee selection processes, including guidelines for accommodation under the Americans with Disabilities Act (ADA).

How Can Staffing Contribute to the Organization's Long-Range Quality Strategic Plan? The transition toward a quality-driven organization is often a long, gradual process. Human resource planning (HRP) is an important means through which the organization systematically prepares its workforce for meeting the long-range strategic objectives of quality. In chapter 5 we outline an approach to HRP in the context of quality improvement, and we raise issues regarding contemporary HRP practices, such as the use of contingent workers in a quality improvement setting.

What Recruiting Strategies and Sources Will Yield a Desirable Pool of Quality-Oriented Applicants? An important determinant of the success of any staffing process is an effective recruiting process. In chapter 6 we present guidelines, strategies, and sources for recruiting applicants with interest and experience in quality improvement. An important theme underlies our discussion of recruiting: the manner in which the applicant is recruited and subsequently dealt with at each stage of the selection process sends important signals regarding the extent to which the organization truly values and embraces total quality principles. We argue that the organization must treat the applicant with the respect afforded a valued customer, communicate total quality values, and operate by those values at each stage of the staffing process.

What Tools (Interviews, Written Tests, Performance Tests, Reference Checks) Will Yield Useful Information About Applicants?

There is a rapidly emerging set of valid, useful assessment tools that focus on specific attributes needed in quality-oriented settings. The core content of this book, chapters 7 through 10, is a user's manual for these tools.

We begin chapter 7 by profiling the variety of assessment tools available for use in the quality setting. We then use the rest of chapter 7 and chapter 8 to take a closer look at specific tools. Chapter 7 deals primarily with paper-and-pencil measures that focus on individuals' ability to learn and perform in quality settings. For the most part, the measures profiled in chapter 7 are highly reliable, cost-effective tools that are most often used in early stages of the selection process. Specifically, we look at cognitive ability tests, basic reading and quantitative ability tests, and various biographical predictors such as application blanks and biographical inventories.

In chapter 8 we present instruments that go beyond measuring a person's ability to perform by measuring his or her fit within a quality culture and his or her willingness or motivation to perform. One instrument we profile is the Quality Orientation Inventory (QOI).[12] It measures six aspects of temperament relevant to the demands of a quality improvement setting (openness to learning, development, and retraining; flexibility/adaptability; team orientation; customer orientation; and conscientiousness). In addition to paper-and-pencil measures such as the QOI, the Personnel Decision Inc. (PDI) Customer Service Inventory (CSI), PDI's Employment Inventory (EI), and Hogan's Personality Inventory (HPI), a variety of assessment exercises can be constructed to measure these qualities.[13]

As you will see, there are some intriguing applications of testing for quality attributes. For example, in staffing a new manufacturing facility, 3M Canada used a variety of assessment tools that included work simulations. Applicants worked in a mock assembly process and at specific stages in the exercise were asked to work as a group to improve the production process. Trained judges observed the interactions of team members and their process improvement efforts. We will present more detail about this exciting project throughout the book. Simulations such as that used at 3M Canada represent an effective strategy for determining what the applicant actually can do, as well as how he or she will adapt to, and respond in, real work situations.

Chapters 9 and 10 focus on the most widely used (and misused) assessment technique, the employment interview. Unfortunately, as it is typically used, the interview is a poor predictor of the subsequent success or failure of applicants. Because it is so widely used, and can, in fact, be substantially improved through a set of best practices, we devote two chapters to the topic. In chapter 9 we review the underlying flaws in the typical interview process and present an approach to effective interviewing that has been demonstrated to improve the accuracy of selection decisions. In chapter 10 we present a guide for conducting an effective quality-focused interview.

What Should the Organization Do to Foster the Continual Development of Its Internal Workforce? Effective staffing requires proactive, continual development of the internal workforce. However, it is important that development be targeted at specific needs likely to produce the greatest individual and organizational return on investment (ROI). In chapter 11 we discuss issues and strategies related to individual career development in quality settings.

How Can Quality-Oriented Leaders Be Identified, Selected, and Developed? Joseph M. Juran notes that ineffective leadership does much damage to quality initiatives.[14] Chapter 12 deals specifically with the recruitment, selection, development, and promotion of leaders skilled in steering and nurturing quality improvement efforts. One critical characteristic required of the new leader is an understanding of the means by which to accomplish organizational change. Whereas executives and managers in traditional organizations were typically focused on financial strategy and planning, leaders in the new workplace must possess sophisticated knowledge and skill in steering organizational change. We conclude chapter 12 with example interview content for assessing managerial applicants' readiness to lead a quality improvement effort.

What Factors Should Be Considered When Staffing Teams? Chapter 13 addresses staffing processes in teams. First, we present a profile of the attributes needed within various forms of teams. Then, we alert the reader to issues regarding the role of teams in selection and promotion decisions.

Finally, we present example content for a behavioral-based interview focused on teamwork.

What Impact Will the Issues of Downsizing and the Use of Contingent Workers Have on the Quality Effort? In chapter 14 we address current issues related to staffing the new workplace. In particular, our focus is on downsizing and the wide and expanding use of contingent workers. We examine issues regarding the impact of contingent workers in the ASQC Survey of Staffing Practices. We present survey data addressing both the use of contingent workers and the perceived effects (costs and benefits) associated with their use.

How Should the Staffing Process Be Evaluated and Improved? The spirit and technologies of continuous process improvement and reengineering are applicable to the staffing efforts of organizations. Consequently, we devote subsequent sections of this introductory chapter to a framework for measuring, evaluating, and improving the staffing process. We'll turn to that topic shortly.

Staffing the New Workplace: Best Practices and Recommendations In chapter 15 we summarize the current view of best practices in staffing the new workplace and present what we believe are the priority best practices for making staffing supportive of the quality initiative.

About This Book

We would like to make a few observations about the objectives and content of this book. First, our intent is to give both the big picture of the staffing process as well as the details involved in implementing and conducting each phase of the process. Second, our goal is to give you a sound conceptual base in staffing issues *and* practical guidance in conducting staffing activities. We want this book to serve as a total quality staffing consultant as you plan, conduct, and evaluate staffing activities. We've incorporated a number of devices that we believe will help meet this goal. For example, we've included numerous illustrations from benchmark companies, detailing how each company has dealt with an important staffing issue. We've also incorporated a detailed look at one exemplary organization, 3M Canada Manufacturing. We'll share more about that example shortly.

We've organized this book as a discussion of staffing for quality. Consequently, we've focused our discussion and examples specifically on the attributes (knowledge, skills, temperament) needed for the employee to succeed within the total quality framework. However, although it is not our focus, it is important to note that selection and promotion processes must incorporate other employee attributes (for example, technical and functional skills) necessary for effective job performance. While our cases and examples focus on total quality attributes, the techniques we present are equally relevant and can be used to identify these additional attributes necessary for effective performance in the organization. This will be clear as you read each chapter.

We've structured the book so that it is relevant and applicable to both small and large organizations. However, this presents a bit of a challenge in that—at one level—the needs appear different in these two settings. The process we outline is probably more typical of a large organization that plans, recruits, hires, and promotes large numbers of applicants for a number of positions. Much of what we present is modeled after those settings. The small organization, on the other hand, is likely to have jobs with only a few, or even one, incumbent. Therefore, it clearly will not develop a very elaborate staffing process. However, it is our contention that it does make sense for the small organization to emulate the standards and values for staffing reflected in large-scale staffing efforts. For example, although the small organization may not conduct a comprehensive job analysis for hiring one person for one position, it will benefit by thinking systematically about the requirements for success in the position and in the organization. Similarly, while the small organization may not design an elaborate assessment center, it will improve its selection or promotion decisions by expanding its assessment process beyond the typical unstructured interview. In fact, we hope to highlight a number of effective tools (standardized tests, assessment exercises) that are cost-effective for the small employer.

Finally, we raise a number of issues regarding how staffing practices must change to support the new workplace. Some of these issues we address; others will require further research, evaluation, and input from staffing researchers and compliance agencies. One thing is clear: Staffing is changing and there is much to be resolved. The coming years will be an important, dynamic period in staffing.

Benchmark Illustrations

You will encounter numerous illustrations of exemplary staffing practices. We've assembled these examples though dialogue with numerous quality and HR professionals and through our own work within organizations. In addition, we present a recurring cohesion case that provides illustrations of effective staffing for quality. We'll introduce the organization now, and refer to it throughout the remainder of the book.

Cohesion Case: 3M Canada Manufacturing Group. The authors are exceptionally pleased with 3M Canada's willingness to participate in this effort and share information related to its staffing process. This organization was selected because of its long history of total quality values and because it has incorporated a number of innovative approaches to staffing for quality. Its long-held embrace of quality-oriented values in management of its workforce is evident in the following quote (circa 1943) from then-chairman William McKnight.

> *Challenge of Management . . . As our business grows, it becomes increasingly necessary to delegate responsibility and to encourage men and women to exercise their initiative. This requires considerable tolerance. Those men and women to whom we delegate authority and responsibility, if they are good people, are going to want to do their jobs in their own way. These are characteristics we want, and people should be encouraged as long as their way conforms to our general pattern of operations. Mistakes will be made, but if a person is essentially right, the mistakes he or she makes are not as serious in the long run as the mistakes management will make if it is dictatorial and undertakes to tell those under its authority exactly how they must do their job. Management that is destructively critical when mistakes are made kills initiative, and it is essential that we have many people with initiative if we are to continue to grow.[15]*

That spirit of empowerment is alive today, according to technical director Judith Benham. She notes, "One of my very first supervisors said, 'Don't ask permission, Judy, ask forgiveness. And, you really only need to ask forgiveness if you've done something seriously wrong. Even if you make a mistake, we'd rather have you take the initiative. Management wants to give employees at every level a long rope and see what they do with it.'"[16]

Known for its ability to nurture creativity and innovation, 3M has consistently been described as one of America's "best-run companies" and as one of the top companies to work for in America.[17]

A Survey of the Staffing Practices of ASQC Sustaining Member Organizations

In addition to the examples and case profiles, we've also included the results of a survey of quality-oriented organizations sponsored by ASQC. As you may well have noticed, we're so intrigued by some of the findings that we've already cited a few of the results, and we will share much more in the chapters that follow. At this point, we would like to provide some background on the project. The survey, conducted in July and August of 1994, investigated the staffing practices of ASQC sustaining member organizations. Each one of 720 organizations received a copy of the survey. Two hundred and six organizations participated by returning completed surveys, representing a participation rate of 30 percent. We focused our study on this segment of the ASQC population with the rationale that it represents those organizations that have the longest history with quality-improvement efforts. While the return rate of 30 percent limits our inferences to the larger population of sustaining member organizations, the magnitude of the sample—approximately 206 of the leading quality-oriented organizations—prompts us to contend that the descriptions provided by these organizations represent a worthwhile snapshot of the current status of staffing for quality.

What Issues Did the Survey Address?   The survey explored the specific quality programs; how those organizations recruit, assess, select, and promote for their quality efforts; and how emerging issues, such as downsizing and contingent workers, affect their quality effort. We've integrated discussions of survey findings throughout the book. Specific questions we investigated include the following.

- What quality tools are these organizations using, and how long have they been doing so? We detail these results in chapter 2.

- What attributes are most critical in a quality-oriented hourly workforce? What attributes are most important in the professional/technical workforce? What managerial attributes are most important to successful quality initiatives? We present these results in chapter 4.

- To what extent are quality organizations utilizing contingent workers? What positive and negative experiences result from the use of contingent workers? We explore these results in chapter 14.

- To what extent are organizations systematically evaluating the quality readiness of their applicants? Do they plan to increase or decrease their focus on selecting and promoting for quality?

- What assessment tools are being used to evaluate quality-relevant attributes?

- To what extent are new hires deficient in quality-related knowledge, skills, and temperament? To what extent must organizations train their new hires to make up for these deficiencies?

Improving the Staffing Process

The new workplace is focused on improvement of all work processes. Because the processes by which we manage human resources have such a strong impact on organization success, it follows that there will be substantial incentive to improve those processes. It makes perfect sense that the values and methods (tools) of process improvement and reengineering can be used to redesign or improve all phases of HR management. We believe that these tools are especially relevant to the staffing process. In the sections that follow, we lay the groundwork for the application of process improvement and reengineering methods to the staffing process. We draw on these principles throughout the remainder of the book.

Fundamentals of Systems Thinking

Components of a System. We can break any system down into components. The typical system consists of *inputs,* a series of interconnecting *transformation processes* (steps), and, hopefully, some kind of valued-added *output.* Suppliers provide inputs, and customers receive outputs of the system. Figure 1.3 depicts the systems model.

Inputs to Staffing (Suppliers). Systems thinking leads us to identify the inputs to the staffing process, and the suppliers of those inputs. Once identi-

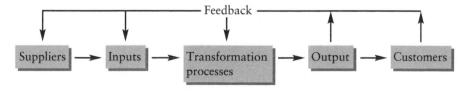

Figure 1.3. The process model.

fied, we can begin to improve the quality of those inputs. Does the staffing process have inputs? Absolutely, every recruit or candidate for an open position is an input to the process. The suppliers of those candidates consist of the various internal and external recruitment sources (internal postings, employment agencies, schools, search firms, temporary agencies). The hiring specification (success profile) is a second critical input to the process. Suppliers include all of the organization members who have input into its formulation. Can we improve the quality of hiring specifications by looking carefully at the sources and methods by which they are formulated? Can we improve our relationships with external recruitment sources? In our opinion, without doubt!

In general, process improvement says that we should select suppliers based on measures of quality as well as cost, reduce the number of those suppliers, and work more closely with those remaining to ensure high-quality inputs to the process. We'll discuss the management of HR suppliers in chapter 6. We'll talk more about the suppliers of input to success profiles in chapter 4.

Customers of the Staffing Process. A recent article contends that HR typically acts in a production, rather than in a service mode. "In other words, the HR function is carried out as if it were a manufacturing operation turning out uniform products for a homogeneous market rather than a service organization promoting unique offerings matched to diverse client needs."[18] Toward the goal of customer service, it is critical that we identify our staffing customers and take systematic steps to improve the extent to which the output of our process (new hires) meet and exceed the needs of those customers. HR researchers David E. Bowen and Edward E. Lawler note,

> A service-driven HR department functions like a high-quality service firm—a world-class resort, a gourmet restaurant, or an elite consulting firm. These firms thrive on satisfying clients. They emphasize the intangibles, customize their offerings to different clients, and involve their clients in decisions that affect the services rendered. HRM must learn to thrive on satisfying its clients (e.g., line managers). Services need to be offered that fulfill the unique and changing needs of different groups of managers and employees.[19]

An advantage of process thinking is that it focuses our attention on the internal and external customers of the process.

Who are the customers of the staffing process? We believe that we must think more broadly, beyond simply the hiring manager, when we define staffing customers. Customers certainly include the hiring manager, but also the peers and team members of the new hire, and speaking more broadly, all of the internal customers whose own work is affected by the new hire. As work has become more team based, cross functional, and cross level, the customer base affected by a specific staffing decision has expanded. An effective staffing process involves these customers in all phases of the process (the customers become input sources). For example, while the HR representative may have the specialized knowledge needed to formulate complete and useful staffing specifications, the content input of the end users is critical to both the quality and acceptability of the specification. Similarly, human resources must continue to collect data from its customers on, in the words of Bowen and Lawler, "how well it is doing."[20]

One important step in customer orientation is to remain attentive to customer needs and service satisfaction. This principle was applied recently in the state of Wisconsin. A survey process was used to measure managers' satisfaction with five aspects of the state's central staffing function: communication, timeliness, candidate quality, test quality, and service focus. Definitions of these dimensions of staffing customer satisfaction, and example survey items, are presented in Exhibit 1.1. The survey was administered to line and HR managers throughout the government, and the survey results were then used to guide the implementation of "several initiatives to improve service" leading to "increases in speed of service delivery, elimination of paperwork, higher reported applicant quality, and positive applicant reactions."[21]

The Role of Measurement. A fundamental premise of process improvement is that the processes we identify are *measurable*. We can identify and measure important aspects of inputs to the process, transformation, and the outputs that are produced by them. For example, we can measure the time consumed by each step of the process. We can measure the quality of the output of the processes against various customer-relevant standards (for example: What training costs must we incur to make the new hires ready for our workplace? What proportion of new hires succeed? What proportion stay with the organization?). Measurement is a fundamental theme running throughout this book. It is the basis of effective staffing, and it is the basis on which we improve the staffing process.

Measuring any process produces two benefits. First, it forces us to specify what is important. What aspects of the process (time, costs, ac-

Exhibit 1.1. Dimensions and example items from staffing service satisfaction survey.

The items selected are representative of the 53 items that make up the survey.

Communication: How well are you kept informed on the staffing process ("staffing process" included recruitment, examination, and selection)?

How satisfied are you with . . .

1. the clarity of instruction and explanation you receive on the staffing process
4. communication regarding new exam alternatives and options

Timeliness: How do you feel about the speed of recruitment, examination, and selection services?

How satisfied are you with the time required to . . .

10. obtain central administrative approval to begin the hiring process
17. hire someone who has been interviewed and selected

Candidate quality: How do you feel about the quality of the job candidates on the employment list? "Quality" means the extent to which the candidates possess the required knowledge and skills for the job.

How satisfied are you with . . .

20. the quality of candidates on new registers
23. the number of people you can interview and select from (if you check 1 or 2, please circle: TOO FEW   TOO MANY)

Test quality: How do you feel about the quality of the civil service exams (for example, paper and pencil tests, work samples, oral boards, and so on)?

How satisfied are you with . . .

34. your involvement in exam construction
37. the extent to which exams are testing for new technologies used on the job

Service focus: To what extent do you believe that your personnel/staffing representatives are committed to providing high-quality service?

How satisfied are you with . . .

41. the way your ideas and suggestions are received
46. the extent to which personnel/staffing representatives understand and respond to your particular work unit's needs
50. the manner in which personnel/staffing representatives follow through with services they promise to deliver

---

Source: Herbert G. Heneman III, Dennis L. Huett, Robert J. Lavigna, and Debra Ogsten. "Assessing Managers' Satisfaction with Staffing Services," *Personnel Psychology* 48 (1995): 163–172. Reprinted with permission of Personnel Psychology, Inc.

curacy of decision) are important? Similarly, what aspects of output are important (low training costs, successful hires, low turnover)? Later in this chapter we discuss a number of process and outcome measures for staffing, and we continue to revisit this topic in subsequent chapters as we look at each separate component of the staffing process.

The second advantage of measuring our processes is that measurement is the basis for improvement. Only by measurement can we track and evaluate the effects of changes we make in the process. Only by measurement will we be confident that we've actually improved the performance of the process.

Focus on the Process. A fundamental principle of process improvement is that the majority of the problems are in the process. Improvement efforts must focus on fixing the process, not blaming people. When things go wrong in the staffing process, and they invariably do, the impulse is to blame someone for the misstep. If, for example, a position is not filled in a timely manner, the finger pointing begins. HR blames the line manager for not completing the employment requisition on time, or for not being available to interview candidates. The line manager, in turn, faults HR for delay in placing the ad or for holding up a final decision because it had trouble scheduling a physical exam. Process thinking tells us that we should not waste our time trying to decide who is at fault but rather concentrate our efforts on improving the process. What steps can be taken to standardize the process? What steps can be taken to streamline the process? What steps can be taken to increase the validity of decisions produced by the process?

Quality Designed into the Process. It is better to build quality into the process than to take action to address problems after they occur. The real cost of poor process quality is much higher than most of us realize. It has been estimated that, for many organizations, the costs associated with poor quality (rework, poor use of people, delays, lost candidates, customer complaints) may run as high as 20 percent to 40 percent of the total HR budget. Once we understand the true cost of poor quality, and that better quality yields savings that exceed costs, we can spend less time dealing with crises and more time improving the process. In fact, one of the basic standards we use to evaluate the staffing process is utility or ROI. For each enhancement we recommend, we ask you, the reader, to put it to the test of whether or not it will result in dollar savings above and beyond dollar costs.

In HR, building quality into the process translates into fundamentals such as (1) designing the staffing process around attributes that really do make a difference in success within the organization; (2) clear communication of necessary attributes to credible recruits who possess these attributes; (3) using effective (reliable, valid) assessment devices (interview content, tests, and so on) that measure these attributes; (4) treating recruits like valued customers as they go through the process; and (5) using data-based assessments to make selection (or promotion) decisions.

Improvement Strategies and Principles

Once we view the tasks we perform in staffing as steps in a process, we can then apply reengineering and process improvement methods to improve the measurable performance and output of the process. We can remove bottlenecks and streamline the process. We can examine how other (benchmark) organizations conduct the process. We can design changes in our process, conduct experiments or trial runs, and measure the improvement produced by the changes we tried.

Quality Tools. There exists a number of tools available to plan, track, evaluate, and improve the staffing process. The seven traditional QC tools are essentially methods to visualize and analyze process data.[22] They represent the foundation of most process improvement efforts. We've profiled and illustrated the basic tools in Exhibit 1.2. In addition to the traditional seven, seven new tools are principally used in the planning process.[23] In subsequent chapters we present a number of examples illustrating the application of these tools. In addition to the tools of process improvement, it is helpful to understand the role of the plan-do-study-act (PDSA) cycle (the Shewhart cycle, named after Walter A. Shewhart) and reengineering as the framework of process improvement or redesign.

The PDSA Cycle. If we are to improve our processes it is often necessary that we investigate the underlying cause of process deficiencies and examine the impact of any changes we make in a systematic fashion. The PDSA cycle provides the structure for trying and evaluating process changes. It is essentially what a scientist would refer to as *the experimental method*. The first step of this rational approach to process improvement is to *plan* a change. Our plan is based on our examination of the problem and an informed hypothesis about what change will resolve the problem. For example, we've noted that we receive fewer applicants responding to ads placed in the local paper than do our competitors. We study the problem. We formulate a belief about the

Exhibit 1.2. Basic quality and process improvement tools.

Flowchart/process chart is a graphical representation of the steps in a process. Flowcharts are drawn to better understand processes and inspect for inefficient or unnecessary steps. We can make major improvements in a staffing process by simply charting the steps, revealing deficiencies in the process such as bottlenecks or redundant steps.

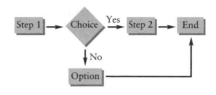

Scatter diagram (correlation plot) provides a graphical display of the relationship between two variables. For example, we could examine whether or not there is a systematic relationship between interviewer ratings and subsequent applicant performance. The linear relationship in a scatter diagram can be summarized statistically by a correlation coefficient.

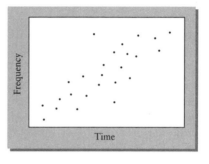

Benchmarking is an improvement process in which an organization measures its performance against that of best-in-the-class companies, identifies gaps that exist, determines how those firms achieved their performance levels, and uses that information to improve its own performance.

Brainstorming is a technique that teams use to generate creative ideas on a particular subject. Members are encouraged to generate as many ideas as possible, withhold evaluation or criticism of ideas, and piggyback off others' ideas or suggestions. One application is in generating potential causes of problems (perhaps then organized in a fishbone diagram). A second application is in generating potential solutions.

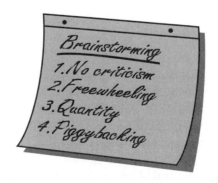

Exhibit 1.2. Continued.

Cause-and-effect (fishbone) diagrams are techniques developed to represent the relationship between some effect and all possible causes or influences. At the end of the horizontal line is the problem to be addressed. Each branch pointing to the main stem represents a possible cause. Branches pointing to the causes are contributing factors. This is used to identify potential causes, so that additional data about the causes can be collected.

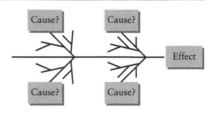

Pareto chart is a graphical tool for ranking causes from most significant to least significant. Typically, analysis of a Pareto chart suggests that most effects come from relatively few causes.

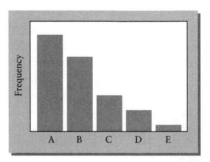

Run (trend) chart is used to visually display data trends over a specified time period. This simple, but very useful, tool aids in the identification of meaningful trends or shifts in the average. It is particularly useful in tracking and evaluating the effects of changes made in the process. For example, we could track applicant numbers before and after a change in recruiting strategy to determine if the program had the intended effect.

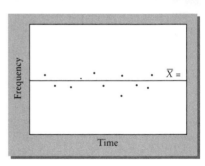

Control chart is a run chart with statistically determined upper (upper control limit) and lower (lower control limit) lines drawn on either side of the process average. Used to determine the amount of process variation due to random variation (common causes) and how much is due to unique events or individual actions (special causes). Spikes that exceed the control limits tell us that a special cause disrupted the process. Investigation of these special causes typically leads to process improvement opportunities.

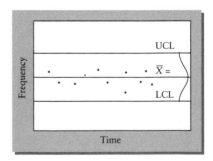

cause. The objective is to ensure that we are focused on the underlying cause of the problem (the root cause). We collect data and use the seven statistical tools to confirm or deny that belief. For example, we consult our staff, examine competitor ads, and conduct a brainstorming session in which we generate potential reasons why our response rate is lower. We organize them in a fishbone diagram. Once we've focused on a cause, or causes, we construct a plan to address it. In this instance, our analysis has led us to believe that our ads are deficient in that they neglect to stress the quality values that support our culture. Consequently, we believe, applicants with a preference for a quality-oriented setting are not responding. We seek to test our hypothesis about the cause of and solution to our problem.

The *do* phase is the implementation of our change. We insert new language in our ads, describing our quality culture, including the broadened responsibilities of our employees and the new attributes they must possess. We run the new ads.

The *study* phase of process improvement is our systematic evaluation of the change. We track the applicants we receive in both number and quality. Our base for comparison is the rate and quality of applicants resulting from previous ads. A simple analysis of the data, perhaps configured in a run chart, will reveal the extent to which the change we tried had an effect on our recruitment process. If the data suggest that there is merit in our new approach (and it seems reasonable to believe that there would be), we then implement the change on a broader scale. This is termed the *act* phase. The process improvement cycle is continuous. Consequently, we'll continue to track, experiment, and modify our recruitment process, always following the systematic, rational, data-based approach to planning, testing, evaluating, and implementing change. As you can see, the PDSA cycle is the core of continuous improvement. (If you are interested in more detail about the PDSA cycle, William W. Scherkenbach presents an excellent description in which he breaks each step into components.[24])

Reengineering. The reengineering concept popularized by Michael Hammer and James Champy is a variation on process improvement in that it takes the ethic for improvement to the extreme, and poses the question: If we were to start anew, with no constraints from how we currently conduct a process, what would the process look like?[25] Adding the availability of new technology, nonexistent when our process was originally conceived, gives us even greater flexibility in thinking through how it might best be structured today. While we sidestep the debate regarding whether or not reengineering is in fact different than process improvement, we will note that, increasingly, there are opportunities to start fresh and design a component of the staffing process anew. Forget the existence of your current staff of recruiters, your current sources of applicants, and your current methods for sourcing them. How today would you get the talent you need?

Benchmarking. In a sense, benchmarking represents the best aspects of the "keeping up with the Joneses" phenomenon. It is a process of comparing one's own practices and outcomes to those of other organizations, with the intent of setting a standard to work toward. Specifically, this process of comparison and emulation involves (1) the selection of a staffing process for which improvement would be beneficial; (2) the identification of a relevant comparison organization(s)—typically an industry leader, or leader in the activity you wish to benchmark; (3) the systematic collection of information about the performance and practices of those organizations (for example, how did they do it?); (4) the comparison of the performance of your organization against the exemplary standards maintained by the comparison organizations and, through that comparison, the identification of performance gaps; and, (5) the formulation of a plan to reduce the "gap" in performance. Companies such as Digital Equipment Corporation, United Technologies Corporation, and Ford Motor Company have used benchmarking to gauge and improve their own HR and staffing practices.[26] While a detailed presentation of how to benchmark is outside the realm of this book, a number of excellent references offer guidance in the design and conduct of a benchmarking effort: Robert C. Camp's two works, *Benchmarking: The Search for Industry Best Practices That Lead to Superior Performance* and *Business Process Benchmarking: Finding and Implementing Best Practices,* provide a comprehensive discussion of the techniques and practices; and Fitz-enz's *Benchmarking Staff Performance* provides an excellent how-to guide to benchmarking in the context of human resource functions.[27] Fitz-enz presents numerous insights and resources for planning and conducting a benchmark program.

What to Measure in Staffing

We cannot close our introductory chapter without a closer look at the issue of measurement in staffing. The measures we choose should be systematically collected and charted to determine how well the system is presently operating and to evaluate the effectiveness of various change strategies. Exhibit 1.3 presents four categories of possible measures useful for tracking how well the system is meeting its objec-

Exhibit 1.3. Potential measures for staffing.

A variety of quantitative and qualitative measures are relevant to each component of the staffing process. They are listed below with an example.

Input or supplier measures:

Timeliness: Does the system provide new hires when they are needed?

Quality or readiness: Do the applicants and new hires possess the necessary attributes, or must they undergo extensive remedial training?

Completeness: Arc hiring specifications thorough and reflective of what applicants need to succeed?

Convenience and usability: Are position specifications understood by recruiters and by applicants?

Cost-effectiveness: Does the addition of a standard test result save money through improved selection decisions?

Value-added transformation measures: Quantitative or qualitative measures of performance within the boundaries of the process being measured.

Task/activity or subprocess cycle time: How long does it take to process employee requisitions? How much time lapses between the final interview and candidate notification?

Quantity measures: How many hours of labor does it take to process applications? What proportion of females and minorities are screened out at each stage of the process?

Quality measures, errors, or defects at various steps: What percentage of applications have deficient or missing paperwork? What is the time lag between a decision and notification of the rejected applicants? What proportion of offers are rejected by the applicant?

Number of tasks, activities, or steps (for example, nonsequential or redundant steps). What steps does the internal posting go through?

Costs (labor hours at each stage of the process): What does it cost to interview a managerial candidate?

Output measures: Quantitative or qualitative information or data that indicate how well a system, subsystem, or process is producing its outputs for its customers.

System or process cycle time (time to fill a new position): How long does it take (from requisition to reporting day) to place a new team member?

Quantity or productivity measures (number of candidates processes): Which recruiting source generates the most responses?

Exhibit 1.3. Continued.

Quality measures: Which recruiting sources generate the most capable new hires? Which assessment devices are most predictive of subsequent job performance? Which interviewer judgments are most predictive of subsequent job performance?

Cost measures (cost per hire, utility analysis): What dollar savings accrue from the use of a standardized test?

Performance: Does the addition of a standardized test result in improved on-the-job performance (utility)?

Turnover: Does the addition of an assessment tool increase the proportion of employees who fit the job and stay with it?

Training costs: Does the addition of an assessment tool upgrade the skills of new hires and reduce training costs?

Return on investment: Do the savings associated with the addition of a selection tool exceed the costs of using the tool?

Customer measures: Customer satisfaction.

Satisfaction surveys (management and employee satisfaction with new hires; candidate satisfaction with the process).

Customer complaints (verbal or written concerns).

Focus groups (discussion with managers, employees).

tives and producing value-added output. The examples are not comprehensive and you will likely add others appropriate to your specific setting. These measures also reflect the criteria we might choose to benchmark. How quickly, for example, does the industry leader fill a position? Or, how predictive of subsequent job performance is the industry leader's selection process? We will in subsequent chapters present more examples of measures for each component of the staffing process.

Finally, Figure 1.4 presents two components of the staffing process, the generation of hiring specifications and the generation of recruits into process components and measures (suppliers, inputs, transformation, output, customers).

Summary

The premise on which this book is based is that the quality-oriented organization requires a very different mix of workforce knowledge, skills, and temperament. Second, there has been much progress in the

Process 1

Suppliers →	Inputs →	Measures →	Transform process →	Measures →	Output →	Measures →	Customer satisfaction measures
Managers Supervisors Peers Incumbents HR specialists	Job information	Time in getting information from various sources Reliability of information by sources Face validity of information by source Content validity	Integrate information, create job descriptions and job specifications	Process time	Valid position descriptions and position specifications	Face validity, content validity, reliability of job description and job specifications	Recruiter's satisfaction with description and specification Hiring manager's satisfaction Peer and team member satisfaction Applicant's understanding and satisfaction

Process 2

Suppliers →	Inputs →	Measures →	Transform process →	Measures →	Output →	Measures →	Customer satisfaction measures
Schools Employment agencies Employee referrals Newspaper ads Executive recruiters Walk-ins Internal postings	Applicants Position descriptions Recruiters	Number of applicants by source Cost per applicant Time lapse in application steps	Evaluation of applicants against position specifications	Process time Reliability of evaluations Validity of evaluations	Pool of credible applicants	Time lag by source Cost per applicant by source Number of passing applications by source Ratings of applications by source Minority applications by source	Hiring manager's satisfaction with applicant pool Applicant's satisfaction with process

Figure 1.4. Example process components and measures for two staffing processes.

31

development of methods for evaluating these new, complex attributes. Third, the process by which staffing is conducted is an appropriate point of focus for improvement. Finally, there will be a tremendous return on investment to the organization that systematically applies the process improvement tools, as well as new staffing technologies, with the goal of upgrading its workforce to meet the competitive challenges of the future. The remaining chapters of this book will guide you in your effort to make staffing a strategic strength of your organization.

Notes

1. Lynn R. Offermann and Marilyn K. Gowing, "Personnel Selection in the Future: The Impact of Changing Demographics and the Nature of Work" in *Personnel Selection in Organizations*, Neal Schmitt and Walter C. Borman, eds. (San Francisco: Jossey-Bass, 1993).

2. L. C. Thurow, "Who Owns the Twenty-First Century?" *Sloan Management Review* (Spring 1992): 5–17; Robert Reich, *The Work of Nations* (New York: Knopf, 1991).

3. G. Fushberg, "Despite Layoffs, Firms Find Some Jobs Hard to Fill," *The Wall Street Journal* (January 22, 1991): B1, B3.

4. Julie Schmit, "Ritz-Carlton: Room for Employees," *USA Today* (Thursday October 15, 1992): 6B.

5. David E. Terpstra and Elizabeth J. Rozell, "The Relationship of Staffing Practices to Organizational Level Measures of Performance," *Personnel Psychology* 46 (1993): 27–48.

6. Richard Blackburn and Bensen Rosen, "Total Quality and Human Resources Management: Lessons Learned from Baldrige Award-Winning Companies," *The Academy of Management Executive* (August 1993): 49–66.

7. Jack Smith and Ronald Morgan, "Staffing for Quality Improvement: A Survey of ASQC Sustaining Member Organizations," technical report (White Lake, Mich.: HR Processes, and Northville, Mich.: Organization Solutions, 1994).

8. Ibid.

9. Ibid.

10. Richard Blackburn and Bensen Rosen, "Human Resource Management and Total Quality Management," in *Research in Quality Management,* D. Fedor and S. Ghosh, eds. (Greenwich, Conn.: JAI Press, in press). These authors report correlations between TQ-related staffing changes and both commitment to TQM ($r = .35, p < .01$) and effectiveness of the TQM effort ($r = .36, p < .01$).

11. W. Edwards Deming, *Out of the Crisis* (Cambridge, Mass.: MIT Center for Advanced Engineering Study, 1986), 177.

12. Jack Smith and Ronald Morgan, "Development of the Quality Orientation Inventory," technical report (White Lake, Mich.: HR Processes, and Northville, Mich.: Organization Solutions, 1995).

13. Personnel Decisions, "The Customer Service Inventory (Minneapolis, Minn.: PDI, 1993); R. Hogan and J. Hogan, *The Hogan Personality Inventory,* 2nd ed. Hogan Assessment Systems, 1992. Available through the Psychological Corporation, 800-228-0752.

14. Joseph M. Juran, *Juran on Quality by Design* (New York: The Free Press, 1992), 428.

15. William McKnight, "Philosophy of Management," paper presented in 1941. The quote reprinted with a 3M promotional pamphlet *3M Who We Are, 3M* (St. Paul, Minn.: 3M, 1993).

16. R. Levering and M. Moskowitz, *The 100 Best Companies to Work for in America* (New York: Plume, 1993), 298–299.

17. Ibid.

18. David E. Bowen and L. E. Greiner, "Moving from Production to Service in Human Resources Management," *Organizational Dynamics* 15, no. 1 (1986): 35.

19. David E. Bowen and Edward E. Lawler, III, "Total Quality–Oriented Human Resources Management," *Organizational Dynamics* (spring 1992): 33.

20. Ibid.

21. Herbert G. Heneman III, Dennis L. Huett, Robert J. Lavigna, and Debra Ogsten, "Assessing Managers' Satisfaction with Staffing Services," *Personnel Psychology* 48 (1995): 163–172.

22. James W. Dean Jr. and James R. Evans, "Tools and Techniques for Quality Planning and Improvement," *Total Quality: Management, Organization, and Strategy* (Minneapolis/St. Paul, Minn.: West Publishing Co., 1994); Michael Brassard, *The Memory Jogger Plus* (Methuen, Mass.: Goal/QPC, 1989).

23. Ibid. These books profile the traditional seven and the new seven tools for quality.

24. William W. Scherkenbach, *Deming's Road to Continual Improvement* (Knoxville, Tenn.: SPC Press, 1991).

25. Michael Hammer and James Champy, *Reengineering the Corporation* (New York: Harper Business, 1993).

26. Ellen F. Glanz and Lee K. Dailey, "Benchmarking," *Human Resource Management* (Spring/summer 1992): 9–20; John D. Arnold, "Benchmarking Salaried Selection: Overview of Best Practices," paper presented at the Tenth Annual Conference of the Society for Industrial and Organizational Psychology, Orlando, Fla., May 20, 1995.

27. Robert C. Camp, *Benchmarking: The Search for Industry Best Practices That Lead to Superior Performance* (Milwaukee, Wis.: ASQC Quality Press, 1989); Robert C. Camp, *Business Process Benchmarking: Finding and Implementing Best Practices* (Milwaukee, Wis.: ASQC Quality Press, 1995); Jac Fitz-enz, *Benchmarking Staff Performance* (San Francisco: The Saratoga Institute, 1992).

chapter 2

The New Workplace

It is a big culture change. Our moms and dads raised us to do what the boss says—and now the boss is asking us what we should do.[1]

Overview

As the preceding quote suggests, the workplace is changing, and the changes are creating new expectations for workers at all levels. In this chapter we address three issues related to ongoing changes induced by quality improvement. First, what is quality improvement? Because there are so many separate components and approaches (TQM, process improvement, benchmarking, self-managed teams, reengineering) and they are applied differently in various settings, we believe that it will be helpful to identify some of the tools and processes that underlie our conception of quality improvement. As you will see, we take a broad, encompassing approach to quality improvement.

The second issue we address is: How are organizations changing as they adopt quality improvement philosophies and processes? In particular, we explore changes in how organizations are structured, changes in organization culture, and changes in how work is conducted in total quality organizations. These changes are important because they've created the need to staff the new workforce we describe in this book.

Third, for us to understand and to get a grasp on the dynamics of performance in these new settings, it will be helpful to step back and think about performance within a work process. To do that, we address the question: What are the individual factors that affect worker performance? We then present a framework for understanding worker performance within any work process and within any particular quality improvement effort. Based on this model of performance, and the changes in structure, culture, and jobs in the total quality setting, we then present a profile of worker attributes required in these settings.

What Is Quality Improvement?

Most of us recall being told that no two snowflakes are exactly alike. To our astonishment, we were told that an infinite number of shapes exist, each formed by a unique set of meteorological circumstances. As children, we stared into a snowfall, amazed at that prospect. Many of us tried to refute it by capturing and comparing many snowflakes.

Similarly, no two quality improvement efforts appear to be exactly alike. A seemingly infinite variety of methods, tools, and processes exist. In Figure 2.1, we present a partial listing of quality improvement philosophies, tools, and processes (we've borrowed the umbrella concept from Masaaki Imai).[2] We believe that the list is representative, but

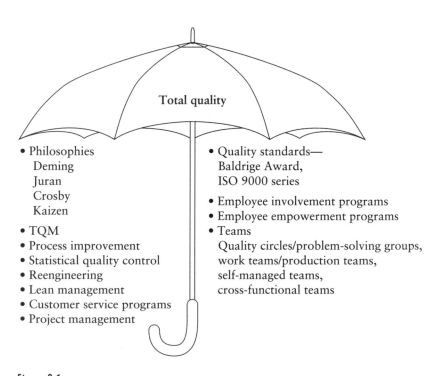

Total quality

- Philosophies
  Deming
  Juran
  Crosby
  Kaizen
- TQM
- Process improvement
- Statistical quality control
- Reengineering
- Lean management
- Customer service programs
- Project management

- Quality standards—
  Baldrige Award,
  ISO 9000 series
- Employee involvement programs
- Employee empowerment programs
- Teams
  Quality circles/problem-solving groups,
  work teams/production teams,
  self-managed teams,
  cross-functional teams

Figure 2.1. Approaches to quality improvement.

by no means is it comprehensive. As you scan the list, one thing to note is the tremendous philosophical and operational diversity in approaches to quality improvement. There's a lot going on out there!

A further complicating factor is that these varied approaches can be configured in unique arrangements designed to fit the particular circumstances of each organization. For example, one organization implements Deming-based philosophy and tools for improving the quality of its production process, but does not alter the authority and decision-making process. It's calling it TQM. Another organization implements the same quality improvement tools in the context of self-managed teams. It's also calling it TQM. According to a recent review of various TQM processes, this is not an unusual scenario. The results of that study revealed that companies varied considerably in the extent to which their TQM programs incorporated genuine employee involvement and empowerment efforts.[3] In fact, some implementations of TQM fail to engender either involvement or empowerment, relying simply on the implementation of job-focused process improvement. The important point is that such fundamental differences in the nature of the quality improvement effort have implications for the plan and design of the staffing process.

What Quality Programs Are in Use? We examined the extent to which various quality improvement tools are being used in our sample of ASQC sustaining member organizations. Figure 2.2 presents the various programs, the percentage of companies using each, and the average years of experience companies have had with each program. Process improvement and customer service programs emerge as the most widely used. Customer service, SPC, and process improvement have the longest tenure in organizations.

This, then, is our dilemma: We intend to provide you, the reader, with useful guidance as you construct staffing plans for your organization. Doing so requires that we deal with specific attributes needed within your specific quality improvement setting. While generic descriptions may be of interest, and a good starting point, they are less useful to your needs than specific profiles for your unique setting. The stumbling block is that the variety in approaches to quality improvement makes such a one-size-fits-all prescription an impossible objective for this book. Our challenge is to make the discussion useful for all readers as they grapple with these issues in their specific quality improvement settings.

We do two things to accomplish this objective. First, we present profiles based on generalizations about the nature of quality im-

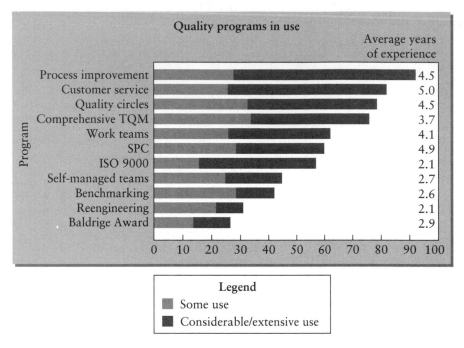

Figure 2.2. Quality programs in use.

provement organizations. In doing so, we will draw on emerging models of TQM, reengineering, and various approaches to the use of teams.[4] However, even as we do so, we stress that these are generalizations, and your organization may not fit the prototype. As you will see, there are attributes that do appear to be highly relevant across a wide range of new workplace initiatives (such as quality improvement). For example, conscientiousness; flexibility/adaptability; openness to learning, development, and retraining; and general mental ability are attributes highly valued in a wide array of quality improvement settings.

The second thing that we do to help you plan for your specific setting is provide the resources and a process for constructing an organization-specific quality success profile. The resources include a comprehensive taxonomy of quality-relevant attributes—the quality attributes inventory—and a format for selecting and prioritizing these attributes. The taxonomies have been constructed to be relevant to the diverse list of quality improvement strategies presented in Figure 2.1. These resources and guidelines appear in chapter 4. Using the materials and processes provided in that chapter, you can construct a detailed quality success profile specific to your organization.

We like to think of it this way: We'll provide detailed menus. To make them most useful to the diverse settings of our readers, the menus consist of an extensive list of à la carte items (knowledge, skills, abilities, temperament) relevant to quality improvement efforts. These materials can be used to assemble a profile tailored to the unique setting of each organization. However, because constructing a quality attributes profile is more challenging than assembling a dinner menu, we also provide guidelines for choosing the attributes on which to focus in the process of building a staffing plan.

With this background in the diversity of quality improvement techniques and our approach to dealing with that issue, we now turn our attention to the transformation organizations go through as their quality efforts mature.

Changing Nature of Organizations: The Quality Transformation

Quality improvement efforts (TQM, process improvement, the use of teams) are transforming organizations—changing their internal design, structure, and culture, as well as changing how work is designed and conducted. These changes have important implications for staffing within these organizations. The links between quality improvement efforts, organization characteristics, job characteristics, and staffing requirements are depicted in Figure 2.3. As we noted earlier, the specific nature of the quality improvement effort determines changes in how the organization is structured, in the cultural values that emerge, and in the way work is designed and conducted. The changes in structure, culture, and jobs create needs for new knowledge, skills, aptitudes, temperament, and interests in the workforce of the organization. Because there are implications for who you hire, develop, and promote, and how you go about doing so, we now take a look at some of the changes in structure, culture, and work. A number of references are listed for the reader interested in a more detailed discussion of organization characteristics.

The Changing Structure of Quality Organizations

Organization structure refers to the formal arrangement of the organization—specifically, the jobs, reporting relationships, functional and departmental divisions and demarcations, and the hierarchical levels that characterize the organization. The concept of structure is best

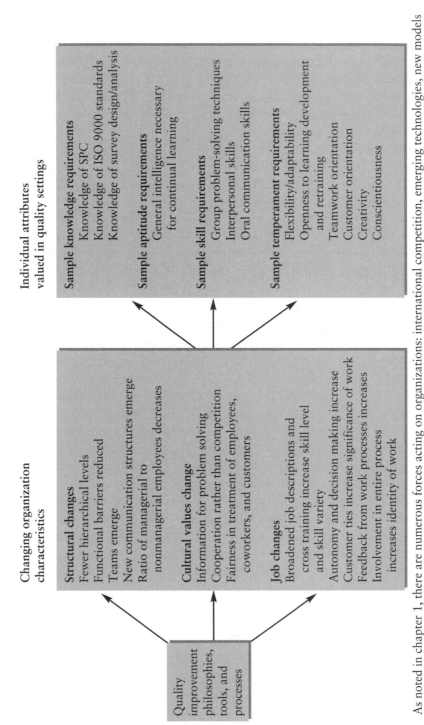

Individual attributes
valued in quality settings

Sample knowledge requirements
Knowledge of SPC
Knowledge of ISO 9000 standards
Knowledge of survey design/analysis

Sample aptitude requirements
General intelligence necessary
for continual learning

Sample skill requirements
Group problem-solving techniques
Interpersonal skills
Oral communication skills

Sample temperament requirements
Flexibility/adaptability
Openness to learning development
and retraining
Teamwork orientation
Customer orientation
Creativity
Conscientiousness

Changing organization
characteristics

Structural changes
Fewer hierarchical levels
Functional barriers reduced
Teams emerge
New communication structures emerge
Ratio of managerial to
nonmanagerial employees decreases

Cultural values change
Information for problem solving
Cooperation rather than competition
Fairness in treatment of employees,
coworkers, and customers

Job changes
Broadened job descriptions and
cross training increase skill level
and skill variety
Autonomy and decision making increase
Customer ties increase significance of work
Feedback from work processes increases
Involvement in entire process
increases identity of work

Quality
improvement
philosophies,
tools, and
processes

As noted in chapter 1, there are numerous forces acting on organizations: international competition, emerging technologies, new models for organizing. Many of those phenomena contribute to the changes occurring in quality-oriented organizations.

Figure 2.3. Systematic links between quality improvement, organization characteristics, and individual requirements.

conveyed through that venerable document, the organization chart. A number of phenomena, including the maturation of quality improvement efforts, are changing the structure of the new workplace in the following ways.

Fewer Hierarchical Levels.   A number of quality processes act to flatten organizations. First, efforts at genuine employee involvement and empowerment programs tend to reduce the number of organization levels. As many of the decision-making responsibilities are pushed downward to the level at which the work is done, the need for levels of managerial hierarchy is reduced. In essence, what happens is that the decision making, monitoring, and control performed by many of the hierarchical levels in the traditional organization are pushed back down to the level at which the work is done. The recent book, *Empowered Teams,* cites survey data in which 68 percent of the organizations adopting teams reduced the number of managers and levels, with almost universal (98 percent) satisfaction with the process.[5]

An additional pressure to reduce organizational levels comes from the joint effects of customer orientation, process improvement, and reengineering in total quality settings. The hierarchy of traditional organizations erected barriers between the customer and organizational decision making. The application of process improvement, with the objective of increasing internal and external customer satisfaction, results in the reduction of levels of organizational insulation. Flatter organizations are required in order to become more attentive and responsive to customer needs. A very compelling argument for reducing levels and getting nearer to the customer was presented in the classic work, *In Search of Excellence.*[6]

The move toward flat organizations creates plenty of challenges and opportunities for staffing. For example, it fuels the need for a more knowledgeable, skilled, and motivated workforce—in effect, a workforce with many of the attributes traditionally associated with managerial performance. These same qualities, in the past, would have opened doors for upward mobility (promotion). However, flatter organizations have reduced traditional opportunities and lines of promotion. So, on the one hand, we have a workforce with increasingly sophisticated attributes and experiences (including traditional managerial skills), but far fewer opportunities for upward promotion. We'll discussion some of the implications for career development in chapter 11.

Horizontal Barriers Reduced.   Traditional organizational barriers—functions, departments—have been a major obstacle to quality, productivity, and organization effectiveness. This has been observed by organization scholars and by quality proponents. In fact, one of Deming's 14 points focused specifically on this issue: "Break down barriers between departments" because "people in various departments must work as a team."[7] Consistent with Deming's point, quality improvement efforts typically dissolve these barriers. Cross-functional teams, task forces, and reengineered work processes cut across traditional organization boundaries, foster horizontal and vertical communication, and act to reduce traditional internal barriers to quality. The joint effect of a customer orientation and the use of process improvement tools also results in dissolving departmental, functional, and divisional barriers. *Reengineering the Corporation* cites a number of examples of how redesigning work processes (by reengineering or by process improvement) reduces internal barriers.[8]

Span of Control . . . Span of Empowerment. Span of control refers to the size of the work group accountable to any one supervisor. In traditional organizations, where supervisors act to direct, decide, evaluate, and control, any one supervisor could effectively manage only a small group of employees—usually about six or seven. However, in total quality settings, the supervisor's role is much different. As organizations empower employees to plan, direct, monitor, and evaluate their own work, the number of employees reporting to any one manager typically increases. Managers serve less as monitors, evaluators, or decision makers, and more as facilitators, teachers, and coaches. The end result is that the optimal span of control that typified the traditional organization no longer applies. Empowered, competent employees no longer need the close supervision that characterized traditional organizations. Whereas the traditional organization required a span of control of one supervisor for six or seven employees, the total quality organization relies on a much broader base, a span of empowerment (see Figure 2.4). The Chrysler Corporation is an excellent illustration of this trend. Between the years 1992 and 1994 it went from an average ratio of 1 supervisor for every 25 hourly workers to 1 supervisor for every 45 hourly workers.[9]

Emergence of Teams. Teams emerge in various forms in total quality organizations. Work teams, cross-functional teams, problem-solving teams, and, in some settings, self-managed teams, represent major structural changes in how individuals in the organization interact to get their work done. It is a structural change with tremendous implications for staffing. It simply takes a different kind of person to function effectively in a team environment.

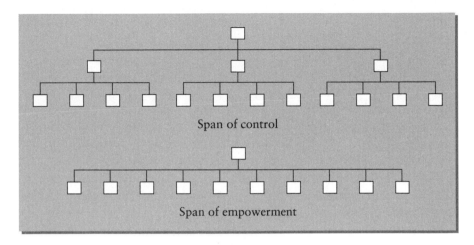

Figure 2.4. The span of empowerment.

Disappearance of the Box. A final structural change is the disappearance of the box on the organization chart. That is, the organization of work into specific, clearly defined, narrow descriptions is being replaced by broadened roles. "It's not my job" is an industrial era phrase out of step with the customer-oriented values of the new workplace. We'll take a closer look at the changes in work shortly.

The Changing Culture of Quality-Oriented Organizations

Organization culture refers to the shared philosophies, values, beliefs, and norms held within an organization. While the concept may appear ambiguous, culture is a critical, determining factor in accounting for why people behave as they do in a particular organization. Culture is important because it provides everyone in the organization with a common framework for, in a general sense, "how we do things around here." Culture affects behaviors such as how superiors treat subordinates, how employees treat customers, and what and how information is communicated upward, downward, and laterally. For a quality improvement effort to succeed in an organization, it must develop a culture based on values, beliefs, and ways of doing things consistent with the philosophical base of quality. Many quality efforts and, in fact, many organization change efforts of the past—such as quality control (QC) circles—have floundered because they have been inserted within incompatible cultures. Because culture is such an important determinant, we ask the questions: What is a quality culture like? What employee attributes are required in those cultures?

What Is a Total Quality Culture Like? A number of authors have addressed this question and characterized the cultural attributes of quality-oriented organizations.[10] In fact, many of Deming's 14 points address aspects of culture needed to support a total quality effort (for example, drive out fear, create trust, create a climate for innovation).[11] While there may well be great variety in quality improvement tools and processes, and great variety in the culture of quality-oriented organizations, some aspects do stand out as being favorable for quality improvement. (As we noted earlier, these generalizations may be more or less true for any particular organization.) Exhibit 2.1 contrasts the cultural values of traditional and quality-oriented organizations. In doing so it presents a profile of a quality-oriented culture, consistent with the model underlying a comprehensive quality improvement effort.

Implications for Staffing. In terms of our interest in staffing, the key point is that the profile of the individual likely to succeed and draw satisfaction from the quality-oriented setting differs from that of the traditional organization. Those likely to succeed are certainly different in temperament. As noted in Figure 2.3, total quality cultures place great value on individual flexibility and adaptability; on openness to learning, development, and retraining; on teamwork; and on customer orientation. Many organizations are investing effort in matching their new hires to their total quality culture; a number of these examples will be presented later.

Building a Quality-Oriented Culture. Implementing a quality improvement effort often involves a process of actively changing the cultural values of the organization. Doing so requires a concerted effort to integrate quality values into every aspect of day-to-day life in the organization. There are multiple strategies through which an organization transforms its culture to make it consistent with the quality improvement tools in use. Among those means are the recruiting, selecting, and promoting practices. Simply put, the criteria used to select, develop, and promote say volumes about the true values of the organization.

Incorporating new cultural values and beliefs into the recruitment, selection, and promotion processes speeds the cultural change. New recruits learn quickly of the values of the organization, and their selection and promotion is based on their fit with those cultural values. When quality-related attributes and experiences are incorporated into the selection and promotion criteria, the importance of quality is rein-

Exhibit 2.1. Changes in organization culture.

Cultural dimension	The traditional culture	The quality-oriented culture
Use of information	Uses information from work processes to control, punish, and instill fear	Uses information to identify and solve problems and to improve work process
Distribution of authority	Authority and decision making are centralized and retained by management	Employees are given the authority needed to make decisions and effectively perform their work
Rewards for results	Employees are rewarded for individual achievement	Employees are rewarded for group and organization achievement
	Rewards focus on short-term measures	Rewards are based on long-term measures
	Rewards stress *productivity*	Rewards stress *quality*
Cooperation *vs.* competition	Fosters internal competition between individuals, departments, and functions	Fosters internal cooperation between individuals, departments, and functions
Job security	Treats employees as variable resources through practices such as employment at will, ineffective HRP, and overreliance on temporary contract workers	Treats employees as long-term stakeholders in the organization; minimizes layoffs; minimizes the use of temporary contract workers
Climate of fairness	Treats employees arbitrarily	Treats employees fairly
Equitable compensation	Attempts to minimize compensation at lower levels and maximize compensation at higher levels	Establishes equitable compensation across organization levels
Customer focus	Focuses on satisfying shareholders	Focuses on satisfying customers
Learning/development	Is job specific and limited	Focuses on continual learning and development

Note: All except the "Customer focus" and "Learning/development" dimensions are adapted with permission of the publisher from M. Sashkin and K. J. Kiser, *Putting TQM to Work*, Berrett-Koehler Publishers, Inc., San Francisco, CA. All rights reserved.

forced among applicants, new hires, and current employees. The message is clear: Quality values and practices really are important here.

Changing Workforce

A recurring theme throughout this book is that quality-oriented organizations require workers with a complex mix of knowledge, skills, and temperament. The structural and cultural changes we've discussed thus far are in part responsible for these new requirements. In particular, there is increased movement toward selecting the individual not solely on the basis of specific job requirements, but rather, on the basis of the fit between the individual and the organization culture. The total quality culture places a premium on certain aspects of temperament—flexibility/adaptability; openness to learning, development, and retraining; conscientiousness; creativity; and teamwork (cooperativeness). Consequently, we will focus much attention in later chapters of the book on matching individuals to the total quality culture.

Changing Nature of Work

> In the next five years, four out of five people in the industrial world will be doing jobs differently from the way that they have been done in the last 50 years. Most people will have to learn new skills.[12]

As the quote illustrates, work and the skills needed to conduct it are changing. Exhibit 2.2 contrasts work in traditional organizations with work in a prototypical quality-oriented setting. The terms used to organize the work are based on dimensions of the job characteristics model developed by organizational researchers J. R. Hackman and G. Oldham.[13] Their model identifies the underlying dimensions of jobs and the relationship of those dimensions to worker motivation. They've identified five dimensions along which jobs vary. These five dimensions are used to organize contrasts in traditional and quality-oriented jobs.

Jobs in Quality Improvement Settings: Restoring Meaningfulness to Work

One generalization that can be made is that the various quality improvement efforts are reversing the work simplification trend that had typified jobs since the emergence of modern industrialization and

Exhibit 2.2. The changing nature of work in quality settings.

Traditional organization	Total quality organization
Skill variety	
Workers specialize in a single or in a few tasks	Workers are cross trained and perform a wide range of tasks and processes
Work is engineered to minimize skill levels required	Work requires various knowledge and skills
Work is designed to minimize the need for learning and development	Work requires continual learning and development
Task identity	
Workers see only their own, isolated function in work process	Workers see how their own activity fits into the larger work process
Work is engineered to minimize the intrinsic motivation of worker	Requires workers who seek challenge and derive sense of accomplishment from work
Workers work on a single, isolated piece of overall product	Workers work on whole, identifiable product or component of product
Workers lack identification with meaningful product	Workers see personal input into product or service
Autonomy, participation, and empowerment	
Design and planning of how work is performed is a managerial responsibility	Workers participate in planning how work is performed
Work quality is evaluated externally	Quality is a central concern of workers
Authority and decision making are separated from workers; a managerial responsibility	Workers are given great discretion and authority
Task significance	
Worker contact with internal and external customers is minimized	Contact with internal and external customers is a natural part of doing the job
Communication with internal and external customers is minimized	Communication with internal and external customers is a natural part of the work process
Feedback	
Feedback is from management or from a separate quality function	Feedback is directly from the work process

mass production. For example, a manufacturing facility of 3M Canada has organized the production work for an entire facility into two broad job descriptions—operators and technologists. These two broadly defined jobs are described in the 3M Canada *Applicant Information Booklet*.[14] The descriptions are reproduced in Exhibit 2.3. As you can see, the work that traditionally had been performed by occupants of specialized positions is now performed by occupants of two broad job descriptions.

Impact of Changing Work. The variety and complexity of skills required of workers increases in settings like 3M Canada. The ability of workers to envision and participate in an entire work process increases. Because operators at 3M Canada are involved in all phases of production, they are more likely to experience meaningfulness in their work. Worker empowerment and involvement in decisions about the job increases (although, as noted by organization researchers, many TQM efforts fail to involve or empower employees).[15] Quality improvement efforts stress the relationship of the worker to various internal and external customers. Workers see themselves as customers and suppliers in highly interdependent work processes. This increases the worker's realization that the work has impact on others both inside and outside the organization. This, in turn, increases workers' sense that their jobs have significance. Finally, by getting the worker involved in the measurement, problem identification, and problem solving of work processes, quality improvement increases the direct, systematic feedback workers receive from the work process. These five dimensions of

Exhibit 2.3. Jobs in the modern manufacturing facility.

The 3M Canada manufacturing facility at Brockville has organized the production work for the entire facility into two broad job descriptions.

An *Operator* is someone who performs the tasks necessary to run the production line. This includes ordering materials and ensuring quality, as well as running production. Operators are responsible for routine machine and equipment maintenance. In addition, an Operator rotates jobs on a regular basis and takes turns acting as the coordinator of team activities. A *Technologist* is responsible for maintenance of the equipment and machinery as well as assisting in the development of new processes. Technologists are members of the production team and also assist as needed in production.

Source: *3M Canada Applicant Information Booklet: Preparing for the Selection Process*, 1992. Used with permission.

work design (skill variety, task identity, autonomy, task significance, and feedback) foster, in those employees who are ready for such challenges, increased satisfaction and motivation.

Summary: The New Workplace

To summarize, total quality efforts change—albeit slowly in some settings—the structure, culture, and work design of the organization. As the quote from the Levi Straus worker at the beginning of this chapter illustrates, the changes require distinctly different capabilities and motivation from employees. That is what this book is about: locating, assessing, selecting, developing, and promoting workers for this new workplace.

Worker Performance in Total Quality Settings: Attributes of the New Workforce

"Statistical thinking will one day be as necessary for efficient citizenship as the ability to read and write."[16] This quote from H. G. Wells was prescient. The changing culture and design of work typifying the new workplace have created the need for new attributes in the workforce. We now present a framework for identifying and organizing the individual attributes that underlie the performance of work in quality-oriented settings.

What Factors Affect Individual Performance?

To understand the performance of workers in a work process, it is helpful to think systematically of performance and the role of the person in the process. Generally speaking, performance is a function of three factors: the individual's ability to perform in the context of the system (the can-do factor), the individual's willingness or motivation (the will-do factor), and situational constraints (the work process and organization context). These three factors are incorporated into the following worker performance function.

Individual performance =
$$f \text{ (ability} \times \text{motivation)} \times \text{situational (process) factors}$$

Ability (the can-do factor) and motivation (the will-do factor) interact in a manner that determines effective performance in each particular setting. The joint consideration of these two factors is consistent with calls for the assessment of the whole person in staffing.[17] The multiplicative relationship of the function indicates that one component cannot make up for the total lack of another. We must jointly consider ability and motivation in our staffing process. Scherkenbach recounts an excellent illustration, attributable to Deming, of the mutual importance of ability and motivation in understanding worker performance. He recounts the following demonstration.

I want you to participate in a process which thousands of people have done before you. It is the process of proofreading. You are the people. Use whatever method you choose. Your material is the highlighted sentence. The characteristic which is critical to the customer is the number of f's in the sentence. Read the sentence and note exactly how many occurrences of the letter "f" you see.

FINISHED FILES ARE THE RESULT
OF YEARS OF SCIENTIFIC STUDY
COMBINED WITH THE
EXPERIENCE
OF MANY YEARS

Many people see exactly three f's. Many people see exactly six f's. A few people see two, four, five, seven, and even zero f's. (Actually the only people who saw zero f's were those who were given a blank sheet of paper because of a copy machine malfunction. I don't hand out this test on paper any more!) There are two lessons to be learned here. The first one is that teaching adults is a lot more difficult in many ways than teaching children. Each of you brings with you the length and breadth of your experience and knowledge. You were carefully taught many things. You were carefully taught how to read English. Most of us learned to read the language phonetically. This seems to be true whether you learned English as a first, second, or third language. This could explain the results of those who saw exactly three f's (approximately 40 percent). The f in the word "of" sounds like a v and people typically skip over it. Those who saw exactly six f's (approximately 50 percent) were probably using a different method. Some read backwards or force themselves to scan each letter and not read the words. The reasons for those who saw other than six or three (approximately 10 percent) have not been scientifically explained. In any event only about half the people were able to meet the customers' needs.[18]

In terms of our interest in staffing, the important point to be drawn from this demonstration is that, even in this simple task, where presumably everyone is motivated to perform, differences in ability create differences in performance. These underlying differences in ability are traceable to differences in knowledge, skill, and experience. We could similarly design a demonstration in which motivation played the defining role. In formulating our staffing plans and designing staffing processes, we must carefully consider the mutual role that ability and motivation play. We now turn our attention to a more systematic look at ability and motivation and the effect they have on worker performance in TQ settings.

The Individual and the Work Process: Who or What Is to Blame?

Before we proceed, it is important that we deal with an important issue related to the role of the individual in work performance. Simply put, workers have traditionally taken the blame for poor performance. In fact, much of the effort of HR management has been directed at fixing or replacing the worker as the way to improve productivity or quality. The rationale went something like this: "If we can only get the right people and get them motivated, our products and services will prevail." This costly oversimplification resulted in a neglect of the role of the work process (tools and methods) in performance. For too long, we simply blamed the worker for flaws that were attributable to the process. This is perhaps one of Deming's most enduring contributions—this focus on the role that the work process plays in performance.

It is important, however, that we not neglect the impact that variability caused by the worker does have on performance. A perfected work process will function more effectively with some individuals and less so with others. Matching the right workers to the process will improve its performance.

Do not misinterpret our focus on selection and promotion as a means to effective work processes. We're not saying that you can, as in the days gone by, attempt to cover up a shoddy work process or a poorly designed product by replacing the people. If work processes are shoddy, discarding the people and hiring others will not solve the problem. However, it is equally important that we recognize the impact that the person has in the quality setting, in terms of both improving the process and functioning effectively within that system. As we've noted repeatedly, some are more suited than others for the unique challenges of the total quality setting.

Understanding Performance: What Is Success in the Organization?

To predict worker performance we must first specify more clearly what exactly constitutes effective performance. Practically speaking, we cannot recruit, assess, and select until we have thought out what, exactly, it is that our organization values in its workforce. What defines success? A number of authors have noted that the new workplace, in general, and the quality setting, in particular, define successful performance differently than the traditional organization.[19]

At this point, we wish to identify some of these contrasts, and we will return to them and treat them more completely in chapter 3. For now, here are some of the distinctions we see. First, in the traditional organization, success meant showing up, conforming to some fairly clear rules and guidelines, producing widgets (often repetitive and countable), and avoiding accidents. As we've noted earlier, work is now much broader, requiring much greater discretion, responsibility, and authority. Successful performance often requires the whole person. Consequently, although we have no data to support the assertion, we would venture to suggest that the contribution (value added) of the typical worker is greater in the new workplace. The ROI associated with a successful hire is consequently much higher.

Second, traditional criteria of success such as retention and trainability are far more central to success. Because of the investment companies make in their employees (for example, continuous training), turnover is far more costly to the total quality organization. Similarly, the need for continual learning leads us to contend that trainability is a critical component of success.

Third, success is less likely individual based and more likely team or process based. This creates intriguing challenges in staffing and causes us to look more closely at the situational factors and incorporate them into the staffing process.

The fourth contrast we'd like to draw is this: In the traditional organization, the superior defined success. In the new workplace, each employee has a much broader mix of internal and external customers to satisfy. Team members, cross-functional peers, and other internal customers in the work process, as well as external customers, all have a stake in the performance of the new hire. Consequently, we must take their expectations of success into account as we design and evaluate the staffing process.

Finally, the traditional organization required an employee that would adjust to principally one thing: the task to be performed. The new organization requires and defines success as adjusting and contributing to the broader work process, to the mission, to the culture of the organization, and to continual change.

We will return to this discussion when we talk in more detail about predicting success in the organization. For now, given this more complex standard for success, we can return to our review of the person factors (ability, motivation) that affect success.

Ability: The Can-Do Factor

Individual ability to learn and perform a particular activity is affected by four attributes of the individual: aptitudes/abilities, knowledge, skills, and personality/temperament. Aptitudes represent underlying individual differences in capacity to learn specific knowledge, skills, and temperament. A number of aptitudes define the speed and extent to which individuals can learn and master quality improvement knowledge and skills. Perhaps the most widely cited aptitude, relevant to various quality improvement processes, is general intelligence. Exhibit 2.4 presents a profile of relevant aptitudes.

Knowledge represents the second attribute employees must draw upon in performing work. Knowledge refers to specific bodies of information. The information consists of theories, principles, and facts,

Exhibit 2.4. Quality-relevant aptitudes/mental abilities.

- General intelligence
- Mechanical aptitude
- Creativity
- Reading comprehension
- Verbal comprehension
- Quantitative aptitude/abilities
- Critical thinking, analysis, and reasoning

organized in some systematic way and learned through systematic study. Quality improvement efforts have greatly increased the mix and depth of knowledge required. At the core of TQM knowledge is what Deming termed *statistical thinking*. Scherkenbach notes,

> *Statistical methods are not proprietary. They are available to anyone able to use them (and even to those not able to use them). In this new economic age, you would be dumb not to use them. No one method alone will suffice in your effort to understand what you are managing. Each tool has its strengths and weaknesses, and there is no substitute for knowledge in this area.*[20]

Exhibit 2.5 presents knowledge bases relevant in quality improvement settings.

Skills represent the third attribute underlying individual ability. Skills involve the application of knowledge and some learned, practiced technique such as giving an oral presentation, mediating a dis-

Exhibit 2.5. Sample quality-relevant knowledge bases.

- Basic descriptive and inferential statistics
  (sampling, central tendency, variability, correlation, regression, ANOVA)
- Statistical quality control
- Statistical process control
- Quality theories and approaches (Deming, Juran, Crosby)
- Quality improvement models
- Reengineering
- Problem identification techniques
  (cause-and-effect diagrams, Pareto charts)
- Statistical analysis tools
  (histograms, pie charts, flowcharting, check sheets)
- Design of experiments
  Taguchi methods
- Survey design and analysis
- Solution generation techniques (nominal group technique, brainstorming)
- Quality standards
  Benchmarking
  ISO 9000 series
  Baldrige Award criteria

Exhibit 2.6. Sample quality-relevant skills.

- Basic math skills
- Basic reading skills
- Skill in use of data analysis tools
    Designing and interpreting a flowchart
    Designing and interpreting Pareto charts and histograms
- Skill in group problem-solving techniques
    Leading a group discussion on production run data
    Encouraging input from quiet team members
    Steering a group discussion back to the topic at hand
- Skill in communication
    Listening to others
    Persuading others
    Oral communication
- Skill in coaching others
- Skill in developing and facilitating teams

agreement between two coworkers, or reviewing the data on a run chart. Quality improvement efforts require a variety of skills in the workforce. Exhibit 2.6 presents examples of some of these skills.

Motivation: The Will-Do Factor

As we've noted, there is increased interest in matching the whole person to the requirements of the work and the organization (its strategy and culture). This translates into increased attention to the personality/temperament and interest attributes that determine motivation, fit, and individual satisfaction.

Personality and temperament are the principal attributes that affect motivation to learn, perform, and derive satisfaction from different job responsibilities. Although there are competing definitions, most describe personality as an enduring characteristic of the person that affects how he or she responds to situations. One noted psychologist describes personality as "a relatively stable set of characteristics, tendencies, and temperaments that have been significantly formed by inheritance and by social, cultural, and environmental factors. This set of variables determines the commonalities and differences in the behavior of the individual"[21]

While it has long been argued that personality plays a critical role in performance, the measurement and use of personality in selection

Exhibit 2.7. Example quality-relevant personality/temperament dimensions.

- Flexibility/adaptability (openness to change)
- Openness to learning, development, and retraining
- Teamwork orientation (group identification, involvement)
- Customer orientation (friendliness, agreeableness, empathy)
- Creativity (thorough, responsible, hardworking)
- Conscientiousness (thorough, responsible, hardworking)

and promotion has generally lagged behind the assessment of other attributes such as knowledge, skills, and abilities. However, two facts have contributed to the emergence of personality in selection and promotion. First, it is generally recognized that personality and motivation are far more important to success in the new workplace than they were in the traditional organization. The fit between the individual and the work and culture of the new workplace is much more driven by personality and temperament. We've already noted examples of individual personality and temperament important in the new workplace, and they are presented in Exhibit 2.7. The second development is that there has been tremendous progress in identifying and measuring workplace-relevant dimensions of personality and motivation. We will present some of the alternative tools (inventories, simulations) in chapter 8.

The Situation. The final determinant of performance is the situation—the job and the conditions under which it is performed, the broader work process, the coworkers and team members, and the organization (structure, culture, policies). In chapter 4 we discuss systematic ways to examine these situational influences on performance with the goal of identifying the specific individual attributes likely to contribute to success in that setting.

Summary

In this chapter we've traced some of the changes induced by a focus on quality improvement. Specifically, we've noted that the structure, culture (values), and work design change in the high-involvement quality setting. More importantly, these organizational changes require a workforce with new knowledge, skills, abilities, and temperament. That is what this book is about.

Notes

1. Joan Arnold, Levi Straus worker, commenting on change to self-managed work teams in N. J. Perry, "The Workers of the Future," *Fortune,* special issue (Spring–Summer 1991): 71.

2. M. Imai, *Kaizen: The Key to Japan's Competitive Success* (New York: McGraw-Hill, 1989).

3. Edward E. Lawler, "Total Quality Management and Employee Involvement: Are They Compatible?", *The Academy of Management Executive* (February 1994): 68–76.

4. M. Sashkin and K. J. Kiser, *Putting TQM to Work* (San Francisco: Berrett-Koehler, 1993); James W. Dean Jr. and James R. Evans, "Tools and Techniques for Quality Planning and Improvement," *Total Quality: Management, Organization, and Strategy* (Minneapolis/St. Paul, Minn.: West Publishing Co., 1994); Michael Hammer and James Champy, *Reengineering the Corporation* (New York: Harper Business, 1993); Richard S. Wellins, William C. Byham, and Jeanne M. Wilson, *Empowered Teams* (San Francisco: Jossey-Bass, 1991); P. R. Scholtes, *The Team Handbook* (Madison, Wis.: Joiner and Associates, 1988).

5. Wellins, Byham, and Wilson, *Empowered Teams.*

6. Thomas J. Peters and Robert H. Waterman, *In Search of Excellence* (New York: Harper and Row, 1982).

7. W. Edwards Deming, *Out of the Crisis* (Cambridge, Mass.: MIT Center for Advanced Engineering Study, 1986).

8. Hammer and Champy, *Reengineering the Corporation.*

9. Richard Willing, "Big Three Retools to Meet Demands of Future," *The Detroit News and Free Press,* 11 June 1995, A1.

10. Sashkin and Kiser, *Putting TQM to Work,* chapter 8.

11. Deming, *Out of the Crisis.*

12. J. F. Coates, J. Jarratt, and J. B. Mahaffie, "Future Work," *The Futurist* (May-June 1991): 15.

13. J. Richard Hackman and Greg R. Oldham, *Work Redesign* (Reading, Mass.: Addison-Wesley, 1980).

14. 3M Canada, *3M Canada Applicant Information Booklet: Preparing for the Selection Process* (1992), 2–3.

15. Lawler, "Total Quality Management and Employee Involvement: Are They Compatible?"; see Bob E. Hayes, "How to Measure Empowerment," *Quality Progress* 27, no. 2 (1994): 41–46 for an excellent treatment of the measurement of employee perceptions.

16. William W. Scherkenbach, *The Deming Route to Quality and Productivity* (Washington, D.C.: CEEPress, 1987), 95.

17. Lynn R. Offermann and Marilyn K. Gowing, "Personnel Selection in the Future: The Impact of Changing Demographics and the Nature of Work" in *Personnel Selection in Organizations,* Neal Schmitt and Walter C. Borman, eds. (San Francisco: Jossey-Bass, 1993), chapter 12.

18. Scherkenbach, *The Deming Route to Quality and Productivity,* 27.

19. Offermann and Gowing, "Personnel Selection in the Future: The Impact of Changing Demographics and the Nature of Work."

20. Scherkenbach, *The Deming Route to Quality and Productivity,* 95.

21. Salvatore R. Maddi, *Personality Theories: A Comparative Analysis* (Homewood, Ill.: Dorsey Press, 1989), 63.

chapter 3

Technical and Legal Standards for Staffing Practices: A Primer on Value-Added Staffing

We begin our discussion of standards for staffing by looking in on a selection process in progress at Ajax Manufacturing: The plant HR manager, Barb; Mike, the team leader from production team 12; and three team associates from team 12, Sally, Joan, and Leslie, are gathered in the conference room. The purpose of the meeting is to discuss the candidates each had interviewed earlier in the week. Joan, a team associate, looks over at the paper in front of Barb and the heading catches her attention, "Position Description—Production Team Associate." She nudges her coworker Sally and in a semiwhisper says, "I didn't know there was a new write-up on the team associate job. When did we get that?" Sally shrugs and the others who overheard her look equally dumbfounded. "I didn't get one," adds Mike Miller. Barb (the HR manager) breaks in, "I didn't have it ready before you interviewed the candidates . . . so, I thought that you could just use the one for production that we've always used in the past. They're pretty close, anyway . . . I have copies for you and you can use the new description to evaluate the candidates you already interviewed. I'm sure that you talked about the kind of things that you'll need in order to rate the four of them." She passes the position descriptions around the room. "OK, let's go around the room and each of you give me your rankings of the four candidates, with #1 being your first choice. Rank them in terms of who you feel will bring the most to the job and to the company."

One by one they go around the room as Barb writes the names on the board. As he finishes the last list, the room is silent. She steps back and everyone stares at the results.

Barb	Sally	Joan	Mike	Leslie
1. Joyce	Pete	Sara	Tom	Joyce
2. Tom	Joyce	Pete	Pete	Sara
3. Sara	Tom	Tom	Sara	Tom
4. Pete	Sara	Joyce	Joyce	Pete

Barb breaks the silence: "Let me figure out the average ranking for each candidate," and she adds the data to the chart.

Candidate	Average ranking
Joyce	2.4
Tom	2.4
Sara	2.6
Pete	2.6

Their expressions convey the question, what went wrong? Why are the rankings so inconsistent? The greatest agreement is about Tom, and three people ranked him third. How is it that the top choice of both Barb and Leslie (Joyce) is ranked last by both Joan and Mike? With this kind of inconsistency, could any one ranking possibly be the correct, accurate one?

How did this happen? They all interviewed the same people and they all had the same job in mind—at least they thought so. After all, four of them work in the job and they think that they know it fairly well, they're all fairly good at interacting with people, and they all express confidence in their ability to size up a good applicant. Barb asked them to rank the candidates on how well they would do the job and who would make the best contribution to the team. It all seemed so straightforward!

Because their rankings are so different, could it be that each interviewer was ranking something different? While they all know the job, did something unique to each individual cause him or her to pursue different questions or hear answers differently? Could this explain the lack of consistency? Let's look back at some of their discussion to see if we can get some idea.

Barb starts the discussion, "OK, let's go around the room and discuss each candidate. I'll start. I ranked Joyce first because she really knows her statistical process control [SPC] . . . she's done it for more than four years now. I think she would bring us some strong experience in that area." "Well," interrupted Joan, " I put her last because I don't think that she will get along with any of us . . . and I think that is more important than her SPC background." "Oh, I like her a lot," noted Leslie. "She is definitely self-confident. I don't think we'll have a problem getting along with her, as long as we are open to new ideas." "Oh, you mean as long as you see things her way," added Joan. Sally joined in, " Well, I put her in the middle, but not for the reasons you've mentioned. I don't think she will stay here—we'll be hiring again in six months. I asked her what she enjoyed most and she said 'training others,' something she's not going to get to do here."

Mike was the last to offer his opinion. "Well, I ranked her last because I thought that she was too pushy. She didn't let me get a word in edgewise. She did almost all of the talking in the interview." "So, you met your match," Leslie interjected, and everyone in the room roared with laughter. "Well, all I know is that if I were to go to an interview, I would show more respect to the interviewer. I wouldn't talk the interviewer's ears off," Mike replied. He continued, "Any woman who is that pushy is going to be trouble!" In unison, Leslie, Joan, and Sally erupted in boos and hisses, while Barb glanced at her watch. She realizes that it is going to be a long afternoon.

Overview

Does this scenario sound familiar? If it does, then this chapter will be of interest to you. We present and review four standards used to evaluate all staffing tools and processes: reliability, validity, fairness, and utility (ROI). These standards differentiate effective from ineffective staffing. While they address statistical, legal, and administrative aspects of effective staffing, for the most part, they translate nicely into measures of process effectiveness along the line we discussed in chapter 1. Mastery of these standards will help you design an effective staffing process; identify and select appropriate assessment procedures (interview questions, tests, and so on); and avoid unnecessary, costly legal entanglements. Most importantly, the design of these standards into the staffing process will help deliver greater value (utility) to the organization. We close this chapter with a case illustration of the validation of a test relevant to the new workplace—PDI's Customer Service Inventory in a hospital setting.

Reliability in Staffing

A test, an interview, or even the evaluation of a resume are all measurements of the applicant. You collect information and use it to compare one applicant to another, or to rank the applicants, or to compare them against some standard. In doing so you are measuring the applicants. Because of this, we evaluate assessment devices used in staffing along the same standards we use for physical measurement. The first and perhaps most fundamental standard is reliability.

Reliability is a well-established concept to quality practitioners. When they speak of reliability, they refer to concepts such as product dependability and consistency. It is appropriate to apply a similar expectation for consistency to the staffing process. In using the term *reliability*, we evoke concern for *consistency of measurement*. As a basis for comparison, consider the consistency attained from measurements provided by a ruler. A ruler measures the physical property of distance. You can measure an object using one ruler and obtain a result. You can return and remeasure the same object again and obtain the same result. Similarly, you could substitute one ruler for another and get the same result. Rulers, as measuring devices, provide highly consistent results. We strive to attain the same consistency from the measurements we make of human attributes.

Reliability is, in many respects, the most fundamental of standards in staffing. To the extent that a measure is lacking in reliability, we are unable to use the measurements it produces. This fact is illustrated in the scenario described at the beginning of this chapter. The lack of agreement among our interviewers creates a suspicion that they are not all measuring the same aspect of each candidate. Furthermore, their individual comments lead us to believe that they probably didn't apply the same standards to each applicant. From Mike's comment you might suspect that he applies different standards to women than to men. All of these factors contribute to inconsistency. Such inconsistency leaves us at a loss as to the true ranking of the candidates. Under these circumstances, which person's judgment do you go with?

Because reliability is such a critical component to the design of an effective staffing process, we would like to give you a well-rounded feel for the concept. We're about to lead you on a user-friendly discussion of what is a highly technical, statistically based topic. For those of you who are statistically inclined, this discussion may whet your appetite for additional information, so we supply additional references and additional discussion in later sections. However, if you count yourself among those who grow weak in the knees at the mention of statistics, we ask that you bear with us. Understanding the statistical basis of reliability will pay great benefits in understanding and dealing with the staffing issues encountered in later chapters.

Reliability: Freedom from Random Error

When you administer a test, you obtain an observed score for the applicant. We think of that score as consisting of two components: the true score and error in measurement.

Observed test score = True score + Measurement error

The observed score represents our best estimate of the true level on the attribute (for example, the true level of knowledge, skill, or ability). However, you must remember that this observed score is only an estimate of the person's true ability. This estimate is distorted by various errors of measurement. For example, temporary changes in the person being assessed, changes in the person administering the selection measure (for example, an interviewer), or changes in the physical conditions under which the test is administered are all potential sources of measurement error. You can think of reliability as freedom from these sources of random error.

It might be helpful to think of measurement error and reliability another way. Imagine this situation: You administer a test to the same individual repeatedly (in fact, an infinite number of times—a theoretical option available to statisticians). Assume that each administration is independent of the others; that is, each time the person takes the test, he does so without any recollection of the previous administrations. We then plot a frequency distribution of the scores he attains. The result is a distribution like that depicted as *a* in Figure 3.1. The first important point that we can take from distribution a is that, although the person's true level of ability does not change from administration to administration, the observed scores do change. This variability in observed scores is due to measurement error. On some occasions, errors

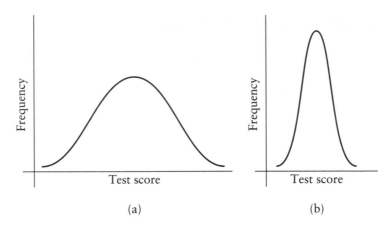

Figure 3.1. Distributions of test scores attained by one individual over repeated administrations of the same test: a, unreliable test; b, reliable test.

of measurement result in an *overestimate* of the individual's true ability. On other occasions, errors of measurement result in an *underestimate* of the individual's true ability. This is an important principle to remember as you use any test: Any one administration of a test provides only an estimate of the individual's true ability. The fact is that the observed score you record for the applicant is very likely to be an underestimate or an overestimate of the true score—the true ability.

A second important point to remember is that tests differ in reliability. Some tests produce scores with less variability due to random error. Figure 3.1b depicts the distribution of scores attained by the same individual on a highly reliable test. Note that, compared to 3.1a, there is less variability in the scores obtained by the individual. The less the effects of random error in a test, the less the variability in the test scores attained by an individual, and the more we can rely on any one administration of the test.

If the measures (interviews, tests) used are perfectly reliable, that is, free of random error, the person's score will be exactly the same with each administration of the test. In that situation, with random measurement error equal to "0," we would be confident that the observed score we get from testing the applicant is his or her exact true score—his or her exact level on the attribute being measured.

For those familiar with SPC, perhaps another perspective will bring the concept of test reliability into focus. Imagine a run chart of repeated administrations of a test. As before, assume that the same person is tested repeatedly and assume that each administration is independent of the other administrations (the person has no memory of the test items). The scores obtained by this person would vary due to measurement error (see Figure 3.2). They would vary between an upper and lower limit. Over the course of the run, the variability we see would take on a normal distribution—with equal proportions of underestimates and overestimates. We can identify the upper and lower control limits and the probability of extreme scores. The modal (most frequent) score of this run represents the best bet on the individual's true ability. Our objective is to choose tests for which the spread (the control limits) is minimized and to standardize and control the administration of the testing process to minimize error-induced variation.

Coping with Unreliability. If the fact that the observed scores obtained from tests are only estimates of the applicants' true abilities, and if the fact that the results may well be either underestimates or overestimates of the applicants' actual abilities troubles you, we have some comforting news. First, it's good to be troubled by these facts. That means that you are very likely to make appropriate, responsible use of tests. Well-selected, standardized tests have much to offer in improving the identification and selection of quality-oriented employees. But they must be used responsibly and consistently with their design. Second, we can offer as comfort the fact that well-developed standardized tests provide reliability-based statistics that allow us to determine, in advance of actually using the test, a confidence interval around the observed scores our applicants will obtain. A confidence interval is simply a range—an upper and lower bound—around the observed score. (It's analogous to the upper and lower control limits on a control chart.)

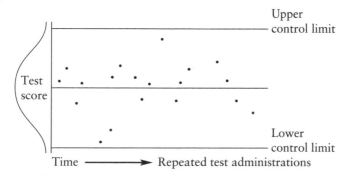

Figure 3.2. Run chart for repeated administrations of the same test.

The basis for computing a confidence interval is termed the *standard error of measurement* (SEM). The SEM is essentially a translation of the test reliability into the same unit of measurement as the test scores. The greater the reliability, the lower the SEM.

We can compute confidence intervals with varying degrees of assurance. For any given test, the greater the assurance we require that the applicant's true score lies within the confidence interval, the wider that interval will be. Typically, we wish to be 95 percent certain that the score is within the confidence interval. This produces a wide range to depict the individual's score, but it gives us strong confidence that the true score lies within. The actual computation of confidence intervals is fairly straightforward.

For 68 percent assurance that
the confidence interval includes   = observed test score $\pm (1 \times \text{SEM})$
the individual's true score

For 95 percent assurance   = observed test score $\pm (1.96 \times \text{SEM})$

The confidence interval allows us to use test scores more responsibly. For example, we can use the confidence interval to determine if the observed scores obtained by two applicants are truly different. In addition, we can use the confidence interval to determine if an applicant's score falls above a cut-off or passing score we've established, and so forth.

An example may be helpful. Suppose you administer a basic math test. The observed score for applicant A is 70. The observed score for applicant B is 65. Does applicant A appear to know more math than applicant B? The way to address this question is to determine whether or not the confidence intervals for each observed score overlap. If they don't, we can conclude that applicant A knows more math than applicant B. To compute a 95 percent confidence interval for each applicant,

Applicant A's = $70 \pm (1.96 \times 2.21)$ Applicant B's = $65 \pm (1.96 \times 2.21)$
$\quad\quad\quad = 70 \pm (4.33)$ $\quad\quad\quad\quad\quad\quad\quad = 65 \pm (4.33)$
$\quad\quad\quad = 65.67 - 74.33$ $\quad\quad\quad\quad\quad\quad = 60.67 - 69.33$

We can conclude (with 95 percent assurance) that applicant A's true math ability lies between 65.67 and 74.33. Similarly, we can conclude (with 95 percent assurance) that applicant B's true math ability lies between 60.67 and 69.33. However, because the confidence intervals overlap, we can't say with assurance that applicant A has greater mastery of math than applicant B.

To summarize, the SEM and the confidence interval give us a practical way to deal with the fact that any test score we obtain is distorted by error in measurement. Reputable standardized tests will present test scores in terms of confidence intervals devised from SEM expressions of test reliability. (Fortunately, the computations presented earlier are usually unnecessary.) The implication is, of course, to choose or construct assessment devices that are highly reliable. They produce more precise estimates of the applicant's true ability (more narrow confidence intervals), and because of that you can place greater confidence in the obtained scores.

A final point we'd like to make is that increasing the reliability of the data used in the staffing process is a principal means to improving performance of the process. The content of this book and the recommendations we will make are intended to assist you in your effort to standardize the staffing process and minimize random error. The net effect of reduced error will be to increase the reliability of the staffing decisions made in your organization.

A Closer Look at Different Aspects of Reliability

Now that we've dealt with the basis of reliability—consistency—and the basic challenge of minimizing random error, we'd like to take a closer look at these concepts.

Different Aspects of Reliability. There are four aspects to the concept of reliability in measurement. We strive to achieve

1. Consistency in composition

2. Consistency over time

3. Consistency over different forms

4. When human judgment is employed, consistency over different judges, termed *interrater reliability.*

Each of these aspects of reliability is presented in Exhibit 3.1 and is discussed here.

The first aspect of reliability is *internal consistency* (consistency in composition). Most measures of human attributes are constructed of numerous components. For example, a knowledge test consists of numerous questions or items. Internal consistency reliability is a reflection of the extent to which there is consistency across the various

Exhibit 3.1. Aspects of reliability in staffing.

Aspect	Definition	Source of error	Statistical expression
Internal consistency (consistency in composition)	Do the items that make up the test measure the same attribute?	Diversity in test content	Intercorrelation of test items (coefficient alpha; KR-20, eta-squared)
Stability (consistency over time)	Are the results obtained stable over time?	Temporary changes in the *person* (mood, attention, health); in the *situation* (room conditions, heat, light, noise levels); and in test *administration* (directions, timing)	Correlation of test scores from two administrations of the test
Alternate forms (substitutability)	Do different forms of the test measure the same attribute(s)?	Item differences in the different test forms	Correlation of results from alternate forms of the test
Interrater reliability	Are judgments provided by different judges equivalent?	Differences in attention, perception, and memory of judges; differences in understanding of job and hiring criteria	Intercorrelation of ratings produced by different judges

items that make up the test. It refers to consistency in the composition of the test. The underlying principle is that, for a test to be consistent, its composition must be internally uniform. The greater the internal consistency of a test, the greater our assurance that the overall score on the test is a reflection of one specific attribute. If a measure lacks internal consistency, it alerts us that the items on the test are measuring different attributes.

Internal consistency is assessed by the intercorrelation of the items that make up the test. These data assure us that the total score we obtain for the applicant is a reflection of a single, uniform attribute.

Because internal consistency is a test design issue, there is little you can do to affect internal consistency reliability. The best advice is to avoid using assessment tools for which there is no clear evidence of internal consistency reliability. A reputable, published test will present evidence of internal consistency in the test manual or in other documentation.

A second aspect of reliability is termed *stability* (consistency over time). We would expect the scores obtained by applicants on a test of SPC knowledge administered today to be consistent with the scores that the applicants would obtain if the test were readministered next week. Just as we can remeasure physical distance with the same ruler at two different times and obtain consistent results, we expect the same stability over time in our staffing measures. The essential factor of interest in the concept of stability over time is that we want our measures to be as free as possible from the effects of random or temporary changes in the person or in the setting in which the test is administered. Clearly, the actual underlying attribute will change over an extended time period. For example, the applicant may, over the course of two to three weeks, learn more about SPC. An effective test will detect change if the applicant's true level of ability has changed. We accept and, in fact, welcome that variability. Our concern and our interest is in eliminating error in measurement attributable to transitory changes in the applicant or in the test setting.

There are various sources of error that reduce the stability of a test score. Essentially, any temporary factor that changes the individual's performance is a source of error. Individual factors such as level of fatigue, mood, or health at the time a test is taken affect reliability. Factors in the setting such as the conditions of the room (heat, light, distractions, and so on) affect the reliability of test scores. Finally, administration procedures such as the reading of the directions, or the timing of the test, can affect the reliability of the test. Our goal in staffing is to standardize all of the factors and minimize the extent to which they change from one administration to the next. Throughout the book we will talk about the practices that build standardization into each component of the staffing process (resume reviews, interviews, test administration, assessment exercises, and so forth).

One way to increase the stability of a test score is to increase the number of items that comprise the test. To draw a parallel to sampling for quality control, the more items we select from a batch, the more accurate (stable) our estimate of that batch will be. The same is true of test construction. Think of each item as a sample of the person. The more samples that make up the test, the more stable the assessment will be. This concept is particularly useful when we apply it to the interview. The pooled judgments of four interviewers will be a more stable reflection of the applicant than will be the pooled judgments of two.

Standardized tests provide estimates of the stability of the test over time. They typically report correlations between test scores for two administrations of the test. It is important that we follow the administration guidelines for using the test to assure reliable measurement.

The third aspect of reliability is termed *alternate forms reliability* (substitutability). Many standardized tests are available in more than one form. Just as we can substitute one ruler for another and be assured that we are measuring the same thing with each, we seek the same substitutability in the use of tests. Although the actual test items differ on each form of the test, the test is constructed so that each form is measuring the same attribute. Alternate forms of a test provide both practical and theoretical advantages. First, they allow for retesting of applicants without concern that the retested applicant will benefit from practice or memory of items on the first administration of the test. Second, they improve the security of the test when there are multiple administrations. You can administer the test on multiple occasions without concern that applicants will disclose specific content to others. From a theoretical perspective, the existence of multiple forms of a test, all of which are highly correlated with one another, gives us greater assurance that the tests are well constructed in that the items that make up each form are sampling a definable, stable attribute.

If alternate forms of a test are available, the test manual should provide evidence of alternate form reliability. Typically, these are based on studies in which the different forms are administered to a sample of individuals and the correlation between performance on the alternate forms is reported. If you are interested in testing numerous applicants or allowing for the retesting of individual applicants, the availability of alternate forms is a desirable feature to consider as you review and choose tests.

The fourth aspect of reliability is *interrater reliability*. It estimates the extent to which the judgments provided by different raters are intercorrelated. It is relevant whenever there is judgment in the scoring of a test or measure. For example, the five interviewers at Ajax Manufacturing each met with and evaluated all of the candidates for the team associate vacancy. We would expect their judgments to correlate. If their judgments do not converge (correlate), the review process lacks reliability. As we noted earlier, a lack of consistency raises a number of serious implications regarding the interview and rating process. For example, if judgments made by the interviewers do not correlate, we cannot place great confidence in the process. From the perspective of the applicant, whether or not he or she receives a job offer is as much dependent on which interviewer met him or her as it is on his or her competency. Just as you are assured that you can substitute one ruler for another and rely on the measure it produces, you want the same substitutability in the various judges that participate in each step of the staffing process. How, for example, could you increase the reliability of the interview judgments made at Ajax? For now, there are a number of recommendations we would make to improve the interjudge reliability at Ajax. The theme that characterizes these recommendations is *standardization*.

- First, we must ensure that all candidates are interviewed by each interviewer.

- Second, we must ensure that each interviewer follows the same structure (outline, questions) with each applicant he or she sees (each applicant experiences the same test).

- Third, we must ensure that each interviewer focuses the discussion on content (knowledge, skills, abilities, temperament) clearly related to success at Ajax. In effect, we will implement one consistent, standardized interview process from which all interviews are conducted.

Following these guidelines is a first step toward assuring that judgments produced by different interviewers are reliable and substitutable. We will elaborate on these guidelines in chapters 9 and 10 and provide a detailed plan for standardizing the interview and increasing the reliability and validity of judgments produced by different interviewers.

Finally, the reliability of judgments made at each stage of the process is a highly relevant process measure. To the extent that the process lacks reliability, the output (selection decision) will be deficient.

Validity in Staffing

Validity: Is What We Are Measuring Related to Performance?

Reliability assures consistency and repeatability. However, it does not ensure that the differences in scores on the measures we've selected reflect differences in underlying attributes we believe we are measuring or that they are related to job performance. Furthermore, it does not ensure that those attributes are the ones we should be measuring. To return to the ruler analogy, we may find that we are using a distorted ruler that consistently provides inaccurate results. We get the same results over and over, but the results do not characterize the object we're attempting to measure. Or, we may find that the ruler measures height accurately, but what we should be measuring is weight. Similarly, consistency in staffing measures, while a fundamental requirement, does not assure that what we are measuring is relevant or appropriate for the job and work setting. Did the questions asked by the interview team at Ajax get at information relevant to the individual's subsequent success as a team member at Ajax? Would the interview judgments accurately predict subsequent performance and fit of the worker into the quality culture at Ajax? These are questions of validity. As suggested by these questions, there are different aspects of validity, and you will encounter references to each as you search for and review different assessment devices. We take a look at four aspects of validity shortly: criterion-related, content, construct, and process validity. Before doing so, we must address a more fundamental question: What is it we are trying to predict?

Predicting Success

The intent of staffing is to predict success in the organization. Essentially, the problem becomes choosing among numerous applicants those who are most likely to succeed in the organization. We assemble assessment devices to measure applicants in advance of hiring them, and use the results of those measures to predict success or failure. The assessment devices we term *predictors*. The focus of our prediction, various definitions of successful performance, we term the *criteria*. However, before we can predict successful performance, we must first define it. If we fail to clearly define successful performance, we'll fail in our efforts to predict it. From this perspective, the question of validity becomes: Do the assessment devices (the predictors) relate to (predict) subsequent success in the organization?

Defining Successful Performance. Traditionally, there has been a wide range of criteria used to define and measure successful performance. Cascio summarizes the dimensions by which performance has traditionally been measured.[1] *Output measures* express productivity in quantifiable terms—for example, number of widgets produced or dollar value of sales achieved. *Quality measures* express performance in terms of product or service quality, such as number of customer complaints or measures of scrap or waste. *Lost time measures* treat individuals' attendance as a performance measure—for example, measuring number of times tardy or number of absences. *Turnover measures* treat longevity as an expression of performance—for example, counting voluntary terminations and involuntary terminations. *Trainability* measures performance in terms of the extent to which training is needed, the time it takes a new hire to reach proficiency, or the level of performance reached. *Promotability* measures performance in terms of the employee's rise in the organization—number of promotions or time between promotions. *Performance evaluations* rely on subjective ratings of employees by others (typically supervisors) on trait or performance dimensions.

While many of these traditional criteria do define, in whole or in part, the successful employee, in many settings they may well be inappropriate or deficient. That is, while they may be a part of what defines a successful employee, they may also miss much of what defines success. They seem particularly deficient in capturing success in the quality setting.

The following are some contrasts we see between how traditional and quality-oriented organizations define success. First, in the traditional organization, predicting success may simply have meant predicting who could show up on time, produce the most widgets, and avoid accidents. Successful employees today are multidimensional: Rather than performing a job with specific output, they are more likely to be part of a larger process. They plan, analyze, experiment, and change the work process. They coach and teach their peers. Although we have no data, we venture to suggest that the value-added contribution of their effort is more substantial than in the traditional organization.

Second, traditional criteria of successful performance have greater impact and carry greater weight in our conception of the successful employee in a quality setting. Two prominent examples are turnover and trainability. The traditional organization treated turnover as an important criterion, but gauged its impact only in terms of replacement costs. A number of authors have suggested that the real cost of turnover is lost quality, service, and customer satisfaction.[2] Others have pointed out that the investment made by quality-oriented organizations in their workforce makes turnover much more costly, and consequently, a more important factor in defining success.[3] In a *Quality Management Journal* article, Robert E. Cole makes a compelling argument for the cost of turnover to quality.[4] (In fact, later in this chapter you will see some fascinating results on the dollar impact associated with decreased turnover attributable to testing.) Consequently, the quality-oriented organization is more likely to include longevity as a central component in its definition of successful employees. Similarly, success in initial training has long been used as a measure of success. However, this aspect of the successful employee has taken on greater importance in the new workplace where trainability—both the ability and willingness to learn—is central to success.

Third, whereas traditional organizations defined success as individual results (number of units produced, dollar value of individual sales, and so on), the quality setting is more likely to define success in terms of team-based results or organization results. Richard A. Guzzo notes, "individual output is but one component of productivity. Only by analyzing the entire organizational environment (the situation) or process factors and all outputs (outside variables) will accurate predictions be made regarding the individual attributes required for affective functioning within organizations."[5] This compels us to broaden our attention in staffing to the work process and the organization mission and culture.

Fourth, in the traditional organization, promotability was a key criterion of managerial success (used to define and measure success). Many studies of management selection practices used promotability as the standard for success. The flatter, multi-track organization, typical of the quality improvement setting, has altered the relevance of this as a definition of success. Fifth, in the traditional organization, successful performance was defined by the superior. In some cases the individual had input through programs such as goal setting, management by objectives, and so on. In the quality setting, others (peers, subordinates, customers) have a clear stake and should have input in defining individual success.

Finally, performance dimensions critical in the new organization are different than those on which the traditional organization based its definition and appraisal (performance appraisal) of success. New dimensions such as coaching, teamwork, group facilitation, continual learning and development, and creativity are central to success in the quality setting. Other dimensions that may have had some importance in the traditional setting, such as conscientiousness, are far more important in the quality setting. An excellent source for the discussion of the definition and measurement of success in quality settings is provided by the Steven B. Knouse book, *The Reward and Recognition Process in Total Quality Management.*[6]

Our point is simply this: Before we can identify appropriate assessment devices (predictors) and build a staffing process, we must think through more clearly what exactly it is we wish to predict. When we know what success in the organization entails, we can then better select assessment tools to predict those outcomes.

Different Aspects of Validity

Criterion-Related Validity. Criterion-related validity involves examination of the statistical relationship between performance on the assessment device (interview, test, reference check) and some measure of performance in the organization. The criterion-related validity of a test is examined by correlating the assessment scores obtained by a group of current employees or applicants with measures of current or subsequent success in the organization. The question of interest is: Does performance on the test correlate with measures of success? For example, Figure 3.3 presents a hypothetical scatter plot of two variables—individual scores on a test of quality principles and ratings of the individual's subsequent job performance. As you can see, those who attain high scores on the test tend to receive higher ratings on job performance, while those who receive lower scores on the test tend to receive lower ratings on job performance. Such a relationship between a test and subsequent job performance allows you to use the test to improve your prediction of the subsequent job performance of applicants. Because this statistical approach to validity presents such promise for staffing decisions, we will present an extended example in a later section.

There are alternate designs for conducting a criterion-related validity study, the advantages and disadvantages of which are beyond the scope of this book. Each approach has as the central objective the identification of a statistical relationship between the test and

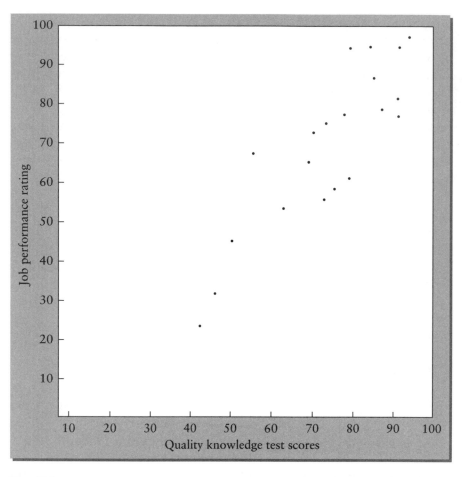

Figure 3.3. Scatter plot of quality practices tests scores and job performance ratings for a sample of quality technicians.

subsequent on-the-job behavior and success within the organization. Manuals for reputable standardized tests will report the results of validation studies by typically reporting correlations between test performance and job performance on specific jobs of interest.

Content Validity. Content validity reflects the extent to which the items or tasks on an assessment device sample the attribute we intend to measure. Evidence for content validity is based on the process by which a test, or an interview, was assembled, and it is typically expressed in terms of the judgments of experts that the items used in constructing the device, or the behaviors required in performing the test, are essential components of the attribute or performance we seek to measure.

It is acceptable to rely on evidence of content validity when the performance on the test is very much like (samples) the actual performance required on the job. For example, content validation is an approach often used to demonstrate the job relatedness of work samples and simulations. These devices are slices or samples of the job and, because of that, the validation process rests on showing that behavior (or performance) on the test samples actual behaviors (or performance) required on the job. One example of a content-valid work simulation is the use of an assessment exercise to evaluate various team effectiveness skills. The key justification for the content validity of such a test is the premise that the situation the applicant finds herself in is a replication of the situations she will find on the job. The behaviors we look for as she performs the simulation are behaviors we expect from proficient employees on the job. Exhibit 3.2 presents the rationale for the content validation of a team assessment exercise by presenting the link between key behaviors required on the job and on the test.

Exhibit 3.2. Content validity of team leader assessment exercise.

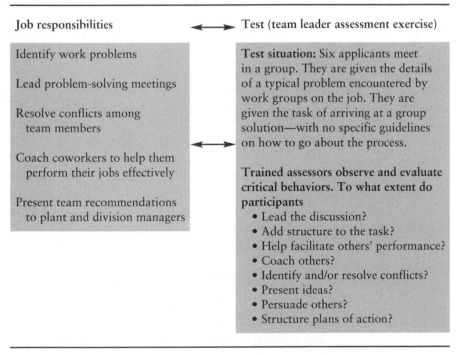

Job responsibilities	←→	Test (team leader assessment exercise)
Identify work problems Lead problem-solving meetings Resolve conflicts among team members Coach coworkers to help them perform their jobs effectively Present team recommendations to plant and division managers	←→	**Test situation:** Six applicants meet in a group. They are given the details of a typical problem encountered by work groups on the job. They are given the task of arriving at a group solution—with no specific guidelines on how to go about the process. **Trained assessors observe and evaluate critical behaviors. To what extent do participants** • Lead the discussion? • Add structure to the task? • Help facilitate others' performance? • Coach others? • Identify and/or resolve conflicts? • Present ideas? • Persuade others? • Structure plans of action?

Because work samples can play such a prominent role, and their development and validation is relatively straightforward, we devote portions of chapters 7 and 8 to their use.

Construct Validity. A third frequently cited aspect of validity is construct validity. Essentially, construct validity deals with the more fundamental question of what, exactly, the test measures. The test claims to measure a specific attribute (for example, creativity or flexibility). In studies of the test we do see that differences in test scores correlate with differences in subsequent job performance. However, the underlying question remains: Are the differences we see caused by differences in this specific attribute? Evidence for construct validity is essentially a collection of all that we know about a test, including evidence for its content validity and evidence regarding what behaviors it correlates with and predicts. Admittedly, it is of greater interest to the scientist than it is to the practitioner. For you, the manager, wishing to use a test to improve selection decision making, knowing that performance on the test correlates with and can be used to predict subsequent performance is the primary concern.

Process Validity. A final perspective on validity addresses the means by which the selection process has been assembled. In a sense, process validity asks: Who have been the suppliers of the information on which the staffing process is based? The essential point is that the design of the process must draw on representatives from throughout the organization. To ensure process validity, include a demographic mix (race, gender, age) reflective of the organization (and your customers within the organization) when designing and implementing each phase of the selection process. For example, include diverse input in constructing the hiring specifications. Utilize a diverse group of recruiters and interviewers. And perhaps most important, source an applicant pool that reflects racial, gender, and age diversity. Such diverse input increases the process validity and user acceptance of the process.[7] Finally, process validity also means ensuring that the forms and procedures used in the process are customer friendly.

A Statistical Approach to Staffing: Using Data to Predict Performance

An advantage of criterion-related validity is that it establishes a statistical relationship between an assessment device (the predictor) and some measure of success (the criterion). A statistical relationship allows you to use one measure, the assessment device, to explain and predict the other (job performance). The statistical tool most frequently used is correlation and regression. If our criterion-related validity study has been conducted correctly, we can apply the results of that study, conducted on a sample of participants, to future applicants. This allows us to use the test performance of future applicants to improve our prediction of their likely job performance. The following hypothetical example provides a brief depiction of the logic and advantages associated with criterion-related validation of a staffing procedure.

Table 3.1 presents partial data from a hypothetical criterion-related validity study. Seventy-five participants completed a 100-item quality practices knowledge test, assessing their mastery of the seven basic

Table 3.1. Quality practices test scores and job performance scores for a sample of quality technicians.

Employee ID	Test score	Job performance rating
1	86	74
2	97	91
3	51	67
4	41	31
5	60	52
6	70	70
7	73	74
8	79	59
9	46	44
10	67	61
11	71	52
12	88	75
13	81	92
14	40	22
15	53	74
16	77	74
17	79	91
18	84	83
19	91	91
20	90	72

quality tools. After six months of employment, supervisors, unaware of individual test performance, rated each participant on a 100-point measure of job performance. The test scores and job performance scores are presented for 20 of the 75 participants.

Figure 3.3 presents a scatter plot of test and job performance scores. Each point represents the coordinates for test and job performance for one individual. The linear relationship between these two variables can be summarized by a statistic, the Pearson product-moment correlation. The correlation for this data for the entire group of 75 participants is $r = .40$, $p < .05$. The probability value, p, represents the results of a statistical test of the correlation. In effect, it indicates that a correlation of this magnitude, for a sample of size $N = 75$, is likely to occur by chance only 5 percent of the time. This gives us greater comfort that the relationship between the two variables measured in our study is reflective of a true relationship between test performance and job performance, rather than merely a chance occurrence.

The desirability of criterion-related data such as that presented in the example is that it allows us to use one variable to account for or predict another. To do so, we compute a regression line and regression equation. A *regression line* is a line that summarizes the linear relationship between two variables. It is termed the *best-fit line* because it is derived so as to minimize the total distance between the observations and the regression line, or to minimize the errors in predicting one variable from another. Figure 3.4 presents the correlation scatter plot with the mathematically determined regression line.

Accuracy of Predictions Based on Regression Line. The regression line is the best-fit line. For any test score obtained by subsequent applicants, the regression line can be used to make a best-bet prediction of job performance. However, when the regression line is applied to the data and used to predict job performance from test performance, there will be errors in the predictions. You can evaluate the effectiveness of the regression line by comparing predicted job performance scores with those actually achieved on the job. This can be done because we have actual job performance scores for our sample. We use the data to examine how *closely* the predicted job performance scores correspond to actual job performance. For example, employee 8 and 17 each scored 79 on the quality practices test. Based on the regression line, the predicted job performance score is 75. In actuality, 17 scored 91 on job performance and 8 scored 59. The regression line underestimates 17's job performance and it overestimates 8's job performance. Despite these errors in prediction, over the range of test scores the re-

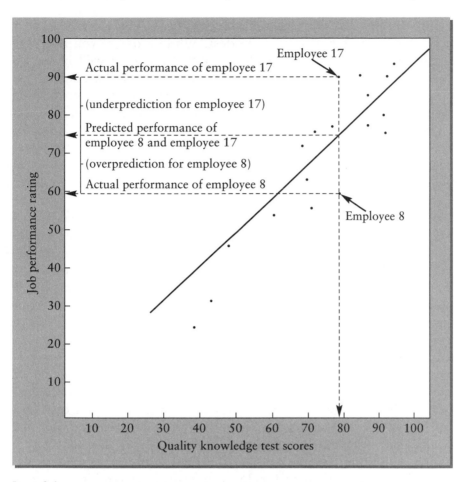

Figure 3.4. Regression line for quality practices test scores and job performance ratings for a sample of quality technicians.

gression line represents a tool for improving the prediction of job performance from test performance.

The Regression Equation. Although the example is presented in graphical form, the data from a criterion-related validity study yield a mathematical expression of the relationship depicted by the regression line. A *regression equation* expresses the slope and intercept of the line. The regression equation is useful because it can be used to transform any test score into a predicted job performance (success) score.

Interpretation of the Correlation. One point that will become clear as you read about testing in chapters 7 and 8 and on the use of the interview in chapters 9 and 10 is that the correlations between predictors and criteria are typically very modest. While those of you from the quality disciplines (the engineering disciplines) may well be accustomed to correlations of magnitude $r = .80$ and $r = .90$, criterion-related validity correlations in staffing are, unfortunately, much more modest. The prediction of human behavior is more challenging. Even our best predictors (cognitive ability tests and work samples) typically produce correlations of about $r = .40$ to $r = .50$ in criterion-related validity studies. However, as we will demonstrate shortly, even modest correlations can result in improved selection and promotion decisions.

To interpret correlations it is typical to use what is termed the *coefficient of determination*, which is simply the square of the correlation. This statistic expresses the percentage of variance the correlated variables share. This statistic is useful in describing how effective one variable is in accounting for or predicting another. For example, the correlation between cognitive ability tests and subsequent job performance of managers is about $r = .50$. Expressed as the coefficient of determination (r^2), we can describe the relationship in a more meaningful way by noting that cognitive ability tests explain, or account for, or predict, about 25 percent ($.5^2$) of the variability we see in job performance. The coefficient of determination can be represented graphically as a Venn diagram. In Figure 3.5a the predictor overlaps, or accounts for, 25 percent of the variance in job performance. The coefficient of determination gives us a practical, user-friendly way to express, interpret, and compare correlations. (By the way, a correlation of $r = .50$, accounting for 25 percent of the variability we see in job performance, is pretty good for a single predictor [test] to attain.)

This leads us to an important point: While individual correlations may explain only modest portions of subsequent job performance, together, multiple predictors can explain considerably more. While separate predictors such as the interview, an ability test, and a performance test typically exhibit modest correlations, together they can dramatically improve prediction of job performance. Multiple regression is the means for combining these individual predictors, all of which individually are quite modest, into a more predictive tool.

Multiple Regression. Typically, we have many sources of data to use to predict job performance (interviewer ratings, multiple test scores, experience ratings, and so forth). An extension of the regression model, multiple regression, allows us to obtain a regression equation that simultaneously weights scores on numerous assessment devices. The re-

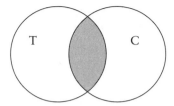

a. Relationship between one predictor (test score) and one criterion (job performance), r = .50.

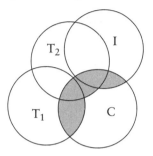

b. Relationships between three predictors (test #1, test #2, and interview ratings) and one criterion (job performance), r = .60.

Figure 3.5. Venn diagrams depicting the relationship between test scores and job performance.

gression equation produces a best-fit combination of the assessment tools, allowing you to capture the predictive power of multiple assessment tools. By using multiple predictors in combination we can often improve the accuracy of our predictions of job performance. This is displayed graphically in Figure 3.5b. Each predictor (T_1, T_2, I) explains (predicts) a unique portion of job performance (C).

There is a consequence of using the multiple regression approach to prediction that is worth noting: Doing so results in a compensatory selection model, meaning that an applicant weakness in one attribute can be made up for by a strength in another. Sometimes this is appropriate, and sometimes it is not. The alternative model, multiple hurdle, identifies a minimum score for each attribute and the successful applicant must pass each cutoff.

We will present additional detail on the use of multiple predictors in chapter 10. In that chapter we review strategies for assembling, weighting, and making decisions based on the variety of data you will typically have about applicants; specifically, how best to combine or use the interview judgments, biographical data, standardized test scores, and reference judgments to optimize the selection decision.

Our intent here is merely to introduce you to the logic and power of statistically based prediction. For the reader interested in an extended discussion of statistical-based prediction, Wayne Cascio's book, *Applied Psychology in Personnel Management* provides an in-depth treatment of these and related topics.[8] Also, Robert Gatewood and Hubert Feild's text *Human Resource Selection* and Benjamin Schneider and Neal Schmitt's, *Staffing Organizations,* provide an excellent, though less quantitative, discussion of these and other staffing topics.[9] Finally, the *Principles for the Validation and Use of Personnel Selection Procedures,* published by the Society for Industrial and Organizational Psychology, provides a detailed treatment of these testing issues.[10]

Statistical Prediction, in Context. As we noted earlier, we know that there is error in our prediction of job performance. By using an appropriate test we will make fewer errors in selection than we would otherwise make. Furthermore, we can gauge the extent to which our tools are leading to errors in selection. That is, as we argued in the first chapter, the advantage of measuring and using statistically based procedures in staffing: We can improve prediction of important aspects of successful performance.

Fairness in Staffing

The third standard by which the staffing process is evaluated is fairness. There are many aspects of fairness. In general, the issue of fairness is concerned with the impact that the use of selection and promotion procedures has on women, the handicapped, and various minority groups protected by equal employment opportunity (EEO) legislation. There are a number of important concepts, and we will discuss them in a manner useful to those readers who wish to design or evaluate a staffing process. However, we can only present an overview of these important concepts and issues. Of course, we identify references for those who seek additional detail about the technical and legal issues in employment fairness.

A series of state and federal laws, court decisions, and administrative rulings have established public policy regarding the conduct of staffing. The intent of public policy has been to eliminate illegal discrimination in all aspects of personnel practices: recruitment, screening, selection, training, compensation, promotion, and treatment of

Exhibit 3.3. Fair employment laws and court cases.

The following represents a partial listing of the laws and court cases that have shaped employer practices.

Law	Major provisions
Title VII Civil Rights Act of 1964	Prohibits discrimination on the basis of race, color, religion, sex, or national origin. Set the basis for subsequent EEO and affirmative actions laws and executive orders. Applies to all personnel actions: recruiting, selecting, training, performance appraisal, compensation, and termination.
Civil Rights Act of 1991	Reestablishes the "Griggs rule" whereby a pattern of underutilization of a protected group places the "burden of proof" on the employer to demonstrate the validity of the hiring or promotion decision. Bans the practice of "race norming" standardized tests.
Americans with Disabilities Act of 1990	Prohibits discrimination against the disabled who can perform the "essential functions" of the job in question with or without reasonable accommodation.
Age Discrimination in Employment Act of 1967	Prohibits discrimination on the basis of age for individuals over the age of 40.

Court cases	Major provisions
Griggs v. Duke Power (1971)	If selection or promotion procedures have disparate impact (differential hiring rates) the burden of proof is on the employer to demonstrate job relatedness.
U.S. v. Georgia Power (1973)	Identified appropriate professional standards for validation of selection procedures. Reaffirmed the EEOC guidelines as standards employers should follow.
Connecticut v. Teal (1982)	Employers must examine all steps in the selection process (resume screen, interview, test, and so on) for disparate impact.
Watson v. Ft. Worth Bank & Trust	If interview has disparate impact it must be validated by same procedures used to validate any other test.

employees. Exhibit 3.3 presents a profile of the major laws and landmark court cases dealing with staffing practices.

As public policy has evolved, a number of concepts have emerged related to staffing practices. These are very important because they have direct implications for the design, conduct, and evaluation of staffing.

The first important concept is *discrimination*. Actually, there are two forms of employment discrimination relevant to staffing. The first, *disparate treatment,* is a form of discrimination in which employment standards, procedures, or conditions are applied differently for members of a particular group. For example, asking interview questions regarding arrests and convictions only of minority applicants, but not of nonminority applicants, would be considered disparate treatment. Asking only women "Are you planning to have children?" would be disparate treatment. Asking members of one group (women) to take a physical strength test, but allowing others (men) to bypass the test, would be considered disparate treatment. Hiring men with young children, but rejecting women with young children, would, as well. Oh, and let's not forget our peek into the interview process at Ajax. It is our belief that Mike holds opinions that lead him to approach interviews with women differently than he approaches interviews with men. He undoubtedly pursues different topics and interprets what he hears differently based on the gender of the candidate. These are all examples in which members of one group are treated differently than members of the majority group. As a generalization, it is said that, compared to other bases for a discrimination suit, it is easier for a rejected applicant to bring a disparate treatment case of employment discrimination. While establishing a disparate treatment discrimination charge is a relatively straightforward process, defending such a charge is equally straightforward (or, at least, straightforward relative to other discrimination charges an employer might face). The basis for the initiation of and the subsequent defense against a disparate treatment case is profiled in Exhibit 3.4.

Standardization of the staffing process is the key to eliminating either the appearance or reality of disparate treatment. The following practices will serve to eliminate disparate treatment.

1. Develop clear, objective hiring criteria, directly related to the actual work to be performed. Chapter 4 outlines the process for doing so.

2. Treat all applicants the same, with objectivity and professional courtesy.

3. Provide decision makers in the staffing process with objective tools for making staffing decisions, and orient them to the need for objective, job-related decision making.

A second form of discrimination is *disparate impact* (also termed *adverse impact*). Disparate impact occurs when the use of a selection standard or a particular assessment device, though applied uniformly and equally to all applicants, results in a disproportionate rate of rejection for members of a protected group. For example, physical strength tests will typically lead to the rejection of a greater proportion of female than of male applicants. Consequently, physical strength tests typically result in disparate impact. A second example, educational criteria such as certification tests, may result in disparate

Exhibit 3.4. Initiating and defending a disparate treatment suit.

To establish disparate treatment, the plaintiff must establish four facts.

1. He or she belongs to a protected minority group.
2. He or she applied for and was qualified for a job for which the company was recruiting.
3. He or she was rejected for the position, despite being qualified.
4. After this rejection, the position remained open and the employer continued to seek applications from persons with the complainant's qualifications.

Employer's defense

- Employer may rebut the charge by showing that a legitimate, nondiscriminatory reason was the basis for rejecting the applicant.

Plaintiff's Rebut

- If employer's defense is successful, plaintiff may attempt to refute the basis for the rejection. Courts have accepted various arguments for disparate treatment, including statements made by company managers that were sexual or racial slurs, records that the company's treatment of the plaintiff was inconsistent with that of individuals of other demographic groups, and statistics showing the demographic group of the plaintiff was underrepresented in the company's work-force.

Source: Based in part on a chapter in Robert Gatewood and Hubert Feild, *Human Resource Selection* (Fort Worth, Tex.: Dryden Press, 1994).

Exhibit 3.5. Selection criteria and procedures likely to produce disparate impact.

The following represent what, on the surface, are objective standards, but when applied tend to have a disparate impact on particular groups.

High school diploma	As of 1992, nonminorities graduate at a rate higher than that of minorities.
Minimum height requirements	The average height of men exceeds the average height of women. The average height of Asians is less than that of Caucasians.
Arrest records	Minorities are more likely to have been arrested than are nonminorities.
Home ownership	Minorities are less likely to be home owners.
Availability of transportation	In some areas, minorities are less likely to own an automobile.
Mental ability tests	On average, some racial and ethnic minority groups tend to score lower on paper-and-pencil ability tests.

---

impact for some racial minorities. Exhibit 3.5 provides examples of other selection criteria likely to have disparate impact.

How different must the acceptance rates be to indicate disparate impact? According to the *Uniform Guidelines on Employee Selection Procedures,* a specific threshold for determination of disparate impact exists: "If the rate of selection for minority group members is less than 80% of the rate of selection for majority group members, the selection device has disparate impact."[11] An example may be helpful. One hundred applicants are screened for a position vacancy, and 50 of them are hired. Twenty percent (20) of the applicants are female. Of the 50 that are hired, 5 are female.

	Applicants	Hires	Within-group selection rate
Male	80	45	56%
Female	20	5	25%
Total	100	50	

Disparate impact threshold (80% × 56) = 45%

The important issue is the rate of selection within each group. The rate of selection for males is 56 percent. In contrast, only 25 percent of the female applicants are hired. The rule of thumb established by the EEOC and upheld by the courts is that disparate impact exists if the rate of selection for the minority group is less than 80 percent of the rate at which majority group members are selected. Eighty percent of 56.25 is 45 percent. Because only 25 percent of the female applicants were hired and 25 percent is less than 45 percent, disparate impact exists.

The presence of disparate impact has been accepted by the courts (including the Supreme Court in *Griggs v. Duke Power*) as the basis of a prima facia case of unfair discrimination.[12] The Griggs rule provides that, once disparate impact is established, the employer assumes the burden of proof to show the legitimacy (validity, job relatedness) of the decisions produced by the selection process. The Griggs rule does not mean that disparate impact is, in and of itself, illegal; it merely puts the employer in the position of proving that the differential rates of hire (or promotion, or termination) are related to differences in ability to perform the job. The next section addresses this point in more detail.

Legal Status of Disparate Impact: Is It Legal to Use a Selection or Promotion Device That Has Disparate Impact? Disparate impact is clearly an undesirable situation in that it will act to reduce the diversity of the employer's workforce and raise the challenge of unfair staffing practices. However, it is not, in and of itself, illegal. From the perspective of employment law, the existence of disparate impact requires that the employer (if challenged in a discrimination suit) demonstrate the following.

1. *The validity of the selection device or selection criteria.* The employer must produce evidence in support of the validity or job relatedness of the selection device; or

2. *A business necessity for use of the hiring criteria* (the courts have been very stringent in accepting business necessity arguments); or

3. *The selection criterion is a Bona Fide Occupational Qualification (BFOQ).* A BFOQ is typically raised when the selection criterion is based on gender, age, race, or some other individual characteristic. For example, arguing that the part of a women in the play must be played by a woman would assert that gender is a BFOQ for acceptable job performance. The courts have been very stringent in accepting BFOQs, and typically do not allow the use of the characteristic when it is merely associ-

ated with lower levels of job performance. For example, even though men are, on average, physically stronger than women, gender cannot be used as a selection criterion. However, the measurement and use of the underlying attribute (for example, a physical strength test) may be used in the same circumstance.

If the employer can demonstrate the job relatedness of the selection procedure, or that its use is a business necessity, or that the criterion being used is a BFOQ, and that no alternative exists which is substantially equally valid, the employer is on reasonably sound footing to use the test. While it is by no means a desirable circumstance, a valid test can be used, even if it produces disparate impact.[13]

As a generalization, work samples and simulations (detailed in chapters 7 and 8) tend to have less disparate impact than do traditional written tests or educational credentials and certification.[14] Consequently, work samples and simulations are very desirable components of the staffing process. Finally, because the composition of the workforce is such a critical issue, chapters 5 (HRP) and 6 (recruiting) revisit the use of the 4/5ths (80-percent) rule in assessing workforce utilization.

Establishing Job Relatedness

When disparate impact is shown, the burden of proof switches to the employer who must produce evidence supporting the job relatedness (validity) of the selection procedure (the Griggs rule, noted earlier). Many employers have argued that this reversal of the burden of proof is a hardship, and is contrary to the general principle of "innocent until proven guilty." The Supreme Court agreed in 1989 in *Wards Cove v. Atonio,* and reversed 18 years of precedent.[15] However, that ruling was quickly reversed by the Civil Rights Act of 1991.[16] That legislation has restored the principle that once a pattern of disparate impact is shown, the employer must then prove the job relatedness of the employment practice.

Finally, it is important to note that the 4/5ths rule is also used as the basis to evaluate the fairness of other staffing decisions. For example, differential rates of promotion, retention (such as during downsizing), and access to career development (such as training) are also evaluated against the 4/5ths standard.

Building Validity into the Staffing Process. How then, does an employer build job relatedness into the selection procedures and ensure that the staffing process is fair and will meet any challenge? The challenge of job relatedness is essentially one of demonstrating the validity of the procedures. If one systematically designs validity into the staffing process, it will improve the selection decisions made and will put your organization in a position to defend its hiring and promotion practices. We begin by outlining the steps of that process.

- **Step 1: Identify what comprises success on the job and in the organization.** What are the important duties or responsibilities? What are the frequent and/or critical work activities (tasks) performed by workers in the job? What organization culture factors must the person adapt to (for example, the values of a quality-oriented culture)? All subsequent staffing actions are then examined in relationship to the work to be done. For example, ADA of 1990 requires that the employer be able to identify the essential functions of the job—those responsibilities for which the position exists.[17] It is unlawful, under that legislation, to reject a disabled applicant who can perform the essential functions with or without accomodation. All staffing processes should be based on an understanding of the work to be performed.

- **Step 2: Identify the attributes—knowledge, skills, aptitudes, personal characteristics (KSAPs)—and experiences needed to perform those activities in the context of your organization.** Collect input from a team of individuals familiar with the job, the work process, and the organization culture. Be sure to consider the job, work process, and culture as they exist now, and as they will exist in the envisioned quality culture. (We'll focus on this point in chapter 4.) For quality-related attributes, use the QAI described in chapter 4 as a guide when choosing KSAPs.

- **Step 3: Identify which specific attributes new hires must possess before they begin work.** These are the attributes the organization cannot train in the short run. For example, temperament factors such as flexibility/adaptability, openness to learning, creativity, and teamwork orientation are individual differences that are not readily developed in an organization training effort.

- **Step 4: Choose selection procedures that measure the underlying KSAP or directly measure performance of the work (such as work samples).** Subsequent chapters in this book will assist you in this process.

Chapter 4 presents greater detail about this process of analyzing work and organization culture to identify critical attributes on which to screen and select.

Utility in Staffing

The ROI of Systematic Staffing

Suppose that a consultant claimed that an assessment process she was selling would increase the proportion of hires who achieved superior performance from 50 percent to 78 percent, and would decrease turnover from 15 percent to 8 percent, and that the associated savings would net your company $1,280,000 per year. Would you like to hear more? Her claims address the fourth standard by which we evaluate the staffing process—utility—and the claim is not out of line with reality. In fact, later in this chapter we will profile a project in which the implementation of a test led to a net savings of about $16 million for a national quick service restaurant chain.

In raising the standard of utility, we deal with questions about the value-added payoff or return on investment (ROI) of staffing processes: Would implementation of a recruiting plan, or implementation of a testing program, improve the performance of the work process sufficiently to justify the cost incurred? Or, stated differently, does the ROI we will get from improving the staffing process justify the expense? Utility, then, is a way to make strategic decisions about where best to invest in the staffing process. Also, it is important to note at the onset that the standard of utility (value-added, ROI) is applicable to each component of the staffing process. In the following sections, we highlight different approaches to addressing questions of ROI. It is our belief that the perspectives and tools of utility analysis will aid you in decisions about how best to allocate resources for staffing.

The Traditional Approach to Utility: Improving the Proportion of New Hires Who Succeed on the Job. The first approach to utility, attributed to two researchers, H. C. Taylor and J. T. Russell, defines the value-added contribution of testing in terms of the extent to which the selection tool increases the proportion of employees who succeed on the job.[18] This classical approach defines utility as a function of three factors: the validity of the test we wish to use, the selection ratio (how selective we can be), and the base rate (the rate at which new hires currently succeed, without use of the test we are considering).

Taylor and Russell demonstrated that these three factors interact to determine utility. They produced a series of tables used to estimate the proportion of workers who will succeed under different conditions of validity, selectivity, and current rates of success. Table 3.2 presents a Taylor Russell table for the circumstance in which 50 percent of the new hires currently succeed.

Table 3.2. Use of Taylor Russell tables to estimate the utility of a selection or promotion procedure.

Proportion of employees considered satisfactory = .50

Selection ratio

r	.05	.10	.20	.30	.40	.50	.60	70	.80	.90	.95
.00	.50	.50	.50	.50	.50	.50	.50	.50	.50	.50	.50
.05	.54	.54	.53	.52	.52	.52	.51	.51	.51	.50	.50
.10	.58	.57	.56	.55	.54	.53	.53	.52	.51	.51	.50
.15	.63	.61	.58	.57	.56	.55	.54	.53	.52	.51	.51
.20	67	.64	.61	.59	.58	.56	.55	.54	.53	.52	.51
.25	.70	.67	.64	.62	.60	.58	.56	.55	.54	.52	.51
.30	.74	.71	.67	.64	.62	.60	.58	.56	.54	.52	.51
.35	.78	.74	.70	.66	.64	.61	.59	.57	.55	.53	.51
.40	.82	.78	.73	.69	.66	.63	.61	.58	.56	.53	.52
.45	.85	.81	.75	.71	.68	.65	.62	.59	.56	.53	.52
.50	.88	.84	.78	.74	.70	.67	.63	.60	.57	.54	.52
.55	.91	.87	.81	.76	.72	.69	.65	.61	.58	.54	.52
.60	.94	.90	.84	.79	.75	.70	.66	.62	.59	.54	.52
.65	.96	.92	.87	.82	.77	.73	.68	.64	.59	.55	.52
.70	.98	.95	.90	.85	.80	.75	.70	.65	.60	.55	.53
.75	.99	.97	.92	.87	.82	.77	.72	.66	.61	.55	.53
.80	1.00	.99	.95	.90	.85	.80	.73	.67	.61	.55	.53
.85	1.00	.99	.97	.94	.88	.82	.76	.69	.62	.55	.53
.90	1.00	1.00	.99	.97	.92	.86	.78	.70	.62	.56	.53
.95	1.00	1.00	1.00	.99	.96	.90	.81	.71	.63	.56	.53
1.00	1.00	1.00	1.00	1.00	1.00	1.00	.83	.71	.63	.56	.53

Source: H. C. Taylor and J. T. Russell, "The Relationship of Validity Coefficients to the Practical Effectiveness of Tests in Selection," *Journal of Applied Psychology* 23 (1939): 565–578. Used with permission.

To illustrate how the Taylor Russell approach to utility can be used, consider the following scenario.

Currently, without use of a test, 50 percent of those hired succeed. You are considering adopting a test with an established validity of $r =$ .40. Will the use of the test prove worthwhile? That is, will use of the test result in a greater proportion of successful hires? Given that 50 percent currently succeed, the answer to that question depends on two factors: the validity of the test you are considering ($r = .40$) and the degree to which you can be selective from the applicants you have generated (the selection ratio, SR). How selective can the organization be? Assume that there are 10 vacancies and 100 applicants have been tested. The SR is therefore equal to .10 (10/100). You'll take the top 10 percent of the applicants you test. Based on Table 3.2 we can estimate that the use of a test with validity $r = .40$ and a selection ratio of .10 yields a success rate of 78 percent. Seventy-eight percent of the applicants hired with this test will succeed. Because 50 percent would have succeeded if we'd simply used the process we had in place, use of the test results in a 28 percent increase in successful hires and a 56 percent change in the rate of successful hires [(78 – 50)/50 = 56%]. Clearly, the use of the test would have a meaningful impact. Remember, however, that the rate of selection is a critical factor to the usefulness of any test. Suppose that rather than the favorable selection rate of 10 percent, we only generated and tested 20 applicants. The reduced number of applicants could occur because of ineffective recruiting practices, a negative organization image, or a labor shortage for that particular skill. For whatever reason, we now must choose 10 from only 20 applicants, giving us a less favorable selection ratio of .50 (10/20).

From the Taylor Russell table we can estimate that use of the test in these circumstances will result in 63 percent of the new hires succeeding. This represents a 13 percent increase above the success rate without use of the test. The 63 percent represents only a 26 percent change in the rate of successful hires [(63 – 50)/50]. This illustrates a useful generalization that we can make: For a test of a given validity, r, the greater our selectivity, the more useful the test will be. Conversely, as we are forced to take a higher proportion of our applicant population, the usefulness of any test will decrease. To confirm this point, scan any row of Table 3.2 (validity) and read the values from left to right. You will see that, for a test of any validity (any row), the success rate of new hires decreases as a higher proportion of applicants are selected. It is because of this that a test of even modest validity can be useful when the organization can be highly selective. Consequently, the organization's recruitment strategy, process, and efforts become an important factor in making the selection procedures useful. In chapter 6, we again discuss the importance of generating a favorable ratio of credible applicants and we present examples of how favorable SRs have been used in state-of-the-art staffing projects. Finally, the recruitment resources presented in appendix C will help you make the most of the selection procedures you adopt by improving efforts at recruiting quality-oriented applicants.

Expectancy Charts and Tables. We can express the value-added impact of a test in probabilistic statements about the success of future applicants. Table 3.3 presents the results of the hypothetical validity study for a quality practices test. The table breaks test performance into various ranges and presents both the count and proportion of those employees who were rated as superior performers. Expectancy charts express such data in graphic form. An *individual expectancy chart* shows the likelihood that a person with a given test score will become a superior performer on the job (see Figure 3.6). An *institutional expectancy chart* expresses the proportion of new hires that will succeed at different test cutoff (pass) scores (see Figure 3.7). As you can see, lowering the test cutoff score (typically because of an insufficient supply of recruits—the SR), results in the hiring of lower proportions of potentially superior employees. The data from a validity study, done within your company or by the test publisher across many companies, allows you to make these kinds of projections in advance.

Table 3.3. Percentage of employees receiving superior job performance for difference score ranges on the quality practices test.

Test score	Other performers	Superior performers	Total	% superior performers
Top 20% 30–34	3	12	15	80
Next 20% 23–29	5	10	15	67
Middle 20% 15–22	6	8	14	57
Next 20% 7–14	9	8	17	47
Low 20% 1–6	9	5	14	36
Total	32	43	75	

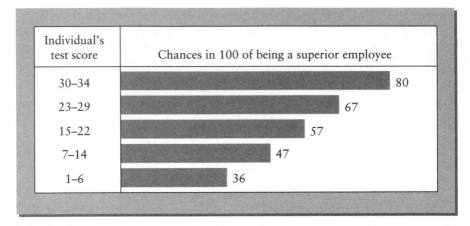

Figure 3.6. Individual expectancy chart illustrating applicant's chance of success for various ranges of test scores.

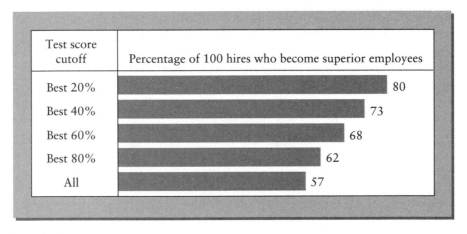

Figure 3.7. Institutional expectancy chart illustrating proportion of applicants who succeed at various test pass scores.

Putting It in Dollars and Cents: The Economic Impact of Value-Added Staffing

Assessing Costs and Benefits. Thus far, we've discussed value-added utility in terms of improving the rate of success in the employees we hire, promote, or retain. While this is a reasonable approach to value-added staffing, a more elaborate approach to utility allows us to estimate the economic costs and benefits of staffing alternatives (ROI). A number of models are available for costing out the cost and impact of a test. Exhibit 3.6 presents one widely used model, attributable to researchers Frank L. Schmidt and John E. Hunter. The approach is an

Exhibit 3.6. The economic benefits of a testing program.

The following is based on a description appearing in Gatewood and Feild's *Human Resource Selection* and based on a study by F. Schmidt, J. Hunter, R. McKenzie, and T. Muldrow.

Frank Schmidt and his associates applied a utility model to examine the expected net gain in dollars obtained by using a valid test for selection as compared to random selection or another predictor that was not valid. Their utility was as follows:

$$\text{Expected gain (\$)} = N_s r_{xy} SD_y z_x - N_t c$$

where

r_{xy} = validity coefficient of the selection measure

SD_y = standard deviation of job performance in dollars

z_x = average test score of those selected in z-score form

c = cost of testing per job applicant

N_t = number of applicants tested

N_s = number of applicants selected

Suppose we have conducted a concurrent validation study of a test and found a validity coefficient of .50. Of every 100 applicants that apply for the job under study, 10 are hired; thus the selection ratio is .10, or 10 percent. Assuming that individuals are hired on the basis of their test scores, and the top 10 percent is hired, the average test score in standardized z-score form is 1.29. The standard deviation in dollars for job performance is assessed at $5,000 per year. Standard deviation in dollars represents individuals' contributions to productivity for the organization. An individual who is one standard deviation above the mean on job performance is worth $5000 more to the organization than an individual with average job performance. Finally, suppose that the cost of purchasing, administering, scoring, and filing the test is $20 per applicant. When these values are substituted in the equation the result is

$$\text{Expected gain (\$)} = 10(.50)(\$5,000)(1.29) - 100(20)$$
$$= 30,250$$

Use of the valid test (versus random selection or a nonvalid predictor) for one year to select workers would yield the organization an expected net gain in productivity worth $30,250 for every 10 employees hired. Gain per worker selected can be derived by dividing the expected gain by 10, that is, the number of workers selected. Thus the gain per worker selected per year would be $3025.

Source: Robert Gatewood and Hubert Feild, *Human Resource Selection* (Fort Worth: Tex.: Dryden Press, 1994). Frank Schmidt, John E. Hunter, Robert C. McKenzie, and Tressie W. Muldrow. "Impact of Valid Selection Procedures on Work-Force Productivity" *Journal of Applied Psychology* 64 (1979): 609–626.

enhancement in three ways. First, it presents a more refined estimate of the extent to which the use of a new staffing procedure will increase performance. This approach recognizes that performance is a continuum, not a success-fail dichotomy (among those who have succeeded, some have excelled). Second, this approach provides estimates of the economic value (in dollars) of improved performance. How much, in dollars, does the organization benefit by each incremental increase in performance resulting from improved selection and promotion? Third, these models incorporate the costs associated with use of the staffing tool (cost of the test, cost of testing each applicant, and so on). The net result is an estimate of the economic impact resulting from the use of a selection or promotion device. In the study profiled in Exhibit 3.6, the gain (payoff) associated with the use of the test is $3025 per worker hired.[19] Ten workers hired yields $30,250 of added value per year attributable to systematic selection. (It is worth noting that the estimate used in that example is in 1979 dollars—inflation alone would increase the magnitude of the ROI.)[20]

Exhibits 3.7 and 3.8 present the economic impact experienced by a national quick service restaurant associated with the use of the PDI Employment Inventory (EI). Exhibit 3.7 illustrates how the impact of a test can be measured and expressed in terms of specific on-the-job behaviors. That exhibit profiles the differences in on-the-job behavior (as rated by managers) seen in employees receiving a passing score on PDI's EI contrasted to those receiving a failing score. For example, 64.6 percent of those passing the EI "take the initiative to find another task when finished with their regular work" compared to only 52.2 percent of those who fail.[21] Other behavioral contrasts between those passing and failing the test are detailed in Exhibit 3.7.

Exhibit 3.8 translates the behavioral changes into dollars. In the quick service restaurant, implementation of the test resulted in a net savings of $16,961,100. The estimate takes into account $475,800 in savings attributable to reduced turnover; $5,920,000 in actual savings associated with improvement in on-the-job behavior; $1,800,000 in actual reduced product costs; $7,385,300 in savings in actual managerial labor costs; and $1,680,000 estimated savings in workers' compensation costs.

Exhibit 3.9 presents the results of the implementation of PDI's EI in a national discount retailer. In that project the employer experienced annual savings of $16,457,760.

The cases illustrated in Exhibits 3.7, 3.8, and 3.9 are situations where very large organizations with very high turnover realized huge financial gains by incremental changes in turnover and on-the-job behavior. What is the potential payoff in the small organization, or in

Exhibit 3.7. Contrasts in on-the-job behaviors associated with use of the PDI Employment Inventory in a national quick service restaurant chain.

One traditional expression of utility is the extent to which the implementation of a test results in an increased proportion of successful employees. We can examine the impact of a test by comparing how those hired with the test differ from those who would be rejected by the test. The following charts show the contrast in on-the-job behavior associated with implementation of one quality-relevant test, PDI's EI.

Specific EI Behavior Improvements

64.60 percent of those who pass the EI usually or always *"take the initiative to find another task when finished with their regular work,"* compared to only 52.20 percent of those who fail.

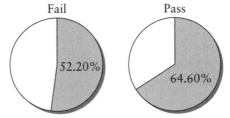

56.10 percent of those who pass the EI usually or always *"keep working, even when other employees are standing around talking,"* compared to 48.30 percent of those who fail.

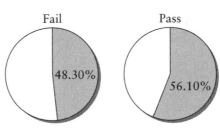

65.20 percent of those who pass the EI usually or always *"during a slow period, help out in another area which is very busy,"* compared to 58.90 percent of those who fail.

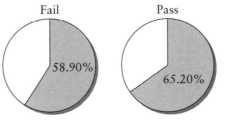

58.40 percent of those who pass the EI rarely or never *"let joking friends be a distraction and interruption to work,"* compared to 47.30 percent of those who fail.

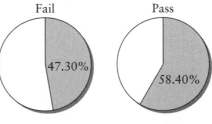

72.30 percent of those who pass the EI rarely or never *"allow work to get behind schedule without notifying anyone,"* compared to 62.60 percent of those who fail.

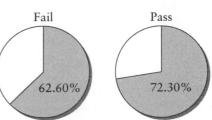

Exhibit 3.7. Continued.

Specific Customer Service Behavior Improvements

69.60 percent of those who pass the EI usually or always *"ask customers if there is anything more he/she can do to assist them,"* compared to 54 percent of those who fail.

67.90 percent of those who pass the EI usually or always *"restate customers' needs before acting,"* compared to 53 percent of those who fail.

77.20 percent of those who pass the EI usually or always *"tolerate rude customers calmly,"* compared to 63 percent of those who fail.

82.50 percent of those who pass the EI usually or always *"give customers full attention,"* compared to 71.80 percent of those who fail.

88 percent of those who pass the EI rarely or never *"make fun of customers behind their backs,"* compared to 73.30 percent of those who fail.

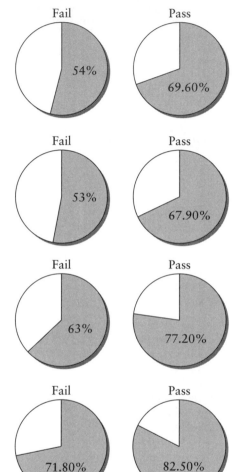
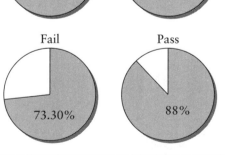
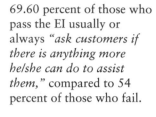

Source: Personnel Decisions, Inc. (PDI), Minneapolis, Minn. Validity of the PDI Employment Inventory for Quick Service Restaurants. Copyright © 1992, Personnel Decisions, Inc.

Exhibit 3.8.   ROI associated with use of the PDI EI in a national quick service restaurant chain.

Savings in staffing costs (estimates based on validation research)

Company norm: 52,000 team members turn over at $183 = $9,516,000

With EI: 49,400 team members turn over at $183 = $9,040,000

A 5% reduction in turnover (3600 team members/year) = $475,800

Savings based on increased productivity (based on actual results)

Conventional test utility analysis (using Schmidt and Hunter formula presented in Exhibit 3.7) calculates that EI-hired team members show more productive behavior worth $160 per year.

$160 × 37,000 team members = $5,920,000

EI saves product costs (based on company actual results @ $1B sales)

Company norm: Product cost = 38.35%

With EI: Product cost = 38.17%

0.18% reduction in product cost = $1,800,000

EI saves management labor costs (based on company actual results)

Company norm: Average management cost per period = $3,517

With EI: Average management cost per period = $3,218

$299 reduction per period for each of 1900 restaurants = $7,385,300

EI reduces worker compensation costs (based on PDI validation research)

Company norm: $16,800,000 per year

With EI: $15,120,000 per year

10% reduction in worker compensation claims = $1,680,000

Total potential savings	$17,261,100
Cost of employment inventory	–$300,000
Total net savings	$16,961,100

ROI = 56:1 or $326 per team member

Source: Personnel Decisions, Inc. (PDI), Minneapolis, Minn. Validity of the PDI Employment Inventory for Quick Service Restaurants. Copyright © 1992, Personnel Decisions, Inc.

Exhibit 3.9. ROI associated with use of the PDI Employment Inventory in a national discount retail chain.

---

1. **Test Decreases: Involuntary Terminations**
   A. Without test = 27,318 involuntary terminations
      With test = 17,574 involuntary terminations
      Test Result: 9,744 (5.6%) fewer involuntary terminations
      Savings: 9,744 × $525/involuntary terminations = $5,115,600

   B. Without test = 50,808 job abandonments
      With test = 45,936 job abandonments
      Test Result: 4,872 (2.8%) fewer job abandonments
      Savings: 4,872 × $250/job abandonment = $1,218,000

2. **Test Increases: Productive Job Behavior**
   A. Without test = 117,624 satisfactory hires
      With test = 129,458 satisfactory hires
      Test Result: 11,832 (6.8%) more satisfactory hires
      Savings: 11,832 × $200/employee = $2,366,400

   B. Without test = 145,464 rehires
      With test = 153,294 rehires
      Test Result: 7,830 (4.5%) more hires
      Savings: 7,830 × $400/hire = $3,132,000

3. **Test Increases: Service-Oriented Job Behavior**
   Without test = 119,538 acceptable hires
   With test = 129,804 acceptable hires
   Test Result: 10,266 (5.9%) more "Acceptable" hires
   Savings: 10,266 × $360/hire = $3,695,760

4. **Test Saves: Shrinkage**
   Annual Sales = $20 billion
   Annual shrinkage costs @ 1.0% of sales = $200,000,000
   Employee theft @ 20% shrinkage = $40,000,000
   EI reduces by 2.2% = $800,000 savings

5. **Test Saves: Workers' Compensation Claims**
   Payroll = $2,000,000,000
   Workers' compensation @ .3% of payroll = $6,000,000
   Test reduces by 5.0% = $300,000 savings

Annual Savings Using EI

1A. Involuntary term.	=	$5,115,500
1B. Job abandonment	=	$1,218,000
2A. Satisfactory hire	=	$2,366,400
2B. Rehires	=	$132,000
3. S.O. job behavior	=	$3,695,760
4. Shrinkage	=	$880,000
5. Workers' comp.	=	$300,000
Total Savings	=	$16,707,760
Cost of EI	=	$–250,000 (435,000 tests @ $.58/test)
		$16,457,760 (65:1 ROI)
Cost Savings		$94/opening

Source: Personnel Decisions, Inc. (PDI), Minneapolis, Minn. Validity of the PDI EI in a National Discount Retail Chain. Copyright © 1991, Personnel Decisions, Inc.

the organization built on jobs with low turnover and higher salaries? To illustrate the applicability of the utility analysis to smaller settings, a later section presents the validation and utility analysis of PDI's Customer Service Inventory (CSI) in a small health care facility.

The Arrangement of the Selection Process and ROI

The arrangement of the staffing process, that is, the order in which applicants work through the various assessment devices, affects the overall cost and ROI of the process. The principle is simply to place the most efficient and valid assessment tools up front, early in the process, and the most costly later in the process. Typically, that means placing valid, efficient tools like paper-and-pencil tests early in the process, and the very costly on-site interview late in the process. This arrangement is illustrated in Figure 3.8.

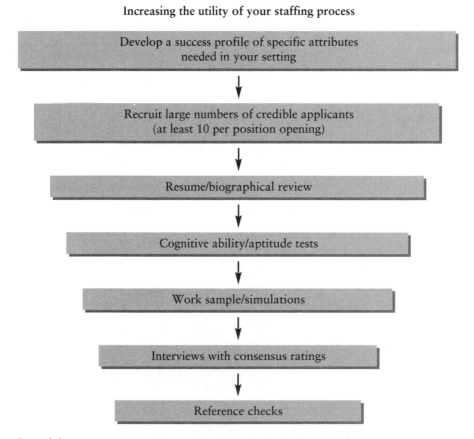

Increasing the utility of your staffing process

Develop a success profile of specific attributes needed in your setting

↓

Recruit large numbers of credible applicants (at least 10 per position opening)

↓

Resume/biographical review

↓

Cognitive ability/aptitude tests

↓

Work sample/simulations

↓

Interviews with consensus ratings

↓

Reference checks

Figure 3.8. Optimal arrangement of selection process.

Case Example: Criterion-Related Validation of the PDI CSI in a Small Health Care Facility

Overview of a Validation Project. A criterion-related validity study seeks to demonstrate the relationship between a test (the predictor) and important aspects of successful job performance (the criterion). There are alternate research designs, appropriate for different circumstances. The design we profile here is termed a *concurrent validity study* because it collects test measures and measures of job performance at the same point in time, using current employees as the study participants. It is the most cost-effective method and, when appropriate steps are taken, can provide an effective basis for substantiating and implementing a testing program.

Figure 3.9 presents the validation process. As you can see, it is based on an analysis of the job, work process, and organization culture. Simply put, we can't choose an appropriate test until we can identify the KSAPs needed in our workforce, and a clear definition of successful performance (criteria). We will discuss job analysis methods in chapter 4. For now, suffice to say that it is a systematic study of the job, the work process, and the organization culture to identify what it is successful employees do and what attributes they must possess to be successful.

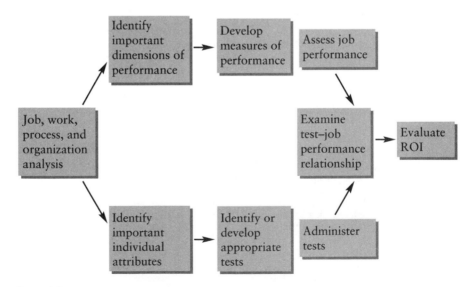

Figure 3.9. The test validation process.

The process begins with a definition of successful employee performance. Typically, this results in the identification of specific attributes. These attributes are then used to identify appropriate tests (presumed to measure the attributes of successful performance) and simultaneously, a measure of performance. The validation study will then collect test scores and measures of job effectiveness from a current group of employees.

An Illustration. A concurrent test validation project conducted in a health care facility will illustrate the logic and steps of the process. Twelve job categories were examined to identify dimensions of performance important to all jobs in the hospital setting. In this example, the relative importance of the attributes was evaluated by employees (those working and supervising the job). Exhibit 3.10 presents the questionnaire used to collect the judgments of the relative importance of some of the 41 attributes. Based on the ratings of those familiar with each job, profiles of important dimensions of job performance were identified for each job. The profile of dimensions for the Human Resource Assistant and for the Nursing Assistant positions is presented in Exhibit 3.11. This profile is used to establish the relative importance of performance dimensions, the underlying attributes, and to substantiate the relevance of particular tests designed to measure the KSAPs.

Exhibit 3.10. The questionnaire.

Instructions

The following pages contain brief descriptions of 41 characteristics that contribute to one's success as a Nutrition Service Aide at this health care organization. We are asking you, as a person who is familiar with the Nutrition Service Aide job, for your help.

First, think about all of the characteristics that contribute to a person's ability to be a good Nutrition Service Aide. Second, read each of the 41 characteristics. Third, make your ratings using the nine-point scale described below.

Please note that we are asking you to rate the *relative* importance of each characteristic.

- Rate 7 to 9 if a characteristic is *much more important* than other characteristics.
- Rate 4 to 6 if a characteristic is *about as important as* other characteristics.
- Rate 1 to 3 if a characteristic is *less important than others*.

Thank you for your participation.

Exhibit 3.10. Continued.

Job Characteristic

How important is each of the following characteristics in comparison with all the others?
(Circle your ratings.)

	Extremely less	Very much less	Moderately less	Slightly less	About equal	Slightly more	Moderately more	Very much more	Extremely more
1. Quickly combining new information into meaningful patterns; identifying a known pattern embedded in other material; quickly and accurately comparing letters, numbers, objects, pictures, or patterns.	1	2	3	4	5	6	7	8	9
2. Performing in the expected or agreed-upon way; reliably keeping promises; telling the truth; following through on commitments.	1	2	3	4	5	6	7	8	9
3. Acting with assurance and assertiveness; being optimistic and self-confident; accepting constructive criticism nondefensively.	1	2	3	4	5	6	7	8	9
4. Having specific knowledge about the job and industry or about company policies and procedures.	1	2	3	4	5	6	7	8	9
5. Learning job knowledge easily and finding good solutions to problems; being competent and perfectionistic.	1	2	3	4	5	6	7	8	9
6. Using muscle force to briefly lift, push, pull, or carry objects; supporting or moving one's own body or objects repeatedly over time.	1	2	3	4	5	6	7	8	9
7. Having a positive and optimistic outlook; being emotionally healthy; feeling satisfied and happy with life.	1	2	3	4	5	6	7	8	9
8. Quickly and correctly performing standard arithmetic operations; understanding basic mathematical principles.	1	2	3	4	5	6	7	8	9

Source: Personnel Decisions, Inc. (PDI), Minneapolis, Minn. Validation of the PDI Customer Service Inventory for a Health Care Facility, Copyright © 1994, Personnel Decisions, Inc. Used with permission.

Exhibit 3.11. Job analysis profiles for nursing assistant and human resource assistant.

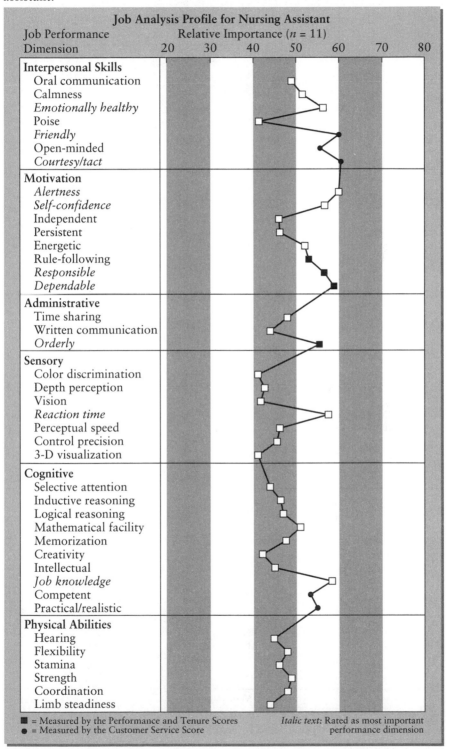

Job Analysis Profile for Nursing Assistant

Job Performance Dimension	Relative Importance (*n* = 11)
	20 30 40 50 60 70 80

Interpersonal Skills
Oral communication
Calmness
Emotionally healthy
Poise
Friendly
Open-minded
Courtesy/tact

Motivation
Alertness
Self-confidence
Independent
Persistent
Energetic
Rule-following
Responsible
Dependable

Administrative
Time sharing
Written communication
Orderly

Sensory
Color discrimination
Depth perception
Vision
Reaction time
Perceptual speed
Control precision
3-D visualization

Cognitive
Selective attention
Inductive reasoning
Logical reasoning
Mathematical facility
Memorization
Creativity
Intellectual
Job knowledge
Competent
Practical/realistic

Physical Abilities
Hearing
Flexibility
Stamina
Strength
Coordination
Limb steadiness

■ = Measured by the Performance and Tenure Scores
● = Measured by the Customer Service Score

Italic text: Rated as most important performance dimension

Exhibit 3.11. Continued.

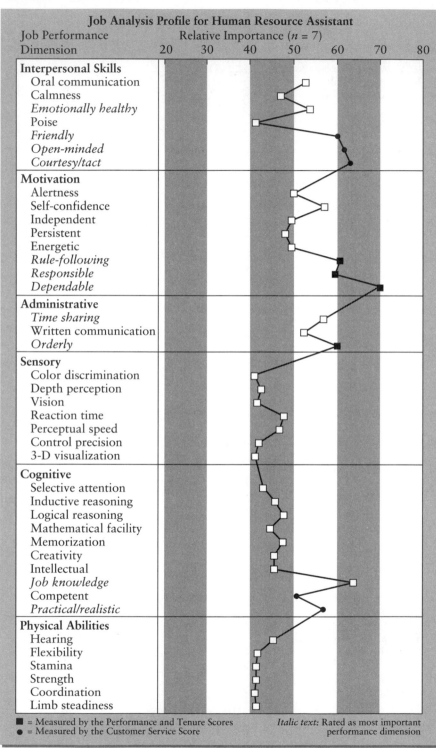

Job Analysis Profile for Human Resource Assistant

Measuring Job Performance: Criteria Measurement. With effective performance defined, the next step is to identify and/or develop specific measures of the attributes and of on-the-job performance. A number of criteria or expressions of effective performance were identified. Four criteria were identified as central to the definition of effectiveness for all 12 job groupings: friendliness, self-control, handling information and solving problems, and job commitment. A tool for measuring these four aspects of effective performance was developed. The definitions and behavior descriptions are presented in Exhibit 3.12.

Test Selection: Identifying an Appropriate Predictor. The PDI CSI was selected as the predictor most appropriate to measure attributes that predict the on-the-job behaviors of interest.

Data Collection. The next step involved is collecting the data. Current employees in all 12 job classifications completed the CSI. Concurrently, supervisors of those employees completed the behavioral anchored ratings scales profiled in Exhibit 3.12, and also ranked employees. In addition, performance appraisal data were retrieved from each participant's personnel file.

Data Analysis. The key question to address becomes: Is there a systematic relationship between performance on the test and performance on the job, as measured by the criteria? Table 3.4 details the correlations between supervisor judgments of employee behavior and employee test performance. As you can see, there are systematic relationships between performance on the test and performance on important criteria of effective performance.

Utility Analysis: Changes in Behavior. To identify the ROI that would be associated with the use of the test in the health care facility setting, a number of analyses were conducted. The first step was to examine the extent to which those passing the CSI behave differently than the total current workforce. The supervisor ratings of employee behaviors depicted earlier were the basis of these behavioral descriptions. As you can see in Exhibit 3.13, hiring based on the CSI would increase the frequency of friendliness, self-control, handling information and problem solving, and job commitment behaviors appreciably. Finally, the expectancy chart displayed in Exhibit 3.14 expresses the impact of use of the test and of choosing different pass scores on the average performance level in the workforce. As you can see, setting higher passing scores results in higher average performance appraisal scores.

Exhibit 3.12. Example measures of job performance used to validate CSI.

1: Friendliness

Definition: Approaching or moving toward others, both physically and emotionally; demonstrating interest in other people; initiating and maintaining interpersonal relationships within the context of the job.

Example behaviors . . .

• Doesn't smile at other people very much. • Often looks like he/she wants to be left alone. • Rarely starts a casual conversation. • Doesn't make very good eye contact. • Interacts with others only when his/her job demands it; doesn't seem interested in others.	• Looks approachable most of the time. • Listens to people and acknowledges what they say. • Usually looks comfortable when interacting with other people. • Usually notices when a patient needs assistance, and approaches to help.	• Always seems to greet people with a smile. • Consistently stands out as sociable and outgoing; makes a lasting impression. • Frequently uses humor to create a positive atmosphere. • Often makes casual small talk with patients. • Often asks patients if they need anything more.

Circle your rating:

1	2	3	4	5	6	7

(Low)   (High)

Exhibit 3.12. Continued.

2: Self-Control

Definition: Staying calm, objective and tactful in tense situations; showing courtesy and respect for other people, even when they are abusive; controlling the impulse to vent anger or hostility.

Example behaviors . . .

• Makes sarcastic remarks to patients. • Swears or uses vulgar language. • Complains about the organization in front of patients. • Acts irritated at request from patients or coworkers; shows anger quickly. • Often frowns or scowls at people.	• Usually even-keeled, but might sometimes get visibly agitated by angry or abusive patients. • Occasionally lets a bad mood affect how he/she treats people, but not for long. • Gets neither complaints nor compliments on how he/she handles difficult people.	• Tolerates rude or abusive patients calmly. • Always shows basic respect for people, regardless of how they act. • Almost always is able to calm an irate patient; has exceptional sensitivity and perseverance. • Compromises willingly, or even cheerfully.

Circle your rating:

1	2	3	4	5	6	7

(Low)   (High)

111

Exhibit 3.12. Continued.

3: Handling Information and Solving Problems

Definition: Giving information, soliciting information, and using information to resolve problems and meet clients' needs.

Example behaviors . . .

• Responds "I don't know" to questions without trying to find an answer. • Often misunderstands patients; makes them work hard to get their point across. • Consistently makes inaccurate or incomplete reports or notes. • Hasn't mastered some basic job knowledge.	• Usually understands patients without much trouble. Sometimes doesn't catch their meaning at first, but asks for clarification. • Is able to answer the most common questions. • Will usually refer a patient to someone else for more complete information. • Has a good grasp of basic job knowledge.	• Offers more information than patients ask for. • Asks clear and concise questions to determine what a patient needs. Rarely misunderstands. • Almost always directs patients to the right resource (person, department, material, etc.). • Gives answers that inspire confidence.

Circle your rating:

1	2	3	4	5	6	7

(Low)   (High)

Exhibit 3.12. Continued.

4: Job Commitment

Definition: Showing job commitment and willingness to fulfill basic job requirements; not giving up readily on difficult tasks; responsiveness during times of peak work activity.

Example behaviors . . . .

- Needs a lot of supervision to get his/her work done; does only enough to get by.
- Easily distracted from work; would rather socialize with others than complete tasks.
- Knowingly repeats mistakes and doesn't care.
- Avoids work by telling people to ask someone else for help with things he/she could do.

- Usually gets the job done, but might cut corners at times. Sometimes puts off distasteful tasks.
- Usually works faster when things get busy.
- Makes a reasonable effort to make sure things are done right, and that patients get what they need. Generally responsible and reliable.

- Figures out what needs to be done, without needing to be told. Lots of initiative.
- Keeps working, even when others are standing around talking. Makes suggestions to improve the way things are done. Shows personal commitment.
- Really hustles during busy times.

Circle your rating:

1	2	3	4	5	6	7

(Low)   (High)

Source: Personnel Decisions, Inc. (PDI), Minneapolis, Minn. Validation of the PDI Customer Service Inventory for a Health Care Facility, Copyright © 1994, Personnel Decisions, Inc. Used with permission.

Table 3.4. Correlations between the PDI CSI and performance measures.

Criterion	Supervisory rating	Supervisory ranking
Friendliness	0.32**	0.25**
Self-control	0.29**	0.25**
Handling information and solving problems	0.21*	0.21*
Job commitment	0.18*	0.16
Sum across dimensions	0.29**	0.24**
Annual performance appraisal	0.31**	N/A

n for ratings = 143; n for rankings = 144
*$p < .05$
**$p < .01$
Note: The reported correlations were for a portion of the total sample. The portion used was that for which the performance rating data were deemed most accurate.
Source: Personnel Decisions, Inc. (PDI) Minneapolis, MN. Validation of the PDI Customer Service Inventory for a Health Care Facility, Copyright © 1994, Personnel Decisions, Inc. Used with permission.

Utility Analysis: Costing Out the ROI. As you recall from our earlier discussion of utility, an additional expression of utility expresses the behavior changes associated with a test in dollar ROI. The application of a utility model similar to the Hunter and Schmidt model profiled in Exhibit 3.7 results in the annual utility per hire displayed in Table 3.5. The annual utility per hire represents the amount of added value during one year for each employee hired with the CSI, compared to hiring with the procedures currently in place. For example, each HR assistant hired by the test brings $1560 of added value compared to one hired under the current method. Each speech pathologist brings $3280 of added value, and so forth. When the total number of employees, and the turnover rate for each job, is factored in, the total utility of the CSI at this organization is $140,000 in its first year of use. When the gains in performance are estimated over nine years (the average tenure rate at the facility), the total benefit of using the test is $1,260,000 (140,000 × 9 years). For the reader interested in the actual computation of these estimates, Table 3.6 reproduces the entire set of calculations.

Summary

Effective staffing requires that we design reliability, validity, fairness, and utility into the staffing process. We've outlined the conceptual and statistical basis of these concepts in this chapter and provided a de-

Exhibit 3.13. Increase in customer-oriented behavior associated with use of the CSI.

Performance Dimension	Percent of Employees Given a Rating of 6 or 7	
	Current sample norm	Those passing CSI
Friendliness—11.8% Improvement Rating of 6 or 7 means: • *Always greets people with a smile* • *Stands out as sociable, outgoing* • *Uses humor to create positive mood* • *Often makes casual small talk* • *Often asks patients if they need anything more*	44.8%	56.6%
Self-Control—12.2% Improvement Rating of 6 or 7 means: • *Tolerates rudeness calmly* • *Shows respect for people, regardless of how they act* • *Calms irate patients through sensitivity and perseverance* • *Compromises willingly*	48.3%	60.5%
Handling Information and Solving Problems—9.1% Improvement Rating of 6 or 7 means: • *Offers more information than requested* • *Asks clear, concise questions to determine patients' needs* • *Directs patients to the right resource* • *Gives answers that inspire confidence*	37.8%	46.9%
Job Commitment—5.7% Improvement Rating of 6 or 7 means: • *Shows lots of initiative* • *Keeps working, even when others are standing around talking* • *Makes improvement suggestions, shows personal commitment* • *Really hustles during busy times*	46.2%	51.9%

Source: Personnel Decisions, Inc. (PDI), Minneapolis, Minn. Validation of the PDI Customer Service Inventory for a Health Care Facility, Copyright © 1994, Personnel Decisions, Inc. Used with permission.

Exhibit 3.14. Performance level for different test pass scores.

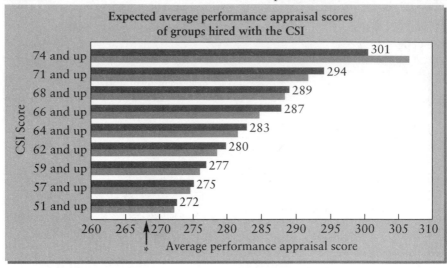

Table 3.5. Annual utility (added value) for each job.

Annual utility summary for each job			
Job	Annual salary	Annual utility per hire	First year net ROI ratio
Human Resource Assistant	$18,658	$1560	39.0 to 1
Unit Clerk/Monitor Tech.	$19,802	$1655	41.4 to 1
Nurse Assistant	$17,056	$1426	35.6 to 1
Radiologic Technologist	$25,542	$2135	53.8 to 1
Escort	$15,558	$1301	32.3 to 1
Phlebotomist	$16,723	$1398	34.8 to 1
Receptionist	$15,891	$1328	33.1 to 1
Housekeeper	$14,810	$1238	30.7 to 1
Speech Pathologist	$39,229	$3280	83.1 to 1
Registration Clerk	$17,576	$1469	36.7 to 1
Nutrition Services Aide	$14,997	$1254	31.1 to 1
Accounts Receivable Clerk	$18,678	$1561	39.0 to 1

Table 3.6. Complete utility analysis calculations.

Job	Selection ratio	Annual salary	Standard deviation of salary	z	Utility per hire	Annual hires	Total utility	Total cost	Net total utility	Net ROI ratio
Human Resource Assistant	33%	$18,658	$7,463	1.10	$1,560	0.50	$780	$20	$760	39.0
Unit Clerk/Monitor Tech.	33%	$19,802	$7,921	1.10	$1,655	13.34	$22,075	$520	$21,555	41.4
Nurse Assistant	33%	$17,056	$6,822	1.10	$1,426	19.35	$27,591	$755	$26,836	35.6
Radiologic Technologist	33%	$25,542	$10,217	1.10	$2,135	6.80	$14,520	$265	$14,255	53.8
Escort	33%	$15,558	$6,223	1.10	$1,301	3.11	$4,039	$121	$3,917	32.3
Phlebotomist	33%	$16,723	$6,689	1.10	$1,398	7.70	$10,771	$300	$10,470	34.8
Receptionist	33%	$15,891	$6,356	1.10	$1,328	3.33	$4,424	$130	$4,294	33.1
Housekeeper	33%	$14,810	$5,924	1.10	$1,238	16.40	$20,305	$640	$19,666	30.7
Speech Pathologist	33%	$39,229	$15,692	1.10	$3,280	3.66	$12,013	$143	$11,870	83.1
Registration Clerk	33%	$17,576	$7,030	1.10	$1,469	5.29	$7,774	$206	$7,568	36.7
Nutrition Services Aide	33%	$14,997	$5,999	1.10	$1,254	12.41	$15,559	$484	$15,075	31.1
Accounts Receivable Clerk	33%	$18,678	$7,471	1.10	$1,561	0.50	$781	$20	$761	39.0
Total Across All						92.39	$140,631	$3603	$137,028	38.0

Utility per hire = (.19 × standard deviation of salary × z), where:
- .19 is the increase in validity of the selection system when using the CSI (.31 − .11 = .19)
- Standard deviation of salary = annual salary × .4 (a value that Hunter and Schmidt and others have shown to produce conservative ROI estimates)
- z is the standardized value of the SR; in this case, a z of 1.10 corresponds to a selection ratio of 33%.

Annual hires was computed by multiplying the total number of incumbents by the turnover rate for each job. The organization indicated a turnover rate of 0% for two jobs, and in those cases a value of 0.5 was used to portray hiring one employee every two years. Total utility = Utility per hire × Annual hires. Total cost = Annual hires × $39 test cost per hire ($13 × 3 tests/hire). Net total utility = Total utility − Total cost. Net ROI ratio = (Utility per hire − Test cost per hire) ÷ Test cost per hire.
Source: Personnel Decisions, Inc. (PDI), Minneapolis, Minn. Validation of the PDI Customer Service Inventory for a Health Care Facility, Copyright © 1994, Personnel Decisions, Inc. Used with permission.

tailed example of a criterion-related validation of a test designed to predict effective customer service. Subsequent chapters will help you design your staffing process in conformance with the standards illustrated in the chapter. In particular, we now turn to the process of identifying the specific attributes needed in your setting.

Notes

1. Wayne Cascio, *Applied Psychology in Personnel Management,* 4th ed. (Englewood Cliffs, N.J.: Prentice Hall, 1991).

2. James L. Heskett, Thomas O. Jones, Gary W. Loveman, W. Earl Sasser, Jr., and Leonard A. Schlesinger, "Putting the Service/Profit Chain to Work," *Harvard Business Review* (March-April 1994):164–174.

3. Lynn R. Offermann and Marilyn K. Gowing, "Personnel Selection in the Future: The Impact of Changing Demographics and the Nature of Work" in *Personnel Selection in Organizations,* Neal Schmitt and Walter C. Borman, eds. (San Francisco: Jossey-Bass, 1993), chapter 12.

4. Robert E. Cole, "Learning from Learning Theory: Implications for Quality Improvement of Turnover, Use of Contingent Workers and Job Rotation Policies," *Quality Management Journal* (October 1993): 9–25.

5. Richard A. Guzzo, "Productivity Research: Reviewing Psychological and Economic Perspectives" in J. P. Campbell, R. J. Campbell, & Associates, *Productivity in Organizations: New Perspectives from Industrial and Organizational Psychology* (San Francisco: Jossey-Bass, 1988), 63–81.

6. Stephen B. Knouse, *The Reward and Recognition Process in Total Quality Management* (Milwaukee, Wis.: ASQC Quality Press, 1994).

7. Joseph L. Moses, Michael Beer, Melvin Sorcher, and Milton D. Hakel, *Making it Happen: Designing Research with Implementation in Mind* (Beverly Hills, Calif.: Sage, 1982).

8. Cascio, *Applied Psychology in Personnel Management.*

9. Robert Gatewood and Hubert Feild, *Human Resource Selection* (Fort Worth, Tex.: Dryden Press, 1994); Benjamin Schneider and Neal Schmitt, *Staffing Organizations,* 2nd ed. (Glenview, Ill.: Scott, Foresman, and Company, 1986).

10. Society for Industrial and Organizational Psychology, *Principles for the Validation and Use of Personnel Selection Procedures,* 3rd ed. (College Park, Md.: SIOP, 1987).

11. *Uniform Guidelines on Employee Selection Procedures,* Federal Register 43, no. 166 (August 25, 1978): 38290–38315.

12. *Griggs v. Duke Power Co.,* 401 U.S. 424, 1971.

13. *Uniform Guidelines on Employee Selection,* Sec. 1607.3 "Discrimination Defined: Relationship between Use of Selection Procedures and Discrimination," 43 Federal Register 38, August 1978.

14. Wayne Cascio and Niel Phillips, "Performance Testing: A Rose Among Thorns?" *Personnel Psychology* 32 (1979): 751–766.

15. *Wards Cove Packing Co. v. Atonio,* 49 FEP Cases, 1989, 1519–1535.

16. Civil Rights Act of 1991, *Congressional Record.*

17. Americans with Disabilities Act, 1990.

18. H. C. Taylor and J. T. Russell, "The Relationship of Validity Coefficients to the Practical Effectiveness of Tests in Selection," *Journal of Applied Psychology* 23 (1939): 565–578.

19. Gatewood and Feild, *Human Resource Selection,* p. 244; Frank L. Schmidt, John E. Hunter, Robert C. McKenzie, and Tressie W. Muldrow, "Impact of Valid Selection Procedures on Work-Force Productivity," *Journal of Applied Psychology* 64 (1979): 609–626.

20. For a more detailed discussion, see Cascio, *Applied Psychology in Personnel Management;* and Cascio, *Costing Human Resources: The Financial Impact of Behavior in Organizations* (Boston: Kent, 1982).

21. Personnel Decisions, Inc., "Validity of the PDI Employment Inventory for Quick Service Restaurants," technical report (Minneapolis, Minn.: Personnel Decisions, Inc., 1993), 7.

Using Job Analysis Techniques to Build a Quality Success Profile

Overview

This chapter provides the background and the tools needed to develop an organization-specific quality success profile. By following this job analysis–based approach, you can identify the quality attributes critical to success within your organization. This profile can then serve as the basis for the design of the entire staffing process: You plan, recruit, assess, select, train, evaluate, and promote based on those attributes.

The process we've outlined departs from the traditional job analysis approach in at least two ways: First, we incorporate a broader base of input (peers, team members, quality professionals). Second, we focus on identifying the attributes that make a difference in the current work and organization (mission, culture) but also incorporate the envisioned work, mission, and culture.

The job analysis process outlined in this chapter adds value to staffing in two ways. First, by integrating quality-related attributes into the staffing decision-making process, the organization reinforces the importance of quality. It becomes clear that to join and progress in the organization, each individual must possess and develop attributes supportive of quality improvement. The process we present will help you identify and prioritize what specific individual attributes are needed in your setting. Second, the systematic approach we present will increase the reliability, validity, fairness, and utility (ROI) of staffing decisions. Simply put, your organization will make better selection and promotion decisions—choices more in line with, and supportive of, the quality strategy.

What Defines Success in the New Workplace? What are the specific attributes needed for successful performance in the quality organization? The answer is, it depends. It depends on the job or position in question (the work to be done), the organization (mission, structure, culture), the quality approach or methodology in use, and how far along the organization is in its transition to a quality culture. This is the basic reason we need to conduct such an analysis. Clearly, we can draw some generalizations, and we've done so in previous chapters: cognitive ability; flexibility/adaptability; and openness to learning, retraining, and development are principal examples of attributes that emerge across various forms of the new workplace. These may apply in your setting, as well. Nonetheless, it will be valuable for you to build on the generalizations we present and focus the question in terms of your specific organization. What quality processes have you adopted, how far along that transition has your organization progressed, and what does the envisioned work and organization look like? Given these conditions, what attributes are needed and will be needed in your organization?

The Role of Job Analysis

Staffing is a process of matching the person to the work to be done and to the organization setting. To do so, we must have an understanding of the work and organization as well as the person's attributes. Some nomenclature will be helpful. *Job analysis* is the systematic process of examining the work, the work process, and the organization culture to determine what is done by the worker, and from that, what individual attributes are needed. The process produces varied outputs or products; first, a narrative description of the work, traditionally termed the *job description;* second, the analysis produces a *specification,* identifying worker attributes (knowledge, skills, ability, personality/temperament) and the experiences (previous education, training, jobs) needed to perform the work and succeed in the organization. This profile of attributes becomes the basis for the entire staffing process. If done correctly, the development of interview questions and the selection of written tests, work samples, and simulations become a very straightforward process, and the resulting staffing decisions become more effective (reliable, valid, fair, and useful). Failure to identify the specific attributes needed leads to the use of invalid methods and poor selection decisions. For example, if your organiza-

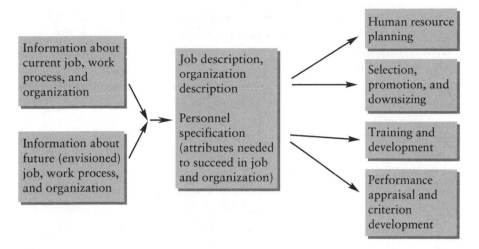

Figure 4.1. Staffing-related uses of systematic job analysis information.

tion is still focused on attributes needed to succeed before its quality transformation, it may well be that the staffing process is inhibiting the success of that effort. Figure 4.1 illustrates the useful output provided by a systematic job analysis.

As the figure illustrates, information about the job, work process, and organization (current and future) becomes the first step and the foundations for human resource planning; selection, promotion and downsizing; training and development; and performance appraisal and criterion development. This is as true in the new workplace as it was in the traditional work setting. In later chapters we detail the choice and development of assessment and selection devices. While there are many exciting quality-relevant assessment tools to share with you, all of them require that you first establish, in your setting, the relevance and importance of the attributes measured.

Are Job Analysis Concepts and Processes Out of Step with the New Workplace?

Our guess is that, if you've heard about job analysis, or if you've experienced it in your own organization, or, for the human resources professionals among our readers, if you've conducted a job analysis project, your preconceived notion of this chapter and of this topic is not wholly favorable. You might well say that job analysis has its detractors. In fact, there are some who are openly questioning the relevance of the process, contending that it is a relic of the past.[1] We thought we might best explore this issue and present our case for why we must change the job analysis process but not abandon the function it serves.

There are three fundamental reasons why some have questioned the relevance of job analysis procedures. First, work is no longer specialized and, consequently, doesn't require the focused analysis. Second, work is no longer stable. It changes too readily to warrant systematic analysis. Third, the impact of culture and the need to fit the person to the culture is said to be more important than fit to "a" job.

Work Is No Longer Specialized. In many respects, it is true that the process of job analysis is a product of the traditional workplace, where jobs were broken down into very specialized and often very narrow activities. In those settings, the job analysis methods and output mirrored the numerous, but minute, differences in jobs. But the trend is certainly toward less task specialization. As we've already noted, many of those minute differences between jobs are no longer relevant in the new workplace: jobs are broadened, and the numerous classifications that once existed are typically collapsed into a few. There is no better example of this than at 3M Canada manufacturing where the work performed by occupants of the two jobs cuts across what would have been, in a traditional facility, 12 to 15 different jobs, each with their own set of specific, narrowly defined tasks.[2]

At the extreme, some suggest that the changes in breadth we now see are only the beginning of a transition to a totally new form of organization. A recent *Fortune* magazine article suggests that the concept of job as we think of it may well have outlived its usefulness.[3] The flexibility needed in the organization of the near future will make practices such as rigidly defined jobs a thing of the past. It remains to be seen if that extreme projection becomes reality.

Whether or not the traditional job disappears, it is a safe bet that organizations will still have work to be done, and individuals will differ in the ability and willingness to do the work. Some rational process of fitting individuals to work and to organization settings will remain necessary. Furthermore, it is our belief that the process of identifying what's done, and the attributes needed to do the broadened jobs that clearly are characteristic of the new workplace, is even more relevant than it was in the traditional organization. The work is more challenging, more complex, more knowledge-based, and, consequently, requires a more complex, broader base of attributes. It requires the whole person. It is more important than ever that you identify clearly the attributes your new hires will need in order to learn and succeed in the organization. Consequently, we believe that it will be important for you to raise and address this question: What does it take to succeed in your work process and organization?

Work Is No Longer Static. The second reason the relevance of job analysis is questioned again relates to its role in the traditional setting. The traditional setting viewed jobs as relatively stable. Unfortunately, the process, as it has traditionally been practiced, results in a snapshot of the job at a specific point in time. The job descriptions produced from this snapshot often convey a rigid inflexibility about the job that is inconsistent with the transition toward a quality-oriented structure, culture, and workforce.

However, as we noted in chapter 2, jobs within quality improvement settings are often in a state of transition. The systematic changes characteristic of quality improvement take time. Simply put, jobs will continue to change and evolve as organizations' experience with quality improvement matures. Because of this, jobs in the new workplace are like moving targets—they're dynamic, and they're in a state of change. The implications of this are twofold. First, we must incorporate this reality into our job descriptions and job specifications. That is, we must make the dynamic nature of the work and organization clear to applicants, to recruiters, and to others involved in the hiring process. We must make it clear that individuals will need certain attributes to function effectively—at a minimum, a flexible/adaptable temperament and an openness to learning development and retraining. In effect, we must focus more on attributes that will endure as the work changes and less specifically on what exactly the person does. To do this, our job analysis process must also be dynamic and accommodate information about how the job is, as well as how it will be changing. The second thing we must do is to, in advance, envision what that change process will look like. What will the envisioned work look like? In effect, we can anticipate how work will change as the quality process matures. Will teams be in use? Will they take on some degree of self-management? Will employees be given increased authority to make on-the-spot decisions to satisfy customers? These are the kinds of work changes we must begin to prepare for now in the staffing process. Our job analysis process must incorporate the reality of change.

Fitting the Person to the Job and to the Organization. The third limiting factor of traditional job analysis is that it often focused on fitting the person to the specific job tasks, and neglected to fit the person to the broader organization culture. There has been a number of researchers calling for increased effort in fitting the person to the organization.[4] Neglecting to account for the culture increases the chance that the person will become dissatisfied or unmotivated, and perhaps leave the organization. The churn of turnover is costly both in terms of damage to the quality effort and to building the values of a quality culture.[5] And, as others have noted, it is legitimate to define success in terms of factors such as retention.[6] (Recall the utility examples presented in chapter 3: The quick service restaurant chain saved about $500,000 through reduced turnover. The national discount retail chain saved a total of $6,333,600—$5,115,600 through decreased involuntary terminations and $1,218,000 through decreased voluntary turnover.)

We concur that the job analysis process must identify individual attributes needed to fit into both the work and the broader organizational context (mission, strategy, and culture). This is related to the concept of whole person measurement cited in chapter 2. To accomplish this whole person—work/culture fit—the job analysis process must identify both the individual attributes needed to succeed in the work and in the culture. There is no better example of this than the increased use of personality and temperament measures to fit the individual with the work and the culture of the organization. Again, we believe this should, and will, be a central theme in staffing the new workplace, and you will read many instances of this as we profile the measurement of fit and motivation in chapter 8.

Reconciling Job Analysis and the Needs of the New Workplace

Before we present our process model and a step-by-step guide for conducting a job analysis, we thought a few points may help you see how we reconcile some of the deficiencies of the traditional approach.

An Attribute Focus. Because of the broadened nature of work, and the fact that the specific tasks may well change over a short time period, one key difference we see is in a need to focus less on specific tasks, and more on broader individual differences (attributes) that cut across tasks and specific job assignments. Consequently, one of the ways we resolve the dilemma of job analysis in the new workplace is to make individual attributes the focus of the analysis. We believe that attributes have greater relevance across time and across work processes than do traditional task-based job analysis practices. We believe that you will be able to identify a core set of attributes that cut across various jobs in your organization, particularly in regard to quality.

In our focus on attributes, we do not dispose of traditional focus on what work is done. To do so would be imprudent. (Compliance agencies and the courts still require that we show the link between the work to be performed and the selection processes.) We think it is still important to be able to describe why particular attributes are important to success in your organization. We simply say, think more broadly about the individual attributes that cut across the work, as it exists now and as the quality initiative matures. We believe this is important when analyzing an individual job, but also when dealing with all of the jobs in your organization. You may well see that a small set of attributes is relevant to all of the jobs in your organization—an organizationwide success profile. Recall the case of the health care facility described in chapter 3. In that setting, the job analysis revealed that the customer service attributes were important across all jobs in the facility. Our sense is that a quality initiative makes a number of attributes (such as customer orientation) similarly relevant across all of the jobs in your setting.

Incorporate Fit to the New Culture. Second, we propose that you overtly think through and incorporate the attributes the person will need to fit into the broader organization culture. This is particularly important in fitting individuals to the quality values of your setting. Our recommendation is right in line with a renewed interest in and renewed methods for measuring personality and temperament relevant to the new workplace. In chapter 8 we profile specific instruments appropriate for measuring fit within your quality strategy and culture.

Incorporate the Envisioned Work and Organization. In addition to the fact that jobs change, it is also the case that, in some circumstances, the job, the work process, and even the organization to be analyzed is evolving or does not yet exist. The basis for the staffing process is a vision of what the organization will become. This is especially true in organizations that are about to embark on a reengineering of work processes, or on the long-range transition to a quality-focused culture. The change will be radical—requiring a workforce with different attributes. To be successful in that long-range makeover, you must begin now to staff for that vision of the future organization. To staff based on your existing or past view of the organization will be self-defeating.

It is our belief that, in the context of the new organization, it is not enough to simply analyze the job in terms of present tasks and duties. Rather, that analysis should be conducted with the strategic quality initiative of the organization firmly in mind. If the vision of the organization is one of teamwork, empowerment, broad-based skills, flexibility/adaptability, and customer orientation, then jobs should be analyzed with those envisioned changes in mind. Analyzing jobs in terms of the status quo would be a big mistake for any organization attempting to foster a transition. (If you look again at Figure 4.1 you will see that we propose analysis of the job both as it now exists and as it will exist after the quality effort matures.)

When the culture, work processes, and the design of jobs are in such transition, the work as it will be done must be envisioned. How will the organization culture differ? How will the work process be performed? What is it that individuals will be expected to do? What attributes will they need?

Analyzing the envisioned work creates new challenges. Researchers Benjamin Schneider and Neal Schmitt describe an approach for dealing with envisioned jobs that essentially involves analyzing both the current job and separately, the future, envisioned job.[7] It is important to note that you should not be cavalier in establishing hiring criteria for jobs that do not yet exist. Later in this chapter we will present specific benchmark examples of job analysis for envisioned jobs, including the use of job analysis procedures to design a selection program for two newly designed positions—the technologist and operator in a plant startup at 3M Canada manufacturing.

It is our premise that the changes associated with the new workplace—and the envisioned jobs that will result—will place a greater emphasis on multiple skills, flexibility in temperament, and a willingness to continually learn, retrain, and develop. These are workforce attributes on which the organization can base its future. However, we also believe that these attributes will be at a premium in the available workforce. The organization that constructs a workforce based on these attributes will be more responsive and more likely to achieve its envisioned future.

Staffing for the future does carry an element of risk. For example, if the organization lacks sincere commitment to the future vision, and you do recruit employees ready for and seeking this new workplace (perhaps one stressing empowerment), but the organization then reverts to a traditional, hierarchical, authoritarian system, you will experience a severely disgruntled workforce. This issue gets at the core of the quality transformation. Is there commitment to, and support for, the transformation from a traditional to quality-focused setting? As we noted in chapter 1, there appears to be a systematic relationship between the extent to which the firm has progressed in its transformation and the extent to which it has revised its staffing practices to support the transition.

In summary, we assume that you intend to build a success profile for an organization that is in the process of transition, moving from a traditional organization (narrow, static jobs) to a true quality-focused organization (broad, dynamic jobs). Therefore, we will present strategies for analyzing, describing, and selecting for jobs in these new dynamic settings.

The Job Analysis Process

The job analysis process is one of collecting information about the work, the organization, and the attributes needed to succeed and then transforming that information into customer-useful output needed to plan, recruit, screen, assess, select, orient, and train the new employee. The output includes what traditionally have been termed *job descriptions* and *job specifications*. Figure 4.2 characterizes the components of that process.

Suppliers of Job Information

There are varied sources for collecting information about the work setting. We can solicit input from those who perform the job, those who supervise the job, those who interact as clients or customers, and HR professionals and the quality professionals familiar with the job. If we must envision future jobs, it is important that we involve the technical experts familiar with the new work (for example, the engineers, consultants, and managers who have designed the new work process). To rely solely on those currently doing the work may well produce misleading results. Similarly, we can benchmark other organizations to see how they have designed work and treat that as input. You may recall our discussion of process validity in chapter 3 where we noted that the involvement of various internal personnel affected by the job contributes to the thoroughness and acceptability of the materials produced (the hiring specifications). As with other suppliers, we seek to select them on the basis of the quality of their input. Do they know the work and broader work process? Do they know the quality initiative? In many circumstances it is useful to interview, observe, and sometimes even survey representatives from these groups. We'll incorporate the input of others in the step-by-step job analysis process we outline at the end of this chapter.

Inputs. The information we seek from them typically includes detail about what the individual actually does (traditionally, tasks or duties), the conditions under which the work is done, the equipment to be op-

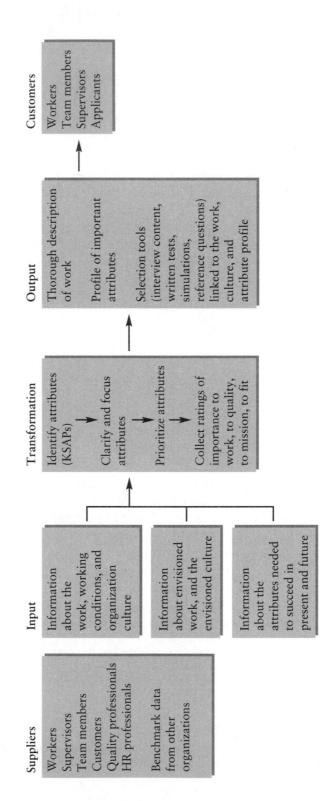

Suppliers

Workers
Supervisors
Team members
Customers
Quality professionals
HR professionals

Benchmark data
from other
organizations

Input

Information
about the
work, working
conditions, and
organization
culture

Information
about envisioned
work, and the
envisioned culture

Information
about the
attributes needed
to succeed in
present and future

Transformation

Identify attributes
(KSAPs)

Clarify and focus
attributes

Prioritize attributes

Collect ratings of
importance to
work, to quality,
to mission, to fit

Output

Thorough description
of work

Profile of important
attributes

Selection tools
(interview content,
written tests,
simulations,
reference questions)
linked to the work,
culture, and
attribute profile

Customers

Workers
Team members
Supervisors
Applicants

Figure 4.2. A process model of job, work, and organization analysis.

erated, how he or she impacts the broader work process, the nature of the organization culture, and what attributes are required to succeed. Sometimes we merely interview these experts and other times we collect more structured input using questionnaires. Sometimes we do both.

Transformation. The key objective of the process is to translate the input about the current and future work, and the current and future culture, into a set of job-related attributes: that is, specific attributes that differentiate successful employees. We'll designate a set of guidelines for identifying, clarifying, and prioritizing attributes. The goal is to take the input and characterize the important attributes needed before hire. The transformation typically involves identifying what experiences (education, training, work experience) will provide the level of mastery we need in our applicants. In all cases the goal is to make the attribute and experience requirements useful to customers of the process.

How does the transformation occur? The transformation process is sometimes completed by a knowledgeable individual, or perhaps based on ratings provided by focus groups or questionnaires administered to samples of employees. We based our approach on collective judgments of the importance of the attributes. We'll present a number of examples of how structured questionnaires can be used to arrive at measurements of the relative importance of specific attributes.

Output. Ideally, the output of this process is a clear description of the work and culture, and most important, clear specifications (KSAPs, and the education, training, work experience needed). These products should be in a format usable to the customers of the process.

Customers. The customers of the process include all those involved in managing the human resources of the organization: HRP, staffing, training and development, and performance appraisal. All of these processes are improved when they are based on a set of clear, relevant attributes (the organization success profile). Furthermore, the human resource processes are more effective when they are all based on the same set of attributes. The specific customers of staffing include the hiring manager, the coworkers and team members, and others inside and outside the organization affected by the work of the new hire. Also, as we noted in chapter 1, we see the applicant as a customer of this process. Distortion in the process (for example, incomplete or inaccurate criteria) can have an even greater effect on the applicant (rejected from a job he would excel at or hired into a job he's not suited for).

What does the voice of the customer call for in job analysis? While this is a question you should investigate within your own organization, we can speculate on some generalities. First, we'd expect that the hiring manager, or work team, typically wants speed. Traditional job analysis has often been a long, methodical process. The time line is a recurring point of conflict between human resources and its customers. A second standard of interest to customers is validity. That is, they need specifications that really do differentiate between those who will and won't succeed. (We won't speculate on how customers differ in their value of speed versus validity.) Those organizations that have built the most effective staffing processes (3M Canada, for example) began by identifying what attributes really do differentiate successful from unsuccessful employees. A poorly thought-out description and specification will be of little use to staffing customers (including applicants) or to the organization. To assure that the process has integrity, there must be confidence in what we are using to make assessments and decisions.

Measures. There are various measures appropriate to each step of the process. We can measure the reliability of judgments collected in the process. We can measure the time the process takes. We can gauge customer satisfaction with the process. We can measure the consensus (reliability) regarding the importance of various KSAPs to the work and organization. We can assess the long-term impact (validity) of the decisions produced by the process.

Methods for Analyzing Jobs

While a number of methods exist for analyzing jobs, the approach we present here is organized around identifying and substantiating the attributes (KSAPs) workers need to succeed in the job, the broader work process, and the organization. The approach we present systematically examines the knowledge, skills, abilities, and personal characteristics (KSAPs) required to successfully perform the job in question. (By the way, many are using the term *competencies* to describe KSAPs.) There are a number of useful strategies for generating and substantiating job-related KSAPs, and we present these next. While we cannot overview all of the approaches to job analysis, we present for the interested reader a number of sources that profile different approaches.[8] Figure 4.3 depicts a simplified flowchart of the steps in a KSAP-based job analysis process we now profile.

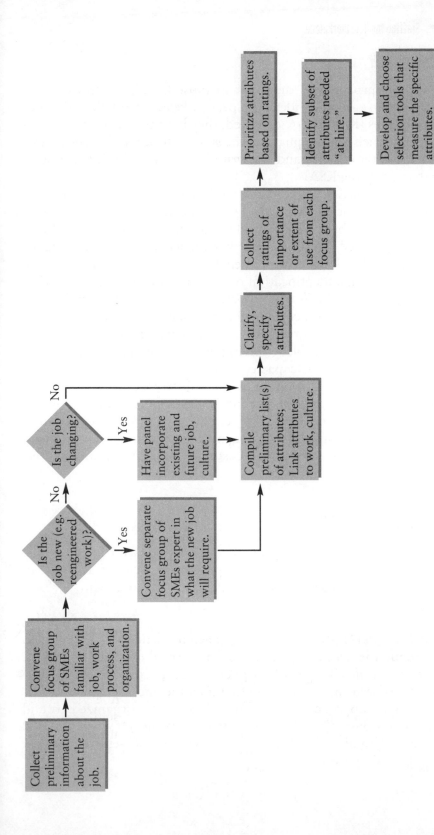

Figure 4.3. Simplified flowchart of a typical job and organization analysis.

133

The KSAP Approach

The KSAP approach uses the input of those familiar with the work and the organization to identify specific, relevant attributes. Once these attributes (KSAPs) are identified, they become the focus of a systematic approach to each phase of the staffing process. (We select tests that measure the KSAPs, and we write interview and reference questions that assess the KSAPs).

As we discussed in chapter 2, *knowledge* represents mastery of information (principles, facts, and so on) associated with a subject matter area. Much of the work required in quality-oriented settings draws on specific knowledge bases such as knowledge of applied statistics or knowledge of SPC, knowledge of benchmarking, or knowledge of design of experiments. Identification of these knowledge bases is critical to effective staffing. *Skills* are proficiencies involving the application of some knowledge or practiced techniques such as giving oral presentations or mediating disagreements. *Abilities* are cognitive or physical proficiencies such as problem solving and reasoning. A related concept, aptitude, reflects the capacity to learn a knowledge or skill. *Personal characteristics* include individual differences in personality, temperament, values, interests, or motivation. Some examples of personal characteristics required in typical quality improvement settings include flexibility/adaptability; openness to learning, development and retraining; conscientiousness; customer orientation; and creative thinking.

Identifying Job-Related KSAPs

There are various methods for identifying KSAPs. Two that we profile are work and organization analysis and critical incident analysis. In essence, these ask what attributes differentiate those who perform from those who fail.

Work and Organization Analysis. The first approach to identifying KSAPs is to think about the work that must be performed (the duties, tasks, processes) and the context (physical conditions, organization culture) in which it is performed, and from that infer the underlying worker attributes. In this approach, the job analysis process is organized around two key questions: What does the individual do in the work process? And what attributes (KSAPs) must the worker possess to perform these responsibilities?

The key to identifying attributes is a thorough understanding of the work to be performed. As we have noted, it is advisable to collect the input from individuals who know the work process and are affected by the role of the new worker. In job analysis nomenclature, our suppliers of information are typically referred to as subject matter experts (SMEs). SMEs may include those who have performed the job, those who have supervised the job, knowledgeable HR professionals, quality professionals, and in some circumstances customers/clients. In addition to knowledge of the work process, SMEs must also possess a thorough understanding of the quality initiative. This is a critical point. We want our job analysis input to reflect the substance of the quality effort. That is, we want our SMEs to generate and focus on attributes needed to succeed with the quality tools and processes. Once we've assembled this sample of knowledgeable SMEs, the key questions to ask are

1. What's done on the job or work process (or, what do we envision will be done), and under what conditions must the worker perform (physical, psychological)?

2. What organizational characteristics (structure, mission, culture) affect success?

3. Given that, what knowledge, skills, abilities, and personal characteristics are needed to accomplish the work in this culture?

If, in fact, we are analyzing a job that does not yet exist, or the changes will be so profound that those familiar with the current work cannot accurately anticipate how the work will change, we might well convene a second, independent focus group composed of those familiar with the new work (the engineers, quality specialists, management specialists, HR specialists, industrial psychologists specializing in human performance and assessment, and consultants who have designed the new work). We then guide them through the same questions, oriented toward the new work.

The Critical Incident Method. A second approach useful for revealing important KSAPs is the critical incident (CI) method. This approach is based on the question: What critical behaviors distinguish effective from ineffective employees? This method involves collecting large numbers of anecdotes of job behavior that describe particularly good or poor job performance. Each of these behavioral examples describes the following:

1. The setting or circumstances that led up to the performance example

2. Exactly what the person did that was effective or ineffective (the behavior)

3. The results or perceived results of the behavior

These descriptions of critical behaviors are then used to reveal important KSAPs. Exhibit 4.1 presents examples of critical incidents from a manufacturing setting illustrating both effective and ineffective performance. Exhibit 4.2 presents quality-relevant CIs for the job of sales manager in an insurance company. As you can see, the

Exhibit 4.1. Critical incidents illustrating effective and ineffective behavior in a manufacturing setting.

Incident 1: Effective behavior

Setting: A major customer called managers to inform them that the trial production parts did not perform up to the standards of the prototype.
Behavior: Instead of sending out a salesperson, an engineer from research and development (R&D) and an engineer from manufacturing were sent to the customer site. The R&D engineer worked with the prototype while the manufacturing engineer made the trial production parts. **Result:** Problems were resolved within a few hours and the customer was impressed and happy. Since then, the customer has been receiving parts that meet expectations, and the customer has already placed orders for its 1997 project.

KSAPs indicated by the CI: Customer orientation and problem analysis.

Incident 2: Ineffective behavior

Setting: A client called the after-market sales manager complaining about a shipment being delayed. **Behavior:** The sales manager immediately made a conference call to the warehouse manager concerning the matter. Unaware that the customer was on the line, the warehouse manager chewed out the sales manager for making empty promises to the customer. **Result:** This incident demonstrated the incompetence of the sales manager for not understanding the company's operating capabilities and made him look bad for trying to blame someone who was obviously not responsible for the problem. Although the sales manager apologized, the customer voiced concerns about the competency of the company.

KSAPs indicated by the CI: Personal integrity, customer orientation, knowledge of process.

Exhibit 4.2. Critical incidents illustrating effective and ineffective behavior in an insurance sales management position.

Incident 1: Effective behavior

Setting: A new agent and sales manager were performing joint fieldwork. The agent discussed with the client the possibility of replacing a permanent life policy held with another company. **Behavior:** After the meeting, the sales manager discussed the situation with the agent and showed how replacement was not in the client's best interest. Although it would have been an easy sale, the agent returned and explained the issues surrounding the policy. **Result:** The sale was not made, but the client later expressed appreciation for the honesty and service received.

KSAP illustrated: Customer service.

Incident 2: Effective behavior

Setting: A client contacted the insurance office and indicated that he was having a problem with his auto insurance. **Behavior:** The sales manager made a conference call to the Property and Casualty Center and put the client in touch with the person who could best solve the problem. The manager also called the client one week later to verify that the problem was resolved. **Result:** The client felt that the problem was handled by an expert who really cared about the problem.

KSAP illustrated: Customer service

Incident 3: Ineffective behavior

Setting: A sales manager received a call from a client complaining about the service received from an agent. **Behavior:** The sales manager told the client she would talk to the agent about the complaint but then failed to do so. **Result:** The client became very upset when he found out that the manager had failed to follow through on her promise.

Incident 4: Ineffective behavior

Setting: A new agent sought advice from the sales manager on the proper way to submit a large premium life case involving trust agreements. **Behavior:** The manager—with little or no knowledge of estate planning—had the agent prepare the application as if it were a normal life case and submit it for underwriting. **Result:** The agent all but lost the case after the client's attorney and an experienced financial planer became involved. The agent was embarrassed and ultimately refused to deal with the manager.

KSAPs illustrated: Conscientiousness, customer orientation.

---

incidents illustrate which individual attributes made a difference in critical situations.

Once generated, CIs are typically grouped into performance dimensions or attributes (customer service, group problem solving, and interpersonal relations). CIs can be used to infer the importance of KSAPs or used on their own merit. CIs are particularly useful for developing behavioral interview questions (discussed in chapter 9) and various work samples and simulations (discussed in chapters 7 and 8).

Ideally, CIs should be generated as they occur. For example, supervisors, employees, or team members may be asked to make note of particularly good or poor employee performance as it is observed. In a hospital where one of the authors consulted, nursing supervisors and managers were given three-inch-by-five-inch cards and asked to record such behaviors for a one-month time period. Once generated, CIs were clustered into performance dimensions and used to identify critical attributes on which to base the selection process.

While concurrent generation of CIs is desired, more often SMEs are asked to think back over time to generate examples of good and poor employee behavior. This is typically accomplished in a conference or group setting with an expert or consultant present to facilitate the process.

As with KSAPs, the generation of CIs should be accomplished with an eye to the organization's quality initiative. For example, SMEs might be encouraged to record or generate CIs that demonstrate attributes such as customer service, continuous improvement, teamwork, problem solving, or employee involvement. And, as we have noted, be sure to include knowledgeable quality professionals in the process.

A related approach to identifying KSAPs was popularized by Robert Mager.[9] He suggests that managers examine those characteristics that distinguish between successful and unsuccessful employees. Managers should ask: Who are good employees, and what is it that they do that convinces me that they are successful employees? Conversely, who are poor or problem employees, and what behaviors do they exhibit that persuade me that they are unsuccessful?

Applying Mager's methodology for determining how to know one when we see one, we can begin to identify those characteristics that are important for successful job performance. Mager's approach tells us to visualize a room full of present employees and then asks us to separate them into two groups. In one group would be all of our best employees—perhaps those who have adopted quality principles and practices. The second group would contain those employees considered ineffective.

Once you have separated them, begin to examine those characteristics that distinguish between the two groups. What characteristics do the top performers exhibit? Why do the poor performers fail?

Top-performing group	Low-performing group
• Makes a lot of good suggestions for improving products and services	• Is reluctant to join and participate in company's improvement teams
• Knows products and services	• Doesn't understand products and services
• Follows up on customer calls and complaints	• Is slow in responding to customers
• Is eager to learn new skills	• Resists additional education or training

Once identified, these descriptions can easily be translated into KSAPs and then used to develop assessment procedures for selection or promotion. For example, from the previous list we can infer that our workforce may need the following attributes: conscientiousness, customer orientation, initiative, and openness to learning and development.

Functional and Quality KSAPs

Although our focus is on quality attributes, it is important to remember to include other (functional) attributes that may be critical to successful performance. Programmers need skill in programming, secretaries need word processing skills, forklift operators need manual dexterity, and so forth. Note that the profile of attributes required in 3M Canada manufacturing facilities presented later in this chapter includes both functional and quality attributes.

Sources for Attributes

Developing clear, specific, meaningful attributes is a very important step in the job analysis process. Rather than thinking of these on your own, or having other SMEs generate and define them, there are a number of taxonomies of KSAPs to which you can turn. They are useful in that, for the most part, they are typically well-defined and sometimes confirmed through research. In many cases there are assessment tools specifically designed to measure these attributes. Exhibit 4.3 presents a newly developed taxonomy of interpersonal skills relevant to business. A number of taxonomies appear in various parts of this book. We thought that it would be useful to list some of them here.

Attributes	Taxonomy	Location in book
Cognitive ability	Employee Aptitude Survey Flanagan Industrial Tests	Chapter 7 (Exhibit 7.2) Chapter 7 (Exhibit 7.3)
Personality	Personality Characteristics Inventory	Chapter 8 (pages 296–298)
Managerial skills	PDI's Profilor Dimensions	Chapter 11 (Figure 11.4)
Quality	Quality Attributes Inventory	Appendix B

If specific knowledges are relevant in your workplace, college and technical school catalogues are excellent sources for identifying how specific bodies of knowledge are configured.

Identifying Quality-Specific Attributes. In an effort to help identify the quality-relevant attributes in your organization, we have developed an extensive list of quality-relevant KSAPs. The QAI is a structured, quality-related, job analysis checklist that can be used for identifying critical attributes for various positions, jobs, or functions.

The inventory contains 100 attributes divided into four major categories.

1. Quality knowledge and skills

2. Personality and temperament traits

3. Certification and professional affiliation

4. Engineering and quality assurance

These four categories are further divided into subsections. We have left spaces at the bottom of each subsection for users to add attributes unique to their quality initiatives. This was done because the QAI can't be a totally comprehensive and definitive listing. We have attempted to list only the more familiar attributes, along with those

Exhibit 4.3. A taxonomy of interpersonal skills.

Sensitivity to others—Skill in understanding others' intentions during inter-action, attending to, anticipating/meeting their needs, respecting their wishes, and projecting courtesy and friendliness.

- High performers attend to others, read situations well, and act appro-priately during interactions, appearing warm and friendly.
- Low performers tend to ignore others, to misperceive the dynamics of an interaction, and to act inappropriately, appearing disrespectful and rude.

Flexibility—Skill in handling the requests of others, responding to new ideas, and appearing willing to bend or compromise rules in order to solve interpersonal problems.

- High performers tend to be adaptable, accommodating, easy-going, and willing to compromise in order to meet others' needs.
- Low performers tend to be rigid, stubborn, and unable/unwilling to set aside rules to meet others' needs.

Leading—Skill in persuading, motivating, encouraging, teaching, and inspir-ing others thereby creating a positive work climate. This skill has less to do with behavior, per se, than with the attitude generated as a result of those behaviors.

- High performers tend to be inspiring, to make others feel good about their work, to teach, and to use power appropriately, thereby making others want to work hard.
- Low performers tend to be arrogant or unassertive, to make others feel defensive or inadequate, to ignore training others, and to alienate sub-ordinates through the inappropriate use of power, intimidation, or lack of support.

Trust and confidence—Skill in acquiring the trust of others by appearing honest, sure, competent, and knowledgeable.

- High performers tend to be fair, trustworthy, competent, and serious/confident about delivering services, which sustains relationships.
- Low performers tend to be unfair, incompetent, casual or careless about meeting commitments, and they create little faith in their reliability which erodes relationships.

Consistency—Skill in handling pressure over time and across individuals and in dealing positively with problem interactions and changing situations.

- High performers tend to be steady, level-headed, resilient, and to keep personnel feelings/emotions out of interactions with others.
- Low performers tend to be unpredictable, erratic, easily rattled or un-nerved, and to introduce negative/hostile feelings into interactions with customers/coworkers.

Exhibit 4.3. Continued.

Responsibility and accountability—Skill in handling obligations, putting forth energy to follow through on promises and commitments, and taking responsibility for the actions of oneself, coworkers, and subordinates.

- High performers tend to solve problems, find solutions, go the extra mile, and take responsibility for good and bad situations.
- Low performers tend to ignore obligations, not respond to requests, blame others for faults or mistakes, pass the buck, and not admit errors.

Communication—Skill in extracting information from others and disseminating it in a clear and accurate fashion.

- High performers listen well, ask good questions, understand others' information needs, and present information in a clear and straightforward manner.
- Low performers tend to be poor listeners who don't ask questions and misunderstand the information needs of others, leaving them feeling uninformed or confused.

Source: Joyce Hogan and Jard Lock, "A Taxonomy of Interpersonal Skills for Business Interactions," presented at the 10th Annual Conference of the Society for Industrial/Organizational Psychology, Orlando, Fla.: May 1995.

---

attributes we considered important for success in a quality-oriented organization. Because the quality literature is rich with philosophies, methods, tools, and descriptions of the behaviors and traits that are important to quality success, additions are being made weekly to this burgeoning field. Consequently, we encourage you to expand the list to meet your own unique needs. The list can be used to assemble the quality-oriented content of a KSAP questionnaire like that presented later in Exhibit 4.4. The QAI is provided to help generate a list of the critical quality attributes needed for a particular job and organization. In addition, the inventory reinforces the importance of staffing for quality and points out the broad scope of KSAPs and qualifications directly linked to quality. Given the scope of the list, it is no wonder that Deming referred to it as "profound knowledge."

Guidelines for Writing KSAP-Based Job Specifications

As practitioners, the authors have considerable experience helping managers and work teams with the details of formulating profiles of job-related KSAPs. Based on that experience, we have formulated guidelines that are helpful to individuals unaccustomed to generating job specifications.

1. Ensure that the KSAPs are specific and clearly defined
2. Ensure that the KSAPs are important to job performance (job related)
3. Ensure that the KSAPs capture all aspects of the job
4. Ensure that the KSAPs are needed prior to hire.

Each of these guidelines is discussed next.

Are the Attributes Specific?

When it comes to doing job analysis and outlining job specifications, it is safe to say that we cannot be too clear and specific in defining what we mean by a particular attribute. The more specific the description of the attributes, the easier it is to identify minimum hiring qualifications, identify appropriate standardized tests, and develop relevant interview questions. If you start with a credible taxonomy, it is likely that the KSAPs you identify will be clear and specific.

The advantage of clarity is simply this: The more specific we become in describing attributes and experience requirements, the easier it is to develop valid selection and promotion procedures and to find the best possible person for the position. Unfortunately, most efforts at describing job specifications are overly general. Typically, we think about qualifications in terms of generalities and abstractions and not in terms of the specific attributes that are necessary to successful performance. Thus we ask for somebody who is motivated, dedicated, fits into our culture, and has good communication skills. We also get lazy and list indicators rather than the specific KSAPs needed to perform the job (for example, three to five years of experience and/or a bachelor's degree in business communication, or some related field).

How, then, do we go about creating effective job specifications? Let's review the often-cited job qualification seen in about half of the help-wanted advertisements—"good communication skills." Kept in this general form, it is useless for both the candidate (all of us think we have good communication skills) and for the individual doing the selecting ("What do we really mean by good communication?"). How do we go about making this abstract qualification meaningful and useful? We begin by asking what kind of communication is important.

Oral? Written? Both oral and written communication can be further refined in terms of level or degree.

Oral?	Written?
• One-on-one?	• Memos and letters?
• Group?	• Reports, executive summaries?
• Sending (talking)?	• Writing technical manuals or reports?
• Receiving (listening skills)?	• Charting?
• Persuading or selling others?	• Computer memos (E-mail)?
• Negotiating with others?	
• Stand-up presentation skills?	

These lists provide us with much better information for assessing and selecting the right person for the job. It's a lot easier to develop selection procedures for assessing stand-up presentation skills than for good communication skills. And these skills can be further refined by describing the context in which the skills should be exhibited. Is the communication conducted with customers? With peers? With subordinates? Done correctly, a final list might better resemble the following.

- Group facilitation skills: to guide problem-solving groups (for example, a team leader for the employee involvement group)

- Listening skills: ability to listen and respond to customer concerns and complaints

- Oral presentation skills: to develop and present training material in a classroom or workshop setting

- Written communication skills: to respond in writing (letters) to customer concerns and complaints

Once this level of specificity is obtained, the development of selection instruments and interview questions becomes an easy and straightforward process. Witness the following example one of the authors recently encountered during an interviewing skills workshop for administrators at a large senior citizen residency complex.

One of the workshop exercises required participants to generate a list of job qualifications for one of their positions. One manager had on her list, in addition to other qualifications, the following competencies.

- Good communication skills
- Good computer skills
- Sensitivity

While these may well be important, as they are stated they are too general to serve as a framework for staffing.

Discussion with the manager revealed that a major duty of the position was to respond in writing to the concerns voiced by the families of the various elderly residents. With some orientation and encouragement, the list was refined to read as follows:

- Good communication skills
  - Compose letters
  - Correct grammar
  - Correct spelling

- Good computer skills
  - Basic word processing using a standard program
  - Interface with laser printer (letter, envelopes, addresses)

- Sensitivity
  - Concern and willingness to work with the elderly and their families
  - Customer orientation for both internal and external customers (elderly families, community)

Once KSAPs are defined clearly, it is much easier to collect concensus ratings of importance (because they are specific, SMEs can concur that they are used on the job and that they are important). It is then easier to design a selection exercise for measuring many of these competencies. In the future, candidates for the position at the complex will be given two or three scenarios (simulations) that reflect various kinds of family complaints (possibly taken from CIs) and asked to compose a computer-generated response letter to those concerns. This straightforward and job-related simulation will provide the organization with valuable information concerning the candidate's ability to "use the computer to prepare grammatically correct letters that respond in a positive and caring way to the concerns and complaints of residents' families."

Are the KSAPs Important for Job Performance, for Culture Fit?

The ultimate test of each KSAP (current as well as envisioned) is the importance of the attributes to performance on the job and in the organization. Once a preliminary list of KSAPs has been generated, it is a worthwhile exercise to scrutinize each attribute for job relatedness. One way to do this is to identify two or three critical work activities that require the KSAP. If the analysis has suggested a KSAP, but you can't clearly describe how it is or will be used on the current or future job, the attribute is probably not appropriate for staffing decisions.

Once we've identified an initial list of KSAPs, we are often interested in prioritizing them. The ultimate test of each KSAP (current and envisioned, quality and functional) is the importance of the attribute to the performance on the job, the work process, and in the organization. While many are clearly relevant, we're interested in identifying those which are most important to successful performance in the job and organization. An advantage of the KSAP approach is that it allows us to collect quantifiable judgments about the attributes. One way to prioritize KSAPs is to use surveys to collect judgments from knowledgeable SMEs. There are a number of judgments (ratings) we might collect and use in prioritizing the KSAPs needed in the job. These include

- The importance of the KSAP to job performance and success in the organization

- The importance of the KSAP to the quality initiative

- The level of the KSAP the individual must possess

- The trainability of the KSAP

- The extent to which the KSAP is needed prior to hire

- The experiences (education, work experience, and training) through which a person could be expected to develop the attribute

Exhibit 4.4 presents an example of a rating scale for the job of customer information representative at a utility company. You could construct a questionnaire like this to collect data that assure you that the KSAPs are important.

What Attributes Are Important to Quality Efforts? At the onset of the chapter we posed the question: What attributes are needed in quality-oriented settings? That same question was incorporated into the ASQC Survey of

Exhibit 4.4. Questionnaire used to collect ratings of KSAPs for customer information representative.

Please rate each of the following KSAPs in terms of their relationship to successful job performance and the extent to which each is necessary upon entry to the job.

> **Relationship to successful performance** refers to the degree that the attribute (KSAP) is needed to perform the important tasks and duties of the job. The following scale is used to rate the relationship to successful performance.
>
> 1 = Never required for successful job performance
> 2 = Seldom required for successful job performance
> 3 = Occasionally required for successful job performance
> 4 = Often required for successful job performance
> 5 = Always required for successful job performance
>
> **Extent to which each is necessary upon entry to the job** refers to distinguishing KSAPs required for immediate performance of the job upon entry from those that will be acquired through normal orientation, training, or on-the-job experience. Extent to which each is necessary at entry is rated using the following scale.
>
> 1 = Learned or acquired through normal experience on the job
> 2 = Desired upon entrance to the job
> 3 = Needed upon entrance to the job

KSAP	Performance	Entry
1. Skill in one-on-one communication	1 2 3 4 5	1 2 3
2. Skill in customer interaction	1 2 3 4 5	1 2 3
3. Openness to learning and development	1 2 3 4 5	1 2 3
4. Flexibility/adaptability	1 2 3 4 5	1 2 3

Staffing Practices. Respondents (principally quality directors) rated the importance of 28 KSAPs to their organization's quality effort. Table 4.1 presents the relative importance of these attributes for hourly/blue-collar and professional/technical employees across a wide range of quality-oriented organizations. Table 4.2 presents the attribute ratings for three levels of management. We've arranged the KSAPs in rank order based on the mean importance rating provided by our respondents. To help you interpret these judgments, a rating of

Table 4.1. Importance of total quality attributes in hourly/blue-collar and technical/professional workforce.

Hourly/blue-collar workforce		Technical/professional workforce	
Attribute	Average importance rating	Attribute	Average importance rating
Conscientiousness	4.20	Basic reading	4.63
Flexibility/adaptability	4.10	Basic math	4.46
Basic reading skills	4.08	Skill in relating to others	4.45
Openness to learning and development	3.97	Customer orientation	4.43
Customer orientation	3.96	Flexibility/adaptability	4.43
Teamwork orientation	3.95	Conscientiousness	4.41
Skill in relating to others	3.80	Openness to learning	4.32
Basic math skills	3.71	Skill in oral communication	4.30
Skill in oral communication	3.41	Teamwork orientation	4.26
Skill in involving others	3.40	Skill in involving others	4.21
Creative thinking	3.27	Creative thinking	4.18
Knowledge of quality tools	3.24	Skill in written communication	4.18

Item	Rating	Item	Rating
Knowledge of process improvement	3.23	Skill in coaching others	4.17
Skill in coaching others	3.21	Skill in empowering others	4.09
Skill in problem solving	3.04	Skill in problem solving	4.06
Skill in written communication	2.92	Knowledge of process improvement	4.02
Skill in empowering others	2.78	Knowledge of quality tools	3.96
Skill in facilitating teams	2.68	Skill in facilitating teams	3.91
Basic PC skills	2.58	Basic PC skills	3.89
Knowledge of SPC	2.51	Skill in organizational change	3.84
Knowledge of ISO 9000	2.41	Knowledge of SPC	3.36
Knowledge of quality theories	2.21	Knowledge of applied statistics	3.16
Skill in organizational change	2.14	Knowledge of benchmarking	3.13
Knowledge of applied statistics	1.98	Knowledge of quality theories	3.11
Knowledge of benchmarking	1.86	Knowledge of ISO 9000	3.09
Knowledge of Baldrige Award criteria	1.76	Knowledge of reengineering	2.80
Knowledge of reengineering	1.69	Knowledge of experimental design	2.77
Knowledge of experimental design	1.46	Knowledge of Baldrige Award criteria	2.57
Average rating	**2.98**	**Average rating**	**3.86**

Table 4.2. Importance of total quality attributes in managerial workforce results of ASQC Survey of Staffing Practices.

First line/supervisory		Middle management		Senior management	
Attribute	Average rating	Attribute	Average rating	Attribute	Average rating
Basic reading	4.48	Basic reading	4.59	Skill in organizational change	4.67
Skill in relating to others	4.45	Skill in relating to others	4.52	Customer orientation	4.65
Flexibility/adaptability	4.39	Flexibility/adaptability	4.52	Oral communication	4.61
Skill in coaching others	4.38	Customer orientation	4.55	Basic reading skills	4.61
Customer orientation	4.37	Skill in coaching others	4.45	Flexibility/adaptability	4.53
Conscientiousness	4.36	Skill in oral communication	4.43	Skill in empowering others	4.52
Teamwork orientation	4.34	Skill in empowering others	4.42	Skill in relating to others	4.51
Skill in involving others	4.26	Conscientiousness	4.40	Creative thinking	4.49
Openness to learning	4.24	Skill in involving others	4.37	Written communication	4.49
Skill in empowering others	4.19	Openness to learning	4.37	Skill in involving others	4.43
Basic math	4.19	Teamwork orientation	4.36	Skill in coaching others	4.40
Skill in oral communication	4.18	Basic math	4.30	Conscientiousness	4.40
Skill in facilitating teams	4.14	Creative thinking	4.28	Openness to learning	4.33
Skill in problem solving	4.03	Skill in written communication	4.27	Teamwork orientation	4.27

Skill/Knowledge	Rating
Knowledge of process improvement	3.95
Creative thinking	3.87
Skill in written communication	3.84
Knowledge of quality tools	3.81
Skill in organizational change	3.58
Basic PC skills	3.54
Knowledge of SPC	3.42
Knowledge of quality theories	3.01
Knowledge of applied statistics	3.00
Knowledge of ISO 9000	2.98
Knowledge of benchmarking	2.84
Knowledge of reengineering	2.63
Knowledge of experimental design	2.46
Knowledge of Baldrige Award criteria	2.35
Average rating	3.76

Skill/Knowledge	Rating
Skill in organizational change	4.27
Skill in facilitating teams	4.23
Knowledge of process improvement	4.12
Skill in problem solving	4.06
Knowledge of quality tools	3.86
Basic PC skills	3.75
Knowledge of benchmarking	3.44
Knowledge of SPC	3.41
Knowledge of quality theories	3.38
Knowledge of ISO 9000	3.24
Knowledge of applied statistics	3.23
Knowledge of reengineering	3.21
Knowledge of experimental design	2.83
Knowledge of Baldrige Award criteria	2.74
Average rating	3.99

Skill/Knowledge	Rating
Basic math skills	4.22
Skill in facilitating teams	4.01
Knowledge of process improvement	3.94
Skill In problem solving	3.82
Knowledge of quality theories	3.66
Knowledge of benchmarking	3.63
Knowledge of quality tools	3.58
Basic PC skills	3.38
Knowledge of ISO 9000	3.32
Knowledge of reengineering	3.32
Knowledge of applied statistics	3.06
Knowledge of SPC	3.06
Knowledge of Baldrige Award criteria	3.04
Knowledge of experimental design	2.53
Average rating	3.98

5 indicates "critical," a rating of 4 indicates "very important," a rating of 3 indicates "important," a rating of 2 indicates "slightly important," and a rating of 1 indicates "unimportant." Think about these attributes in your own setting. Would the ranking from your setting depart from this cross-company prioritization?

Do the KSAPs Capture the Entire Job?

The third recommendation for generating job specifications is to ensure that the list of attributes is comprehensive and all-inclusive. It should include all of the important attributes. That is, it should completely capture what differentiates the successful from the unsuccessful employee. The first way to ensure this is to incorporate input from the varied sources we've outlined earlier (those who have performed the job: supervisors, customers/clients, HR professionals, and quality professionals). This diversity of input will help ensure that all important aspects of the job are included. The second way is to make sure that all of the job activities have been considered. This means being systematic to ensure that each important aspect of the job is considered. This is especially important because of the breadth of jobs in the new workplace. If the work of the individual now cuts across what were, previously, boundaries between jobs, be sure to consider all of those activities. Relevant questions to consider include: Does the work change over different seasons? Are there rare but critical activities that must be performed? The third way is to incorporate, if appropriate, the envisioned job as well as the job as it actually exists. In addition to profiling the present job, we must also include a careful analysis of the envisioned job that reflects the strategic quality direction of the organization. To summarize, collect diverse input, consider all job responsibilities, and consider how the job is changing as the quality effort matures.

Examples of job analysis-based KSAPs relevant to the new workplace are presented next.

Example 1: Envisioning KSAPs at a New Plant Startup at 3M Canada Manufacturing. Staffing the 3M Canada manufacturing facility, organized around two broad job descriptions (operator and technologist), required a redesign of the staffing process. A comprehensive job analysis was conducted. This case represents an example of how to approach the analysis of envisioned jobs.

John Arnold, VP of the consulting firm HRStrategies, describes their approach to analysis of the envisioned jobs at 3M Canada.

We took a two-pronged approach. We assembled a focus group of SMEs familiar with the new technology (industrial engineers, the plant manager). We had them identify a skills profile. At the same time we selected an existing job that was as similar as possible to the new work and had a second group of SMEs analyze it. We used a questionnaire to collect task and KSAP ratings from both groups. Once we had the data on the new and the traditional job, we then looked for gaps between what the two groups were telling us, gaps in the skills profiles between the envisioned and existing job. Often groups working on the envisioned work tend to be too high in their characterization of the compentencies. The job analysis of the existing position is very useful in that it presents a reality test that can serve as a basis for focusing on places where the envisioned job analysis may be inaccurate. So, for example, at 3M we then led the SMEs working on the envisioned job through a process of assuring that the differences we saw in the ratings reflect real differences in the jobs.[10]

The questionnaire used to measure the relative importance of the 38 attributes at 3M Canada manufacturing is presented in Exhibit 4.5 (a questionnaire was also used to measure the importance and frequency of 179 job activities). An example of important job activities and the associated ratings are displayed in Exhibit 4.6.[11]

The reconciled ratings of the 38 attributes and their link to the work to be performed were analyzed and the resulting list of attributes is displayed in Exhibit 4.7. As you can see, the final list includes both functional and quality-relevant KSAPs. In chapters 7 and 8 we will see how a systematic selection process was constructed to measure these specific, documented attributes.

Example 2: Generating KSAPs for the Envisioned Job at the Detroit Medical Center. The envisioned job and organization might include a rather specific change already on the drawing board (for example, a job that has been reengineered, such as the 3M Canada example, or a move to self-directed work teams) or it may simply reflect some of the strategic quality directions of the organization (customer orientation; openness to learning, development, and retraining). The DMC, a large health care system, has incorporated such an approach in its selection interviewing workshop for managers. In 1992 the DMC began a full-scale quality initiative that included a clear statement of its mission and values (see Exhibit 4.8).

Exhibit 4.5. Job analysis questionnaire used to measure importance and skill level required in 3M Canada manufacturing.

---

1. Applied reading

The ability to read, understand, and apply written text of a technical nature, that may or may not be written in traditional sentence form, in order to answer questions, solve problems or complete job tasks. This includes the ability to identify major points, make inferences, and draw conclusions which accurately reflect the material.

Skill level	Skill level description and examples	Skill level required for effective job performance
High	The ability to read, understand, and apply complex written material of a technical nature: • Read, understand, and apply a written description of machine operation in order to set up and operate the machine. • Read, understand, and apply information from several technical manuals in order to troubleshoot a machine problem.	9 8 7
Moderate	The ability to read, understand, and apply moderately complex written material of a technical nature: • Read, understand, and apply instructions for machine maintenance. • Read and understand an outline of machine specifications in order to answer a question about a particular setting.	6 5 4
Basic	The ability to read, understand, and apply simple written material of a technical nature. • Read, understand, and apply a few simple checks on a machine. • Read, understand, and apply simple safety procedures.	3 2 1
N/A	Skill not required	N/A

How *important* is this skill to effective job performance?	Not at all important	Minor skill	Important skill	Key skill	Critical skill
	N/A	1	2	3	4

Exhibit 4.5. Continued.

---

2. Learning
The ability to study, master, and apply a series of steps, rules, or guidelines needed to perform a variety of specific tasks.

Skill level	Skill level description and examples	Skill level required for effective job performance
High	Master a sequence of steps, rules, or guidelines and apply them in order to perform new tasks: • Learn a new multistep procedure that involves several decisions to operate a new piece of equipment. • Use one's knowledge of familiar equipment in learning to operate new, but similar, equipment.	9 8 7
Moderate	Study, master, and apply a short sequence of steps, rules, or guidelines necessary to perform a daily task: • Learn and apply a five step procedure to operate a machine used every day. • Learn and apply safety procedures and precautions in daily job activities.	6 5 4
Basic	Study, master, and apply a simple step, rule, or guideline necessary to perform a basic, repetitive task: • Learn and apply a two-step material handling procedure. • Use the correct procedure to lift heavy objects in order to avoid back injury.	3 2 1
N/A	Skill not required	**N/A**

How *important* is this skill to effective job performance?	Not at all important	Minor skill	Important skill	Key skill	Critical skill
	N/A	1	2	3	4

Exhibit 4.5. Continued.

	11. Troubleshooting
	The ability to use established physical, mechanical, or scientific principles and perform appropriate tests to identify and solve problems encountered on the job. This includes the ability to locate and isolate the problem, identify possible solutions, and select approaches which are practical and effective.

Skill level	Skill level description and examples	Skill level required for effective job performance
High	Use principles and appropriate tests to identify the nature of the problem, generate alternate solutions, identify criteria for use in choosing among alternatives, and decide on solution: • Identify the cause of a machine failure due to the interaction of several machine components. • Examine interconnections between machines and logs of machine outputs to identify source of output decline, and determine possible solutions and resolve problems.	9 8 7
Moderate	Approach problems in a logical, systematic manner, identify practical solutions, and conduct appropriate tests as needed to ensure soundness of solutions: • Locate a stuck value in a hydraulic system containing several valves. • Determine which of several electrical components caused a board to short out.	6 5 4
Basic	Follow a logical series of steps when solving problems, and determine source of equipment problem by planning and conducting general troubleshooting tests: • Determine source of equipment error based on a trend in an equipment reading. • Detect problems in a piece of equipment based upon a change in noise and vibration.	3 2 1
N/A	Skill not required	N/A

How *important* is this skill to effective job performance?	Not at all important	Minor skill	Important skill	Key skill	Critical skill
	N/A	1	2	3	4

Source: HRStrategies, Grosse Pointe, Mich. Used with permission.

Exhibit 4.6. 3M Canada manufacturing group job task survey results.

HRStrategies	Job task importance and frequency	
	Brockville team member	Skill-based job analysis
Listing of key job tasks	Average importance rating	Average frequency rating
Setting up equipment and machinery		
11. Set up and make adjustments to equipment or machinery.	3.57	3.57
12. Check equipment setting(s) against specifications before operation, making adjustment(s) when necessary.	3.43	3.29
Reading and understanding written communications		
131. Read and understand production and quality forms and reports.	3.57	3.86
132. Read and understand brief written summaries, such as traceability slips, log entries, work orders, or shift pass downs, that describe work status, repairs, inspections, or problems.	3.14	3.43
Working with numerical material		
143. Perform basic arithmetic operations (e.g., addition, subtraction, multiplication, and division) with whole numbers in order to complete charts and forms.	3.00	3.57
144. Perform basic arithmetic operations with fractions, decimals, and percentages in order to complete charts and forms.	2.71	3.43
145. Record numerical data relating to testing, inspection, or operating performance.	2.71	3.14

Exhibit 4.6. Continued.

Listing of key job tasks	Average importance rating	Average frequency rating
Providing information to others		
154. Notify supervisor or appropriate personnel of problems, status of work in progress, or other work-related matters.	3.14	3.71
155. Explain the nature of simple equipment, material, or machinery problems to coworkers, supervisors, or appropriate personnel.	3.29	3.29
156. Explain simple procedures, methods, or guidelines to others.	3.14	3.00
157. Provide technical or procedural instructions, descriptions, or training to others.	2.71	2.57
158. Provide suggestions to supervisors or others to help resolve production problems.	2.86	2.71
Working with others		
159. Discuss work in group discussions, such as production meetings, safety meetings, or job briefings.	3.57	3.14
160. Work together with others in a cooperative manner.	3.71	3.86
161. Work closely with others as part of a team.	3.71	3.86
162. Volunteer to assist coworkers without direction from supervisor	3.00	3.14
Standard	≥ 2.50	

Task importance scale: 4 = critical; 3 = key; 2 = important; 1 = minor; 0 = not at all important.
Source: HRStrategies, Grosse Pointe, MI. Used with permission.

Exhibit 4.7. 3M Canada manufacturing attribute profile.

Skill category	Important skill
Learning and analytic skills	Procedures learning
	Applied learning
	Planning and organizing
	Classifying
	Judgment
	Troubleshooting
Language skills	Applied reading skills
	Reading comprehension
	Referencing written materials
	Forms completion
Perceptual skills	Checking
	Inspection
	Monitoring
	Spatial visualization
Math skills	Arithmetic computation
	Arithmetic reasoning
	Measurement
Interaction skills	Active listening
	Communicating with others
	Interpersonal interaction
	Teamwork
Technological literacy	Diagram and blueprint reading
	Table and graph comprehension
	Instrumentation
	Mechanical comprehension
Personal characteristics	Work orientation
	Adaptability
	Stress tolerance
Physical characteristics	Strength
	Stamina
	Physical flexibility
	Manual dexterity
	Arm-hand steadiness
	Hearing
	Visual acuity

Source: HRStrategies, Grosse Pointe, Mich. Used with permission.

Exhibit 4.8. Detroit Medical Center values statement.

In fulfilling our mission, we are driven both by our vision of national preeminence as a vertically integrated, academic health system, and by a set of values which will help us provide the best possible services to our patients and make us proud to be members of the DMC team. These values are:

Community welfare

We are committed to improving the health of the communities we serve, and to being a socially responsive member of those communities.

Quality

We are committed to the pursuit of excellence and to the never-ending improvement of all processes and outcomes.

Respect and involvement

We are committed to the creation of an environment characterized by: ethical behavior; mutual trust; personal and professional development; fair, competitive compensation and recognition systems; and equal employment opportunity.

Teamwork

We are committed to collaboration and teamwork throughout the organization. Individuals and work groups are interdependent, and overall success can only be achieved through recognition of each other as "internal customers."

Communication

We are committed to open and effective communication among all levels of the organization. Every individual will have an awareness of the DMC's overall direction, as well as a clear understanding of their own role and relationship to the success of the organization.

Innovation and education

We are committed to the discovery, transmission, and application of new knowledge, as well as openness to innovation, creativity and change.

Efficient and effective resource use

We are committed to effective and efficient use of the resources with which we have been entrusted by the community.

Source: Detroit Medical Center. Used with permission.

Managers attending an interviewing skills workshop were given the task of envisioning the future staffing priorities of their facility in the context of the mission and organization values (culture). The managers were first provided with a list of those values, along with some examples of possible attributes consistent with the value statements (see Exhibit 4.9). They were then asked to generate their own list of value-based KSAPs for inclusion in their interviewing process for both selection and promotion. A consensus discussion was used to arrive at a profile of the attributes on which the hospital would base its staffing effort.

Once an agreed-upon list of KSAPs has been generated, the same (or comparable) job experts should systematically rate the KSAPs in terms of importance, trainability, or any of the other aspects identified earlier. Those attributes considered important should then become the basis for developing staffing procedures and instruments.

Example 3: Generating KSAPs to Capture the Mission of the North Allegheny Pennsylvania School System.

Exhibit 4.10 presents the results of an analysis of KSAPs judged to be important for principals in the North Allegheny Pennsylvania School System. This too is an example of translating the organization's quality mission into the attributes needed to carry it out.[12] In this case, a focus group familiar with the educational mission of the district, the Baldrige Award criteria, and the role of the principal in the quality initiative were used to generate the profile.

The generation of envisioned KSAPs must be done very carefully. Those attributes should reflect actual, envisioned job changes or directly mirror the strategic plans and direction of the organization. They should not merely be a wish list of nice-to-have attributes. Also, just like other attributes, it is important that it be shown how the attribute will be used on the job.

Is the KSAP Needed Before Hire?

Once a profile of the necessary attributes (KSAPs) and behaviors (CIs) has been completed, it is then necessary to choose those attributes and behaviors that should be evaluated in the selection process. Some important questions must be addressed when making that decision.

Must the attributes or behaviors be present prior to employment or can they be learned on the job? As a rule, the selection process should focus on attributes that must be developed before employment or promotion and should avoid those that can be learned and

Exhibit 4.9. Value-based attributes important for success at the DMC.

Examples of quality requirements
- Awareness of both external and internal customers
- Knowledge of quality improvement theories or models (for example, Deming)
- Process improvement knowledge/experience
- Willingness to treat the customer/client as king
- Continuous improvement philosophy and history

Examples of teamwork requirements
- Group facilitation skills
- Knowledge and experience with problem-solving tools (Pareto charts, brainstorming, run charts, fishbone diagrams)
- Knowledge of group behavior and dynamics
- Willingness to work with other units/departments
- Willingness to listen to others and allow for employee involvement

---

Source: Detroit Medical Center. Used with permission.

developed in a reasonable period of time (orientation period) on the job.

To what attribute or behavioral level should the worker have progressed? For example, if knowledge of statistical quality control is critical, must that knowledge be at an introductory or advanced level? It is important to focus subsequent assessment procedures (interview questions, tests) at the identified appropriate level.

Documentation. Finally, we encourage those involved in job analysis to carefully document their activities and outputs (for example, the job experts involved, list of KSAPs, ratings of importance, final listing used for staffing). This information is invaluable in case of litigation and can be very helpful to others engaged in similar future projects.

The Output

The output of the process is a relevant, useful job description and job specification.

The job description provides a narrative description of the work, the work process, the setting, and the organization culture. The job

Exhibit 4.10.   Example mission and KSAP profile for school principal.

Mission

The Principal, who serves as a positive role model, exemplifying mutual trust and respect, is a fearless advocate for children. As a visionary leader, the Principal cultivates and enhances an atmosphere of continuous improvement. As an instructional leader, the Principal promotes professional development while encouraging team dynamics and decision making based on data collection and analysis. Above all, the Principal supports the district mission and continually enhances the teaching/learning process that occurs on a daily basis.

Nature and scope

It is the Principal's accountability to perpetuate and develop the quality process through

Leadership. The Principal is a positive role model who creates a climate of mutual respect and trust which empowers people to share responsibility. The Principal collaborates with clients, individually or in teams, to facilitate problem solving, decision making, and risk taking, which promote continuous improvement. As a fearless advocate of quality educational programs, the Principal inspires clients to rise above self-interest. The Principal monitors, supports, evaluates, and develops the curriculum; effectively manages resources; and serves as a liaison among clients.

Information and analysis. The Principal collects, synthesizes, and analyzes qualitative data and quantitative data. The Principal uses comparable benchmarks in order to make educational and management development decisions.

Strategic quality planning. The Principal is an advocate for children and quality programs. The Principal shares the vision by fostering communication, facilitating consensus, and seeking commitment. The Principal enlists appropriate resources to achieve the goals and objectives of the vision. In addition, the Principal is proactive in responding to existing challenges and in anticipating future concerns.

Human resource development, selection, and management. The Principal promotes an interdependent team concept, which enlists, seeks, and encourages support and participation among all clients. The Principal is an effective communicator with all clients, creating a climate of trust while providing feedback, safety nets, and the structure needed to identify concerns, goals, and outcomes. The Principal is a cheerleader, rallying around clients to take responsible risks and celebrate team success.

Quality and operational results. Using the mission as the yardstick, the Principal explicitly identifies the goals and outcomes of the organization and promotes "systems thinking" in evaluating the process of continual

Exhibit 4.10. Continued.

---

development and improvement. The Principal encourages an understanding and appreciation of all roles, procedures, and key elements in the system through training and practice, focusing on problem solving in order that the total quality process is utilized in arriving at decisions and policies—the identification and use of appropriate data and information, the incorporation of a team approach, and the recognition of cause-and-effect relationships.

Management of quality process. The mission is the message and serves as the basis for all decisions, activities, and assessments. The Principal is the messenger who encourages and allows leadership development, takes risks without fear of retribution, models proactively desired behaviors, and uses quadrant II thinking in prioritizing. The Principal sets realistic expectations and strives diligently to achieve them, with client needs as the primary focus.

Client focus and satisfaction. In supporting the development of the learning organization, the Principal seeks data and information from all clients to utilize knowledge and understanding in the guidance of efforts for continual improvement and client satisfaction. As an agent of change, the Principal has a vision and keeps it as a focus to empower children to become life-long learners. In addition to effectively prioritizing activities, the Principal remains a flexible innovator and a sensitive yet assertive transformer of ideas.

Critical knowledge, skills, and abilities

Child advocacy	Critical listening	Risk taking
Analysis and assessment	Facilitation	Planning
Coaching	Leadership	Problem solving
Communication	Management	Stewardship of resources
Conflict resolution	Negotiations	Vision
Counseling		

Source: Personal communication with Lawrence Bozzomo, Superintendent, North Allegheny Pennsylvania School System, Aug. 1994. Used with permission.

---

specification provides a listing of the important attributes needed to succeed, and typically, additionally, provides a description of the minimum experiences (education, training) needed to develop the KSAPs. Exhibit 4.11 presents the categories of information to include in the job description and specification. As you can see, the description of the work and working conditions, and the list of attributes are detailed enough so that the applicant, and all others involved in the selection process, get a complete picture of the job.

Exhibit 4.11. Example job description and specification.

Job description: Staffing Associate

The staffing associate is part of a team of associates responsible for all phases of recruiting, screening, interviewing, and evaluating applicants for both exempt and nonexempt positions within Superior Products.

Representative activities include the following

Review job descriptions, interview supervisors, and conduct other research necessary to identify job specifications for vacant positions. Formulate job-related questions for use in screening applicants for vacant positions. Build ties to applicant sources (local high schools, colleges, temporary agencies, search firms). Review and evaluate resumes to identify candidates for specific positions. Plan and organize specific interview procedures for use in screening applicants. Conduct fair, objective, and professional interviews with applicants for positions at all levels within the company. Write summaries of applicant strengths and development needs for review by position supervisors and senior managers. Monitor, review, and evaluate hiring procedures within Superior Products to ensure objectivity and fairness in selection processes throughout the organization. Read journals and attend continuing education courses necessary to remain up-to-date on changing laws and procedures related to employee selection. Participate in team-based use of process improvement tools to continuously improve staffing process.

Working conditions

The staffing associate must be prepared to work under time pressure, with evening and occasional weekend work necessary (average work week of approximately 50 hours). Travel 35% of time, including occasional trips of seven or more days' duration.

Job specifications

Candidates for the Staffing Associate position should demonstrate mastery of the following knowledges, skills, abilities, and temperament

Knowledge of interviewing practices: Candidates must have working knowledge of practices and techniques for planning, organizing, and conducting employment interviews.

Knowledge of job and organization analysis techniques: Must have working knowledge of job analysis techniques.

Knowledge of employment law: Must have a working knowledge of employment laws, court decisions, and administrative rulings related to fair employment practices.

Oral communication: Candidates must be able to speak clearly, use correct grammar, and project enthusiasm through voice inflection and intonation.

Written communication: Candidates must be able to write clear, concise reports using correct grammar and syntax.

Exhibit 4.11. Continued.

Interpersonal skills: The applicant must be relaxed and comfortable around others, must be friendly and project a genuine interest in others, and must display patience and empathy for others.

Organization skills: The applicant must be able to organize information (maintain organized files, notes, and records) must be able to organize own time and plan own work day.

Judgment: The applicant must have sound interpersonal judgment and must be able to evaluate information objectively and arrive at logical conclusions.

Process improvement: Candidates should have basic familiarity with process improvement methods (PDSA) and tools.

Flexibility/adaptability: Candidates must be able to consider different approaches, to change old ways of doing things, to incorporate new information or changing circumstances, and to operate without clear guide-lines, and to work beyond narrow job descriptions.

Openness to continual learning, development, and retraining: Derives satis-faction from learning and skill development and seeks out additional training and development.

Minimum **qualifications:** The following experiences represent the minimum amount and level of education, training, and work experience needed to suc-ceed as a Staffing Associate.

> *Undergraduate degree with 15 semester hours in management and eight hours in HRM **or** two years experience in personnel assistant or related administrative positions, 15 semester hours in management and eight hours in HRM.*

Job Analysis and the Legal Environment

In chapter 3 we discussed the importance of fairness in the staffing process and the need for demonstrating the appropriateness (validity, job relatedness) of selection procedures. One of the key means to demonstrate job relatedness is by showing the chain of relationship between each staffing component, the KSAP it measures, and the job or organizational responsibility requiring the attribute.

Government and professional guidelines, as well as case law, make clear the importance of conducting a thorough job analysis. For example, the government's *Uniform Guidelines on Employee Selection Procedures* (Sec. 14A) state: "Validity studies should be based on review of information about the job. Any validity study should be based upon a review of information about the job for which the selection procedure is used."[13] Admittedly, much of our discussion throughout this book has proposed that you think less about specific jobs and more broadly about the work process and quality culture the person must adapt to. Unfortunately, to date, the guidelines developed by compliance agencies have not been revised to reflect the dynamic nature of work in the new workplace.

The uniform guidelines do say that any method of job analysis is acceptable provided it is relevant for the specific validation strategy used. In addition to the uniform guidelines, professional guidelines on selection put out by both the American Psychological Association (APA) and the Society for Industrial and Organizational Psychology (SIOP) reinforce the importance of job analysis in selection, particularly for demonstrating evidence of content validity.[14]

In addition to the government and professional guidelines, the courts, including the Supreme Court (*Albemarle Paper Company v. Moody*), have consistently affirmed the importance of job analysis when implementing selection procedures that result in disparate impact.[15] Recall our discussion in chapter 3. If a selection process results in a disproportionate rejection of a protected group (for example women or racial minorities), the burden of proof is on the employer to show that the process is job related. The job analysis process is the cornerstone of job relatedness.

Finally, the important role of job analysis to staffing has recently been reinforced with the passage of the ADA, which requires organizations to identify the essential functions of the job so that they can provide reasonable accommodation for those individuals defined as disabled. The ADA defines a person with a disability as "an individual who, with or without reasonable accommodation, can perform the essential functions of the job."[16]

Individuals unable to perform the essential functions and requirements of the job need not be selected. But the organization must be able to identify and defend those essential functions. Legal experts generally agree that the first line of defense in such court cases will be current and accurate job descriptions and specifications that clearly identify the essential functions of the job. In particular, the identification of physical requirements will be crucial.

While the primary reason for doing a thorough job analysis is that it is a good and sound practice, individuals involved in staffing should understand the legal ramifications of not using some systematic analysis of work, jobs, and the organization setting to support their staffing programs.

Conducting the Organization-Specific Job Analysis

We now present you with a step-by-step approach to analyzing jobs within the context of the new workplace. We've constructed a process we believe is efficient and will yield a quality success profile the organization can use to build an effective staffing process. Use this process for individual jobs or for developing a quality success profile that is relevant to a group of jobs in your organization.

We've organized the job analysis process into nine steps. While these steps could be completed by one person who thoroughly understands the job, the work process, and the organization, the job profile will be more complete if the steps incorporate the input of additional job experts (either interviewed individually for their input, or through a group discussion format). Input from multiple perspectives will increase the process validity, result in more thorough job descriptions and specifications, and increase the defensibility of the staffing process.

Step 1: Characterize What's Done (or to Be Done) on the Job and in the Broader Work Process. The first step in this systematic analysis is to identify what it is the individual must do in the work process, and the context (culture) in which he or she must perform. What responsibilities, what mix of activities (duties, tasks, accountabilities) are performed? It is often helpful to describe the work using action-oriented verbs that convey a clear sense of what the person actually is doing (the mental or physical activities). For example, action verbs such as *analyze, interpret, read, instruct, coach, listen, facilitate, guide, brainstorm,* and *diagnose* convey a sense of what the person is doing and, more importantly, convey a sense of what KSAPs the person must draw on in the work process. If specific equipment must be operated, be sure to include that in the description of the work to be performed.

An alternate, or additional device to describe the work is to display it in a systematic process flowchart. Mapping the work flow and the individual's actions in that flow is a convenient way to characterize what gets done (or what will be done in the new work process).

Repeat the description for the envisioned work, again generating the specific, action-oriented verbs to describe the activity of the worker in the work process.

There are numerous methods by which to collect preliminary as well as detailed information about a specific job. If other organizations are now using the job as you envision it in your facility, you can benchmark against their experience with the work. To collect information within your own setting, you can observe workers performing the job, you can interview individuals, or you can conduct focus group discussions with those who know the job. Finally, you can use questionnaires to confirm and substantiate the information you've collected.

If you are interviewing individuals, or conducting a group discussion about the position, ask general questions such as: What do our team members do? What are the major responsibilities we ask of team members? As members respond, list the activity, trying always to use the most action-oriented verbs that convey the work that is done. Also, consider trying to generate any CIs that have occurred—instances of renowned successes or blunders.

The objective is to be able to clearly link everything we do in staffing (interview, test, and so on) back to what it is the person must do to succeed. As we've noted, these descriptions are increasingly broad and flexible. Consequently, you may well be listing fairly broad accountabilities in this step (for example, "lead team problem-solving meetings, analyze statistical data to identify sources of variability, coach team members to help them succeed in their work"). Be sure to focus both on important responsibilities and on those activities that are frequently performed, and be sure to describe them with action verbs. The description of the work and work context will also be useful to you as you subsequently recruit applicants.

Consider also the organization context, mission, and culture. What cultural values are so pervasive that they determine how work is done and how successful the new team member may be? Or, stated differently, what aspects of your culture lead to success across a broad range of jobs the person might perform? For example, does the culture value independent decision making or following closely prescribed rules; does it reflect or value change or the status quo; does it value results over analysis; does it value individual achievement or team accomplishment; does it value the customer or the organizational hierarchy? Each of these dichotomies suggest different attributes.

Consider the working conditions (physical conditions, unusual schedules, hazzards). The conditions under which the work is performed often help us see specific attributes that are needed to succeed. For example, time pressure and urgent deadlines suggest that ability to tolerate stress will be an important factor. Changing work schedules may lead us to conclude that flexibility/adaptability is important.

Step 2: Generate Initial Listing of KSAPs. Now that you've described the work and the organization context (culture) the question becomes: What attributes—specific knowledge, skills, abilities, and personal characteristics—must the individual possess to succeed in the work process and organization? Or, stated differently: What KSAPs differentiate those employees who excel in performance from those who merely get by or fail? What KSAPs are suggested by CIs that have occurred on the job? Be sure to think about the job, the work process, and the organization culture both as they now exist and as they are envisioned. Be sure to include quality-related as well as functional KSAPs.

Do not feel compelled to invent and define KSAPs. Instead, refer to established taxonomies of KSAPs listed earlier, including the QAI. For now, the following might reflect the preliminary list of KSAPs for the position of team leader.

- Knowledge of process improvement
- Oral presentation (stand-up training) skills
- Group facilitation skills
- Customer-oriented temperament
- Coaching skills
- Openness to continual learning and development
- Flexibility/adaptability

Step 3: Revise Initial Listing. Add specificity to the list of KSAPs you've generated. For example, "knowledge of process improvement" may be expanded and clarified to include specific elements of the attribute as needed in your setting.

- Knowledge of problem-solving tools
  —Brainstorming
  —Cause-and-effect (fishbone) diagrams
  —Pareto charts
  —Flowcharts

—Root cause analysis

—Run charts

—Control charts

• Knowledge and/or experience with problem-solving models (such as the PDCA cycle, scientific method)

Edit the initial list of KSAPs to ensure that they are specific, clearly defined, and job related. Using the input of the QAI and the specificity criterion discussed earlier in this chapter, revise the listing to be as complete and specific as possible.

Step 4: Job Relatedness. For each KSAP you've identified, list two or three important job responsibilities that require the attribute. Or, alternately, describe incidents that show how the attribute makes a difference in job performance. This step helps assure that you focus on job-related (valid) attributes. You can increase the credibility of the process if you have your panel of experts (SMEs) concur that the tasks are performed and require the attribute. If you can't demonstrate how the attribute is (or will be) used on the job, it's probably inappropriate to include it in the staffing plan.

Step 5: Have the List Reviewed. If the list has been compiled by a group or, more importantly, if it is based on the judgment of only one person, make sure that you broaden the input by giving it to appropriate peers, superiors, and subordinates for review. Ask them to examine the list and make any additions, deletions, or modifications they think are appropriate.

Step 6: Systematic Ratings of KSAPs. It is advisable to collect consensus judgments about the importance, or job relatedness, of the KSAPs. The most efficient means for doing so is to simply assemble a questionnaire. List the KSAPs on a questionnaire with an "importance" scale (or other relevant judgment). Have the SMEs (either in a group setting or individually) rate the importance of the KSAPs to success in the job and company. Identify those KSAPs which generate the highest ratings and the strongest agreement (low standard deviations).

Recall the validation study described in chapter 3. In that case the consultants collected ratings from relatively small samples of job experts (seven to 11 people in each job) to establish the relative importance of the attributes for each job, and by doing so substantiated the appropriateness of a standardized test for all jobs in the hospital.

Step 7: Determine If the Attributes Are Needed Prior to Employment. Edit the list to identify those attributes applicants must bring to the job. (Concensus ratings of the extent to which an attribute is needed for hire from knowledgable SMEs will help in this decision process.) Exclude those attributes that the organization is prepared to develop in the new hire. Those KSAPs that are viewed as most important by many knowledgeable experts and developed to at least a minimal degree before hire become the basis for the staffing and training efforts. The subsequent assessment process should be built on those KSAPs that must be developed prior to employment.

Step 8: Finalize List. Using the input from other sources, finalize the list to be used in the staffing process. If appropriate, differentiate between essential and desired attributes and designate those characteristics that should be communicated in the help-wanted ad or for a posting of the job. The list can then be filed and pulled for use in subsequent staffing decisions.

Step 9: Formulate the Job Description and Job Specifications. Once the attribute profile has been developed, you can prepare the products of the job analysis process. First, a job description is a narrative description of the work to be done, the conditions under which it is done, and the organizational context (including working conditions, how the person fits into the work process, who the position reports to, and elements of the organization culture relevant to potential applicants). The description is written with sufficient detail to give potential applicants a thorough understanding of the work and organization. Make sure that the description conveys the quality-oriented values of your current and envisioned culture. If it is sufficiently detailed and candid, the description can serve a very important function of helping the applicants determine if the work and culture are consistent with their own needs. (The phenomenon is termed *realistic job preview,* and we'll discuss it more fully in chapter 6.) The job specification is a listing of the KSAPs needed before hire and a profile of the experiences typically needed to develop the KSAPs.

A Reminder: Building Validity into the Process

The approach we've outlined is fairly expedient. If you follow it, you will generate credible job descriptions and specifications (success profiles). To meet the expediency criterion, we've collapsed a number of steps typically included in traditional, large-scale job analysis projects.

The most prominent short cut we've taken is that we did not include a task inventory. Typically, a task inventory is done in order to substantiate that the specific tasks we've included in the job description are actually done, their importance, and/or how frequently they are performed. Instead, we focused on documenting the importance of the KSAPs and simply linked the KSAPs to the work that is performed—without ratings of tasks.

There are circumstances under which more comprehensive data regarding duties and tasks should be collected. For example, if the work (what the worker actually does) varies tremendously from site to site, a questionnaire (task inventory) may be the most efficient means to assess the differences in jobs. Or, if the organization has neglected to diversify its workforce, it may well wish to conduct a more complete job analysis prior to implementing selection procedures. Or, if the job analysis information is being used to construct work sample tests, it will likely require that we demonstrate more conclusively that specific tasks are performed in different settings.

In general, you can increase the rigor and the defensibility of the job analysis through the following steps.

- Be sure to involve multiple SMEs in all stages of the process, and make sure that the SMEs are reflective of the race and gender mix in the organization and in the applicant pool.

- Use a structured questionnaire to document the performance of work across different locations in the company.

- Use a structured questionnaire to document the relative importance of the KSAPs (like we described in Step 6, but across the entire company).

Future Trends in Job Analysis

We have already discussed many of the radical changes occurring as a result of the new quality paradigm. As with other organizational factors, the new philosophy is also likely to substantially change the process of job analysis. Following is a brief discussion of some possible changes and future trends in analyzing jobs.

The term *job analysis* may be somewhat of a misnomer in the new workplace. The traditional notion of *job* is rapidly changing and may no longer be applicable in the organization of the future. Pick up any dictionary and the definition provided will look something like this.

job (jb) n. 1. *an action or piece of work that needs to be done; task* 2. *a regular activity performed for payment* 3. *a specific piece of work to be done for a set fee.*

This definition connotes a fixed, single chunk of work that is done by a person in exchange for compensation. But, as we noted earlier, this static and narrow view of work is now the exception rather than the rule. Hiring employees to do a narrow job (some set of tasks) is becoming a thing of the past. What the worker actually does on the job is becoming much broader in scope and will continuously change. We might argue that more appropriate terms might be *function* (the proper, normal, or characteristic activity of a person) or *role*.

While the term *job* is likely to remain as part of our business jargon, the point of this discussion should be clear. We can no longer view what the person does as one of those squares in an organizational chart and select individuals to simply fill that slot. A more dynamic and flexible notion of job is needed in the new organization.

A second but related trend will be a move toward job descriptions that are more process and customer oriented. For example, the description of the future for the job Customer Information Representative might read: "Handle all customer inquiries from inception to resolution such that the customer is fully satisfied." Included in this trend is the view that job descriptions will be written for entire units or for teams or groups. Here, all members of the group will be responsible for the process and will be trained and developed with the goal of being able to perform all process activities. But we'll still be interested in and able to identify attributes needed for these broad work processes.

We also strongly believe that job specifications will be much more comprehensive, include more quality-related attributes, and include higher order requirements and qualifications. Higher order is used in the sense that the new employee has much more responsibility and authority for process output. In the traditional organization, the employee might be asked to collect some performance or quality data but that would be the extent of involvement. The quality-oriented organization asks that same employee to not only collect the data but then to compile it, analyze it, and use that information to make decisions. Likewise, the old paradigm had employees taking instructions and possibly exchanging information with their supervisors and coworkers. The new organization requires employees to actively participate in problem solving, training or mentoring new employees, facilitating group problem-solving sessions, and so on.

Summary

Job analysis is critical to the process of matching the person to the specific job, work process, and culture of the organization. It is the foundation for ensuring that all staffing procedures are reliable, valid, and fair, and have a favorable ROI to the organization. In this chapter we have discussed the KSAP approach for collecting such information and have argued that a broader view of job analysis is needed in quality-oriented organizations. This broadened view must recognize the need to fit the individual not only to a job but also to the work process and to the organization culture.

Notes

1. Richard Hackman, "Is 'Job' Dead? Implications of Changing Concepts of Work for I/O Science and Practice," panel discussion at the Tenth Annual Conference of the Society for Industrial/Organizational Psychology, Orlando, Fla., May 20, 1995.

2. Jim McSheffrey, HR Director at 3M Canada manufacturing plant, personal communication, August 1995.

3. William Bridges, "The End of the Job," *Fortune* (Sept. 19, 1994): 62–74.

4. David E. Bowen, Gerald E. Ledford, Barry R. Nathan, "Hiring for the Organization, Not the Job," *The Executive* (November 1991): 35–51; Lynn R. Offermann and Marilyn K. Gowing, "Personnel Selection in the Future: The Impact of Changing Demographics and the Nature of Work" in *Personnel Selection in Organizations,* Neal Schmitt and Walter C. Borman, eds. (San Francisco: Jossey-Bass, 1993).

5. James L. Heskett, Thomas O. Jones, Gary W. Loveman, W. Earl Sasser Jr., and Leonard A. Schlesinger, "Putting the Service/Profit Chain to Work," *Harvard Business Review* (March-April 1994): 164–174; W. Edwards Deming, *Out of the Crisis* (Cambridge, Mass.: MIT Center for Advanced Engineering Study, 1986), 177.

6. Offermann and Gowing, "Personnel Selection in the Future: The Impact of Changing Demographics and the Nature of Work."

7. Benjamin Schneider and Neal Schmitt, *Staffing Organizations,* 2nd ed. (Glenview, Ill.: Scott, Foresman, and Company, 1986).

8. For comprehensive reviews on different approaches to job analysis, see Robert Gatewood and Hubert Feild, *Human Resource Selection* (Fort Worth, Tex.: Dryden Press, 1994); Wayne Cascio, *Applied Psychology in Personnel Management,* 3rd ed. (Englewood Cliffs, N.J.: Prentice Hall, 1987); Schneider and Schmitt, *Staffing Organizations.*

9. Robert Mager, *Goal Analysis* (Belmont, Calif.: Fearon Publishers, 1972).

10. John Arnold, VP, HRStrategies, August 1995, personal conversation describing company's approach to development of the selection system for 3M Canada.

11. HRStrategies, "3M Canada Manufacturing Project," technical report (Grosse Pointe, Mich.: HRStrategies, 1994).

12. Lawrence Bozzomo, Superintendent of the North Allegheny Pennsylvania School System, August 1994, personal correspondence.

13. *Uniform Guidelines on Employee Selection Procedures,* 29 Code of Federal Regulations, Part 1607, Federal Register 43, No. 166 (1978): 38295–38309.

14. American Psychological Association, *Standards for Educational and Psychological Testing* (Washington D.C.: American Psychological Association, 1986); *Principles for the Validation and Use of Personnel Selection Procedures* 3rd ed. (College Park, Md.: Society for Industrial and Organizational Psychology, 1987).

15. *Albemarle Paper Co. v. Moody,* 422 U.S. 405, 1975.

16. Americans with Disabilities Act, 1990.

Human Resource Planning: Preparing for the Envisioned Quality Organization

Overview

In this chapter we review the HRP process organizations conduct to ensure that they have the requisite workforce attributes for meeting strategic business objectives. It is a process of asking "Where do we want to go?" and "How must we staff to get there?" We begin by describing a number of issues related to planning in the context of quality improvement (downsizing, use of contingent workers, workforce turnover). We then describe the components of an HRP process and focus on the use of these processes to facilitate the quality improvement effort.

Few quality professionals would disagree with the premise that the decision to become a quality-oriented organization should be carried out in the context of strategic business planning. Achieving quality and market leadership requires a long-term outlook and commitment to new values and practices. Respondents to the ASQC Survey of Staffing Practices confirmed this point. They indicated that achieving the values and practices of a total quality organization is a long-term, systematic process. The survey asked respondents to characterize the extent to which their organizations had integrated the values, philosophy, and practices of a total quality organization into their day-to-day operations. As we noted in chapter 1, only a small proportion (about 25 percent) report that their organizations have achieved their quality-oriented transformation. HRP is the tool that will help each organization systematically progress on that long journey toward achieving the vision of a quality culture. Essentially, it raises and addresses the question: "Given what we want to accomplish (our quality objective), what HR actions (staffing, training) will be needed to get us there?" This chapter outlines an approach to HRP in the context of the organization's corporate quality strategy.

Our assumption in preparing this chapter is that an existing HRP process is in place in your organization. Therefore, we do not provide a detailed review of how to design or implement a process. Our focus, for the most part, is on the HRP issues that emerge when planning the transformation to a quality-focused culture. To accomplish that discussion, we do present a generic HRP process, and use it to focus on the issues unique to planning for quality. As a final note, the process we describe for HRP (the steps, the tools) could well occur at the level of the work unit, department, or business unit or systemwide across an entire corporation.

Quality as a Strategic Initiative

Quality professionals generally agree that, to be truly effective, the introduction of any quality improvement process should be integrated into the strategic plan of the organization. Successful quality improvements do not happen without systematic planning. Without planning for quality, the organization will find itself deficient in the attributes (knowledge, skills, temperament) needed to implement quality practices. Or, it will find that it has retained HR policies and practices that thwart the quality effort. Historically, as we've noted before, the planning process has focused on training the existing workforce to the content of the quality initiative. We are arguing that the organizational transformation is much more complex than that, and requires a systematic, planned (upstream) review of a number of organization policies, resources, and practices. That review begins in the HRP process.

The Baldrige Award criteria reinforce the need for quality to be derived from the strategic planning process. Organizations that attempt to win the award, or that use the criteria as a blueprint for their own quality initiative, must address quality as a strategic process. Furthermore, the Baldrige Award criteria focus on how the HR plans and policies are supportive of the quality strategy. The criteria make clear the importance of addressing development of staff to meet the quality objectives. Systematic, targeted development should flow directly from the HRP process. That is, both the staffing and the training plan should be organized around the attributes needed to meet the strategic plan. The link between strategy, HRP, and strategic success or failure is clear and undeniable.

We can think of the strategic process as consisting of three general components.

1. A vision of quality that gives the organization direction

2. A plan for introducing and sustaining the new vision of excellence

3. A structure (staffing, training, compensation) that supports the quality initiative

To be successful, the structure or process for achieving this change must involve each component of HR management: the organization and design of work must change; the structure (levels, reporting relationships) must change; the culture must change; the staffing process must change; the training process must change; and, of equal importance, the appraisal/reward/recognition process must change. Finally, all of the associated HR policies must be examined and revised to support the quality initiative. To be successful, we must be systematic in our approach. A patchwork approach will thwart the quality initiative. Ideally, the planning process becomes the focus for guiding the quality initiative.

For example, the vision may be one of an organization based on empowered employees capable of making on-the-spot decisions to resolve customer complaints. In addition to the structural changes (span of control to span of empowerment, flattening of the organization), the vision of an empowered workforce requires a number of human resources changes. First, we must revise the "success profile" to reflect attributes needed in the new work, structure, and culture which will develop as the quality initiative matures. Our workforce—those who will assume increased authority and responsibility—must possess different attributes. Similarly, our leadership and managerial workforce—those who will relinquish aspects of their traditional authority—must also possess new, different attributes. We must incorporate these new attributes into the recruitment, selection, and promotion processes. Second, we must revise the training curriculum to reflect the vision of empowerment, and to aid our current employees in the transition, we must implement a targeted training effort designed to prepare them for their new roles. Third, we must revise the performance appraisal processes (managerial and nonmanagerial) to begin to support the new behaviors in each group. Fourth, we must examine all HR policies and practices to ensure that they are supportive of these new behaviors in each group.

While the vision, plan, and structure of most quality efforts invariably includes a number of strategic activities such as communication, employee involvement, recognition, and the training of employees, it seldom systematically addresses the issue of staffing for quality. It appears a bit ironic that, when an organization makes other changes in technology or direction, those changes invariably influence its staffing decisions. But all too often, the introduction of a quality improvement effort occurs independent of the staffing plan and process. For example, when an organization replaces its aging machining tools with computer numerical control (CNC) machines, it very quickly modifies its recruiting and selection procedures to meet the needs of the new technology. The same is true of the computerization of industry. Today's clerical person is likely to go jobless without skills in word processing, spread sheets, graphics, and so on. Why then is there so little thought put into staffing decisions when something as dramatic and comprehensive as a quality initiative is introduced into the organization? The same question applies to other efforts at transforming organizations—teams, reengineered work, and so forth.

The Staffing Plan. One purpose of this book is to persuade and encourage both HR and quality professionals to look closely at their own mission statements and strategic quality initiatives and ask the questions: What are the ramifications of the quality initiative for how we staff our organization? What impact should the quality effort have on how we plan, recruit, select, place, train, and develop, and, if necessary, downsize in the organization? If the organization envisions employees who can function effectively in a team environment, then start to select and promote for it. If the organization desires managers who truly involve and empower their employees, then start promoting managers with that ability and history. If the organization requires individuals who are flexible and can adapt to rapid change, then place flexible employees in those units or environments where they will be comfortable with that change. If selecting out (downsizing) is necessary, then retain those managers and employees able and willing to embrace the new paradigm. To be effective, the strategic quality initiative must be translated into specific objectives, policies and procedures, and actions.

HRP in the New Environment

We would like to make an important observation at the outset. The basic assumptions and models of HRP are changing dramatically. The traditional approach to planning has characterized a process through which the organization designs a strategic plan and then from that constructs a staffing plan designed to achieve the strategic objectives. In that model, strategy determines staffing. However, in some instances the sequential relationship between strategy and staffing has been reversed. Today it can be argued that the existing staff of the organization often defines strategy. That is, the staff that the organization has recruited, trained, and developed puts limits on what the organization can set out to do. In effect, organizations are constrained in what they can pursue by the availability of specific workforce attributes needed to pursue their strategic goals. For example, many organizations have been hindered in attaining their quality strategy primarily because they lacked the workforce attributes (managerial and nonmanagerial) needed to succeed.

Admittedly, organizations are responding to this need for adaptability (for example, to pursue different strategic objectives with short lead times) in different ways. Some are using their HRP process to attain and develop the workforce they need to carry out a strategy (for example, what core workforce attributes will give us optimal adaptability?). Others are relying on the use of contingent workers of varying forms to meet strategic goals. Others are engaged in what can best be termed *creation of a virtual organization*. Charles C. Snow and Scott A. Snell describe a firm that relies on a system of loosely coupled arrangements in place of traditional employees. They describe Lewis Galoob Toys of San Francisco, which consists of about 100 core employees. All functions are actually accomplished through a network of independent companies. They note,

> *Independent companies conceive most of Galoob's products, while outside specialists do most of the design and engineering. Galoob contracts for manufacturing and packaging with a handful of companies in Hong Kong, and they, in turn, pass on the most labor-intensive work to factories in China. When the toys arrive in the United States, they are distributed by commissioned manufacturer's representatives. Galoob does not even collect its accounts. It sells its receivables to Commercial Credit Corporation, a factoring company that also sets Galoob's credit policy.*[1]

For Galoob, a change in strategic direction means simply a change in the network. Traditionally, organizations have been more constrained—constrained by the need to get the work done through an established base of employees—in good times more employees; in bad times, or in times of strategic redirection, fewer. Clearly the changing workplace has created a number of HRP issues.

Three Critical HRP Issues

There are three emerging HRP issues with potential impact on the quality effort. We highlight each now.

Downsizing and the Loss of Strategic Advantage. Systematic HRP has taken on increased importance in the wake of organizational downsizing. Downsizing, it seems, has produced very mixed results, in part because it has often occurred apart from the quality initiative. In fact, in his recent review, organization researcher Kim Cameron notes that most downsizing efforts have been counterproductive.[2] A number of authors have pointed out how organizations, in their zest to grow lean and mean, inadvertently discarded critical knowledge and skills.[3] Downsizing strategies such as across-the-board headcount reduction and early retirement incentives have left many organizations deficient of organization knowledge, skills, and competencies needed to pursue new initiatives. Many have now called for the use of more judicious, process-based approaches, such as process improvement and reengineering, in preference to downsizing as a means to avoid tossing away strategic HR strengths.[4] That is why this chapter on planning is so critical. It provides the framework the organization can use to prepare for the future. We address the effect of downsizing on quality improvement more fully in chapter 14. For now, suffice to say that prudent downsizing is conducted with the long-term quality objective in focus.

Use of Contingent Workers as an HR Strategy. Contingent workers of various forms (temps, consultants, and so on) make up a sizable and growing component of most organizations. As Lisa Magi, Staffing Specialist at Computer Aided Engineering Technology, noted, "More and more companies are using contract personnel. It used to be only secretaries, and now engineers and even managers are on contract. It is the trend for the nineties."[5] In fact, estimates are that by the end of this decade about 50 percent of the American workforce will be employed on a contingent basis. In large part, the trend has arisen as a means to maintain strategic responsiveness by securing services as needed, rather than taking on permanent staff. Without question, this enticing alternative has implications for the HRP process. Like other staffing alternatives, there is a clear need to identify the costs and benefits of this trend in general, but most certainly in terms of the impact on the quality initiative. Furthermore, it is necessary to plan for and manage the use of temporary personnel, just as diligently as with permanent employees.[6] Because of the importance of this issue, we devote much of chapter 14 to the tradeoffs associated with the use of contingent workers, and we've assembled recommendations for how best to incorporate this alternate source of human resources into the quality effort.

Turnover and the Impact on Quality. The third critical HRP issue that affects quality is turnover. In a recent article, Robert Cole identifies the cost of turnover to the quality effort. Turnover results in the loss of organizational memory. As people leave, critical knowledge is lost, as is the interpersonal trust that is typically built up over time. As Cole notes, "Loss of such individuals destroys useful historical experiences and thereby dramatically increases the probability of quality failure, much like losing the cook with the recipe."[7]

Cole further notes that, in those industries with the highest turnover (26 percent for child care center workers; 60 percent to 70 percent in the motel business; 60 percent to 100 percent among car salespeople; and 50 percent to 100 percent in some lower-level banking positions), the churn created by the movement is typically at the point of key customer contact. Others have pointed out that, because of this, the real cost of turnover is lost quality, service, and customer satisfaction.[8]

Why is the impact of turnover so great? Cole succinctly notes, "In the end, a customer's contact with a company is through employees. It is with employees that customers built bonds of trust and expectations. When these employees leave, the bonds will break as well." Similarly, "internal customers build up a routine with their internal suppliers; it is based on trust and reliability of expectations. When the internal supplier leaves his or her job or the company, the routine is disrupted at least temporarily while the new replacement learns the routine." In short, the disruption caused by turnover is excessively costly to quality.

While there are many complex factors that affect turnover (the design of the job, the compensation rate, labor market conditions), there is clear evidence that, independent of these circumstances, effective selection practices can dramatically reduce turnover and yield tremendous savings in cost as well as improve the quality of key customer contact. Recall again the utility examples presented in chapter 3. In the national discount retail chain, reduced involuntary turnover resulted in \$5,115,600 in savings; and reduced voluntary turnover resulted in \$1,218,000.

The HRP process can be the point at which we systematically look at the movement through the organization and identify those jobs which, because of high turnover, appear to be weak links in the quality effort. Later in this chapter we present an example of Markov analysis (transitional probability matrix) as one tool to use to identify these jobs.

For now, our message is simple; turnover is costly. Addressing the issue (through various means, including improved selection) has substantial ROI.

With our introduction and review of these HRP issues now complete, we turn to the presentation of an HRP model.

What Is HRP?

Figure 5.1 provides a simplified overview of the key components of HRP. The intent of the HRP process is to construct a plan for meeting the human resources needs of the organization in both the short and

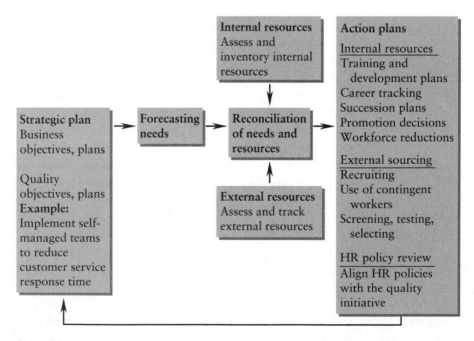

Figure 5.1. The HRP planning process.

long range. The first component on which the process is based is an analysis of the strategic plan—what business objectives does the organization have for the future? What quality objectives, for example, does the organization intend to accomplish in the next six months, year, two years, five years? Clear identification of the strategic goals and objectives is necessary as the basis from which important questions regarding the workforce are examined.

The strategic objective is the set of business priorities the organization has established. Objectives may include targets for market share, cost, or quality, to name a few.

- Increase market share within 18–24 age group by 15 percent.

- Increase customer satisfaction ratings on industry indices by one standard deviation.

The strategic plan charts how the organization will accomplish the objective. It may include factors such as

- Increase product mix of interest to 18–24 age group.

- Implement customer service program.

The second component is the process of forecasting demand, or needs. What units will grow as a consequence of the strategy? How many and what mix of positions will be needed? Which positions will no longer be needed? Will the application of process improvement technologies alter the mix of positions? Will it alter the responsibilities of our management team? Will the move toward production teams alter the mix? Will (and should) efforts toward pushing decisions to the point of the customer reduce the number of levels in the organization? In chapter 2 we discussed specific ways in which organizations change (structure, culture, work design) and the effect of these changes on workforce requirements. It is necessary for each organization to make these projections within the context of its quality effort.

One focal point for these projections is the job, work, and organization analysis process profiled in chapter 4. Ask: What are the attributes required to meet our mission, to perform the new work, and to fit in and succeed in our culture? What constitutes value in our workforce? These questions are just as appropriate at the aggregate level as they are at the level of the specific position opening. What is the attribute profile of your quality initiative? What attributes are relevant across all of the jobs in your company?

The third component of HRP is an inventory of the current internal workforce. Questions include: What are the current capabilities of our workforce relative to the goals and objectives of the strategic plan? Does the organization have the appropriate mix of knowledge, skills, and experience to meet the long-range quality objective? To profile the current capabilities of the organization, an inventory of the human resources typically involves analysis of current data on the internal workforce such as demographics, educational background, knowledge and skills inventories, performance appraisal data, positions held, performance data, training completed, and so forth. This database allows you to quickly determine where HR deficiencies represent barriers to specific quality initiatives.

The fourth component of the process is the assessment and tracking of external labor sources. What knowledge, skills, and experiences are readily available in the external workforce? Which are scarce or difficult to source? With which institutions (K–12, universities, associations, community groups, temporary agencies) should we establish contact to facilitate location of these external resources? Furthermore, with which must we assert an influence to foster our own long-term interests? For example, many organizations, in response to basic skills deficiencies in their entry-level applicants, have chosen to get actively involved in the K–12 education system. In fact, ASQC supports programs for encouraging the teaching of quality in K–12 institutions.[9] By acting to make their needs clear, and in many cases providing resources, they seek to reduce the long-term costs associated with new hires who are ill-prepared.

The fifth component of the process is the reconciliation of needs (demand) and current resources (supply). (See the convergence of the three arrows in Figure 5.1.) Where are the existing gaps between what we will need and what we have? Related to this component is the succession planning process. The availability of workforce data, combined with projections of movement, allows the proactive planning and preparation for natural movement of people into and out of key positions. What positions are critical to the quality initiative? What individuals are now ready to step into key quality positions? Do we have candidates available to step into key positions that affect the quality effort (leaders)? Are we prepared for any movement in personnel that may occur? These are questions of succession planning, an important element of developing leadership for quality. The succession planning process (identifying individuals and their development needs) is a crucial step to ensure leadership of the quality initiative. Our refrain again is: Have you incorporated key quality attributes into the process you use to identify successors for positions important to success of the quality effort?

The sixth step of the process is the development of specific action plans formulated to close the gap between the organization's current resources and future needs. Internal actions are oriented to developing the current workforce. Given the current capabilities of our workforce relative to the strategic goals and objectives, what development (education, training, career moves) must be undertaken to prepare the workforce? Internal action plans may include specific training programs, job-based developmental experiences, transfers and reassignments, succession plans for key personnel, and a revision of all HR policies and procedures to assure that they are supportive of the total quality strategic plan.

In addition to plans for developing the current workforce, external staffing plans are also constructed for bringing new talent into the organization. Given the strategic objective and the current profile of our workforce, what new knowledge, skills, temperament, and experiences must we bring into the organization? Activities include forecasting needs, in terms of the number and kinds of positions, identifying and establishing relationships with recruitment sources, and constructing a recruitment plan. We discuss planning in this chapter and devote all of chapter 6 to the actual recruitment activities. Because of its importance, we address the use of contingency workers as an external resource in chapter 14.

Clearly, the topics of external and internal HR planning are not independent. Rather, we contend that both should be part of a totally integrated system for effectively staffing the organization. We now take a closer look at components of the planning process.

Forecasting Labor Needs

The first component we examine is the process of forecasting labor needs. Forecasting data is used to project future requirements in terms of both the number and type of employees needed to successfully operate the organization. Even with a relatively stable organization, it is important to anticipate future HR needs. Voluntary and involuntary turnover, promotions, retirement, and changes in technology and skill requirements all require planning for replacement. And that need for planning is compounded when the organization is adopting the quality paradigm, undergoing rapid growth, or downsizing its operations.

Like most HR activities, the process of forecasting labor demand runs the gamut in terms of sophistication. Forecasting varies from being very reactive and unsystematic to being proactive and very systematic in the use of various forecasting methods. Obviously, we advocate the latter but do believe that some of the traditional approaches to forecasting may prove to be inadequate in the quality setting. That is because most models for forecasting are based upon a historical perspective of labor demand in the context of a traditional organization structure and philosophy. During the initial stages of your transformation, the historic data may not apply in the new paradigm.

The Traditional Approach to Forecasting. Traditional quantitative methods of labor demand forecasting are based upon the assumption that the future is an extrapolation from the past. Trend analysis incorporates certain business factors (for example, units produced, revenues) and a productivity ratio (for example, employees per units produced) to forecast demand. Thus, the standard, pyramidal organization with its scalable structure allows for a relatively direct approach for forecasting changes in labor demand (see Figure 5.2). For example, with the traditional organization we could easily determine that the average worker produces 50 weeidgets per day (a weeidget is much like a widget, only smaller), and that one supervisor is needed for every 20

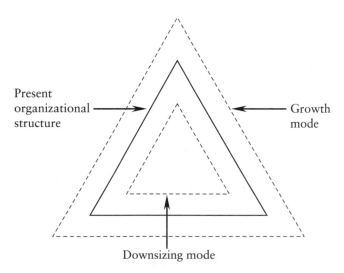

Figure 5.2. Forecasting with a scalable organizational structure.

workers, one support staff member (sales, marketing, purchasing, HR) is needed for every 15 employees, and so on. Learning curves and changes in technology can also be easily factored into the equation. Thus, by projecting changes in either the productivity ratio and/or business factors, forecasting changes in labor demand becomes a relatively straightforward process.

John H. Bernardin and Joyce E. Russell describe six steps that are included in traditional trend analysis.[10]

1. Find the appropriate business factor that relates to the size of the workforce.

2. Plot the historical record of that factor in relation to the size of the workforce.

3. Compute the productivity ratio (average output per worker per year).

4. Determine the trend.

5. Make necessary adjustments in the trend, past and future.

6. Project to the target year.

More complicated models or methods used in forecasting, such as multiple regression and linear programming, also assume traditional organizational structures and the use of historical trends. But what happens when these assumptions are no longer true? How do you forecast labor demand for a specific functional unit or grouping in the organization when those traditional boundaries are now obscured by the use of cross-functional teams and a process approach to getting work done? What happens when the organization radically redesigns or reengineers its processes and now only needs five employees to do what was previously done by 50? What happens when conventional wisdom concerning the ratio of workers to management personnel no longer holds true? Chrysler Corporation, for example, has gone from a worker/supervisor ratio of 25:1 in 1992 to 45:1 in 1994 for its hourly employees, and plans to eliminate the need for skilled trades supervisors by the year 2000. Similarly, Chrysler now produces approximately 450 vehicles per salaried employee versus 236 per salaried employee in 1991.[11] The old ratios for forecasting no longer apply.

Forecasting in the Quality Setting. A quick review of the steps for trend analysis described earlier suggests that we need to rethink much of what we call labor demand forecasting. Virtually none of the assumptions underlying the traditional steps holds true for a total quality organization. Indeed, the quality literature is replete with admonitions to discard such assumptions and padlocks on our creative instincts.

What does all this mean in terms of HRP and forecasting labor demand? Obviously, we still need to anticipate and make provisions for our labor needs and labor supply. While more difficult, forecasting will always remain an important activity. We've identified five ways in which forecasting must change in the quality setting.

1. **More Decentralized.** First, we believe that forecasting will require a more decentralized (versus centralized) approach to projecting labor demand. For example, while the strategic direction of the organization may be to flatten the organization structure and become leaner, it will be the responsibility of individual units, departments, or divisions to translate the directive into action based upon their own unique needs and capabilities. Some functional areas will, no doubt, remain relatively stable or even grow while others provide excellent opportunities for streamlining operations and reducing headcount. Thus, the process of projecting staffing needs will be accomplished by combining input from various functional areas to generate a composite forecast for the organization.

2. **Use of Qualitative Methods.** A second likely trend in the quality setting will be a move toward using more qualitative methods for forecasting labor demand. As previously discussed, quantitative forecasting methods that rely on historical data for modeling labor needs may no longer prove useful. While some quantitative information will always prove useful, managers and HR planners will be forced to use more qualitative or subjective approaches for projecting labor demand. One such method, the nominal group technique (NGT) is familiar to most quality professionals (see Exhibit 5.1).

The NGT provides a way to give each group member an equal voice in the forecasting process by minimizing interpersonal and jurisdictional conflicts. All members of the group are given an equal voice in establishing staffing needs and priorities.

NGT and other qualitative approaches to forecasting will work best with managers and HR planners who are committed to the strategic direction of the organization and are dedicated to the quality paradigm. They are much less likely to be effective using traditional managers bent on building their hierarchical power base or who sub-

Exhibit 5.1. The nominal group technique applied to forecasting labor demand.

---

(1) Team members individually generate their labor forecasts along with a rationale for both the numbers and types of employees needed. This forecasting should be done in the context of

  (a) The strategic direction and action plans of the organization

  (b) Historical (quantitative) data (for example, production data, present staffing)

  (c) Growth, or lack thereof, of the organization (budgetary constraints)

  (d) Their own efforts at becoming lean (flattening the organization structure, automation, process improvement, reengineering)

  (e) Meeting customer needs

(2) Each team member is asked to share his or her forecasts along with a rationale for his or her needs. These should be put in writing for easy reference.

(3) These forecasts are discussed by the group and a number of alternative forecast plans are developed and posted for all to see.

(4) Each plan is lettered (A,B,C . . .) and then ranked by each member of the group. A completed ranking might look like this:

Forecast plan	Team number rankings						Total
	1	2	3	4	5	6	
A	5	4	4	5	5	5	28
B	1	5	3	2	4	3	18
C	2	3	1	3	2	2	13
D	3	1	2	1	3	1	11
E	4	2	5	4	1	4	20

---

scribe to the not-in-my-back-yard (NIMBY) principle when asked to do more with less.

3. **More Attention to Attributes Employees Possess.** A third trend will be an increased emphasis on the types of employees needed rather than just projecting the numbers required. Consistent with everything written in the previous chapters, the quality-oriented organization will place a premium on those employees that can and will function effectively under the new quality paradigm. This will be true for both external and internal HRP. Support for this trend was found in our staffing

survey. Respondents were asked to describe the extent to which quality-related attributes are evaluated when making selection and promotion decisions. First, they were asked to describe current practices. Then, they were asked to describe practices five years ago and five years from now. The results, as shown in Figure 5.3, strongly indicate that the trend will be toward more and more emphasis on these quality-related attributes when making selection and promotion decisions.

Our belief is that staffing truly does dictate, or at least confine, strategy. Therefore, staffing your organization with bright, inquisitive, creative, flexible/adaptable employees will yield great dividends. Your organization will be more agile in the strategic objectives it can pursue.

4. **Active Partnerships with External Groups.** Fourth, we believe that the quality-oriented organization will take a more active role in its dealings with the labor market. This may include mutually beneficial partnerships between organizations and K–12 school systems, colleges, universities, and community organizations. As the shortage of skilled individuals in the workforce becomes increasingly acute, forward-thinking organiza-

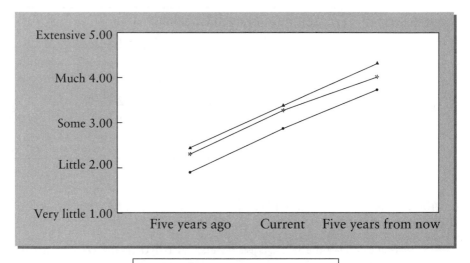

- • Hourly
- * Technical/professional
- ▲ Managerial (all levels combined)

Figure 5.3. Extent to which quality-related attributes are evaluated when making selection and promotion decisions.

tions will increase their interaction with those communities from which their applicants are to be recruited. This proactive approach will be used to nurture those skills considered important to the organization, and to ensure an ongoing flow of viable candidates to the organization. We will present much more about the relationship with your HR suppliers in chapter 6.

5. Flexibility. The fifth trend is toward a more flexible notion of HRP and staffing. Increasingly, a mix of both internal and external individuals will be put together to accomplish a particular task or project. Once completed, these individuals will be reconfigured to work on other projects. As we noted earlier, some have even suggested the demise of the job as we know it.[12] People will be selected to get work done and not to fill slots in a traditional organization chart. The role of those external workers (contingent workforce) will be further explored in chapter 14.

Internal Supply Analysis: What Capabilities Now Exist?

The central component of HRP is internal supply analysis. It involves three activities: keeping inventory of the current workforce within the organization, tracking movement within the organization, and projecting and planning for necessary changes.

Keeping Inventory of the Current Workforce

As the process model (in Figure 5.1) illustrates, a key component of HRP is data regarding our current workforce. Planning for quality requires that we know what resources we have. In fact, as noted by Snow and Snell in their chapter "Staffing as Strategy," the inventory organizations keep will be a significant strategic advantage. Those organizations that know what workforce attributes they have in place will be able to envision and to move more quickly at new opportunities.[13]

There are many sources for data and organizations with systematic HRP functions typically incorporate many of them. Exhibit 5.2 lists examples of workforce data useful in the planning process. Typically, an individual's record begins with data recorded at the time of initial hire and is periodically updated as his or her tenure in the organization unfolds.

Exhibit 5.2. The internal inventory—HRP data.

Biographical information

    Education history (courses, degrees)

    Training programs

    Certifications (such as offered by ASQC)

    Demographics (race, age, gender)

    Previous job history (titles, time)

    Job history in company

    Self-reported interests

    Recruitment/selection data (source, interviewer, ratings, test scores)

Skills data

    Self-reported skills (including attributes from QAI)

    360-degree (peer, subordinate, self-, superior, customer) assessments

    Performance on assessment exercises

    Foreign language skills

Performance data

    Job performance history

    360-degree performance data

Compensation history

    Salary history

Training history

    Programs attended

    Skills mastered

Health and safety history

Periodic HRP data

    Profitability judgments (readiness)

    Specific positions for which person is prepared

    Transferability judgments (willingness, urgency)

    Current training and developmental needs

The existence of an HR database, and the computer technology for conducting analyses, has created an important tool for strategic planning. This tool allows the exploration of various staffing questions such as the following:

- What skills do we possess internally? For example, do we have individuals trained in ISO 9000 implementation?

- What quality-relevant knowledge, skills, abilities, and temperament are lacking or inadequately developed in the organization? Can the current workforce be trained and developed in these?

- What are the key quality-oriented jobs, and what internal candidates are ready or can be ready for these key strategic positions?

- What experiences are needed to prepare key candidates?

- Given our internal resources, what attributes must we seek from the outside?

Attribute Profile. For organizations with an existing HRP process, the major attention may be to provide a framework to inventory quality-oriented attributes. The quality-related taxonomies listed in chapter 4 and appendix B can serve as a model. This comprehensive list of quality knowledge, skills, abilities, temperament, and associated experience can be used to identify quality-related dimensions to incorporate into the HR database. The profile might be used to compile an assessment checklist to be completed by all employees, in conjunction with their managers (or organized into a 360-degree instrument), or it may be used to select more elaborate assessment devices for internal assessment of particular segments of the workforce (for example, those with critical roles in the quality initiative, high-potential employees). For example, we could envision an assessment center used to evaluate the readiness of candidates for the highly visible leadership positions on which the success of the quality effort will hinge.

Tracking Movement Within the Organization

It is often helpful to identify the movement of individuals throughout the organization. One tool for doing so is termed a *transitional probability matrix* (Markov analysis). Essentially, it relies on the history of movement through jobs in the company to understand the relationship among jobs. Doing so allows us to identify key positions (team leaders, quality program managers) and begin to identify the route employees have taken to those jobs. When we see these patterns, we can be more proactive in planning the development and movement of individuals into key positions. For example, Table 5.1 presents an example of Markov analysis.

Table 5.1. Markov analysis of staff movement.

Positions occupied at Time 1		Proportion in each job at Time 2: One year later				
		TM	T	S	M	Exit
Team members (TM)		.75	.06	.04		.15
Technicians (T)		.06	.78	.03		.15
Supervisors (S)		.04	.02	.70	.06	.18
Area managers (M)				.08	.67	.25
	Staffing levels	TM	T	S	M	Exit
Team members (TM)	200	150	12	8		30
Technicians (T)	100	6	78	3		13
Supervisors (S)	50	2	1	35	3	9
Area managers (M)	12			1	8	3
Forecast		158	91	47	11	55

The table reflects the movement into, through, and out of various jobs in the organization (team member, technician, and so on) during a specified period of time. The exhibit displays the movement through four specific jobs at Ajax Manufacturing, over the period of one year. The rows represent the positions occupied at Time 1. The columns represent the positions occupied by the same individuals at Time 2 (one year later). The cells (top matrix) present the proportion of individuals in the position at Time 2 who were in the row position at Time 1. For example, 75 percent of those who were team members at Time 1 are team members at Time 2 ($n = 150$). Six percent of those who were team members at Time 1 are now technicians ($n = 12$). Four percent of those who were team members at Time 1 are supervisors at Time 2 ($n = 8$). Fifteen percent of those who were Team Members at Time 1 have left the company (exit column) at Time 2 ($n = 30$).

The transitional probability matrix is useful in a number of ways. First, the pattern of movement between jobs can be used to identify career paths in the organization. The natural progression between positions alerts us to the need to examine how time in one job can contribute to preparation for later jobs. Second, we can see which jobs are essentially dead ends or developmental blocks. Third, we can examine turnover rates to reveal jobs that lead individuals to leave the company (the exit column). For example, 15 percent of our 200 team members left the company. Finally, we can use the mobility in jobs to identify internal and external recruiting priorities. For example, 25 percent of our team members moved, creating 50 team members vacancies.

Action Planning Process

The final phase of HRP is to reconcile the gaps between identified needs and availability. From that, we prepare specific staffing plans (initiation of strategic downsizing, recruitment of applicants for permanent positions, use of contingents, development of employees for future challenges).

Developing Plans for Individuals.   One outcome of the HRP process is a training needs assessment for individuals. Effective HRP processes produce profiles of the developmental needs of individuals. Some do so for all individuals in the system, with special focus on those individuals in key positions. Others do so only for individuals critical to attaining the strategic plan.

Companywide Development Plans.   The HRP process can serve as an organization training needs assessment process. The aggregated data can identify training and development priorities systemwide. This information can be very helpful in identifying those needs that are prevalent enough to justify purchase or development of an internal training program. For those needs that occur only for unique positions or persons throughout the system, the use of a public workshop may be a cost-efficient alternative.

Realign HR Policies and Practices to Support the Total Quality Strategy.   One deficiency in many settings is the failure to systematically change HR policies and practices to support new initiatives adapted by the organization. This is true of the implementation of teams, of redesigned or reengineered work, and of the transformation to quality improvement values and practices. The planning process is the ideal setting to ask the question: Are our HR policies and practices supportive of the strategic initiative? In terms of quality improvement, do our policies and practices support or inhibit the adoption of this new way of functioning? Each component of HR practice must be examined.

- What must be changed in our culture to support the quality initiative? What structure will support the quality practices? (Do current structural barriers reduce teamwork?)

- What staffing practices support or detract from the quality initiative? What staffing practices must we change? (As you know, that is the content of this book.)

- What training practices support or detract from the quality initiative?

- How does the performance measurement and appraisal process support or detract from the quality initiative? (Are we preaching teamwork, but rewarding individual accomplishment at the cost of teamwork?)

- Do our reward and compensation practices support or inhibit the quality initiative?

In a recent article, Richard Blackburn and Bensen Rosen examined the extent to which Baldrige Award winners had aligned their staffing practices to be supportive of their quality initiatives. They report that these organizations had changed their HR practices in support of their quality efforts in virtually all areas except in the area of staffing.[14] Follow-up research does suggest that there has emerged increased attention to aligning staffing to be supportive of the quality effort.[15] Refer again to Figure 5.3. For each occupational grouping, ASQC sustaining member organizations report, compared to five years ago, there is more attention to quality-related attributes now, and the respondents project that there will be even more in the future. However, much of that effort appears to be unsystematic. Consequently, there appears to be much room for progress.[16]

Blackburn and Rosen identify a number of contrasts in the HR policies and practices of the traditional and total quality organization.[17] First, they note that total quality organizations provide greater voice and involvement to employees than do traditional organizations. Second, total quality organizations train for a broad range of skills rather than narrow job or function skills. Third, whereas traditional organizations attune the performance measurement and evaluation process to individual goals and supervisory judgments, total quality organizations attune the process to team goals and diverse (customer, peer) input. Fourth, whereas traditional organizations allocate rewards on the basis of individual merit, total quality organizations allocate team and group-based rewards. These and other HR policy changes contribute to the development of a true quality-oriented culture. The HR planning process is the focal point at which you can examine all your HR policies and practices to determine if they do, in fact, support the development of a quality culture.

Summary

Planning for the HR contribution to the initiatives of the new organization, such as quality improvement, is more important now than ever before. The tools of contemporary HRP (keeping track of internal and external HR capabilities, identifying HR needs for strategic initiatives, sourcing and developing those resources, and realigning the HR policies of the organization) can serve as the principal means through which the organization moves from the traditional to the quality-oriented paradigm.

Notes

1. Charles C. Snow and Scott A. Snell, "Staffing as Strategy," in *Personnel Selection in Organizations,* Neal Schmitt and Walter C. Borman, eds. (San Francisco: Jossey-Bass, 1993), 463.

2. Kim Cameron, "Strategies for Successful Organizational Downsizing," *Human Resources Management* 33, no. 2 (1994): 189–211

3. Robert E. Cole, "Learning from Learning Theory: Implications for Quality Improvement of Turnover, Use of Contingent Workers and Job Rotation Policies," *Quality Management Journal* (October 1993): 9–25.

4. Cameron, "Strategies for Successful Organizational Downsizing."

5. Lisa Magi, Staffing Specialist, Computer Aided Engineering Technology, August 1995, personal communciation.

6. Laura Rubach, "Downsizing: How Quality Is Affected as Companies Shrink," *Quality Progress* (April 1995): 23–28.

7. Cole, "Learning from Learning Theory: Implications for Quality Improvement of Turnover, Use of Contingent Workers and Job Rotation Policies."

8. James L. Heskett, Thomas O. Jones, Gary W. Loveman, W. Earl Sasser, Jr., and Leonard A. Schlesinger, "Putting the Service/Profit Chain to Work," *Harvard Business Review* (March-April 1994): 169.

9. Connie Faylor, "Pennsylvania Builds Tomorrow's Workforce," *Quality Progress* (July 1995): 71-73; contact Hank Lindborg, NIQI, 17 Forest Ave., Fond du Lac, WI 54935, (414) 923-9600 (e-mail niqi@aol.com) for more information on the implementation of quality into the high school curricula.

10. John H. Bernardin and Joyce E. A. Russell, *Human Resource Management: An Experiential Approach* (New York: McGraw-Hill, 1993).

11. Richard Willing, "Big Three Retools to Meet Demands of Future," *The Detroit News and Free Press,* 11 June 1995, A1.

12. William Bridges, "The End of the Job," *Fortune* (Sept. 19, 1994): 62–74.

13. Snow and Snell, "Staffing as Strategy."

14. Richard Blackburn and Bensen Rosen, "Total Quality and Human Resources Management: Lessons Learned from Baldrige Award-Winning Companies," *The Academy of Management Executive* (August 1993): 59.

15. Richard Blackburn and Bensen Rosen, "Human Resource Management and Total Quality Management" in *Research in Quality Management,* D. Fedor and S. Ghosh, eds. (Greenwich, Conn.: JAI Press, in press).

16. Jack Smith and Ronald Morgan, "Staffing for Quality Improvement: A Survey of ASQC Sustaining Member Organizations," technical report (White Lake, Mich.: HR Processes, and Northville, Mich.: Organization Solutions, 1994).

17. Blackburn and Rosen, "Total Quality and Human Resources Management."

chapter **6**

Recruiting: Putting Your Quality Strategy into Action

Overview

The focus of this chapter is getting quality-oriented applicants into the staffing pipeline. We contend that recruitment sources should be viewed as *suppliers,* candidates should be seen as *customers,* and that the organization should make data-driven decisions concerning both. Recruiting applicants for the quality setting requires a well-thought-out, well-planned process. This process should be structured so that the particular needs of the company will be met in terms of the individuals it hires.

Introduction

The move from HRP to recruitment is a process of translating broad, quality improvement strategies into action-oriented tasks. Both the HR department and line managers are responsible for making that transition effective. In theory, *recruitment* is the process of attracting qualified and interested individuals to fill available job vacancies. *Selection,* on the other hand, is a decision-making process aimed at identifying those persons most able and willing to meet organizational expectations (for example, perform well, stay with the organization, be promotable, and so on). In practice, this distinction blurs considerably.

How the recruitment process is accomplished directly affects selection and the organization's ability to obtain qualified employees. For example, how the candidate is treated during the recruitment process will likely influence his or her own decision to remain in the recruitment pipeline (self-selection). Similarly, the candidate's perception of the staffing process can directly influence the organization's ability to attract good applicants (by word-of-mouth). Consistent with our process theme throughout this book, recruitment affects, and in turn is affected by, other components of the staffing process.

"Get Me a Warm Body"

Mike Magnuson is a Production Manager at the Ajax Plastic and Trim Products plant. Mike's job is a nonstop, 60-hour-plus week that keeps him moving from the time he enters the plant at approximately 6:00 A.M. until he drags himself out of the plant in the late afternoon or evening. It is now Friday, and his already hectic and demanding schedule is interrupted by the news that one of his best supervisors has submitted her resignation and will be leaving the following Friday. Already short-staffed, a panic-stricken Mike calls the HR manager with the plea to "get me somebody—anybody, as soon as possible." The HR manager responds that a staffing requisition is needed to start the process, but that he will do everything possible to expedite the request. Mike quickly fills out the requisition, has his boss sign it, and then submits his request to the HR manager with a final appeal for immediate action.

This *get-me-a-warm-body* scenario is, unfortunately, all too typical and illustrates many of the problems and realities involved in recruiting for a position. What qualifications must candidates possess to successfully fill the position? How quickly can the position be filled without jeopardizing the integrity of the process? Do viable candidates exist within the plant (or organization), or should Ajax look externally? If someone is promoted from within, what problems will that create for other units in the company? How many candidates will be needed in a final pool for Mike's selection? What kinds of EEO goals might affect the plant? These are only a few of the questions that need to be addressed during the recruitment process.

Some General Issues and Guidelines

How can we go about getting Mike qualified candidates in an expeditious manner? Following are some of the more important issues that should be addressed and guidelines to follow when recruiting quality-oriented candidates.

Tie Recruiting Efforts to Quality Strategic Goals. As previously discussed, to be effective, quality should be a strategic initiative. Strategic quality planning is not just an exercise. It is not giving lip service to the concept of quality following a two-day retreat in the Catskills. Rather, strategic planning is a means for providing direction for the entire organization. It is a blueprint for corporate action and, as such, should influence all policies, procedures, and actions. Many of the organizations we surveyed (formally and informally) described themselves as quality driven but had given little or no thought to translating that strategic direction into their staffing practices. Our findings are consistent with a recent study that examined the HR management practices of initial winners of the Baldrige Award. The study looked at a number of HR-related characteristics (for example, training, involvement, communication, job design, performance measurement, and reward) and gave relatively high marks to the winners in terms of those practices. One notable exception in the study was the characteristic entitled "Selection/Promotion and Career Development." Here, the processes of these companies remained relatively unchanged. In the authors' words,

> *When asked to describe changes in selection processes as a result of their organization's TQM emphasis, most of our respondents indicated that the same processes remained in place—find the best available applicant and assume that he or she can be socialized and trained to function effectively in a TQM environment. The underlying assumption for many of these firms is that individuals with the requisite skills can readily be taught to produce quality work.[1]*

Mike's problem at Ajax illustrates this apparent paradox. Like most auto suppliers for the Big Three, Ajax would be under considerable pressure to be a quality-oriented company. Failure to meet certain quality-related criteria and standards typically means removal from the auto companies' acceptable vendor listing. But Mike and the HR manager, much like the companies we surveyed, fail to make the link between their strategic goals for quality and their staffing activities.

Plan Ahead. Our previous discussion of HRP begins to take on real-world meaning when viewed from the perspective of our scenario. If Mike and the HR manager had planned for this eventuality and taken steps to have someone in the pipeline to replace the departing supervisor, then many of Mike's worries would have been eliminated. It's ironic that our production manager, who appears to meticulously plan his production schedule and parts inventory, finds himself short-staffed through a lack of planning. Mike's inability to translate his planning skills to staffing is indicative of many HR and line managers in the workplace and likely represents the norm.

The key is to plan ahead. The supervisor's leaving should not be the trigger mechanism for starting the staffing process. That staffing activity should have been well underway prior to the position opening. For example, a simple Markov forecast analysis, as described in chapter 5, might have shown that, of the 50 supervisors in the plant, approximately 15 would need to be replaced during the year. Whether recruited externally or developed and recruited internally, many of the staffing activities should have been completed in anticipation of those labor demands.

Identify and Incorporate Quality Requirements. We have already pointed out the necessity of doing a thorough job and organization analysis that reflects the requirements for the job in question. In addition to reinforcing that concept, it is important to discuss the need to have that information early on in the recruiting stage of the staffing process.

Most organizations require the completion of some type of employment requisition prior to filling a position. These requisitions are used for justifying need and for budget considerations, but they are also used by HR personnel as an aid in recruiting candidates for the position (for example, placing ads, job postings, screening applicants). Therefore, accurate and complete qualification information on the requisition does much to help in the search for viable candidates. Put simply, the more complete this requisition, the more likely that the individuals involved in recruiting will be able to find the right person for the job.

The following example illustrates the need for putting some serious thought into completing the employment requisition. A few years ago, one of the authors was doing interviewer skills training for a major computer company. In designing the training program, HR personnel were interviewed to determine issues that they felt should be addressed during the training sessions. Among their chief concerns was the complaint that managers seldom put much thought into the completion of the employment requisitions. They complained that this cavalier attitude made it difficult to do their jobs properly and often resulted in the screening in of unacceptable candidates for the position. Much time and effort was wasted by both HR personnel and by the managers who, in theory, had a vested interest in finding qualified candidates in a timely manner. A brief review by the author of recently completed requisitions supported this contention. An actual Job Qualifications section from one of the requisitions for the job of programmer read as follows:

- College degreed

- Some programming experience

- GPA 3.00 or higher

While this example was the worst of the lot, many of the requisitions reviewed approximated this rather poor effort on the part of management. The task of finding qualified candidates becomes very difficult under these circumstances. As discussed in chapter 4, it is imperative that work and organization-relevant attributes be identified. We also contend those attributes be identified early in the process. The success of all other steps in the process depends on this critical activity.

The More, the Better. Suppose that two high schools are scheduled to play each other during the fall season. Both teams are allowed a 50-person roster and proceed to conduct tryouts for the selection of their respective teams. Suppose again, that High School A had 100 hopefuls try out for their team, while High School B had 250 student athletes show up for its tryouts.

	Tryout participants (applicants)	Final roster (selected)	Selection rate
High School A	100	50	50%
High School B	250	50	20%

On which team would a betting person put money when the two teams meet on the gridiron? Obviously, the person would bet on High School B (unless his/her kid was playing for High School A). This is because High School B was able to be more selective in its decision process. Recall the basic tenet of recruitment reviewed in chapter 3— the more credible applicants for a position, the better. Assuming that the selection process has some relationship with job performance (validity) and that there are more applicants than openings for the position or job in question, the ROI (utility) of the selection process depends on the ratio of those hired to those who applied for the position (the SR). All else equal, the lower the SR, the better. If an organization has only 12 applicants for its 10 job openings (a high SR), then it cannot be very choosy in its hiring. However, with 50 applicants for the same 10 job openings (a low SR), the organization can be much more selective. Our advice to Mike (our production manager) is to make sure he has several viable candidates for filling the vacant position. As a rule of thumb, we suggest a minimum of three to five candidates per job opening.

Don't Hire Under Time Pressure. Both HR personnel and operating managers should avoid the temptation to quickly fill a position with the proverbial warm body. While short-term needs may have been addressed, the long-term results of such decisions are typically not so positive. Studies have consistently shown that the performance of employees hired under time constraints is significantly lower than for their coworkers hired in a more conventional manner. When faced with an open position, resist the temptation to simply fill the slot. Doing so may not be worth the long-term grief associated with a poor selection decision. In the case of staffing, haste may indeed make waste.

Reduce Process Cycle Time. The caution to avoid hiring under time pressure does not mean that the staffing process cannot and should not be accomplished in a timely manner. As we state throughout this book, staffing is a process. And like any process, it can be systematically measured, analyzed, and improved. While the recruitment/selection process cycle time is likely to vary from job to job and from organization to organization, studies indicate that the typical time required for this process is likely to be between 60 and 90 days and sometimes even more. A flowchart and analysis of this process typically reveals multiple opportunities to streamline and improve the time needed to recruit for a position (see Figure 6.1).

Any HR manager that fails to maintain this cycle time or time lapse data (TLD), and then use that information to make improvements in the process, does not yet understand the concept of quality. An example of systematically reducing staffing process cycle time is presented at the end of this chapter.

Treat Recruitment Sources as Suppliers. Deming and other quality advocates have consistently pointed out the importance of improving supplier relationships. In particular, they have recommended the selection of suppliers based on quality as well as price and have encouraged businesses to develop a closer and more long-term relationship with

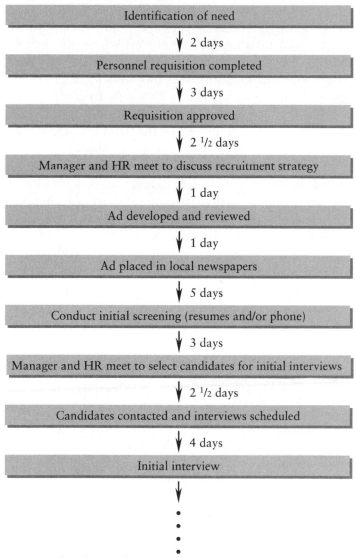

Note: Total cycle time from "completed requisition" to "initial interview" is 22 days.

Figure 6.1. An example of a recruitment process flowchart with cycle-time data for an entry-level position.

those suppliers. Unfortunately, many quality and HR professionals view suppliers as the folks that provide them with door panels for cars or computers for their offices. They seldom think of an employment agency, temporary service, or local university as a supplier, but they are. We would argue that they may be the organization's most important suppliers because they provide the workforce that makes everything else happen. If, as we espouse, employees are the most important part of our organization, then viewing recruitment sources as suppliers becomes critical.

Viewing those various sources as suppliers means that we can and should apply the same set of criteria as we do to companies that supply us with our door panels. First, we should evaluate recruitment sources in terms of their quality. Does the supplier provide us with the kind of employees we need? Indices might include the number of potentially qualified candidates generated by the source, the number or percentage of successful placements made, and the longevity or tenure of those selected from a particular source. Whatever criteria are established, they should be systematically measured, evaluated, and used to make recruitment source decisions.

A second quality principle related to suppliers is to reduce the number of suppliers to a few dependable and quality-driven sources. Only those recruitment sources that truly meet our needs and provide us with quality employees should be used. The key is that the organization utilizes the tools available to systematically measure the quality of those recruitment sources.

This reduction of the number of suppliers based on quality is clearly illustrated by one supplier firm's experience with the Big Three auto companies. CAEtech provides contract labor (contingent workers) to the Big Three automotive manufacturers in the area of computer-aided engineering. In 1993, CAEtech was informed that its major client would be reducing its dependence from more than 1000 vendors to less than 50 in the contract labor area. It was also told that inclusion on the vendor list would be determined by its success at becoming a quality-conscious company. CAEtech had approximately two years to become such a company, which meant a big turnaround for the firm. In the words of Donald V. Sequeira, manager of human resources, *"Quality* was used more as an adjective than as an important function in every aspect of the business—*Kaizen, QOS, TQM,* and *SPC* were all buzz words when we started our adventure with the concept of quality."

During the next two years, CAEtech went through a series of quality audits by the client company while at the same time engaging in a full-scale total quality operations effort. Again, Sequeira explains,

> We put together as a team all the aspects starting with the Quality System which included planning for quality, control procedures, quality documentation, training and development,

reviewing process change, audit functions, key critical processes, team approach to problem solving, and dedicated teams. A quality operating system was drawn up with internal and external indicators, performance appraisals, realistic improvement goals being identified. Leadership's commitment to the pursuit of quality was clearly spelled out. The quality strategy was imbued in the long- and short-term business plan of the company. The organization's overall human resources development plan clearly earmarked the quality strategy and plan as well as addressed all levels and categories of employees. The innovative approaches of the organization were documented.[2]

The end result of CAEtech's total quality efforts has been its continued relationship with the client company. The fruits of its quality operations system (QOS) is evident from the financial growth of the company by 300 percent, doubling the employee strength, and doubling the facilities and the assets of the company. CAEtech has become a total quality supplier of contract labor for its client.

The final quality principle for dealing with suppliers is to improve the relationship between the organization and the particular supplier. Quality-minded professionals have long known the importance of working closely with suppliers to ensure that parts and supplies meet quality specifications and arrive at the location in a timely manner. So, why not do the same in terms of recruitment sources? Begin to develop strong relationships between the organization and those recruitment sources found to be most valuable. Once accomplished, begin working with those sources to improve the quality of their outputs.

For example, some quality-oriented organizations are beginning to target those schools that best meet their needs and then develop close working relationships. One excellent example of this concept is the relationship between Texas Instruments (TI) and Iowa State University (ISU).[3] As is often the case, TI found that, while the ISU graduates it hired were proficient in their respective disciplines, they lacked the specific attributes required to function in TI's total quality environment. Because of this, TI was forced to provide a significant and costly amount of remedial training in TQM principles and practices. In an effort to bridge that gap, TI and ISU made a commitment to work together with the goal of producing better quality-oriented graduates. Here's an example of that working relationship.

TI brought 100 ISU faculty and staff to the Texas Instruments Learning Institute in the summer of 1993 for training. The two organizations have remained in constant contact and work, not as financier and recipient, but as partners working toward implementing TQM principles and practices so ISU can meet its goal of producing better graduates for the workforce.[4]

In addition, ISU has modified its curriculum in several areas to be more consistent with total quality and has taken other steps to meet the needs of its customer (TI).

Other organizations such as Motorola, American Express, IBM, Ford Motor Company, Milliken, Procter & Gamble, and Xerox have engaged in similar partnership activities with academic institutions to develop well-rounded and quality-oriented graduates.[5]

These types of relationships are not unique to large organizations and universities. The 310-employee K-Byte manufacturing plant, a division of Reptron Electronics, in Gaylord, Michigan, is a contract manufacturer for printed circuit boards (PCBs). In an effort to ensure a steady supply of skilled workers for its plant, K-Byte began developing a closer working relationship with the local high school. Initially, that connection meant a plant tour by the electronics classes and K-Byte providing scrap PCBs and parts for use by the school. That initial contact evolved into an active co-op program and improved communication with the school in terms of employment skill needs. Students work six hours per day on the afternoon shift following their day classes. Students involved in the co-op program not only receive the opportunity to acquire work-related skills but also return to the classroom prepared to share those skills with classmates. Many co-op students have gone on to full-time employment with K-Byte following graduation.

At present, K-Byte, in conjunction with the State of Michigan's School-to-Work Program, is working toward funding for the purchase of new electronics equipment to improve further the high school's electronics education program. K-Byte, Gaylord Community High School, faculty members, and students are all winners under this arrangement. K-Byte improves both the skill level and numbers of its entry-level candidates. The high school gains a reputation for being "relevant" and placing its graduates. Faculty members improve their instructional skills. And students graduate with employable skills.

View Recruitment as a Two-Way Street. Individuals involved in recruitment and selection often approach the process from a very narrow perspective. They view it as a one-way affair where they are in the driver's seat in terms of selecting applicants. Much like St. Peter at the Golden Gate, they see their roles as screening out applicants deemed unqualified and screening in those viewed as having potential. While true, this is a somewhat narrow view of the actual process. In reality, at the same time we're doing our screening, the potential candidates are going through their own decision-making processes. They are scrutinizing the organization at each stage of the recruitment and selection process and, like the organization, can make a rejection decision at any point. And, unfortunately for the organization, the more qualified the candidates, the more likely they are to have a number of viable employment alternatives that they are considering.

So how do we ensure that we are competitive in the recruitment marketplace? First, recruiters must be prepared to adequately sell the organization to the prospective employee, as well as the possible downsides of employment. We will discuss this issue later in this chapter, but it is important to point out that most individuals involved in the staffing process have not given adequate thought to this important component. Candidates must be motivated to apply for our openings and then be sold on the value of joining the organization. And monetary considerations are not the only factors included in that decision-making process. While it's true that first-job choice decisions are heavily influenced by the compensation package, studies show that, as we mature and change jobs (a fact of life for 85 percent of workers), other factors, such as job content, opportunity to contribute, challenge, location, and opportunity for advancement become increasingly important when making employment decisions. To the degree that these positive factors do exist in the organization and job in question (and they certainly will if you're truly a quality-oriented organization), they need to be systematically communicated to the candidate pool.

A second way to remain competitive during the entry-level staffing process is to use the golden rule in all dealings with the candidate. In the spirit of having a quality orientation, every candidate, hired or not, should be treated with respect and viewed as a potential customer. What many individuals involved in staffing do not understand is that one of the best ways to sell the organization to its job applicants is to have those applicants view the staffing process as being completely professional. Typically, a candidate's major perception of the organization is obtained during the staffing process. The person will likely generalize from those experiences to all facets of the organization. A negative experience may very well mean the loss of a good employee and leave that individual with a negative image of the company for life, while a positive staffing experience will have the opposite effect. A professionally administered staffing process should include the following elements.

1. Whenever possible, respond to all applications, inquiries, and demonstrations of interest in a position or job.

2. The staffing procedure, particularly the interview schedule, should be carefully planned so that there is little downtime for the candidate. With the interview, it is a good idea to designate one person to oversee the entire interview process to ensure that the candidate is moved smoothly from one interview to the next. The Delphi Division of General Motors provides such a person for site visits by candidates. Delphi assigns a host to each visiting candidate to ensure that the process runs smoothly and professionally. The host is also encouraged to solicit comments for improvement to the staffing process (see Figure 6.2).

3. Candidates should be given a clear understanding of all steps in the process, including time frames, and should be kept informed about the progress of those steps.

4. Finally, someone should be responsible for informing all candidates when a selection decision has been reached.

Ideally, every candidate should reflect on his or her contact with the organization and mentally conclude that "these folks are a class act—they are professionals and really know what they are doing." This reaction will not happen if candidates have been left waiting in some reception room for 20 minutes, shuttled from one ill-prepared interviewer to another, and then forced to call the organization a month after the selection process to find out the status of staffing decisions.

Where to Look: External Recruitment Sources

There are two basic sources for recruiting quality-oriented employees: external and internal. External sources include a wide variety of labor markets that exist outside the organization. Table 6.1 provides a list of those major sources along with extent of use ratings acquired from

Figure 6.2. Host duties and activities sheet at GM's Delphi Division.

Host duties and activities.

The following duties will vary according to scheduled time of arrival per candidate.

> If arrival is between 5:00 P.M.–8:00 P.M.
> the night before visit.

- Meet and greet candidate at airport (use divisional cars if available)
  Arrival:
  Date_____; Time_____; Flight_____
- Take candidate to dinner (use General Motors credit card or obtain money from petty cash fund).
- Deliver candidate to hotel, assure check in.

> Plant visit activities,
> day of the interview

- Meet and greet candidate promptly at 7:30 A.M.
- Secure candidate's luggage in host vehicle.
- Take candidate on a short tour of Saginaw (Bay Road, Michigan, and so on).
- Deliver candidate to Personnel for briefing (30 minutes).
- Conduct plant site tour, lunch.
- Deliver candidate to second interview.
- Return candidate to airport. (Stay with candidate until plane departs; solicit comments for improvement to process.)
  Departure:
  Date_____; Time_____; Flight_____

Reprinted by permission.

our survey. While a full discussion of these sources is beyond the scope of this book, we will examine them briefly with an emphasis on the recruitment sources most frequently used (for example, referrals and ads). But before addressing each source, we would like to engage in a general discussion of the availability of quality-related skills in the workforce population.

Table 6.1. Mean ratings for the extent of recruitment source use.

Rating scale: 1 = Very little use
                2 = Some use
                3 = Much use
                4 = Considerable use
                5 = Extensive use

Recruitment source	Employee group		
	Hourly/ blue collar	Technical/ professional	Managerial
Referrals by current employees	3.23	2.92	2.71
College recruiting	—	2.40	1.87
Local high schools	1.96	—	—
Job fairs	1.82	1.77	1.53
Ads (newspapers, trade publications)	3.06	3.23	3.05
Walk-ins and unsolicited applications	2.45	1.85	1.60
Professional employment agencies	—	2.43	2.59
State employment agencies	2.18	1.43	1.32
Temporary or leasing agencies	2.48	1.68	1.33
Professional associations	—	2.07	2.07
Executive and professional search firms	—	2.25	2.79

Attention to Quality

We believe that the search for quality-oriented employees is very feasible, and that the availability of such personnel has grown considerably in recent years. Ten years ago, a discussion of recruiting for quality-related knowledgeable and experienced employees would have been primarily academic. A recruiter would have been hard-pressed to find candidates with a background in any of the quality improvement tools and methods. Today, however, the number of individuals with both quality knowledge and experience is burgeoning, and every indication is that the trend will continue.

Let's begin to examine why those quality-related attributes are more and more available in the labor market and, more importantly, what that means to us in terms of *where we look* and *what we look for* when filling positions in our quality organization. Our discussion will focus on three areas: existing quality-oriented organizations, educational institutions, and continuing education.

TQM Organizations. To begin with, the number of organizations that have embraced the quality paradigm is impressive. While no exact figures exist on the number and scope of that involvement, we do know that the numbers are substantial and growing. For example, ASQC membership jumped from 45,574 in 1984–1985 to 130,977 members in 1994–1995 and more than 1000 organizations are presently sustaining members with ASQC. Further evidence can be found in the fact that nearly one million copies of the Baldrige Award criteria were distributed between 1988 and 1994. And evidence exists that this interest is being translated into practice.

Final proof of the burgeoning interest in quality can be found in the number of firms that are ISO 9000–certified both in the United States and worldwide. In January 1993, 893 U.S. company locations were certified. As of April 1995 that number had risen to 6112 sites. During that same 27-month period, the number of ISO 9000 certifications in Canada rose from 292 to 1348, Some representative companies include (as of November 1994) Minnesota Mining & Manufacturing (3M) with 62 sites, General Electric with 77 sites, AT&T with 58 sites, Eastman Kodak with 39 locations, IBM with 48 sites, and Hewlett-Packard with 30 locations.[6]

The 1993 ASQC/Gallup survey measuring employee attitudes on teamwork, empowerment, and quality improvement demonstrates that quality initiatives are being implemented in the workplace. Results of that survey include the following:

- Among employees from companies that have team activities, more than six in 10 (64 percent) report they participate in team activities at work. Most (84 percent) participate in more than one team activity. Based on all employees, at least half (52 percent) say they participate in team activities.

- Approximately three in five said they had received training in job skills and/or the use of new technology, and half said they had received training in problem-solving skills and/or skills for working with other people.[7]

This trend can be seen in the specific training and development of various companies. Blackburn and Rosen have described the training practices of Baldrige Award-winning companies, and the results of their survey are impressive.[8] Xerox BP&S, for example, has spent more than $125 million in quality training with every employee receiving a minimum of 28 hours of such training. Federal Express employs more than 650 full-time trainers at sites around the world. Blackburn and Rosen go on to report that Cadillac sent more than 1400 employees to a four-day Deming workshop at a cost of $650 per employee, and both Wallace and IBM Rochester have spent enormous amounts, in terms of direct cost and time, training their workforces.

Thus, one viable source for recruiting is to look carefully at those organizations that have a history of applying the quality philosophy. Many employees in the workforce have already been trained in quality at someone else's expense. And lest the reader become uneasy about the concept of enticing quality-competent individuals from other organizations, we should point out that such practices are commonplace. While the science of benchmarking (adapting practices from the best) may be relatively new, the practice of raiding the competition for good employees is ageless. We raid the competition to get a leg up on technology, marketing, and strategic directions, so why not look for individuals, particularly management personnel, with the training, experience, and enthusiasm necessary to make our quality initiatives successful? That raiding does not always have to be hostile. In today's multinational, multidivisional, multialliance corporation, it is very likely that numerous employees exist with quality-related knowledge and experience (see the discussion on skills inventories in chapter 11). These people can be called upon as needed, especially when the organization is in the startup phase of a quality initiative.

Educational Institutions. In 1991, *Quality Progress* printed its first survey of quality management efforts in educational institutions. Results of that survey indicated that 55 colleges/universities and 12 community colleges had integrated some quality-related management courses into the curriculum.[9] Four years later, the 1995 survey results reported 220 colleges/universities and 83 community colleges now offer courses in quality.[10] Not only have the numbers exploded, but the scope of that education has improved dramatically. The number of programs (engineering, management, statistics, education) at the college and university level has increased substantially. Fifty-five percent of colleges/universities now offer quality-related degrees and minors or concentrations in quality.

This trend in education is likely to continue with the result that more and more degreed individuals will enter the workforce with quality-related knowledge and skills. These recruits do not have to be sold on the value of quality nor will valuable time and resources have to be spent training them in quality concepts. The HR manager of the 1990s would be remiss not to review the latest *Quality Progress* survey of educational institutions prior to sending recruiters on campus visits. Recruiting at such campuses also sends an important message to those institutions—"We are willing to hire your students if they possess the necessary quality-related knowledge and skills."

Continuing Education. Hardly a day goes by that the authors of this text do not receive a mailer describing some quality-related course, conference, seminar, or workshop. We could attend a quality program every day of the week and barely scratch the surface of what is now available. And these programs do not include the various professional association meetings that are held on a regular basis. Educational and training programs vary from two-hour telecasts (listen to Michael Hammer discuss reengineering) to ASQC certification programs (Certified Quality Auditor, Certified Quality Engineer, and Certified Reliability Engineer). While we have no data on the exact number of managers and employees attending these sessions, the proliferation of such programs would indicate that the numbers are enormous and growing.

In summary, what all this means to the recruiter is that a significant portion of the workforce has received some kind of quality-related training. Given the number of organizations providing quality training, the increase in the number of formal education (university and college) courses and degrees, and the rapid growth of continuing education quality-related programs, the recruiter would be remiss not to carefully examine these sources when staffing the organization. Indeed, we would argue that, given the widespread availability of quality-related education, individuals involved in staffing should view with suspicion any professional or managerial applicant who demonstrates ignorance concerning the quality movement.

Recruitment Sources

Following is a brief description of some of the major recruitment sources as identified in the survey.

Referrals by Current Employees. One frequently used source of recruiting is current employee referrals. This internal approach to recruiting is consistent with the quality imperative in terms of both employee participation and low-cost (lean) recruitment. Referrals have the added advantage of being predictive of performance, particularly rate of job survival, in a number of settings.[11] Because such referrals are inexpensive and often very effective, many organizations have instituted a formal process for encouraging and rewarding referral efforts. Our own survey results showed referrals to be the most widely used source for recruiting hourly/blue-collar workers. Surprisingly, referrals were the second most popular source for technical/professional positions and the third most widely used source for managerial recruiting.

While seen as a prime recruitment source, referrals are not without their limits and should be used carefully. Following are a few suggestions for making the most of employee referrals. First, communicate clearly to employees concerning the type(s) of employees needed including position openings, qualifications (functional and quality-related attributes), and time frames. If you have a reward system for referrals, only pay for those candidates that are hired and stay with the company for a reasonable period of time (for example, one year). Both of these activities will help ensure the infusion of viable candidates. Next, be careful to use referrals along with other recruitment sources, and take steps to ensure that the actual selection of individuals is done using valid and standardized procedures. These actions will help reduce the concerns of nepotism and favoritism that often accompany the use of referrals. Finally, be vigilant to the very real possibility that employee referrals may be unfair to certain protected groups or contrary to the organization's position on diversity. Word-of-mouth recruiting methods such as employee referrals tend to replicate the existing demographics of the organization. This can create a problem if the organization underutilizes a particular group. For example, if the organization's present utilization of minorities is lower than that of nonminorities, an overreliance on employee referrals would tend to perpetuate that imbalance and lead to disparate impact in the organization.

College Recruiting. Most of the readers of this book are intimately familiar with campus recruiting, having personally experienced the process from the candidate's perspective. Studies indicate that approximately 50 percent of entry-level managerial and professional personnel are hired using campus recruiting. Our own survey results indicate that college recruiting is an important source, particularly for technical/professional employees.

As previously discussed, few organizations have totally incorporated the philosophy and practices of total quality. Those few know that change and improvement must continue and become a way of life.

Thus, campus recruiting becomes a critical recruitment source because it provides the management personnel that will shape the future direction of the organization. The college graduates your organization hires today are still somewhat malleable and can be shaped to the new quality paradigm. They will be the movers and shakers of the early twenty-first century and will be the key to the organization's transformation to quality. Unlike their predecessors, they have not been shaped by years of operating in the traditional organizational setting. Following are some guidelines for improving the campus recruiting process.

1. Make every effort to improve the relationship with those institutions where you regularly recruit or send students. Instead of complaining about the knowledge and skill level of college graduates and railing against the system, take steps to increase the relevant skill level of those students. Initiatives such as the TI and ISU experience demonstrate that such efforts are possible. And TI is not alone. A number of quality-oriented organizations including American Express, Ford Motor Company, IBM, Milliken, Motorola, Procter & Gamble, and Xerox have created a Leadership Steering Committee to facilitate industrial and academic partnerships through a total quality forum.[12] Other examples of improved interaction may include co-op programs, summer employment, managers or professionals as adjunct instructors, and site visits by faculty or administrators.

2. To be effective, recruiters must be trained to assess important quality attributes. Thomas L. Watkins, Associate Dean for Graduate Studies at the University of Denver's Graduate School of Business, recently took the business community to task for its inconsistent approach to recruiting and selection. Watkins points out that businesses and the media have long criticized business schools for failing to turn out graduates with the necessary skills to perform effectively in today's work environment. He goes on to point out than many business schools have taken that criticism to heart and have adjusted their curriculums to address such issues as communication, problem solving, team building, and quality. In Watkins' own words,

> *Businesses told us they wanted those skills and attributes. But while they "talk the talk" at the top, they don't "walk the walk" on the ground, where recruiting takes place. Time after time, . . . students have come back from job interviews, both on campus and off, and told us that the recruiter never got any closer to asking about "soft skills" than "How well did you do in accounting"?*[13]

Recruiters need to be carefully trained in planning and conducting effective interviews, and in ensuring that the content of the interviews includes a focus on quality-related KSAPs. Chapters 9 and 10 will address this important topic. Recruiters should also be trained to answer the various questions posed by applicants.

3. If you haven't already, begin to investigate the possible use of resume databases to aid in your search for viable candidates. For those firms that do considerable college recruiting, these databases show a great deal of promise and appear to be the wave of the future. The use of such a database system allows corporate recruiters to receive and scan resumes prior to a campus visit. Recruiters can then be more selective in terms of the schools visited and students interviewed.[14] These databases provide one more example of how the firm can develop better relations with its schools (suppliers). Firms can work closely with schools to ensure that resumes include appropriate content (quality in, quality out).

4. Provide more substance and less glitz with your recruiting material. Students want clear and detailed information about the job(s) and organization in question. Complete and accurate information provides students with the kind of information needed to assess a match. Provide ample time during the initial (school site) interview for giving this information.

Advertising. One very common method of recruiting is advertising. Advertising media can range from the typical classified newspaper ad to very complex and glitzy campaigns on radio or television. Major approaches to advertising include newspapers, radio, television, direct mail, magazines (including trade and professional journals and newsletters), and directories. For a full discussion of the advantages and disadvantages of each medium, along with how and when to use each, the reader should review the note references shown at the conclusion of this chapter. However, experts generally agree that ads should include the following minimum information.

1. An accurate, brief description of the job, including primary duties and responsibilities

2. Job specifications, including education, experience, and KSAPs necessary to succeed on the job

3. Compensation range and fringe benefits

4. The location of the job

5. Directions on how and where to apply

In preparation for writing this book, the authors reviewed hundreds of print advertisements in newspapers, trade and professional journals, and newsletters with special attention given to those ads that included quality-related job specifications (qualifications). While we were encouraged by the growing number of ads looking for people with quality-related attributes (for example, CQE certification, ability to work in a team environment), based on our review, we have added a few suggestions for improving advertising effectiveness.

1. **Relate recruitment and total quality strategy.** At the expense of being redundant, our first suggestion is that these efforts at recruitment be consistent with the overall quality strategy of the organization. Ads should emphasize the more intangible benefits of joining a TQM organization. A climate that truly fosters involvement and empowerment, extensive training and development programs, enriched jobs, creativity, and so on gives the organization a recruiting advantage for attracting the superior applicant, and should be communicated to prospective candidates. If the goal of the ad is to sell the job and organization, why not go with your strengths as a TQM organization? Exhibit 6.1 provides an example of such an ad from our 3M cohesion case.

2. **Communicate expectations.** In those situations where special demands or working conditions are required on the job, those requirements should be communicated in the ad. This does not mean a full-blown realistic job preview (RJP) as discussed later in this chapter. It does mean that major or unusual demands should be included in the ad. If the job requires the person to spend two or three weeks each month visiting company plants in Findlay, Ohio, and Madrid, Spain, then that information should be communicated.

3. **Be more creative.** Our final suggestion is to be a little more creative in generating these advertisements. On the whole, the ads we reviewed were extremely bland and unimaginative. It seems a bit ironic that organizations spend millions of dollars developing original and entertaining ads to sell us everything from pickles to pizzas to pantyhose, but are reluctant to go outside established boundaries when generating their employment ads. Remember the company mission statement that pronounced "Our employees are our most important resource"? Well then, translate that into action.

Exhibit 6.1. A quality-oriented ad example from 3M Canada.

PROCESS OPERATORS

At 3M Canada Inc. we believe that success comes through commitment to customer satisfaction and the continuous improvement of our products, quality and services. If you share this vision, we may have a challenging opportunity available for you.

3M Canada has several openings in its new Brockville plant for process operators. Successful candidates will become members of a high-performance, self-managed work team in our state-of-the-art tape making facility.

We are looking for candidates who:

- Have a minimum of Grade 12 education or equivalent
- Are willing to work rotating shifts on a 24-hour, 7-day basis.
- Enjoy working in a diverse team environment
- Are capable of learning and performing all operator job functions in the plant
- Have excellent interpersonal and communication skills

3M offers competitive compensation and a full benefits package. We offer interesting and challenging work in a friendly, safe, supportive atmosphere. Applicants may be asked to complete a number of tests and group exercises, as well as interviews before being offered a position.

All qualified applicants are invited to complete an application at the 3M Brockville site, 60 California Ave., Brockville. We will be receiving applications from March 1–March 6, 1993 only, from 8:30 am–8:00 pm Monday–Friday and from 8:30 am–4:00 pm on Saturday. In order to keep this process as smooth as possible, we ask that people use the following schedule:

Surnames beginning with:

Monday	A–C
Tuesday	D–J
Wednesday	K–M
Thursday	N–S
Friday	T–Z
Saturday	Open

Please note that NO special consideration will be given to those candidates showing up early to complete applications. Also, no phone calls, please!

 Employment and Immigration Canada

3M gratefully acknowledges the support and assistance of the Canada Employment Centre in our hiring process.

3M Canada Inc.
P.O. Box 755
Brockville, Ontario
K6V 5W1

3M

3M Canada Inc. encourages applications from women, men, members of visible minorities, aboriginal peoples and persons with disabilities.

Used with permission.

More creative ads might include catchy or witty headlines, the use of endorsements from present employees, incentives or come-ons (for example, sign-on bonuses, relocation expenses, help for the spouse), light or amusing illustrations, community and recreational attractions, and the pluses of joining a TQM organization. In short, we encourage those involved in recruiting to apply some of their quality training when constructing advertisements. Pull out that TQM training binder, look up the topic *brainstorming,* and use those rules of brainstorming to generate your next recruitment ad. Not only will the process generate a more effective ad, but it will be fun.

Exhibit 6.2 provides an extreme, but actual, example of such a creative job ad sent to a university's Cooperative Education and Career Center office by a prospective employer prior to its recruiting visit. Because the ad reflected what many of that office's recruiters were searching for in student characteristics, the office duplicated the ad and disseminated it to its student clients at the university.

Exhibit 6.2. Example of a creative ad sent to a university's Cooperative Education and Career Center.

Meet the Wolf

A Wolf is one who attacks a job with both zeal and impatience; who recognizes that productivity has dimensions of both quality and quantity; who despises shoddy performance and is intolerant to mediocrity; who has the tenacity and determination to see the tough tasks through to completion.

Being a Wolf does not mean having a degree or taking prescribed courses or having a certain amount of professional experience, though it does embrace some of these elements. It is a way of life, a lifetime of study, a state of mind, and a relentless drive for excellence.

Being a Wolf means being extremely proficient in a specific field and interested in the job. The Wolf has a passionate thirst for it. The Wolf is not only a specialist, but a generalist who understands an organization's overall objectives.

A Wolf is particularly attentive to "the hand that feeds" (the Customer). He/she is acutely aware of what drives his/her existence and is constantly aware of fulfilling those needs and striving to go beyond expectations.

The Wolf understands that, as part of the Pack, he/she is much more powerful than when alone. The Pack members support, nurture, collaborate, learn from each other, and leverage each other's skills. The Wolf lives and dies by the Pack. The Pack's strength comes from the spirit, collaboration, and skills of its individuals.

The Wolf will not be fazed by "that's the way we do things" or "that's the type of organization we are." The Wolf will ask "Why?" and expect to grow, but only through exceptional performance. The motivations of that person are objectives, goals, and accomplishments. The Wolf is hungry, alert, opportunistic, and creative/adaptive. A Wolf gets things done.

Reprinted by permission.

Executive Search Firms. According to our survey results, executive search firms are the second most frequently used external source for recruiting management personnel. Only advertising is described as being used more frequently. It is safe to assume that the frequency of using search firms increases as openings occur further up the organizational hierarchy.

Such firms are often referred to as *headhunters* because their search is frequently targeted at managers who are already employed. Search firms differ from professional employment agencies in several ways, including fee structure, client relationships, time commitments, and so on. Typically, such firms are very expensive and require retainer and payment fees even when the opening is filled through other sources. They also require a very close working relationship with the organization and often take on many of the responsibilities for screening and assessing candidates.

As a major external source for recruiting managerial personnel, executive search firms can become a critical component of any quality initiative. Juran, Deming, and other quality gurus have consistently pointed to the importance of leadership to quality improvement. As previously discussed, top management must provide the vision, direction, resources, and reward systems necessary to achieve quality. Similarly, middle managers must embrace the quality initiative and provide the impetus for making quality happen. These are the folks that are responsible for various organizational systems and subsystems and establishing the climate for process and quality improvement. If management is critical to quality improvement and executive search firms are a major source for filling management slots, then why not align the use of this important source with the organization's quality effort?

While this alignment seems to make sense, the unfortunate reality is that many so-called quality-focused organizations have not made this obvious connection. While we don't mean to beat a dead horse, the new, quality manager must possess more than skills and experience in a particular industry and functional specialty. The critical quality-related attributes for managers previously described (for example, customer orientation, skill in implementing organizational change, flexibility/adaptability) must be incorporated into any recruiting and screening efforts. Following are some suggestions for making the most of this important recruiting source.

First, remember that the search firm is a supplier and, as such, should be evaluated in terms of the quality of its services and products. That means taking a close look at how the firm conducts its business prior to using its services. Possible quality indicators include the following:

1. Does the firm focus on a particular industry (for example, health care) or does it attempt to be everything for everybody? Generally speaking, the industry-specific firms are preferred over those that sell themselves as jack-of-all-trades.

2. Is one individual (or small group) responsible for the search or is the process fragmented? Better service is usually provided when an individual or individuals are responsible for all phases of the search. They research the organization in terms of needs (job analysis), conduct the search, and do the screening and assessment of candidates.

3. Does the firm use systematic and relevant procedures for screening and evaluating candidates? Because executive search firms typically do much of the screening and assessment of candidates, it is important that they use reliable and valid procedures. Applying the principles discussed in chapter 3 can do much to help you select the best possible firm.

4. Does the firm use primary resources for locating potential candidates? Typically, the most effective firms are those that have direct ties with various professionals and industries and do not have to rely solely on secondary resources such as professional directories, resume files, or ads.

Evaluating Recruitment Sources

To this point, our discussion has avoided the question of which of the various recruitment sources is best. Should the organization put its efforts and money into advertising or would the budget be better spent on using an employment agency? Which approach will have the highest payoff to the organization? In an attempt to answer that question, a number of research studies have compared the various recruitment sources in terms of such variables as cost, quality of recruit, longevity with the firm, frequency of use, and general organizational preference. And while those studies have shown mixed results (with the possible exception of the positive effect of internal referrals), two important conclusions are apparent. First, there are significant differences between the various sources in terms of effectiveness. Second, those differences in effectiveness depend on the situation. It depends on the specific job in question, the level (blue-collar, professional, managerial), the geographic location of the firm, and so on. In short, the primary conclusion that can be drawn from the research is that each organization (or possibly division or plant) should systematically collect its own effectiveness data and use that information to determine bottom-line payoff to the organization.

When making such decisions, the quality-oriented organization should refer to the standard adage that "quality begins and ends with data." Rather than relying on intuition or past practices ("we've always done it that way"), the recruitment process can be systematically analyzed and improved. Cascio has identified a number of cost and quality analyses that can be performed on a regular basis to improve the efficiency and effectiveness of the staffing process (see Figure 6.3).

Figure 6.3. Recruitment quality measures.

- Cost of operations
- Cost per hire
- Cost per hire by source
- Total resume inputs
- Resume inputs by source
- Quality of resumes by source
- Source yield and source efficiency
- Time lapse between recruiting stages by source
- Time lapse between recruiting stages by acceptance versus rejection
- Geographical sources of candidates
- Individual recruiter activity
- Individual recruiter efficiency
- Acceptance/offer ratio
- Offer/interview ratio
- Interview/invitation ratio
- Invitation/resume input ratio
- Biographical data analysis against acceptance/rejection data
- Analysis of post-visit and rejection questionnaires
- Analysis of reasons for acceptance and termination
- Analysis of post-reporting-date follow-up interviews
- Placement test scores on hires versus rejections
- Placement test scores versus observed performance
- Salary-offered-acceptance versus rejections
- Salary versus age, year of first degree, and total work experience.

Source: Cascio, Wayne F., Applied Psychology in Personnel Management, 4/e, © 1991, pp. 258–259. Reprinted by permission of Prentice Hall, Upper Saddle River, New Jersey.

Cascio goes on to recommend that those analyses should be presented graphically for ease of interpretation and communication. We wholeheartedly agree with Cascio when he states: "As is true of other organizational subsystems, a highly coordinated, systemic view of the recruiting process is indispensable."[15] Table 6.2 shows how such data can be used to evaluate the effectiveness of different recruitment sources for our hypothetical Ajax plant case. Such data can be used to help make recruitment source decisions and improve the recruitment process. The data provided, coupled with cost per hire by source data, clearly show where future recruiting efforts should focus. Given the success rates for employee referrals and walk-ins, along with the low cost per hire for each, the strategy for improvement becomes obvious.

Attracting and Keeping the Best

We have previously described recruitment as the process of attracting qualified applicants that meet the current and future needs of the organization. So what steps can be taken to attract a skilled and motivated workforce? We contend that one of the best ways is to become a quality-oriented organization in the first place. The more the organization embraces quality, the easier it becomes to attract and retain a top-quality workforce. Several studies have shown the importance of organization reputation when recruiting applicants. The vast majority of quality-oriented organizations have a great reputation as places to work. It is not by accident that many of the best companies to work for are considered quality-oriented organizations (for example, Federal Express, Motorola, Ford, Procter & Gamble, Steelcase, Hewlett-Packard, and 3M).

Employees in today's workforce want to be involved and empowered. They want variety and enriched jobs, and they appreciate the chance to grow and develop in their careers. With its emphasis on training, group problem solving, employee participation, and continuous change, the quality organization affords the employee that opportunity. Thus, the more ingrained the quality culture, the easier it becomes to attract and retain a highly qualified workforce. This, in turn, allows the organization to further increase its quality-oriented culture. This cycle will continue to feed on itself, allowing the organization to steadily improve its workforce and reinforce its quality culture (see Figure 6.4).

This ability of the organization to attract skilled and motivated workers will become increasingly important as we move toward the year 2000. A shortage of skilled and motivated workers is projected for the near future, and more than just dollars will be needed to at-

Table 6.2. Recruitment source analysis for the team member position at Ajax.

Recruitment source	Applicants	Screened as potentially qualified	Took and passed assessment 1. Skills inventory 2. Test	Took and passed interview	Accepted offer	One-year survival rate
Employee referrals	50	36 (72%)	29 (58%)	26 (52%)	25 (50%)	23 (46%)
Newspaper ads	210	97 (46%)	52 (25%)	36 (17%)	32 (15%)	26 (12%)
Walk-ins	40	26 (60%)	18 (45%)	14 (35%)	12 (30%)	11 (28%)
State employment agencies	100	41 (41%)	21 (21%)	14 (14%)	11 (11%)	8 (8%)
Total	400	200	120	90	80	68

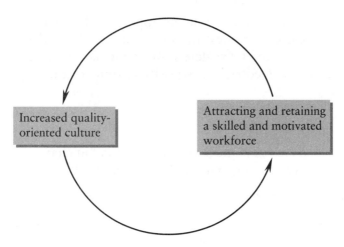

Figure 6.4. The quality culture/attraction cycle.

tract and retain the very best. Total quality directly affects the quality of work life of its employees and greatly enhances the reputation of the organization.

Another approach for improving the firm's ability to attract and retain the very best applicants is to systematically examine the recruiting process and make improvements. For example, one particularly pesky question that often haunts those involved in recruitment is, "Why does a particularly qualified and sought-after applicant drop out of the process or reject a job offer?" The solution is to systematically identify the major causes or reasons for the withdrawal, then take appropriate action to remedy the situation. One such effort was recently undertaken by Prudential Insurance and Financial Services.[16] This study is used to demonstrate how an organization can systematically examine its recruitment process and make improvements, particularly as it relates to qualified applicants.

Prudential examined its recruitment and hiring process for agents over a three-year period and found that more than 200,000 applicants showed interest in the position of agent. Of that number, approximately 11,000 were hired. Of particular interest to Prudential was the finding that of the approximately 190,000 not hired, 75,000 were considered to be potentially hireable (they had successfully passed the tests and screening requirements). This was especially alarming given the fact that most offices around the country were not meeting their hiring objectives. Also of concern was the fact that many of those applicants went on to work for other insurance companies or took jobs in sales.

To find out why these qualified applicants had left the process, Prudential developed a survey and hired an outside marketing firm to contact these individuals to determine why they had dropped out. While much of the feedback was positive, some of the negative findings included

- Being poorly treated by some of the offices

- Having a lack of contact with the person "in charge" (for example, given testing material by clerical or office staff)

- Getting lost in the shuffle

- Being oversold on the position (for example, somewhat deceptive advertising about the position)

Using this information, along with other information collected, Prudential made systematic changes in its recruitment and selection process. Some of those changes included

- The development of a recruitment video to be shown to all applicants (standardized process with an RJP)

- An approval procedure on all ads to ensure their accuracy and credibility

- The creation of specialized recruiting positions at the various offices to ensure proper treatment

- The development of a recruiting manual to train personnel in how to treat candidates in a professional manner

- An improved, standardized system for tracking applicants at various stages of the staffing process

- The development of behaviorally based interview guides for those involved in conducting interviews

The Prudential case clearly shows how any organization, large or small, can systematically collect the data necessary to improve its staffing process. While smaller firms may not be able to hire a marketing research firm (although the cost was nominal), they can most certainly collect data on why potentially qualified applicants reject an offer and then use that information to make improvements.

This issue of getting viable candidates into the pipeline and keeping them there has become increasingly important. For many of the firms the authors work with, the primary staffing issue is not making selection decisions. Rather, it is obtaining enough qualified individuals in the applicant pool to allow for making screening decisions.

Decreasing Employment Process Cycle Time: A Case Study

The following case describes how one organization, the University of Hartford, used a total quality methodology to improve its staffing process. The case does an excellent job of illustrating many of the principles previously discussed and, as such, provides an excellent model for firms interested in improving their staffing processes.[17]

As part of the university's TQM initiative, the Human Resources Development (HRD) office participated in an 18-hour workshop that introduced the basic principles and concepts of total quality, tools and processes used, and guidance into initial improvement activities. One goal of the total quality initiative was to identify critical departmental processes (customer driven) and select one such process for an improvement initiative. As a result, the HRD office's quality improvement team decided to analyze and make improvements in the staffing process. In particular, it focused its efforts on employment process cycle times. Following is an abbreviated description of the process improvement methodology used by the team.

- **Step 1.** The first step was to assemble process cycle time data for the previous two years (see Table 6.3).

- **Step 2.** Next, to assess the stability of the process itself over time, a control chart was constructed (see Figure 6.5).

Table 6.3. Staffing process cycle time statistics.

	Time period	
Category	1993–1994 (pre)	January–May 1994 (post)
Cycle times		
Staffing process	58.0 days	51.1 days
Committee searches	106.8	102.7
Supervisory searches	55.6	47.9

Source: Mark G. Borzi, "Decreasing Employment Process Cycle Time: A Personnel Exemplar" (unpublished paper, 1994): 28. Reprinted by permission.

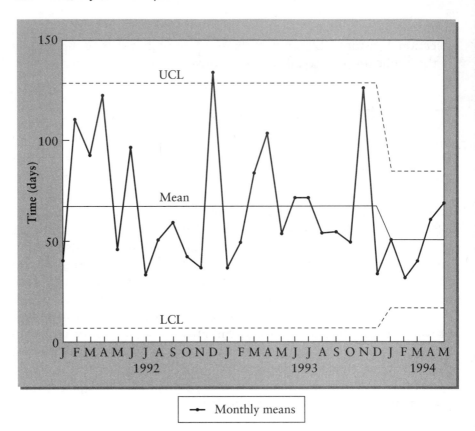

Figure 6.5. Staffing process cycle time control chart.

Source: Mark G. Borzi, "Decreasing Employment Process Cycle Time: A Personnel Exemplar" (unpublished paper, 1994): 29. Reprinted by permission.

Note that the process has special cause variation and would be considered out of control (one point is above the upper control limit of the chart, and two out of three points are outside the two sigma level). The group's goal then became one of reducing that process variation along with the average time ($\overline{X}$) required to fill a position.

- **Step 3.** The group then developed a flowchart showing the critical activities in the staffing sequence (see Figure 6.6).

The team used this process mapping to identify problem areas within their own functions and to make specific improvements to increase the effectiveness of the department process (e.g., elimination of reports, minimizing delays, empowering front-line staff). While these changes helped the HR function operate

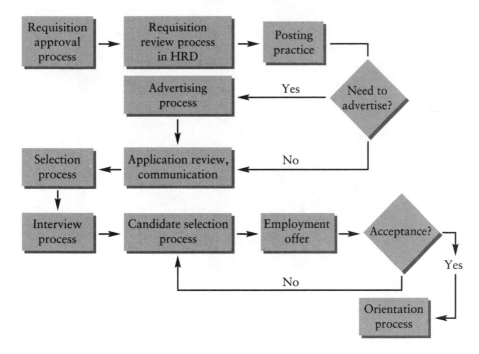

Figure 6.6. Critical activities in the staff process flowchart.

Source: Mark G. Borzi, "Decreasing Employment Process Cycle Time: A Personnel Exemplar" (unpublished paper, 1994): 30. Reprinted by permission.

the process more efficiently, it did not address many of the fundamental causes for delays.

• **Step 4.** All employment searches (1992 and 1993) that took longer than 30 days were examined for causes of delay. Figure 6.7 provides a Pareto chart showing a breakdown of those causes.

The number one cause for delay was found to be supervisory in nature and, as such, became the focal point of the group's effort. Later on, the group discovered this to be a good choice because other vital few causes (interviews and advertising) were addressed in the action steps identified to deal with supervisory delay.

• **Step 5.** To begin the process of assessing the root causes for supervisory delay, a cause-and-effect diagram was constructed and is presented in Figure 6.8. A total of 48 potential reasons for supervisory delay were identified and sorted into the three basic areas of personnel, communication, and process.

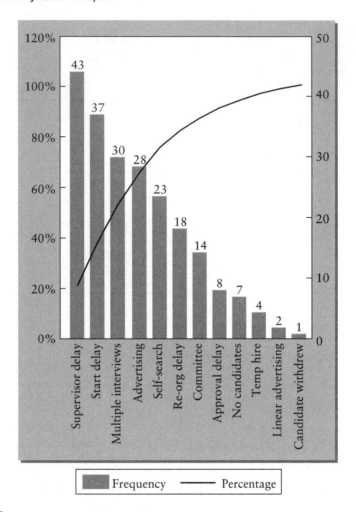

Figure 6.7. Pareto chart of employment search delays.

Source: Mark G. Borzi, "Decreasing Employment Process Cycle Time: A Personnel Exemplar" (unpublished paper, 1994): 32. Reprinted by permission.

- **Step 6.** From the 48 causes and follow-up discussion with supervisory personnel, three general change strategies, along with specific action steps, were developed for implementation. They included the following:

    1. Improved feedback (for example, formalized conversations between the HR staff person coordinating the search and the hiring supervisor, and a job sheet that prompts and documents feedback to the supervisor at critical points)

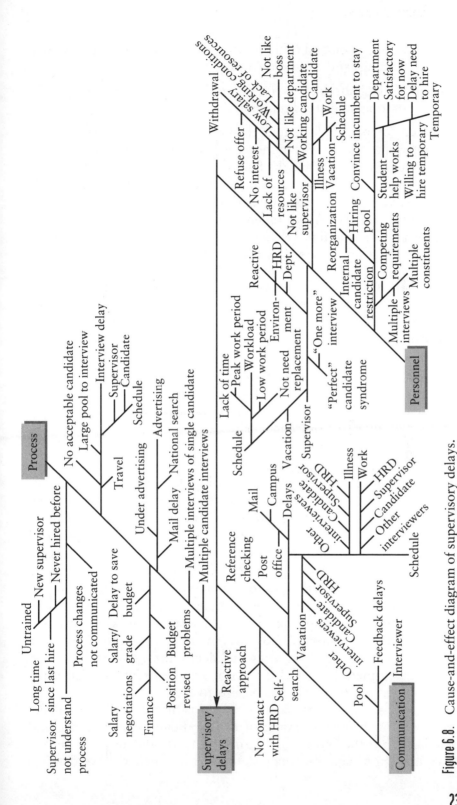

Figure 6.8. Cause-and-effect diagram of supervisory delays.

Source: Mark G. Borzi, "Decreasing Employment Process Cycle Time: A Personnel Exemplar" (unpublished paper, 1994): 30. Reprinted by permission.

2. Information and training (for example, periodic supervisory briefings and a question and answer series)

3. Staffing alternatives (for example, student employment, job sharing, and cross-training)

- **Step 7.** Once implemented, the final step of the process improvement effort was to monitor and evaluate changes in the cycle time data. While the final results of the change effort were not reported, the initial results for the first five months of 1994 were very positive. (See Table 6.3 and Figure 6.5 for post-intervention results.) A two-tailed *t*-test comparing the two groups at time one and time two show that the differences in the data are significant ($t = 15.48$ with $df = 27$, $p > .01$).

We used this case to illustrate possible change initiatives not because it represents the most sophisticated process improvement effort the authors discovered (although we think the initiative is excellent), but because it demonstrates what a process improvement team is capable of doing with minimal (approximately two days') training in total quality and the right mind-set.

Internal Recruitment Sources

In our get-me-a-warm-body scenario at the beginning of this chapter, Mike must replace one of his supervisors. One of the first decisions Mike and the HR manager need to make is whether they should seek applicants from among those already working at the plant (or company) or look externally to fill the position. With the exception of entry-level jobs, the majority of organizations try to fill positions internally, although some notable exceptions do exist.

There are several advantages to internal recruiting when filling positions. First, it enhances employee morale, motivation, and commitment. The perceived opportunity to get ahead in the company is a strong incentive for most employees. Failure to promote or advance from within can be very frustrating and demoralizing to employees. In fact, the resentment from such an action can be so intense that it becomes difficult for an outsider to be effective.

A second reason for internal recruiting is the advantage of having a more thorough understanding of the candidate's performance and potential. While the knowledge of an external candidate's past performance is often meager or nonexistent, decision makers have detailed performance information available concerning internal applicants. Performance evaluation data, progression history, training and development information, and formal or informal feedback from superiors, peers, and subordinates are all data sources that can be used to strengthen the decision process.

A third reason for recruiting from within is that it is generally less costly and time-consuming. Advertising, screening, and site visits for external candidates can be very laborious and expensive. Related to this is the time and cost associated with orienting a new employee to the organization. Internal candidates already know the ins and outs of the company and have established associations and networks. They do not have to learn about the organization.

Finally, the quality-oriented company can use the internal recruiting process to strengthen its quality culture. Incorporating quality dimensions into appraisal forms, including quality attributes and experiences into promotion specifications, and developing quality-related skills with present employees are all ways to reinforce a quality environment. One company where the authors consult, for example, strongly encourages active team participation as a necessary step for promotion. In the words of one professional, "Team membership is one of the tickets you'd better get punched if you want to get ahead." At this firm, team membership typically includes top management personnel, and employees quickly learn that active membership is key to being visible and taken seriously by the organization. Employees at any company will be encouraged to climb on the quality bandwagon when they get the message that the company is serious about quality. No better way exists to send that message than to start rewarding, through promotion, those individuals who have embraced the new paradigm.

With all the advantages of recruiting internally, why would any organization consider going to the outside to fill a position? Basically, because there are some disadvantages to internal recruiting and some sound reasons for looking externally. One argument for going to the outside is the infusion of new blood into the organization. This line of thinking suggests that exclusive internal recruiting perpetuates the status quo and reinforces a narrow perspective. Proponents of this argument can point to numerous examples (Michael Eisner at Disney, Lee Iacocca at Chrysler, or Robert Townsend at Avis) where an outsider has been able to come in and be extremely successful in turning a company around.

A second concern often voiced is the domino effect of making changes internally. One internal move can start a chain reaction of moves that can be very disruptive to the organization. This disruption is often compounded in a quality-driven organization where the roles of employees have been broadened. For example, problem-solving teams can lose a valuable member halfway through a major project. Or, employees who are given much broader responsibilities in a reengineered process are more difficult to replace. Or, coworkers become annoyed when they find out that the unit's computer whiz kid will be moving on to bigger and better things. Many managers become frustrated with these constant changes (unless, of course, it's their own promotion) and are sometimes reluctant to part with their good employees. They are also hesitant to establish long-term problem-solving teams whose membership is likely to change dramatically over the course of the project.

Another disadvantage of internal recruitment is the potential for politics to influence staff decisions. While external candidates can be assessed objectively (unless it's somebody's relative), internal evaluations are often clouded with political and extraneous considerations. This problem can be negated by following the advice given throughout this book.

Finally, sometimes firms are forced to look externally because present employees may lack the necessary attributes required for the position.

Some Rules of Thumb on Internal vs. External Recruiting

What advice should we give Mike and the HR manager at Ajax? Should they look inside for their new supervisor, or would they be better off to go to the outside to fill the position? While no hard-and-fast rules exist for making this decision, professional wisdom suggests that, wherever possible, organizations should look internally when filling positions at the bottom end of the organizational hierarchy. Employees should clearly see the link between their efforts and the potential to get ahead in the organization. Organizations forced to continually look externally for filling first- and second-level management positions would be well advised to take a close look at their training and development efforts. Chances are they are deficient.

While internal candidates should receive favored status at lower levels of the hierarchy, that bias should be tempered as the organization looks to fill higher level management positions. The further up in the hierarchy, the more credence should be given to the new-blood argument. While the majority of openings should continue to be filled internally, the infusion of new ideas and approaches is healthy for the organization. This is particularly true when the organization is considering dramatic and strategic changes in direction, such as the introduction of TQM or reengineering the company. Bringing in a few key management personnel who believe in quality and have the requisite skill and experience to help direct the change effort can do much to help ensure the success of the quality initiative.

Tell It Like It Is: Realistic Job Previews

Attracting potential employees to the organization is a primary goal of recruiting. But attempts by the organization to sell itself as a great place to work may give applicants inflated expectations about the nature and rewards of work. Numerous studies dealing with voluntary turnover have shown that "met expectation" is a critical factor in determining early withdrawal from the organization.[18] Early withdrawal can be extremely costly to the organization in terms of excessive recruiting and training expenses, as well as poor quality and service due to an inexperienced workforce. As discussed in chapter 3, turnover becomes a critical criterion in the quality organization.

Recent theory and research suggest that employers might do better to avoid sugar coating the message to applicants and to start providing RJPs. To avoid unfulfilled expectations and costly turnover, recruiting should initiate the process of accurate communications regarding the job and organization prior to the hiring decision. By providing an accurate description to applicants, the process of job choice is facilitated; those who accept employment will be more satisfied and thus be less likely to leave voluntarily.[19]

Although research results of RJPs have not been entirely consistent, it is clear that RJPs reduce voluntary turnover under certain circumstances. Research results show that survival rates can be expected to improve between 6 percent and 24 percent depending on the existing turnover rates.[20]

RJPs are particularly critical in the total quality setting where employees are expected to exhibit a much broader repertoire of attributes (for example, openness to learning, flexibility, teamwork orientation, and so on) than the traditional environment. RJPs provide an excellent opportunity to communicate to the candidate the organization's customer orientation and commitment to quality. Some of those quality-related expectations might include the following:

- In our organization, the customer is king. Everything we do is aimed at meeting or exceeding the needs and expectations of our customers.

- Change is a fact of life at XYZ. We strive for continuous improvement and ask: "How can we do things better? Faster? Cheaper?"

- Teamwork and cooperation is a must. You will be expected to work in team situations to solve problems and meet organizational goals.

- Our employees must see themselves and their jobs as part of a larger process and system and cooperate with other employees, units, and functional areas to meet organizational goals.

- We have a very flat and lean organizational structure that somewhat limits promotional opportunities.

One useful tool used by the authors for developing RJP interview content is shown in Figure 6.9. Knowledgeable SMEs such as the interview team are asked to complete the "Tell It Like It Is" sheet. The form helps those involved in staffing articulate both the positive and negative aspects of the job and is divided into four areas (job, department or unit, organization, and location) to help SMEs focus on the broader notion of job as previously discussed. Figure 6.9 also shows what a completed form might resemble.

While an RJP should be included in any structured interview format, other RJPs typically offered by organizations include brochures, formal oral presentations, assessment center exercises, and films or videotapes. Most firms place the RJP early in the staffing process to allow for self-selection on the part of the candidate. One home-care firm that we know of has its job candidates (nurses, aides, social workers) spend two days working with its inner-city clients before a final hiring decision is made. This allows candidates to make a more informed decision concerning future employment.

These more elaborate efforts at RJPs typically require a more systematic effort at identifying pluses and minuses of the job. For example, the authors have in the past surveyed employees to determine what they like *most* and *least* about their jobs. Exhibit 6.3 presents results from such an effort for the job of customer information representative with a large utility company. This information can be combined with other data and expectations (quality commitment) and a formal RJP can be developed.

One final note concerning RJPs. Anyone who engages in such an effort will soon discover that what is considered a plus for one person

Figure 6.9. "Tell It Like It Is": Example of what an RJP might look like in practice.

Positive aspects of the job (SELL)	Negative aspects of the job (RJP)
Job:	**Job:**
• Self-directed, a lot of freedom in the job • Involvement in new and major projects that will affect the future of the company • Very technically challenging	• Requires constant training (e.g., new software) • Long hours, odd hours and shifts, and "on-call" may be required (e.g., plan to work two to three Saturdays per month) • May have to sit in front of computer terminal for several hours at a time (e.g., six hours/day)
Department or unit:	**Department or unit:**
• High visibility with top management and other departments/units • Coworkers are good group to work with, friendly and do much outside of work (e.g., softball team, golf league) • Flexible hours (rated on getting the job done)	• Older work environment (e.g., desks and furniture) • Not only an office job but entails working in a plant environment (e.g., wear steel toe shoes, get your hands dirty, perform hands-on tasks, etc.)
Organization:	**Organization:**
• Continued college/university education paid for by the company • Training and education during working hours are encouraged and supported by management • Casual dress code (no tennies or jeans) • Firm continues to be profitable and has a great reputation as a successful enterprise	• Organization structure is very flat and lean with limited opportunities for promotion • Firm has outsourced many of its operations with possibility that both the plant and the division are going to be sold • Extremely high expectations in terms of meeting customers' needs
Location:	**Location:**
• Close to metropolitan area (e.g., restaurants, theaters) • Easy access to major freeways	• Separated from rest of engineering (different building); must make several trips a day to other building to do job • Lots of traffic if choose to live in suburbs

Exhibit 6.3. Most- and least-liked characteristics of the job for customer information representatives.

"Like most"
1. Problem solving when helping customers (satisfying the customer and providing good service)
2. Customer relations and contact with the public
3. Coworker relations
4. Challenging and stimulating work
5. Feeling of accomplishment
6. Variety
7. Meeting and learning about different types of people
8. Salary and benefits
9. Being appreciated
10. Hours (work schedule)

"Like least"
1. Tolerating bad customers (dealing with irate and rude customers)
2. Emphasis is put on production, not quality
3. Other departments not cooperating
4. Treated like a child by supervisor
5. Pressure to meet supervisor's expectations
6. Low pay
7. Not enough help when it's needed, understaffed
8. Oversupervision
9. Short lunch period
10. Can't always follow a problem through to the end

---

may be viewed negatively by another. Witness the issue of salary as shown in Exhibit 6.3. To some customer service reps, the pay provided by the company is good and valued while for others it is too low and seen as negative. Thus, the old adage that "one person's junk is another person's treasure" appears to be true for RJPs. But whether or not some aspect of the job is viewed as positive or negative is of little consequence when developing an RJP. Letting the individual clearly know that the job requires a lot of travel is the inherent value of an RJP—not whether the person enjoys or dislikes the prospect of travel.

Applicant Information

Consistent with the notion of an RJP is the practice of informing candidates about the staffing process they will be expected to undergo if they hope to be selected. In addition to an RJP, many firms provide detailed information concerning the attributes to be measured as well as the assessment tools used in the process. Each candidate is provided with a clear description of the jobs in question and the entire staffing process. For example, in our 3M Canada cohesion case, candidates were provided with an applicant information booklet describing the staffing process. The booklet provided applicants with an overview of 3M Canada's staffing philosophy and expectations (see Exhibit 6.4).

The booklet goes on to describe in detail the entire selection process, including examples of each component and some tips on how to prepare for and take the exams. This no surprises approach to selection truly views the candidate as a customer and meets our previously described criterion of professionalism.

Summary

At this point, you should begin to fully understand our view that staffing is a process that can be systematically measured, analyzed, and improved. The simple fact is that any organization can do a better job of attracting more and better qualified candidates. A firm can also continually improve how it treats those candidates so as to keep the very best in the staffing pipeline and maintain positive perceptions from those who leave the process. Having concluded this chapter you should now be in a better position to step back and carefully examine your own recruitment process. Some of the questions you should be asking include the following:

- Do we have a complete flowchart of our recruitment process? Do all of our customers (internal and external) understand that process? Have we systematically examined that process in terms of cycle time, errors, confusion, rework, loss of high potential candidates, and so on?

- Do we do a good job of evaluating the quality of our recruitment sources? Are there ways to improve our relationships with those suppliers?

Exhibit 6.4. *Applicant Information Booklet* excerpt.

Introduction

Welcome! We are glad you are interested in employment with 3M. We are proud of our company and the people who make it a special place to work. At 3M Canada, we try hard to provide an atmosphere in which employees can make the best use of their skills. Since people are the single most important resource at 3M Canada, we take great care in selecting the people who join our company.

We believe that joining 3M involves two important questions. First, do *you* have the skills and abilities it takes to perform our jobs? Second, do *we* offer the jobs and work environment that you will find rewarding? If you wish to join 3M, *we both* must make a decision. *We* must decide whether *your* skills and abilities match our jobs. *You* must decide whether the opportunities *we* offer fit your goals.

This booklet will help each of us make our decision. It describe the jobs we offer at Brockville, the work settings they involve, and the skills they require. It also describes the steps we follow in evaluating applicants for 3M jobs. It gives a preview of the test you may take and describes the interview we use and other parts of our selection process.

We suggest that you use this booklet to get a clear understanding of our selection process and the jobs we offer. In this way, you can make the right decision too.

Working at 3M

The Brockville plant is new. Our employees work in many different jobs as part of a high-performance, self-managed work team.

We have two sets of job openings at the plant: *Operator* and *Technologist*. These people will comprise our production teams. An *Operator* is someone who performs the tasks necessary to run the production line. This includes ordering materials and ensuring quality, as well as running production. *Operators* are responsible for routine machine and equipment maintenance. In addition, an *Operator* rotates jobs on a regular basis and takes turns acting as the coordinator of team activities. A *Technologist* is responsible for maintenance of the equipment and machinery as well as assisting in the development of new processes. *Technologists* are members of the production team and also assist as needed in production. Both positions require good interpersonal skills, technical skills, and self-motivation.

Our jobs are rewarding. They are also mentally, and sometimes physically, demanding. All of our positions are salaried and require working on shifts that rotate around the clock every day of the week.

Source: 3M Canada's *Application Information Booklet.* Reprinted by permission.

- Are there ways that we can improve our treatment of applicants and enhance their views of our professionalism?

- Do we provide candidates with an RJP for the target position and the organization? Are applicants clear on the various steps included in the staffing process?

Every quality-oriented HR function should be sponsoring problem-solving teams that systematically attack these and other staffing-related issues and it should be continuously improving its processes. That is the message of this chapter, and it will remain the primary theme as we begin to examine the various tools that can and should be used to improve selection and promotion decisions.

Notes

1. Richard Blackburn and Bensen Rosen, "Total Quality and Human Resources Management: Lessons Learned from Baldrige Award-Winning Companies," *The Academy of Management Executive* (August 1993): 49–66.

2. Donald V. Sequeira, CAEtech, personal correspondence, August 1995.

3. H. Fred Walker, "Texas Instruments' and Iowa State University's Experience with the University Challenge Program," *Quality Progress* (July 1995): 103–106.

4. Ibid., 104.

5. Ibid.

6. Mobil Oil Company survey as reported in *ISO 9000 News, The International Journal of the ISO 9000 Forum,* Geneva, Switzerland (Jan.–Feb. 1995). See also *Quality Systems Update,* a publication of CEEM Information Service, Fairfax, Va. (June 1995). See also *ISO 9000 Registered Company Directory, North America:* CEEM Information Services, Fairfax, Va. (November 1994).

7. "Employee Attitudes on Teamwork, Empowerment, and Quality Improvement," ASQC/Gallup survey, 1993.

8. Richard Blackburn and Bensen Rosen, "Total Quality and Human Resources Management: Lessons Learned from Baldrige Award-Winning Companies."

9. Suzanne Axland, "Looking for a Quality Education?" *Quality Progress* (October 1991): 61–72.

10. Anne Calek, "Quality Progress' Fifth Quality in Education Listing," *Quality Progress* (September 1995), 27–77.

11. John P. Wanous, *Organizational Entry: Recruitment, Selection, Orientation, and Socialization of Newcomers* (Reading, Mass.: Addison-Wesley, 1992), 34–39.

12. H. Fred Walker, "Texas Instruments' and Iowa State University's Experience with the University Challenge Program."

13. Thomas L. Watkins, "What Do You Want from Us?" *Across the Board* (June 1993): 11–12.

14. B. Leanord, "Resume Databases to Dominate Field," *HR Magazine* (April 1993): 59–60.

15. Wayne F. Cascio, *Applied Psychology in Personnel Management*, 3rd ed. (Englewood Cliffs, NJ: Prentice Hall, 1987), 252.

16. Ronald M. Festa, "Why Don't They Take the Job? A Discussion of Non-Traditional Recruiting and Selection Issues," presentation at the Tenth Annual Conference of the Society for Industrial and Organizational Psychology, Orlando, Fla., May 20, 1995.

17. Mark G. Borzi, "Decreasing Employment Process Cycle Time: A Personnel Exemplar," unpublished paper, 1994. The case study is abstracted with permission from the author.

18. Lyman W. Porter and Richard M. Steers, "Organizational Work and Personal Factors in Employee Turnover and Absenteeism," *Psychological Bulletin* 80 (1973): 151–176.

19. Wanous, *Organizational Entry: Recruitment, Selection, Orientation, and Socialization of Newcomers*.

20. Ibid.

Personnel Assessment Tools: Assessing and Predicting Ability to Perform

Overview

In this and the following chapter we present a guide to assessment tools. We begin by profiling the variety of tools available for use in evaluating quality-relevant aptitude, knowledge, skills and personality/temperament. After a brief overview, we then take a closer look at the use of each of these tools in the quality improvement setting. In this chapter we focus on paper-and-pencil measures of ability, certification and knowledge tests, and biographical predictors. These measures have in common the fact that they are efficient, cost effective, and are best placed early in the selection process. For the most part, the tools detailed in this chapter assess the ability to perform. In chapter 8, we continue our in-depth look at tools and focus on those tools used to assess the individuals' temperament, fit within the quality culture, and motivation to perform. Throughout both of these chapters we provide you with examples of specific tests and measures and information on where you can inquire about the purchase and use of these tools.

Assessment Tools: Systematic Predictors of Performance

The technology of HR assessment has progressed substantially in recent years. A variety of techniques are available to the organization intent on assessing and predicting the individual's likelihood of performing well on the job. The following sections provide an overview of available assessment tools. We've restricted our discussion to those tools that have relevance to the assessment of quality-related attributes.

What Tools Are Available?

Before we present specific measures for use in the quality improvement setting, we believe it will be helpful to overview the alternate assessment tools and profile some of the strengths and weaknesses of each form of predictor. We introduce standardized written ability tests, work samples and simulations, job tryouts, biographical predictors (application blanks, skills inventories, biographical information blanks), selection interviews, performance appraisals, reference checks, and assessment centers.

Standardized Written Ability Tests. Standardized written (paper-and-pencil) ability tests present the applicant with a series of items designed to measure a specific mental ability. Standardized written ability tests are available to evaluate quality-related aptitudes, knowledge, and abilities. Their use, when appropriate for the job in question, is advantageous for the following reasons. First, the scores attained by standardized written tests are highly reliable. You can generally be assured that the measure is fairly stable and consistent. Second, standardized paper-and-pencil tests can be highly predictive of the applicant's ability to learn and perform the job. That is, they produce very favorable validity correlations. For example, the correlation between cognitive ability tests and subsequent performance in complex jobs (managerial, professional, industrial setup) is about $r = .58$.[1] To put the significance of that correlation in perspective, it means that the test would account for (explain, predict) about 34 percent of the subsequent variability in job performance. Imagine, one 40-minute test provides prediction sufficient to explain about one-third of the variability seen among individuals performing the job. Third, standardized written tests provide a large normative database against which the applicant's performance can be compared. Related to this point, you can also use norm data to benchmark your recruiting process by comparing how your applicants perform relative to others. Fourth, written tests are highly efficient and provide substantial information relative to their cost. You can learn a lot about the applicant's potential in a relatively brief period of time. Because of their efficiency, well-chosen standardized tests tend to meet our criterion of utility or ROI.

The most challenging problem associated with standardized paper-and-pencil tests is that they may result in disparate impact against racial minority groups. As you recall from the discussion in chapter 3, the organization should take steps to minimize the effects of disparate impact. While this does not mean that you should abandon the use of standardized tests, it is important to track and deal with any disparate effects. A second deficiency of standardized tests is that they sometimes do not resemble the job and, because of that, applicants may respond less favorably to them. Nonetheless, they are the most effective means of measuring many attributes, and we will profile a number of examples with potential applicability to your setting.

There are countless published standardized tests. In many cases you will want to obtain objective evaluations of tests you wish to consider. There are a number of reference guides, the most noteworthy of which are *The Mental Measurements Yearbook* and *Tests in Print*.[2] *The Mental Measurements Yearbook* provides critiques of each test, evidence of reliability and validity, and other information that will help you in your selection of appropriate tests.

Work Samples and Simulations. Some tests, by design, measure the extent to which applicants can perform important job responsibilities. Work samples and simulations provide information on how applicants respond to job-relevant situations. That is, the applicant performs activities that are typical of the activities performed on the job. Rather than asking the applicant how he'd respond to working in a team, these devices allow you to observe and evaluate his actual behavior and any products produced during testing.

There is a subtle, but important, distinction between work samples and work simulations. Work samples are actual pieces of the job—specific tasks performed on the job. The evaluation is essentially how well the task is performed, or whether the applicant can perform the test at all. A typing test is an example of a work sample. The test is scored by evaluating the product produced by the applicant.

Work simulations are similar to work samples in that they replicate what it is like to work on the job, but they are different in that the applicant's performance is scored along a set of dimensions (traits, characteristics). A common example is a team leadership assessment exercise. Applicants are assembled as a leaderless group and instructed to work on some job-relevant problem. Trained observers track and subsequently evaluate applicants along dimensions relevant to working in teams. (We discuss the merits of trained observers shortly in our review of assessment centers.)

Work samples and simulations are desirable for a number of reasons. First, when properly constructed, they are valid predictors of subsequent ability to perform the work. On average, the correlation between a well-constructed work sample or simulation and subsequent job performance is .44.[3] Second, applicants tend to respond very favorably to work samples. They look like the job, and consequently, from the perspective of the applicant, seem reasonable. Third, work samples give the applicant a preview of the job. By working through the test, the applicant learns more about what the job is like. Fourth, work samples tend to have less disparate impact against minority groups than do written tests.[4] We will present a number of exciting work samples and simulations used to assess ability and willingness to perform in quality improvement settings.

Job Tryouts. A logical extension of a work sample test is the traditional probationary or job tryout period. The individual is hired on a temporary basis, oriented and trained to the job and organization, and performance is reviewed over the interval of employment. (The surge in the use of contingent workers is, in part, due to organizations' interest in gaining an extended look at potential permanent employees.) The advantage is that you can acquire a thorough sense of the person's strengths and weaknesses, provided that a *systematic* means exists for tracking and evaluating performance over that job tryout period. Ideally, you will assess the temporary employee on a job analysis–based set of KSAPs. Without a systematic, valid tracking of performance, the job tryout loses effectiveness as a selection device.

Biographical Predictors. The best predictor of future behavior is past behavior in similar circumstances. Biographical information about the individual's past behavior and experiences can be collected in various ways, including interviews, application blanks, and the most elaborate of these devices, biographical inventories. We focus this section on the use of paper-and-pencil devices ranging from application blanks to biographical information.

Application blanks are useful in situations where the number of applicants is substantially greater than the number of openings (low

SR). Application blanks are particularly useful in determining whether or not the applicant meets minimum requirements and should therefore continue in the selection process. Consequently, where they are appropriately constructed and scored, they can greatly increase the utility of the staffing process by narrowing the applicant pool. We give a number of recommendations for improving application blanks later in this chapter.

Education and experience (skills) inventories are an innovative refinement of the application. This tool presents applicants with a listing of skills and relies on their self-reports regarding their skill proficiencies. Applicants identify skills they have mastered and present detailed biographical information addressing the experiences (education and training) through which the skills were developed. In a sense, skills inventories are extensions of application blanks and biographical information blanks focused specifically on a detailed listing of how and where the individual acquired various self-identified skills. We present examples of skills inventories used at 3M Canada later in this chapter.

Biographical information blanks and biographical inventories systematically collect information about the individual's past experience and use it to predict future performance. They are distinct from application blanks and weighted application blanks in a number of ways. First, they include a larger sample of items covering a much wider range of biographical, attitudinal, and preference questions. Additionally, question responses are presented in multiple choice format. More importantly, the content of biographical inventories is typically based on well-reasoned hypotheses about how past experiences relate to job performance. For example, we would hypothesize that one who has been active in the community and joined clubs and organizations would tend to function well in team settings. Biographical items would then be written to assess the history of relevant interests and activities. Finally, a well-developed biographical inventory is research based. That is, we conduct empirical research to determine if, in fact, that historic pattern of activity in organizations does relate to effective performance as a team member. Appropriately constructed, biographical information blanks and inventories can add much to the prediction of training, performance, and tenure. For example, the correlations between well-developed biographical predictors and subsequent performance in various occupations groupings are: $r = .38$ for managers, $r = .52$ for clerical workers, $r = .50$ for sales workers, and $r = .41$ for scientific/engineering occupations.[5] We examine various tools for biographical prediction later in this chapter.

Selection Interviews. The selection interview is the most widely used selection tool. Unfortunately, as it is typically configured in organizations, it does not conform to the standards we hold for measurement devices. There has emerged a clear consensus on how the interview can be improved: It can be made more reliable, valid, and contribute greater ROI. For example, validity estimates of the structured, focused interview process we profile approach a range in correlation with subsequent job performance from about $r = .49$ to about $r = .62$.[6] Because of its wide usage and its potential usefulness when appropriately conducted, we devote chapters 9 and 10 to the design and implementation of a valid interview process.

Performance Appraisals. The use of performance appraisals is a controversial issue in quality improvement settings. Many, including Deming, Scherkenbach, and Ronald D. Moen have called for the elimination of systems that focus on and evaluate the performance of the individual.[7] While we cannot address the controversy in detail in this book, we do believe that there is emerging a context in which performance appraisals can contribute to the success of a quality improvement effort. Clearly, we have seen change in the recommendation from some in the quality community, and a performance appraisal process can be designed to serve the goals of the quality initiative. We refer the interested reader to the recent work *The Reward and Recognition Process in Total Quality Management*.[8] With that said, the purpose of this section is not to argue either for or against the use of performance appraisals. Rather, we take the stance that appraisals remain a fact of life in the majority of organizations and are likely to remain so for some time to come. In fact, if you review the data we present in Table 7.1, you will see that the performance appraisal process is among the most widely used sources of data for promotion decisions, and this is true across all occupational groupings. Given that reality, the question becomes: How can we use that information most effectively in staffing decisions?

Reference Checks. Reference checks involve collection of evaluations from those familiar with the applicant. On the surface, it seems reasonable that they would contribute much useful information to the selection process. However, as typically used, they contribute far less to predicting subsequent performance than many would suspect. Studies show that the validity of reference data ranges from $r = .16$ for predicting promotions to about $r = .26$ for predicting subsequent ratings of job performance.[9] Reference checks tend to focus on four categories of information: employment and educational background, appraisal of an

Table 7.1. Use of various assessment devices.

Assessment device	Use reported in ASQC sustaining member organizations					
	Hourly	Technical/ professional	Lower management	Middle management	Top management
Interview	87%	96%	93%	93%	93%
Knowledge tests	34%	16%	8%	7%	5%
Written aptitude/ability tests	46%	21%	11%	8%	6%
Work samples	24%	10%	4%	2%	1%
Team interaction simulations	4%	5%	6%	4%	6%
Standardized personality measures	5%	8%	9%	14%	13%
Assessment centers	5%	2%	6%	7%	9%
Application blanks	80%	81%	78%	71%	61%
Biographical inventories	20%	34%	33%	36%	40%
Reference/background checks	70%	83%	79%	80%	73%
Performance/appraisals (for promotion decisions)	70%	80%	84%	81%	79%

applicant's character and personality, evaluation of an applicant's job performance, and the willingness of the reference to rehire the applicant.[10] Because of the important role that references play in most settings, recommendations for their effective use appear in Exhibit 7.1.

Assessment Centers. We've presented assessment centers last because, typically, they represent the assembly of multiple tools, including most of those we've reviewed thus far. The tools are used to systematically assess the behavior and performance of a small set of participants (usually six to 12). Specifically, assessment centers are characterized by the following: (1) there are multiple assessment tools, including various work samples and simulations; (2) the tools are designed to measure multiple attributes (KSAPs); (3) the participants are observed by multiple assessors; (4) the assessors are trained to observe, record, and categorize behavior; (5) subsequently, the assessors meet and produce consensus profiles of each participant's performance, strengths, and development needs.

Work simulations (typically a component of assessment centers) have great relevance for staffing decisions in the quality setting. For example, what more effective way to evaluate the individual's team skills and temperament than in an intense team-based assessment exercise? In chapter 8 we will present numerous examples of quality-relevant simulations, used alone, and packaged in comprehensive assessment centers.

What Tools Are Being Used?

We have examined the extent to which various assessment tools are being used in quality improvement settings. Table 7.1 presents data on the use of specific assessment devices in a sample of organizations and in the sample of ASQC sustaining member organizations. To our surprise, quality improvement settings have neglected to incorporate state-of-the-art practices. They continue to rely on the interview and reference checks as the assessment tools of choice. As we've noted, there are methods that are more reliable, valid, and provide greater ROI. It is our contention that the selection and promotion process can be improved by using a greater variety of systematic tools, and we will provide examples of how benchmark organizations are doing just that.

With the overview of various assessment tools complete, we now turn to a discussion of the application of these tools to measurement of applicant knowledge, skills, abilities, and personality/temperament.

Exhibit 7.1. Guidelines for collecting effective references.

1. **Reference data are most properly used when the data involve job-related concerns.** Requested data should address KSAs or any other characteristics of the applicant that are necessary for successful job performance. Emphasis should be given to those characteristics that distinguish effective from ineffective performance . . . based on an analysis of the job.

2. **Reference checks are subject to the Uniform Guidelines.** Thus, as for any selection measure, we will need to monitor the fairness and validity of the reference check. If our reference-checking system unfairly discriminates against groups or is not related to job success, we should change or eliminate our system. To do otherwise is not only legally foolish but jeopardizes our ability to choose competent employees.

3. **An objective (for example, a system that focuses on factual or behavioral data related to the applicant) rather than a subjective (such as trait ratings) reference-checking system is less likely to be open to charges of discrimination.**

4. **Applicants should be asked to give written permission to contact their references.** When actually contacting references, information should also be collected on how long that person has known an applicant and the position the person holds. This information can be useful for verifying responses or, if necessary, legally proving that the person contacted is in a position to provide the assessments being requested.

5. **Reference takers collecting information by telephone or in person should be trained in how to interview reference givers.** Preparation will be necessary in how to formulate questions and record responses systematically. Here again, an objective approach to information collection will improve the quality of data ultimately collected.

6. **All reference-check information should be recorded in writing.** If a legal suit is brought against an employer, reference data may serve as important evidence in defending against the suit. Documentation in writing is essential for the defense.

7. **If a job applicant provides reference but reference information cannot be obtained, go back to the applicant for additional references.** Consider not hiring an applicant if complete reference information is not available. Hiring an applicant without such information can be very risky.

8. **Check all application forms and resume information.** In particular, focus on educational background (for example, schools attended, degrees earned, academic performance) and previous employment records (for example, dates of employment, job titles, duties performed). Gaps in information reported are red flags and signal a need for special attention.

Exhibit 7.1. Continued.

9. A caveat on the use of negative information. Negative information received during a reference check frequently serves as a basis for rejecting an applicant. Caution is certainly advised in using any negative data as a basis for excluding applicants. Before negative information is employed, we should (a) verify its accuracy with other sources, (b) be sure that disqualification on the basis of the information will distinguish between those who will fail and those who will succeed on the job, and (c) use the same information consistently for all applicants.

Source: Robert Gatewood and Hubert Feild, *Human Resource Selection* (Fort Worth, Tex.: Dryden Press, 1994), 467–469.

We review three topics in the remainder of this chapter. First, we present a review of various standardized paper-and-pencil ability tests applicable to the quality setting. Second, we profile various paper-and-pencil knowledge tests. Third, we examine the use of biographical predictors in the quality setting.

Quality-Relevant Standardized Paper-and-Pencil Ability Tests

One consistent theme of the new workplace is that it will depend on a workforce that is able to analyze and interpret data, reason, evaluate, generate solutions, and continually learn. We look now at standardized measures of cognitive aptitude and abilities. We've organized our look at these by the specific abilities they measure. We believe that this will aid in your selection and use of specific tests. We begin by profiling measures of general mental ability, and then focus on measuring specific aspects (for example, analytical thinking, reasoning, creativity, problem solving, reading, and basic math).

Cognitive Ability

Across a wide range of jobs, cognitive ability has proven to be a predictor of individual ability to learn and perform. For example, the average correlation between performance on a cognitive ability test and job performance for supervisors is about $r = .64$ and for computing and account-recording clerks it is about $r = .49$.[11] A recent study of 4039 entry-level army personnel found that general mental ability tests predicted technical proficiency ($r = .63$) and general task proficiency ($r = .65$).[12] Correlations of this magnitude can be the basis for making great strides in predicting subsequent job performance and success.

One generalization we can make is that the more complex the job, the stronger the relationship between performance on cognitive ability tests and subsequent training performance and job performance. For jobs of high complexity (managers, technicians, professionals), the relationship between mental ability test performance and subsequent job performance is about $r = .58$. For jobs of low complexity, the correlation with performance in training is $r = .54$, and the test–job performance correlation is $r = .40$.[13] It is generally true that measures of cognitive ability are even more effective at predicting success in training. Finally, specific aspects of mental ability (arithmetic reasoning, verbal ability) produce equally useful validity results for specific occupational groups.

As we noted, the greater the job complexity, the more likely that cognitive ability will be a valid and useful way to assess and predict individual performance. Because the quality setting requires that the individual learn varied, complex knowledge and skills, cognitive ability is a fundamental ability required in the new workplace. The importance of cognitive ability is even more compelling when you consider that your workforce must continue to learn and master new knowledge and skills. A workforce capable of learning will increase the flexibility and agility of your organization. The greater the cognitive ability of your workforce, the more quickly new, future competencies will be mastered, and the more responsive your organization will be to new business opportunities and challenges as they emerge.

Measures of General Mental Ability. There are two approaches to measuring cognitive ability. The first measures *general mental ability*, also termed *general intelligence*. This approach is based on the premise that the variety and complexity of cognitive functioning can be measured and summarized as an overall score. Typically, measures of general mental ability require that the individual work through a variety of test items requiring vocabulary, memory, and reasoning. An overall score is computed on the basis of the individual's responses to these different types of mental exercises. The notion that mental ability can be summarized by one overall score has been controversial, but nonetheless persists. We now preview a number of standardized measures used to assess general mental ability.

The Wechsler Adult Intelligence Scale (WAIS-R) (1981) consists of 11 subtests presenting a variety of items and yielding a general mental ability score.[14] It has been widely used in managerial assessment and selection. It requires an intensive administration process (approximately 60 to 90 minutes). Consequently, it is a relatively costly alternative for the employment setting.

The Thurstone Test of Mental Alertness (TMA) is a mental ability test predictive of the individual's ability to "learn new skills quickly, adjust to new situations, understand complex or subtle relationships, and be flexible in thinking."[15] The test requires 20 minutes and yields scores of quantitative (arithmetic reasoning, number series, and so on), linguistic (same-opposite word meanings, definitions), and general mental ability.[16] Norms and validity data for a wide array of occupations and industries are available from the publisher.

The Wonderlic Personnel Test (1992) is one of the most widely used tests of general mental ability. It consists of 50 items that draw on a variety of mental activities (for example, numerical computations, arithmetic reasoning, vocabulary, common sense reasoning, and scrambled number series). The items are arranged in order of difficulty, and the 50 items yield a general mental ability score. The overall score produced by the Wonderlic is heavily influenced by verbal comprehension, deductive reasoning, and numerical fluency.[17] Systematic studies of the Wonderlic have demonstrated reliability (test-retest correlations range from $r = .82$ to $.94$ and alternate forms reliabilities range from $r = .73$ to $.95$). Evidence of validity as a measure of general cognitive ability is well established with validity coefficients (correlations between test performance and job performance) ranging from $.23$ for jobs of low complexity, to $.56$ for jobs of greater complexity such as managerial and technical occupations.[18]

Because the new workplace requires the mastery of a variety of knowledge and skills, as well as continual learning and development, we believe that general mental ability may prove to be a reliable, valid, and efficient predictor of success. We turn now to the specific components of mental ability relevant to the quality improvement setting.

Measures of Specific Aspects of Mental Ability. As we noted earlier, the premise that mental ability can be summarized in one overall measure is a point of debate among experts. Detractors contend that it is more useful to think of the various components of mental ability. With that as a premise, a number of measures of specific mental abilities are available. The Employee Aptitude Survey (EAS) is one example of an instrument that measures various components of mental ability.[19] Exhibit 7.2 presents the dimensions of mental ability measured by the EAS. We have identified the potential relevance of each subscale for specific roles in the new workplace.

Exhibit 7.2. Cognitive aptitudes measured by the Employee Aptitude Survey.

Verbal comprehension: Ability to use words meaningfully in communication, thinking, and planning. *Potential applications:* Customer service, team leader.

Numerical ability: Ability to work easily with numbers, to do simple arithmetic quickly and accurately. *Potential applications:* Use of process improvement tools, survey analysis.

Visual pursuit: Speed and accuracy in visually tracing lines through an entangled network. *Potential applications:* Work requiring the use of complex schematic diagrams.

Visual speed and accuracy: Ability to see small details quickly and accurately, as required in visual inspection and clerical work. *Potential applications:* Production jobs, quality control inspectors.

Space visualization: Ability to visualize forms in space and manipulate objects mentally. *Potential applications:* Jobs requiring mechanical aptitude, or those requiring that the person understand how individual components of complete work processes interact.

Numerical reasoning: Ability to analyze logical relationships and discover principles underlying such relationships. *Potential applications:* Jobs requiring mastery and use of process improvement tools, SPC, analysis of survey data, and so on.

Verbal reasoning: Ability to analyze verbally stated facts and to make valid judgments on the basis of the logical implications of such facts. *Potential applications:* Jobs requiring group (interactive) problem solving.

Word fluency: Flexibility and ease in verbal communication. In contrast to verbal comprehension, word fluency involves speed and freedom in using words rather than understanding of verbal meaning. *Potential applications:* Jobs requiring extensive oral or written expression (customer service, training positions).

Manual speed and accuracy: Ability to make fine finger movements rapidly and accurately. This type of coordination is sometimes called *finger dexterity.* An important factor affecting a person's score on this test is the temperamental willingness to perform the type of monotonous, repetitive tasks that are required by highly routine clerical jobs.

Symbolic reasoning: Ability to manipulate abstract symbols mentally and to make judgments and decisions that are logically valid. The ability to evaluate whether adequate information is available to make a definite decision is an important aspect of performance on this test. *Potential applications:* Jobs requiring application of process improvement methodologies (experimentation, PDCA) and problem solving.

Source: The Psychological Corporation, *Tests and Related Products for Human Resource Assessment,* 1994. Used with permission. The definitions are from the test manual for the *Employee Aptitude Survey,* The Psychological Corporation. Potential applications are inferences provided by the authors.

The **Flanagan Industrial Test (FIT)** is a second multi-aptitude measure with subtests relevant to the new workplace.[20] The test consists of 18 individually timed subtests. The test is oriented toward supervisory, technical, office, skilled labor, and industrial positions. The 18 subtests are profiled in Exhibit 7.3. Many of the specific subscales for both the EAS and the FIT are profiled in later sections of this chapter when we discuss the measurement of specific aptitudes and abilities.

Other multi-aptitude cognitive ability tests include the **Differential Aptitude Test (1990)** and the **Technical Test Battery (TTB)**, oriented toward technical personnel and technical supervisors. The TTB measures numerical computation, visual estimation, mechanical comprehension, diagraming, spatial reasoning, and spatial recognition.[21] Finally, the **Applied Technology Series** measures six cognitive abilities relevant to technical environments.[22]

In addition to comprehensive tools like the EAS and the FIT, a number of tools are designed to measure only one or a few specific cognitive aptitudes.

Measuring Critical (Analytical) Thinking. Much process improvement is based on the application of systematic experimentation and analysis. The ability to think analytically about problems, to make inferences from data, and to interpret, weigh, and deduce based on experimentation is fundamental to process improvement. There are a number of measures of this important aspect of cognitive ability.

The **Watson Glaser Critical Thinking Appraisal** provides a measure of analytical thinking. The 80-item test takes about 40 to 50 minutes to administer and incorporates a variety of analytical tasks, including making inferences from data, recognizing unstated assumptions, determining if certain conclusions follow from information presented, deciding if generalizations are warranted by given data, and discerning strong and weak arguments to issues presented.[23] A short form requiring 30 minutes is also available.

The **Critical Thinking Test** measures verbal and numerical reasoning appropriate for middle and senior management and professional and technical occupations. The test provides separate tests and scores for numerical critical reasoning and verbal critical reasoning. The numerical reasoning test (making inferences and decisions from numerical data) takes 35 minutes. The verbal critical reasoning test measures the ability to evaluate the logic of various arguments relevant to managerial work and takes about 25 minutes.[24] A similar instrument, **The Critical Reasoning Test Battery**, is designed to assess reasoning skills

Exhibit 7.3. Flanagan Industrial Test.

This paper-and-pencil test is designed to measure a variety of cognitive abilities in lower-level industrial settings.

Arithmetic. Ability to add, subtract, multiply, and divide. 5 minutes.

Assembly. Ability to visualize how separate pieces will look as a whole. 10 minutes.

Components. Ability to identify a simple figure that is part of a complete drawing. 10 minutes.

Coordination. Ability to control hand and arm movements while working through a series of mazes. 5 minutes.

Electronics. Ability to understand electrical and electronic principles as well as analyze diagrams of electrical circuits. 15 minutes.

Expression. Knowledge of correct grammar and sentence structure. 5 minutes.

Ingenuity. Ability to think of ingenious and effective ways to solve problems. 15 minutes.

Inspection. Ability to spot imperfections or flaws in a series of objects. 5 minutes.

Judgment and comprehension. Ability to read and comprehend information. 15 minutes.

Mathematics and reasoning. Ability to reason through mathematical word problems. 15 minutes.

Mechanics. Ability to understand and analyze mechanical principles and movements. 15 minutes.

Memory. Ability to remember codes used in coding test. 10 minutes.

Patterns. Ability to perceive and reproduce pattern outlines accurately. 5 minutes.

Planning. Ability to plan, organize, and schedule various types of activities. 15 minutes.

Precision. Capacity for precision work with small objects. 5 minutes.

Scales. Ability to read scales, graphs, and charts. 5 minutes.

Tables. Ability to read alpha and numeric tables. 5 minutes.

Vocabulary. Knowledge of words used in business and government environments. 15 minutes.

Source: *SRA Human Resources Assessment Catalog* (London House Consultants, 1992), 38. Used with permission.

262 • Staffing the New Workplace

in administrative, junior management, and middle management positions. The verbal evaluation subtest (30 minutes) measures the ability to evaluate logical arguments. The interpreting data (30 minutes) subtest measures the ability to make correct inferences from data, and the diagnostic series subtest measures reasoning with diagrams and requires recognition of logical rules governing sequences.[25]

Measuring Creative Thinking and Problem Solving. Problem solving is a critical requirement in the new workplace. We will discuss the measurement of problem-solving skills in a later section. For now, we want to point out that mastery and application of various problem-solving techniques (for example, the skills and techniques that can be taught) are facilitated by individual differences in specific cognitive abilities, in particular, creativity. The FIT provides a measure of ingenuity, defined as the ability to think of ingenious and effective ways of solving problems. The test takes 15 minutes. An example item from the ingenuity subtest is presented in Exhibit 7.4.

Mechanical Aptitude and Reasoning. Mechanical aptitude is a cognitive ability with particular relevance to the quality improvement process. Although definitions of mechanical aptitude vary, a generic example is the aptitude for learning, understanding, and visualizing processes. Mechanical aptitude is important to understanding the operations of

Exhibit 7.4. Test and example item measuring creativity and problem solving.

FIT Ingenuity Test (15 minutes)

Example Item:

This is a test of your ability to think of clever and effective ways of doing things. Removing old paint can be a problem. A common household appliance can be used to do this in the same way as the newer electric paint removers. The appliance is used to soften the old coats of paint with heat so that the paint can be removed with a putty knife.

$$\bigcirc \quad i \_ \_ \_ \_ \_ d \quad w \_ \_ e$$
$$\bigcirc \quad a \_ \_ \_ \_ \_ \_ e \quad d \_ \_ g$$
$$\bigcirc \quad e \_ \_ \_ \_ \_ \_ n \quad t \_ \_ g$$
$$\bigcirc \quad e \_ \_ \_ \_ \_ \_ c \quad i \_ \_ n$$
$$\bigcirc \quad o \_ \_ \_ \_ \_ \_ r \quad p \_ \_ g$$

Answer: electric iron

Source: *SRA Human Resource Assessment Catalogue* (London House Consultants, 1992), 214.

machinery and production processes. It is related to the ability to think systematically—a critical attribute in the mastery of process improvement tools. Consequently, mechanical aptitude plays an important role in activities directed to work flow and process improvement. Individuals capable of visualizing and understanding production processes will more capably engage in innovative improvements.

The **Bennett Mechanical Comprehension Test (BMCT) 1969, Forms S and T** consists of 68 items requiring the ability to "perceive and understand the relationship of physical forces and mechanical elements in practical situations."[26] According to the test publisher, the "test items are presented in terms of simple, frequently encountered mechanisms that do not resemble text-book illustrations or require special knowledge."[27] The items deal with objects that are generally familiar in American culture: planes, carts, steps, pulleys, seesaws, and gears. The test has a long history of use, and evidence of reliability, with reported reliabilities of $r = .80s$.[28] However, a recent review did criticize the dated appearance of the test and the lack of female and minority figures in the problem illustrations.[29] Exhibit 7.5 presents example items from the Bennett and from the mechanics subtest of the FIT.

Spatial visualization is a related, underlying component of mechanical aptitude. It may prove useful in assessing the applicant's ability to think in systematic terms about processes and to think about the implications of changes in one part of a system. The EAS described earlier includes a space visualization measure.

In addition to the measures of mechanical aptitude profiled thus far, a number of measures have been designed to more closely reflect the work actually done on a job or a job family. Exhibit 7.6 profiles a "Troubleshooting" test designed for manufacturing settings and administered to applicants for the operator position at 3M Canada.

Assessing Basic Cognitive Skills

As you will recall from the ASQC Survey of Staffing Practices, quality directors concurred that a number of skills are important to quality improvement efforts. Basic skills in reading and math are seen as especially critical. In effect, these provide the base on which much quality knowledge and skill must build. If your workforce lacks basic reading and math skills, training and performance will be deficient.

Exhibit 7.5. Tests of mechanical aptitude/ability and example items.

Bennett Mechanical Comprehension Test (BMCT) 1980. Sixty-eight items requiring 30 minutes "assess the ability to apply physical and mechanical principles in practical situations."

Example items

Sample item   *Sample item*

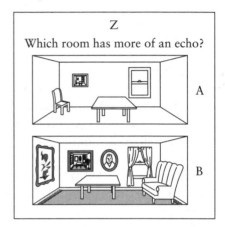

Flanigan Industrial Test (FIT) mechanics' subtest. Ability to understand and analyze mechanical principles and movements (15 minutes).

Example item

This is a test of your knowledge of mechanical symbols, devices, and principles and your ability to understand mechanical relations.

The viscosity of a substance is primarily altered by a change in
    ○ Temperature
    ○ Volume
    ○ Elevation
    ○ Humidity
    ○ Density

Source for BMCT: Tests and related products for Human Resource Management, 1995. Used with permission.
Source for FIT: SRA Human Resource Catalogue, Rosemont, Ill., London House, 1992, p. 38.

Exhibit 7.6. Assessing a job-specific mechanical aptitude, troubleshooting, at 3M Canada.

Troubleshooting

In today's companies, it is important that people be able to troubleshoot problems and find out their source. The Troubleshooting test asks you to figure out problems in systems. You will be shown a diagram of a system similar to what a 3M employee might face on the job. You will also be given rules that show how the system works. Your job will be to find out why the system is not working the way it should, or what would happen if a part in the system failed. Here is an example along with the rules showing how the system works.

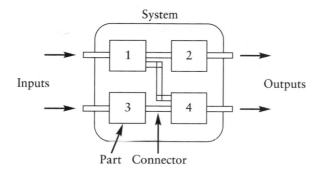

Rule 1: A part will output a signal *only* if it receives an input signal from *all* other parts connected on its left side.

Rule 2: If a part fails, then it *will not* output a signal to any other parts to which it is connected on its right side.

Use the drawing and rules to answer this sample question.

1. Which of the following parts would not have an output signal if Part 3 suddenly failed?

A) Part 1

B) Part 2

C) Part 4

D) None of the above

The correct answer is "C" (Part 4). If Part 3 has failed, there is no output signal from Part 3 to Part 4 (Rule 2). Part 4 will not produce any output signal because no input signal is received from one of its connected parts on the left (Rule 1). You would make the correct answer by filling space "C" on your answer sheet like this:

Ⓐ Ⓑ ● Ⓓ Ⓔ

Exhibit 7.6. Continued.

Here are some tips that can help you find the correct answers when working with Troubleshooting test questions.

- Carefully read all the facts given in the problem and keep them in mind as you solve the problem.

- Review Rule 1 and Rule 2 and apply them to every problem.

- Work through each problem in a logical way.

- Work through the possible connections and signals on scratch paper. Sometimes they can be hard to picture in your mind.

Each question in this test has only one correct answer. The Troubleshooting test has 30 questions. You will have 30 minutes to complete them.

Practice questions like the ones on the Troubleshooting test follow. If you want more practice answering questions like the ones in this test, look for books on shop, mechanics, basic electricity, and troubleshooting guides. Basic electricity courses also can help you practice the kind of thinking to do well on this test.

Troubleshooting Practice Questions

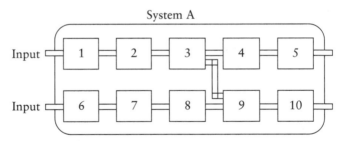

System A

Rule 1: A part will output a signal only if it receives an input signal from all other parts connected on its left side.

Rule 2: If a part fails, then it will not output a signal to any other parts to which it is connected on its right side.

1. Part 10 has an output signal, but Part 5 doesn't because one of the parts in the system has failed. Which of the following could be the failed part?

   A) Part 3   D) Part 9
   B) Part 4   E) none of the above
   C) Part 6

2. If Part 7 suddenly failed, which of the following parts would not have an output signal?

   A) Part 6   D) Part 9
   B) Part 3   E) none of the above
   C) Part 5

Exhibit 7.6. Continued.

3. Which of the following would not have an output signal if part 2 suddenly failed?

A) Part 1   D) Part 10
B) Part 6   E) none of the above
C) Part 8

4. Part 9 does not have an output signal because one of the parts in the system has failed. Which of the following could be the failed part?

A) Part 1   D) Part 10
B) Part 4   E) none of the above
C) Part 5

Practice Answer Sheet

1 (A)(B)(C)(D)(E)
2 (A)(B)(C)(D)(E)
3 (A)(B)(C)(D)(E)
4 (A)(B)(C)(D)(E)

Source: "Preparing for the Selection Process," *3M Canada Applicant Information Booklet.* Used with permission of 3M Canada and HRStrategies, Grosse Pointe, Mich.

The **Wonderlic Basic Skills Test (WBST) (1994)** is a new paper-and-pencil measure of work-related math and verbal skills. The publisher notes it is designed for use with adolescents and adults applying for entry-level employment or entering vocational training programs. Consisting of two subtests (WBST Verbal and WBST Quantitative), the instrument is composed of items developed in reference to skills taught at grades 4 through 12. The items represent common work-related activities and materials familiar to a broad cross-section of the population.[30]

The **Work Skills Series Production** assesses basic literacy—understanding instructions subtest (12 minutes), numerical skills (10 minutes), and visual checking skills (7 minutes) in manufacturing and production environments.[31]

Basic Reading Comprehension

Reading comprehension is a skill of critical importance to the new workplace. The importance of basic reading skills was confirmed in the ASQC survey where it emerged as one of the more important attributes for every occupational grouping. In fact, it emerged as the most important attribute for technical/professional, supervisory, and middle management occupations.

Assessing Reading Skills. There are two approaches to measuring basic reading skills. First, there are standardized tests of reading ability. One such test is the **Industrial Reading Test (IRT)** (1978), a paper-and-pencil test consisting of nine reading passages and 38 test items. It can be administered individually or in groups. The test assesses reading comprehension of written technical material, takes about 40 minutes to administer, and is written at the reading level of grade eight. As the vendor notes,

> *IRT is a power test of reading comprehension rather than a measure of reading speed. Passages are designed to be within the reading ability of the typical student at a vocational high school or an adult with a high school education or equivalent. Reading passages focus on work-relevant topics, such as safety devices used by technical workers, basic first aid principles, and the importance of blueprints in manufacturing. . . . Good performance on the test does not depend on previous knowledge of the subject matter covered in the passages.*[32]

Another standardized test of reading comprehension is the **Wide Range Achievement Test (WRAT-3)** (1993).[33] It assesses basic skills in reading, spelling, and arithmetic. The test requires 15 to 30 minutes. The test is well suited for settings in which applicants may be deficient in basic skills.

Work Sample Reading Tests. A second approach to measuring reading ability is to construct a test of reading materials designed to reflect specific jobs or job families. This approach is modeled after work simulation tests in that the individual must read and respond to reading content typical of that encountered on the job. The reading test used to assess applicants for the technologist position at 3M Canada, profiled in Exhibit 7.7, illustrates this approach.

Basic Arithmetic/Math Skills

A central component of virtually all quality improvement efforts is measurement. The analytical tools of quality improvement require basic mathematical proficiencies. To the extent that the applicant lacks basic math, the training process will be extended, and performance will be deficient. This premise was confirmed in the ASQC Survey of Staffing Practices. Respondents identified basic math as the second most important attribute for technical/professional employees in quality settings. Although receiving a lower ranking for other occu-

Exhibit 7.7. Assessing reading comprehension at 3M Canada.

This description orients applicants to the reading comprehension test used at 3M Canada.

The Reading Comprehension test shows how well you read and understand written material. The test has reading materials like those that 3M employees must be able to read. Don't worry, you do not need to have worked at 3M to be able to answer the questions. The test simply tells how well you can read and answer questions about what you've read. The correct answer to every question can be found in the materials you are given to read.

The test asks you to read several passages. After each passage, you will be asked to answer a set of questions. You will be able to read the material again, if you wish, as you answer the questions. You will not need to memorize it! Here are a few examples of Reading Comprehension test questions. The actual test will have reading passages that are longer than this example. Read the passage and then look at the sample questions.

Being a 3M employee can be very interesting and rewarding. However, all employees should know that safety must come first. Completing a job safely requires a carefully thought out approach to each task. Before beginning a task, an employee must decide how to accomplish it safely. This will help avoid careless mistakes and unfortunate injury.

Sample Questions

1. According to the passage:
   A) Employees are often careless
   B) Careless mistakes always cause serious injuries.
   C) Safety must come first to a 3M employee.
   D) Being a 3M employee is an easy job.
   E) None of the above.

2. Which of the following would be the best title for this passage?
   A) The importance of quality.
   B) The importance of safety.
   C) The work day of a 3M employee.
   D) Common on-the-job injuries.
   E) None of the above.

The correct answer for the first question is "C." The passage says safety always comes first. When you take the test you will mark your answer by blackening in a circle on an answer sheet. You will blacken the circle that goes with the letter for the correct answer. You would mark the correct answer for the first question by filling in space "C" on your answer sheet, like this:

Ⓐ Ⓑ ● Ⓓ Ⓔ

Exhibit 7.7.   Continued.

The correct answer to the second question is "B." This title tells best what the passage is about. Although the other three titles are about work at 3M, they do not stress how important it is to think about the job. You would mark this answer by filling in space "B" on your answer sheet as follows.

(A) ● (C) (D) (E)

Here are some tips that can help you get the right answers on the Reading Comprehension test.

- Read each passage carefully. Pay attention to the major idea of the passage.

- Read each question carefully. Read all of the answers to each question before you choose the answer you think is right.

- If you have trouble answering a question, reread the part of the passage that the question asks you about. Remember, the correct answer to every question can be found in the passage—you just have to look for it!

- Each question in the test has only one correct answer. The test has 32 questions. You will have 30 minutes to complete them.

Practice questions are given on the next page of this booklet. If you want more practice, your local library has many books that deal with improving your reading skills. Adult education programs offer courses on improving your reading skills. Reading instruction books are good places to go for help. Find books that give practice reading tests. Many interesting textbooks on different topics have review questions at the end of each chapter. Reading passages and answering questions will be good practice and could help you on this test.

The following practice test is provided to applicants.

Reading Comprehension
Practice Questions
Two Types of Corrugated Paper

Most people do not realize how versatile boxes can be. They can be made out of regular cardboard or corrugated cardboard. Regular cardboard is flat and made up of paper pulp. But is thicker and stiffer than paper. It is light and easy to fold, making it an ideal container for light food products such as breakfast cereal. Corrugated cardboard is actually made up of three pieces. Two pieces of flat cardboard are held together by a third corrugated

Exhibit 7.7. Continued.

piece of cardboard. The third piece of cardboard is shaped into parallel grooves or ridges and glued in between the two pieces of flat cardboard. Corrugated cardboard is stronger and can take more abuse than regular cardboard. This type of cardboard is most often used to make strong boxes to transport and store heavy items such as cans of food.

1. Regular cardboard is an ideal container for

   A) Light food products.
   B) Heavy items.
   C) Cans of food.
   D) Fluids.
   E) None of the above.

2. Which of the following is the best material to use for the storage of heavy items?

   A) Regular cardboard.
   B) Pasteboard.
   C) Corrugated cardboard.
   D) Paper
   E) None of the above.

3. Corrugated cardboard is made up of

   A) One piece of regular cardboard
   B) Two pieces of regular cardboard
   C) Three pieces of regular cardboard
   D) Four pieces of regular cardboard
   E) None of the above.

4. Glue is used to make

   A) Paper pulp.
   B) Corrugated cardboard.
   C) Regular cardboard.
   D) Paper.
   E) None of the above.

Source: "Preparing for the Selection Process," *3M Canada Applicant Information Booklet.* Used with permission of 3M Canada and HRStrategies, Grosse Pointe, Mich.

pational groupings, it was nonetheless rated as very important to success across all occupational groups. As with reading comprehension, there are two approaches to measuring math and quantitative skills. The first is to use a standardized test; there are numerous arithmetic, math, and quantitative ability tests from which to choose. The second is to construct a company-specific work sample composed of the types of arithmetic and mathematical operations performed on the job. We'll take a look at each.

Standardized Measures of Basic Math. There are a number of standardized paper and pencil tests that measure the applicant's basic arithmetic or mathematics knowledge and skill. The quantitative skills scale from the WBST provides an efficient assessment of the applicant's ability to work with quantitative data. According to the publisher the items measure the following.

Addition, subtraction, multiplication and division of whole numbers and fractional numbers, including those in monetary units and units of measure, as well as the computation of rates, proportions, and percentages. Evaluation and interpretation of line, bar, or pie graphs; Comparison of fractional magnitudes; Algebra, including evaluation, simplification, and solving of variable expressions and equations; Geometry including computation and identification of magnitude of lengths, angles, areas and volumes.[34]

The EAS, profiled earlier as a multi-aptitude measure, includes a numerical ability subtest. The FIT, also profiled earlier, provides measures of four aspects of quantitative skills. It includes a five-minute measure of basic arithmetic; a 15-minute measure of mathematical reasoning; a five-minute measure of the ability to read scales, graphs, and charts; and a five-minute measure of the ability to read tables. Additionally, the **Personnel Tests for Industry** provides a measure of numerical ability that requires 20 minutes to administer.[35] Exhibit 7.8 presents sample items from measures of basic arithmetic, mathematics, or mathematical reasoning.

Work Sample Math Tests. Basic math and arithmetic can be assessed with job sample arithmetic tests, designed to more closely reflect the use of arithmetic in particular jobs or job families. Exhibit 7.9 presents the applicant orientation to the practical arithmetic test used to assess applicants for the operator position at 3M Canada.

Oral Directions

An additional basic skill is attending to, interpreting, and reacting to oral instructions. This basic skill is critical to orientation, training, and performance in many entry-level occupations. Additionally, because of the flexibility of the new workplace, where activities are no longer routine or as clearly specified or documented as in the traditional organization, the ability to attend to and follow oral directions has taken on increased importance. The Personnel Tests for Industry Oral Directions Test provides a measure of this basic competency. The applicant listens to a standardized taped oral presentation and responds to directions by marking appropriate items on the test booklet. Scores on the test reflect both general mental ability and the ability to understand and follow oral directions.[36]

The ability to follow oral directions is critically important to those jobs which require verbal interaction (such as customer service). The

Exhibit 7.8. Sample items from measures of basic math skills.

Example of a quantitative item from the WBST and the FIT.

Use this chart for the following.

Population

Selected cities and villages

Ashdown	5,150	Herber Springs	5,628
Batesville	9,187	Pocahontas	6,151
Crossett	6,282	Wynne	8,817

3. About 2/5 of the people in Ashdown were watching the Ashdown Athletes last Friday. How many people watched the Athletes on Friday?

A. 206   C. 2,488

B. 248   D. 2,060

Example items from the Flanagan Industrial Test

Arithmetic Test

This is a test of your ability to do numerical computations quickly and accurately. Sample problems of the type you will find in the test are given below. The answers have been marked beside the questions. Study the problems, calculate the answers and check your numbers with the answers that are given in the sample answer spaces at the right.

	A	B	C	D	E		A	B	C	D	E
S1. $6 + 3 + 9 + 7 =$	33	15	27	25	29		○	○	○	●	○
S2. $49 + 5 - 3 + 7 =$	66	58	78	74	69		○	●	○	○	○

Scales Test

This is a test of your ability to get information from graphs. This graph shows how many gallons of gas a car uses at different speeds on difficult highway slopes. For example, find out how much gas a car uses on a 2 percent slope at a speed of 50 mph (miles per hour). First find 2 on the percent slope scale along the bottom of the graph. Now follow the line up from 2 to the point where it crosses the 50 mph curve. From that point, follow the line across to the scale along the left side of the graph. From the scale, read the decimal value (in this example, 0.060) showing the fraction of a gallon used per mile.

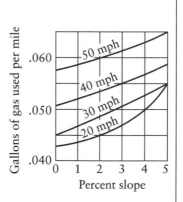

	Speed	Gallons of gas used per mile					Sample
Slope	mph	A	B	C	D	E	Answer column
4%	40	0.055	0.060	0.057	0.050	0.065	Ⓐ Ⓑ ● Ⓓ Ⓔ

Source for WBST: Eliot Long, Victor Artese, and Winifred Clonts, "Wonderlic Basic Skills Test," 1994. Example item from Psychological Corporation, *Tests and Related Products for Human Resource Assessment* (San Antonio, Tex.: The Psychological Corporation, 1995), 31.
Source for FIT: John C. Flanagan, "The Flanagan Industrial Tests (FIT)," example item from SRA London House, *SRA Human Resource Assessment Catalogue* (Rosemont, Ill.: SRA London House, 1992), 39, 42.

Exhibit 7.9. Measuring basic math skills at 3M Canada manufacturing.

Practical Arithmetic

This is a test of your ability to use information provided in a chart or table. An important part of an Operator's job is to adjust machinery, ensure quality, and analyze data to improve a process. These tasks require an Operator to use practical arithmetic to solve problems. Here is a sample table you can use to answer the example question below.

Daily Work Record		
Employee	Parts Completed	Number of Errors
Jones	33	2
Smith	29	1
McDonald	39	2

Example A: How many parts were made by Jones and Smith?

A) 52

B) 53

C) 62

D) 63

E) none of the above

For this example, you should have chosen option "C." The correct answer is obtained by adding the number of parts completed by Jones and Smith (33 and 29). The correct answer would be marked by filling in space "C" on your answer sheet as follows:

Here are some tips to help you get the correct answers on the Practical Arithmetic test:

• Read each question carefully.

• Look at the charts, tables and graphs, carefully.

Each question in this test has only one correct answer. The test has 24 items. You will have 30 minutes to complete them.

Practice questions are given on the next page. If you want more practice, your local library has basic math books that have these types of questions. Look for examples of addition, subtraction, multiplication, and division of numbers.

Exhibit 7.9. Continued.

Practical Arithmetic

Practice Questions

Use the graph below to answer the four practice questions.

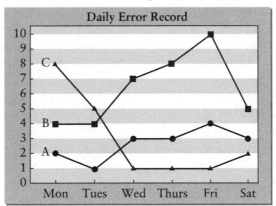

1. How many errors were made by all three departments on Thursday?

    A) 11   D) 15
    B) 12   E) none of the above
    C) 13

2. How many errors were made by department C on Monday, Tuesday, and Wednesday?

    A) 6   D) 15
    B) 13   E) none of the above
    C) 14

3. Combining all three departments, how many more total errors were made Friday than were made on Wednesday?

    A) 2   D) 5
    B) 3   E) none of the above
    C) 4

4. If department B is able to reduce the number of errors made on Saturday by 20%, how many errors will they make on the next working day?

    A) 1   D) 4
    B) 2   E) none of the above
    C) 3

```
        Practice Answer Sheet
    1  Ⓐ Ⓑ Ⓒ Ⓓ Ⓔ
    2  Ⓐ Ⓑ Ⓒ Ⓓ Ⓔ
    3  Ⓐ Ⓑ Ⓒ Ⓓ Ⓔ
    4  Ⓐ Ⓑ Ⓒ Ⓓ Ⓔ
```

Source: "Preparing for the Selection Process," *3M Canada Applicant Information Booklet.* Used with permission of 3M Canada and HRStrategies, Grosse Point, Mich.

oral directions test may be especially relevant for entry-level positions requiring the ability to understand and comprehend the English language (for example, positions requiring interactions with internal or external customers).

A reminder: When using tests of mental abilities, general or specific, it is important that you are able to identify how the attribute contributes to success in your organization. When appropriate paper and pencil mental ability and multi-aptitude tests are used, they can greatly improve the reliability, validity, fairness, and ROI of the selection process. However, because they can be relatively abstract, do not resemble the activities of the job, and tend to have disparate impact, it is advisable that you seek professional advice and assistance in the selection and use of specific tests. HR consultants, industrial/organizational psychologists, and educational psychologists specializing in the use of tests can assist you in that process.

Locating, Evaluating, and Obtaining Standardized Tests

We've cited a number of standardized measures available for use in the employment setting. The reference notes appearing with each test identify the test publisher from which you can obtain additional details about the test. Also, to aid in your search and review of standardized tests, Exhibit 7.10 details how to go about the process of locating and obtaining tests.

Measuring Quality-Relevant Knowledge

We've noted throughout the book that the new workplace requires a workforce with a variety and complexity of knowledge. The fact that work, even production work, has become much more knowledge intensive is perhaps the greatest change to date. Examples of relevant knowledge include quality theories and practices, process improvement techniques, statistics, problem-solving techniques, and appropriate teamwork. Systematic assessment of what potential employees know about quality improvement can be very useful in making the selection decision, as well as determining what specific follow-up training will be needed. There are various standardized tests of quality-relevant knowledge.

Certification Tests. The certification testing process sponsored by ASQC provides the most systematic approach to measuring knowledge of quality theories and practices.[37] Certification tests are designed to

Exhibit 7.10. Locating, evaluating, and selecting standardized tests.

The following guidelines will help as you search for, identify, evaluate, and implement published tests.

What attributes to measure? The first step in choosing assessment tools is to specify the KSAPs you are intent on measuring. Chapter 4 detailed the rationale and methods for doing so. Remember, it is important that you be able to specify how an attribute contributes to performance and success in the organization. (Remember, success can be defined many ways—success in training, staying with the organization, fitting into a team, and so on.)

In chapters 2, 4, 7, and 8 and in QAI, we've supplied a number of attributes relevant to different quality improvement settings. Remember to also include other attributes (functional KSAPs, physical abilities, and so on.)

Locate test titles and publishers. Once you've focused on an attribute or attributes important for success in your organization, a number of reference works can help you locate specific test titles.

A very useful reference source is *The Mental Measurements Yearbook*. It is indexed to help you locate tests, and then after you've focused on a specific published test, it provides evaluative reviews of tests.

For locating potentially relevant tests, the *Mental Measurements Yearbook* provides six indexes. These include an index of titles, an index of acronyms, a subject index, a test publishers directory and index, an index of names, and a score index. The score index is especially useful. It lists tests by the scores the test produces—the attributes the test measures.

The *Yearbook* is published every other year, with a supplement published each intervening year.

Evaluating a test

Once you've identified relevant test titles, you are now ready to take a closer look at the properties of the test. The criteria we use to evaluate standardized tests are profiled in chapter 3: reliability, validity, fairness, and utility.

Objective reviews. An excellent source for objective reviews of tests you are interested in is *The Mental Measurements Yearbook*. It will provide an objective review of most tests you've identified. Typically, the reviewer(s) will focus on whether or not the test meets the appropriate standards: Is there credible evidence of its reliability? Is there credible evidence that the scores measure the attributes the publisher claims it measures (construct validity). Is there credible evidence that the test correlates with measures of job performance for any specific occupational groupings? Are there studies of disparate impact? Does the publisher provide a credible norm base?

Exhibit 7.10. Continued.

Other sources for test titles and reviews include *Tests in Print*. A consulting firm, PRO-ED based in Austin, Texas, provides a number of testing references including, *Tests: A Comprehensive Reference for Assessments in Psychology, Education Business*. This includes descriptions, cost, scoring procedure and publishers for more than 3000 tests; *Business and Industry Testing; Current Practices and Test Reviews*, which provides reviews of 60 tests widely used in employment settings; and *The Consumer's Guide to Tests in Print*, which describes 148 tests.

More detail. If the test appears to measure the attribute(s) you wish to measure, the next step would be to contact the publisher. *The Mental Measurements Yearbook* lists publishers, and most are easily accessible by toll-free numbers. Several of these numbers are also listed in the notes to this chapter. Inquire about the availability of a test user's manual, and if you are still uncertain about the applicability of the test, inquire about any validity studies appropriate to the job and setting you're interested in.

Test manuals. The test manual produced by the test publisher should thoroughly address each standard. It should present evidence of internal consistency and stability (test-retest) reliability. If different forms of the test are available, evidence that the alternate forms correlate should also be presented. Similarly, the test manual should detail validity studies that have examined the test. Many standardized tests will present validity studies for many different job titles. If you've been unable to locate an objective review of the test (such as those in *The Mental Measurements Yearbook*), and the test manuals do not address these issues, it is best that you not use that test in the decision-making process.

Meeting user requirements

For reasons of security (to protect the scoring and to guard against the misuse of tests), most publishers require that the purchaser meet certain criteria. Most publishers use an A-, B-, and C-level categorization of their tests and require that different criteria be met within each level. The following "Requirements to Qualify for Test Purchase" are the standards used by The Psychological Corporation, and are reprinted by permission.

Requirements to Qualify for Test Purchase

The Psychological Corporation has established a policy for qualifying individuals, organizations, or agencies to purchase tests. A three-level (A,B,C) classification system differentiates products according to the types of purchasers to whom tests may be sold.

Exhibit 7.10. Continued.

Requirements	Qualifications Level		
Depending on the Qualifications Level assigned to the product(s) being ordered, the order must also include the following information to qualify an individual, organization, or agency for test purchase.	A	B	C
1. Name of purchasing organization or agency.	•	•	•
2. Address of purchasing organization or agency. *Note: The Psychological Corporation reserves the right not to ship any education test materials to a home address.*	•	•	•
3. Phone number of purchasing organization or agency.	•	•	•
4. Completed Registration Form. *Note: If you have a current account with The Psychological Corporation and have already qualified to purchase A, B, or C level products, it is not necessary to complete a Registration Form. However, The Psychological Corporation reserves the right to require its customers to submit a Registration Form each time an order is placed.*	•	•	•
5. Agency or organization's official purchase order number OR Official letterhead signed by the person authorized to purchase OR (If ordered by an individual) Verification of licensure or certification by an agency recognized by The Psychological Corporation to require training and experience in a relevant area of assessment consistent with the expectations outlined in the 1985 Standards for Educational and Psychological Testing.	•	•	•
6. Verification of a master's level degree in Psychology or Education or the equivalent in a related field with relevant training in assessment. OR Verification of membership in a professional association recognized by The Psychological Corporation to require training and experience in a relevant area of assessment consistent with the expectations outlined in the 1985 *Standards for Educational and Psychological Testing.*		•	•

Exhibit 7.10. Continued.

Requirements	Qualifications Level		
	A	B	C

If the products and services being purchased are for the assessment and development of human resources: They may be purchased by human resource managers, personnel managers, and consultants who are (a) employed by a business or industrial firm using tests for selection, promotion, job analysis, and training and development; (b) trained in issues regarding tests and measurements; and (c) are knowledgeable of the Equal Employment Opportunity Commission's (EEOC) Uniform Guidelines on Employee Selection Procedures (1973) and employment law. The order must be placed by the human resource manager who is responsible for administration of the tests, and the tests may only be used to test applicants or employees of the organization placing the order. Registration is required.

7. Verification of Ph.D.-level degree in Psychology or Education or the equivalent in a related field with relevant training in assessment

OR

Verification of licensure or certification by an agency recognized by The Psychological Corporation to require training and experience in a relevant area of assessment consistent with the expectations outlined in the 1985 *Standards for Educational and Psychological Testing*.

If the products and services being purchased are for the assessment and development of human resources: They may be purchased by human resource managers, personnel managers, and consultants who are (a) employed by a firm using tests for selection, promotion, analysis, and training and development; and (b) licensed or certified by the Human Resource Credentialing Institute (HRCI). The order must be placed by the human resource manager who is responsible for administration of the tests, and the tests may only be used to test applicants or employees of the organization placing the order. Registration is required.

Source: The section "Requirements to Qualify for Test Purchase" is reprinted from *Tests and Related Products for Human Resource Assessment*, The Psychological Corporation, 1995, p. 89. Used with permission.

measure the knowledge associated with a particular discipline. Exhibit 7.11 presents the certification tests offered by ASQC and the knowledge base measured by each test. Each test consists of multiple choice questions designed to sample the relevant knowledge base.

Knowledge of Teamwork. Researchers Michael A. Campion and Michael J. Stevens have developed a paper-and-pencil test of the knowledge required for effective teamwork. This test is unique in that the focus is on what effective team members *know about* conflict resolution, collaborative problem solving, communication, goal setting, and planning and task coordination. Figure 7.1 presents the organization of the major categories of the test. Exhibit 7.12 presents the more detailed dimensions of teamwork measured by the test. The test is short and efficient. Applicants complete 35 multiple-choice items, which re-

Exhibit 7.11. Quality-relevant certification tests provided by ASQC.

Certification is formal recognition by ASQC that an individual has demonstrated a proficiency within and a comprehension of a specified body of knowledge at a point in time. It is peer recognition and not registration or licensure.

Quality Engineer Certification: Designed for those who understand the principles of product and service quality evaluation and control.

Quality Auditor Certification: Designed for those who understand the standards and principles of auditing and the auditing techniques of examining, questioning, evaluating, and reporting to determine quality systems adequacy.

Reliability Engineer Certification: Designed for those who understand the principles of performance evaluation and prediction to improve product/systems safety, reliability, and maintainability.

Quality Technician Certification: Designed for those who can analyze quality problems, prepare inspection plans and instructions, select sampling plan applications, and apply fundamental statistical methods for process control.

Mechanical Inspector Certification: Designed for those who, under professional direction, can evaluate hardware documentation, perform laboratory procedures, inspect products, measure process performance, record data, and prepare formal reports.

Quality Manager Certification: Designed for professionals who understand quality standards and concepts, implement organizational assessments, maintain customer satisfaction and focus. The certified quality manager should manage projects supporting strategic objectives and motivate human resources in the support of organizational goals.

Source: "ASQC Certification," ASQC pamphlet (Milwaukee, Wis.: ASQC, 1994). Used with permission.

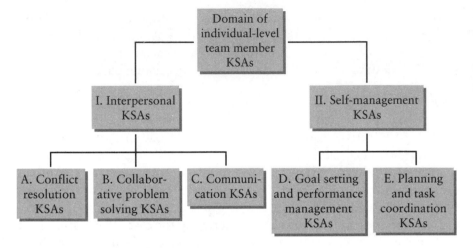

Figure 7.1. The content categories of the knowledge, skill, and ability requirements for teamwork.

Source: Michael J. Stevens, *Managing Employees in a Team Environment* (El Paso, Tex.: Michael J. Stevens, 1995).

sult in an overall assessment of their knowledge of teamwork. We profile the use of this knowledge test in predicting individual performance in teams in chapter 13, and also share example items from the test.[38]

Biographical Information

The use of biographical information for personnel selection has a long history and is used to measure both the can-do and will-do components of the performance equation. Biographical information is widely used when making employment decisions and runs the gamut from the very subjectively developed and scored **application blank** at one end of the continuum to the statistically (empirically keyed) developed **biographical information blank** (BIB) at the other. The basic assumption underlying the use of biographical information is that past behavioral patterns should be predictive of future behavior. This section will be used to describe four approaches for using biographical information.

1. Application forms

2. Education and experience (skills) inventories

3. Weighted application blank (WAB)

4. BIB

Exhibit 7.12. Dimensions measured by the teamwork KSA test.

The essential knowledge, skills, and abilities (KSAs) needed by employees in a self-managing teamwork environment

I. Interpersonal Team Member KSAs

  A. *Conflict Resolution KSAs,* consisting of

    1. Fostering useful conflict, while eliminating dysfunctional conflict

    2. Matching the conflict management strategy to the source and nature of the conflict

    3. Using integrative (win-win) strategies rather than distributive (win-lose) strategies

  B. *Collaborative Problem Solving KSAs,* consisting of

    4. Utilizing the right level of participation for any given problem

    5. Avoiding obstacles to team problem solving (such as domination by some team members) by structuring how team members interact

  C. *Communication KSAs,* consisting of

    6. Employing communication patterns that maximize an open flow

    7. Using an open and supportive style of communication

    8. Utilizing active listening techniques

    9. Paying attention to nonverbal messages

    10. Taking advantage of the interpersonal value found in greeting other team members, engaging in appropriate small talk, and so on.

II. Self-Management Team Member KSAs

  D. *Goal Setting and Performance Management KSAs,* consisting of

    11. Setting specific, challenging, and accepted team goals

    12. Monitoring, evaluating, and providing feedback on performance

  E. *Planning and Task Coordination KSAs,* consisting of

    13. Coordinating and synchronizing tasks, activities, and information

    14. Establishing fair and balanced roles and workloads among team members

---

Source: Michael J. Stevens, *Managing Employees in a Team Environment* (El Paso, Tex.: Michael J. Stevens, 1995). Reprinted by permission.

Application Forms

Most organizations require application forms to be completed as the first hurdle in the selection process. Typically, these forms focus on the education and job history of the candidate. This information has the advantage of being used as an inexpensive but systematic means for screening applicants relative to certain minimum job requirements. Application forms are particularly useful in situations where the number of applicants is substantially greater than the number of openings (a low SR). In our 3M Canada case, for example, 60 applicants were recruited for each opening at the plant (SR = .016). Similarly, Toyota's manufacturing operation received more than 60,000 applications for approximately 2700 positions (SR = .05) at its Georgetown, Kentucky, plant.

We recommend the use of application blanks over such tools as resumes and letters of reference because they can be used to collect information from the organization's perspective rather than the applicant's. As Erwin S. Stanton points out,

> *An applicant's resume will tell us what the applicant wants us to know, not necessarily what we need to know. Some borderline and totally incompetent applicants engage the services of so-called employment consultants to help them design elaborate, attractive resumes that extol their alleged virtues and abilities. These resumes are little more than tributes to the writing skills of the people preparing them.*[39]

Similarly, letters of reference do not have a very good track record for predicting job performance. Application blanks have the added advantage of requiring the candidate to sign a statement that the information contained on the application blank is true and that the individual can be terminated for falsifying the document.

Because of the very subjective nature of the application form, some recommendations and cautions are in order. First, the use of an application form, like any selection device, should be scrutinized in terms of the standards outlined in chapter 3. In particular, the issues of validity and fairness become critical. Only those questions considered job related should be included on the form, and care should be taken to avoid items that may create disparate impact on a protected group or that may be viewed as discriminatory. Application forms should be periodically reviewed and updated to reflect EEO laws and guidelines.

Beyond making sure that the content is focused on job-related information, the application process can also be improved by the addition of objective scoring guidelines, which can be achieved with a weighted application blank. Weighted application blanks have been used in various settings to develop objective scoring schemes that predict behavior such as turnover. In one study, a scoring scheme was devised and used to predict turnover among county government clerical workers and resulted in savings of more than $250,000.[40]

Finally, and most important, the application form should reflect the quality imperative of the organization. Form content can easily be expanded to collect information related to specific training and work-related experiences (for example, quality-related training, technical skills training, experience working in team situations, and so on).

Education and Experience (Skills) Inventories

A further refinement of the application form is the use of instruments designed to collect very specific information related to the candidate's education, training, and experiences. While still subjectively developed, these instruments adhere much more closely to what we previously described as content validity. Based on a thorough review of the job and organization, education and experience (E&E) inventories use a rational approach for demonstrating the relationship between response scores and job success. These E&E inventories are widely used in the public sector and show considerable promise for selecting highly skilled and quality-oriented employees in organization settings.[41]

Exhibit 7.13 presents a portion of a skills inventory used to evaluate applicants in 3M Canada manufacturing facilities.

Weighted Application Blanks and Biographical Information Blanks

WABs, as the name implies, identify statistically significant relationships between responses to questions on the application form (for example: How far do you live from this work location? How old were you when you graduated from high school?) and later measures of job performance (for example, turnover, absenteeism, sales performance). This is done by identifying those application items that differentiate between groups of effective (high tenure) and ineffective (low tenure) employees. Weights are then assigned to each application question in accordance with the predictive power of that item.[42]

BIBs (also termed biographical inventories) are similar to WABs in terms of being self-report instruments and in the methodology used in

Exhibit 7.13. Inventory used to assess applicant skills and relevant experiences.

Last Name	First Name	Middle Initial	SSN	Date Completed

Skill Rating	Skill Code	Skill Area Description
	01	Shipping/Receiving—loading trucks, bills of lading, manifest documentation, transportation of dangerous goods, ordering materials, ensuring material receipt, completing necessary paperwork, lift truck operation.
	02	Preventive Maintenance—development and execution of planned maintenance activities including parts changing, oiling, and lubricating.
	03	Production Machinery—operation, repair, troubleshooting. Please indicate purpose of machinery and your specific duties.
	04	Shop Equipment and Machinery—operation, repair, and maintenance of lathe, mill, grinder, drill press, and CNC equipment.
	05	Tool and Die Use and Maintenance—using, making, repairing, or maintaining tools and dies.
	06	Quality Control Techniques and Systems—SPC, SQC, ISO 9000, etc.
	07	Blueprint Reading—reading prints, layouts, diagrams, schematics, etc.
	08	Preparing Job Documentation—preparing written descriptions of work, including process worksheets, job aids, etc.
	09	Production and System Changeover—changing a line or system to produce different products or configurations.
	10	Health and Safety—occupational health and safety procedures such as machine lock-out, hazardous material handling, first aid, etc.
	11	Continuous improvement—quality control/improvement, suggestion program participation, problem solving.
	12	Assembly—manually place products, parts or materials in trays, rolls, or hoppers. Fit, fasten, or join components or parts. Load and unload parts or products in automatic or semiautomatic assembly machines.
	13	Manufacturing Environment—working in a production/manufacturing environment, operating manufacturing equipment, ensuring quality of product and meeting production standards.
	14	Community Groups—working on community projects, organizing or participating in efforts of social committee or groups.
	15	Auto Repair—maintaining and repairing autos, checking and adding fluids, changing oil, doing tune ups, replacing brake pads.
	16	Home/Building Construction, Repair, Maintenance—completing home repairs, installing large appliances, building additions or decks, roof maintenance, flooding, etc.

Instructions for Completion

We are especially interested in finding individuals who have skills related to those listed to the right. As you describe your skills, please keep in mind that we are interested in skills developed from both job-related and non-job-related experiences (for example, military positions, hobbies).

STEP 1—Rate your ability or experience in each area. Mark the rating in the space provided to the left of the skill. Use the following rating scale:

Blank   No experience in Skill Area

1   Limited Experience

2   Moderate Experience (may need some assistance or direction)

3   Extensive Experience (have performed in skill area with no direction or assistance)

STEP 2—After rating your skill experience, choose the highest rated skills. Then, describe both your experience and how you acquired the skill in the boxes provided on the lower half of this sheet. Place the skill number in the space provided to show the level detail we would like from you. (Don't feel it is necessary to fill out all the boxes. We have provided more boxes than we expect most people to need.)

Exhibit 7.13. Continued.

Code #01	Description of skill and how your obtained skills	Example

At XYZ Company, I drove a lift truck and stocked different line areas. This job involved communicating with operators concerning needed stock and ensuring that none of the 12 operators was ever out of stock.

Are you Certified or Licensed in this Skill?
If Yes, Describe Where and When Obtained. ☐ Yes ☐ No

Code #	Description of skill and how your obtained skills

Are you Certified or Licensed in this Skill?
If Yes, Describe Where and When Obtained. ☐ Yes ☐ No

Code #	Description of skill and how your obtained skills

Are you Certified or Licensed in this Skill?
If Yes, Describe Where and When Obtained. ☐ Yes ☐ No

Code #	Description of skill and how your obtained skills

Are you Certified or Licensed in this Skill?
If Yes, Describe Where and When Obtained. ☐ Yes ☐ No

Please describe any skills, training, or experience you have that prepare you to participate in work teams that are responsible for deciding upon and directing their own activities. (For example, facilitator training, participation in community organizations, leadership exercises, service as an instructor/trainer, participation in problem-solving training, etc.)

Source: HRStrategies, Grosse Pointe, Michigan. Used with permission.

Exhibit 7.14. Example items for inclusion in a WAB.

Q. During your last two years in high school, about how many hours a
   week did you spend on athletics?

     ○ 1 or less

     ○ 2 to 5

     ○ 6 to 9

     ○ More than 10

Q. How many professional development meetings, workshops, or
   seminars have you attended during the last year?

     ○ Zero

     ○ 1 or 2

     ○ 3 or 4

     ○ 5 or more

Q. Did you ever build a model airplane that flew?

     ○ Yes

     ○ No

---

their development. They differ from their WAB cousins in that they include a larger sample of items covering a much wider range of biographical, attitudinal, and preference questions. Additionally,
question responses are presented in a multiple-choice format.[43]

Figure 7.2 displays the use of biographical inventories in the sample of ASQC sustaining member organizations.

Both WABs and BIBs have an excellent track record for predicting
various measures of job performance, particularly turnover. Criterion-
related studies report validities in the range of .25 to .50.[44] Recent research also indicates that BIBs may have validity that is generalizable
across companies and occupations.[45] An example of that predictive
power can be illustrated with the previously described biodata item:
"Did you ever build a model airplane that flew?" This single item was
almost as good a predictor of success in flight training during World
War II as the entire Air Force Test Battery.[46]

The authors of this book believe that the use of biodata has considerable potential for predicting relevant behavior and performance
in quality settings. William A. Owens, for example, has identified a
number of biodata factors that can be reliably measured across samples and that are consistent with various models and theories of personality and human development.[47] For example, his factors *academic
achievement, positive academic attitude,* and *interest in vocational*

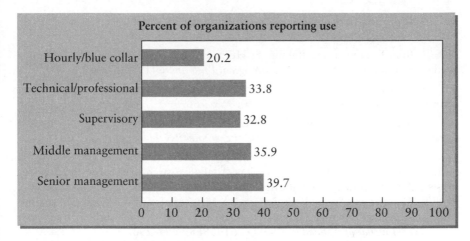

Figure 7.2. Use of biographical inventories for selection and promotion.

courses are doubtless highly related to the quality attributes *openness to learning, development, and retraining.* Similarly, his identified factors *social desirability* and *social introversion* show promise for predicting teamwork orientation and skill in relating to others. Recent research in the military has identified biodata items that measure a number of factors including *team sports/group orientation* (preference for working in groups) and *intellectual/achievement orientation* (involvement in intellectual pastimes).[48]

Summary

In this chapter we've presented examples of measures available to help assess the individual's readiness to learn and perform in the new workplace. We hope that this chapter has given you the basis on which to investigate the potential usefulness of these tools to your specific setting.

Notes

1. John Hunter, "Cognitive Ability, Cognitive Aptitudes, Job Knowledge, and Job Performance," *Journal of Vocational Behavior* 29 (1986): 340–362.

2. Jack J. Kramer and Jane Close Canoley, eds., *The Mental Measurements Yearbook* (Lincoln, Neb.: Buros Institute of Mental Measurements, University of Nebraska Press, 1992); Linda L. Murphy, Jane Close Canoley, and James C. Impara,

eds., *Tests in Print* (Lincoln, Neb.: Buros Institute of Mental Measurements, University of Nebraska Press, 1994).

3. John E. Hunter and Rhonda E. Hunter, "Validity and Utility of Alternative Predictors of Job Performance," *Psychological Bulletin* 96 (1984): 72–98.

4. Wayne Cascio and Niel Phillips, "Performance Testing: A Rose Among Thorns?" *Personnel Psychology* 32 (1979): 751–766.

5. Richard R. Reilly and Georgia T. Chao, "Validity and Fairness of Some Alternative Employee Selection Procedures," *Personnel Psychology* 35 (1982): 1–62.

6. Cynthia Searcy, Patty Nio Woods, Robert D. Gatewood, and Charles F. Lance, "The Structured Interview: A Meta-Analytic Search for Moderators," paper presented at the Society for Industrial and Organizational Psychology, May 1993; Willi H. Wiesner and Steven F. Cronshaw, "A Meta-Analytic Investigation of the Impact of Interview Format and Degree of Structure on the Validity of the Employment Interview," *Journal of Applied Psychology* 61 (1988): 275–290.

7. W. Edwards Deming, *Out of the Crisis* (Cambridge, Mass.: MIT Center for Advanced Engineering Study, 1982).

8. Stephen B. Knouse, *The Reward and Recognition Process in Total Quality Management* (Milwaukee, Wis.: ASQC Quality Press, 1995).

9. Hunter and Hunter, "Validity and Utility of Alternative Predictors of Job Performance."

10. Robert Gatewood and Hubert Feild, *Human Resource Selection* (Fort Worth, Tex.: Dryden Press, 1994).

11. F. Schmidt, J. Hunter, K. Pearlman, and Guy Shane, "Further Tests of the Schmidt-Hunter Bayesian Validity Generalization Procedure," *Personnel Psychology* 32 (1979): 257–281; K. Pearlman, F. Schmidt, and J. Hunter, "Validity Generalization Results for Tests Used to Predict Job Proficiency and Training Success in Clerical Occupations," *Journal of Applied Psychology* 65 (1980): 373–406.

12. J. McHenry, L. M. Hough, J. L. Toquan, M. A. Hanson, and S. Ashworth, "Project A Validity Results: The Relationship Between Predictor and Criterion Domains," *Personnel Psychology* 43 (1990): 335–354.

13. Hunter, "Cognitive Ability, Cognitive Aptitudes, Job Knowledge, and Job Performance."

14. David Wechsler, *Weschler Adult Intelligence Scale,* revised 1981 (San Antonio, Tex.: The Psychological Corporation, 800-228-0752).

15. L. L. Thurstone and T. G. Thurstone, *Thurstone Test of Mental Alertness (TMA)* (Boston: Available through SRA, London House, 800-221-8378).

16. SRA London House, *SRA Human Resource Assessment Catalog for Business and Industry* (Rosemont, Ill.: 1992), 58.

17. R. Guion, *Personnel Testing* (New York: McGraw-Hill, 1965), 234.

18. J. E. Hunter, *The Wonderlic Personnel Test as a Predictor of Training Success and Job Performance* (Northfield, Ill.: E. F. Wonderlic Personnel Test, 1989).

19. F. L. Grimsley, N. D. Warren Ruch, and J. S. Ford, *Employee Aptitude Survey (EAS):* Psychological Services, Inc, 800-331-TEST.

20. John C. Flanagan, *Flanagan Aptitude Classification Tests (FACT)* (Boston: SRA London House Human Resource Assessment, 800-221-8378).

21. George K. Bennett, Harold G. Seashore, and Alexander G. Wesman, *The Differential Aptitude Tests,* 5th ed. (San Antonio, Tex.: Psychological Corporation, 1990); Technical Test Battery (Boston: Saville & Holdsworth).

22. "Applied Technology Series," *Ability Test,* p. 23 (Boston: Saville & Holdsworth, 800-899-7451).

23. Goodwin Watson and Edward M. Glaser, *Watson-Glaser Critical Thinking Appraisal* (San Antonio, Tex.: Psychological Corporation, 1980).

24. *Critical Thinking Test* (Boston: Saville & Holdsworth, 800-899-7451), 12.

25. Peter Saville, Roger Holdsworth, Gill Nyfield, David Hawkey, Susan Bawtree and Ruth Holdsworth, "The Critical Reasoning Test Battery," *Ability Tests* (Boston: Saville & Holdsworth, 1983), 13. 800-899-7451.

26. G. K. Bennett, *The Bennett Mechanical Comprehension Test* (San Antonio, Tex.: Psychological Corporation, 1980.

27. The Psychological Corporation, *Tests and Related Products for Human Resource Assessment* (San Antonio: Tex.: 1995).

28. Gatewood and Feild, *Human Resource Selection,* chapter 13.

29. Hilda Wing, "Review of the Bennett Mechanical Comprehension Test," in *Mental Measurements Yearbook,* Jack J. Kramer and Jane Close Canoley, eds., 106.

30. The Psychological Corporation, *Tests and Related Products for Human Resource Assessment,* 30–31.

31. Saville & Holdsworth, "The Basic Skills Series Production," *Ability Tests* (Boston: SHL, 1994): 19.

32. The Psychological Corporation, *Tests and Related Products for Human Resource Assessment,* 32.

33. Sarah Jastak and Gary S. Wilkinson, *Wide Range Achievement Test—3* (San Antonio, Tex.: The Psychological Corporation, 1993, 800-228-0752).

34. The Psychological Corporation, *Tests and Related Products for Human Resource Assessment,* 30.

35. A. G. Wesman and J. E. Doppelt, *Personnel Tests for Industry,* (San Antonio, Tex.: The Psychological Corporation, 1969, 800-228-0752).

36. The Psychological Corporation, *Tests and Related Products for Human Resource Assessment,* 43.

37. ASQC, 611 East Wisconsin Avenue, Milwaukee, Wis. 53202, 800-248-1946, (414) 272-8575, FAX (414) 272-1734.

38. Contact Michael J. Stevens, University of Texas at El Paso, El Paso, Tex. 79968-0539, (915) 747-5185.

39. Erwin S. Stanton, *Successful Personel Recruiting and Selection* (New York: AMACON, 1977), 80.

40. Raymond Lee and Jerome M. Booth, "A Utility Analysis of a Weighted Application Blank Designed to Predict Turnover for Clerical Employees," *Journal of Applied Psychology* 59 (1974): 516–518.

41. Ronald A. Ash, James C. Johnson, Edward Levine, and M. A. McDaniel, "Job Applicant Training and Work Experience Evaluation in Personnel Selection," in *Research in Personnel and Human Resources Management,* K. Rowland and G. Ferris, eds. (Greenwich, Conn.: JAI Press, 1989).

42. Wayne F. Cascio, *Applied Psychology in Personnel Management*, 3rd ed. (Englewood Cliffs, N.J.: Prentice Hall, 1987), 258.

43. H. John Bernardin and Joyce E. A. Russell, *Human Resources Management: An Experiential Approach* (New York: McGraw-Hill, 1993), 221.

44. Richard R. Reilly and Georgia T. Chao, "Validity and Fairness of Some Alternative Employee Selection Procedures, *Personal Psychology* 35 (1982): 1–62. See also John E. Hunter and Rhonda E. Hunter, "Validity and Utility of Alternative Predictors of Job Performance," *Psychologyical Bulletin* 96 (1984): 72–98.

45. Neal Schmitt, R. Z. Gooding, R. A. Noe, and M. Kirsch, "Meta-Analysis of Validity Studies Published Between 1964–1982 and an Investigation of Study Characteristics," *Personnel Psychology* 37 (1984): 407–422. See also Frank L. Schmidt, D. S. Ones, and J. E. Hunter, "Personnel Selection," in *Annual Review of Psychology*, L. Porter and M. Rosensweig eds. (Stanford: Annual Reviews, 1992), 627–670.

46. E. R. Henry, *Research Conference on the Use of Autobiographical Data as Psychological Predictors* (Greensboro, N.C.: Richard Foundation, 1965).

47. William A. Owens, "Background Data," in *Handbook of Industrial and Organizational Psychology*, Marvin D. Dunette, ed. (Skokie, Ill.: Rand McNally, 1976).

48. Fred A. Mael and Blake E. Ashforth, "Loyal from Day One: Biodata, Organizational Identification, and Turnover Among Newcomers," *Personnel Psychology* (1995): 309–333.

chapter 8

Personnel Assessment Tools: Assessing and Predicting Motivation to Perform

Overview

This chapter builds on the previous chapter's discussion of assessment with an emphasis on the use of personality and motivational staffing tools.

Introduction

In chapter 4, we discussed the relative importance of various quality-related attributes as identified in our survey of ASQC sustaining member organizations. A careful review of those findings shows that the personality and motivational attributes (will-do attributes) are often the ones considered most critical to the successful implementation of quality improvement efforts. Thus, attributes such as *customer orientation, skill in relating with others, creative thinking, flexibility/adaptability,* and so on were considered relatively more important than the specific knowledge and skill attributes (can-do attributes) such as *applied statistics, SPC,* and *knowledge of experimental design.*

When staffing for quality, every effort should be made to identify these will-do attributes and then systematically assess each candidate's tendency or predisposition to behave in that manner. Will the candidate continue to learn and develop once placed on the job? Will he/she function well in a team environment? Will the candidate remain customer oriented once faced with the realities of the work situation? These are the nitty-gritty questions we attempt to answer during the staffing process. But herein lies the major rub of selection. The personality and motivational attributes considered the most important in a quality setting are, in practice, the most difficult to reliably and validly assess. When staffing for quality, it is much easier to measure the candidate's basic SPC knowledge and skills or cognitive ability than it is to determine whether or not the person will be customer oriented, open to change, or function effectively in a group or team environment.

The good news is that, if done correctly, valid assessment of an individual's typical behavior (personality and motivation) is possible. Recent findings suggest that personality assessment may be more predictive of work performance than previously thought. In addition, typical behavior can be assessed through behavior observation (simulations and exercises) and by examining the success history (behavioral interviewing and biographical information) of the candidate. Used appropriately, particularly in combination, these assessment tools can be used to select and promote quality-oriented employees. In this chapter, we will discuss the various assessment devices used to focus primarily on the measurement of the will do component of the performance equation. In particular, the following five assessment tools will be addressed.

1. Personality and motivation tests

2. Interest inventories

3. Simulations and assessment centers

4. Performance appraisals

5. Honesty and integrity inventories

We will also briefly describe the use of two other tools, the polygraph and graphology (handwriting analysis). Before discussing these assessment devices, the reader should be reminded of the job performance equation presented in chapter 2 (see Figure 8.1). It is also important to reiterate that many of these tools are used to measure both the can-do and will-do factors of job performance, particularly, work simulations and performance appraisals.

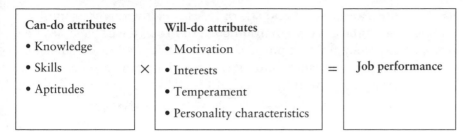

Figure 8.1. Factors contributing to the job performance of individuals.

Personality and Motivational Assessment

Personality tests can be divided into two broad categories: self-report inventories and projective tests. *Self-report inventories,* as the name implies, ask candidates to describe themselves by answering a set of questions or statements related to their attitudes, preferences, behaviors, and so on. For example, the candidate might be asked

I would rather work alone than in a group setting	*Agree*	*Disagree*
If you want something done right, do it yourself	*Agree*	*Disagree*

OR

Which of the following descriptions is most like you?		
A. Flexible	*OR*	*B. Neat and tidy*
A. Show-me attitude	*OR*	*B. Hardworking*

Responses to these statements are scored in terms of various personality scales or dimensions such as emotional stability, personal relations, intraversion/extraversion, and conscientiousness.

The most eminent of these self-report tests is the **Minnesota Multiphasic Personality Inventory (MMPI).**[1] This 566-item test is typically used in clinical settings for measuring such personality factors as depression, paranoia, and schizophrenia. However, the MMPI is used to identify and screen out individuals with pathological problems for such occupations as police officers, firefighters, and high security and nuclear power plant employees.

While a number of personality tests exist that are used in organizational settings (for example, **California Psychological Inventory**

(CPI), 16PF, Adjective Checklist), only a few show direct promise for application in the quality environment. And even fewer have been developed expressly for that purpose. We will begin by discussing some of the personality measures and inventories that show promise in total quality settings, followed by descriptions of five instruments designed specifically for use in the quality/service environment.

The Big Five Personality Factors

Of particular interest to the issue of quality is a line of personality research that has centered on the measurement of five separate and identifiable psychological traits or constructs. Compelling research evidence exists that these Big Five personality factors can be reliably measured through the Personality Characteristics Inventory and are often associated with job-related behavior and performance.[2] These five personality factors are

1. Extraversion/introversion (sociable, gregarious, assertive)

2. Emotional stability (anxious, depressed, emotional)

3. Agreeableness or likability (courteous, good-natured, cooperative)

4. Conscientiousness (hardworking, achievement-oriented, persevering)

5. Intellect (open to experience, curious, intelligent)

In particular, four of the Big Five factors show promise for predicting relevant behavior in the quality setting. Extraversion and, to some degree, agreeableness are likely to be related to such important quality attributes as *customer orientation* and *teamwork orientation.* Likewise, intellect is apt to be predictive of individuals who are creative in their thinking. Intellect may also be related to the important quality attribute *openness to learning, development, and retraining.* Finally, the factor *conscientiousness* was one of the highest rated attributes in the survey of ASQC sustaining members.

We are unaware of any studies that have specifically examined the predictability of the Big Five personality factors in quality-related settings. However, some research findings support their potential for such use. One study used a meta-analysis approach for investigating the relation of the Big Five factors with various job performance criteria, including job proficiency, training proficiency, and personnel data (turnover).[3] Results of that study indicated that the conscientiousness factor was related to all of the job performance criteria measures across a number of occupations. Not surprisingly, it appears that hard-working and achievement-oriented persons are likely to be successful in any work setting.

Of particular interest to our discussion of quality was the finding that extraversion was a valid predictor of success only in those occupations involving high social interaction (for example, sales and management). The obvious inference is that, in work settings where social interaction and customer service skills are valued (the quality-oriented organization), the personality factor *extraversion* will likely be predictive of success. Also of interest was the finding that intellect (open to experience and curious) was a valid predictor of the training proficiency criterion. As previously discussed, success in the quality organization requires that all employees be open to continuous learning, development, and retraining. As such, the measurement of the Big Five personality factor of *intellect* or *openness to experience* and *conscientiousness* seems particularly promising.

In summary, an impressive body of literature has accumulated that points to the robustness and possible predictive power of the Big Five personality factors. Unfortunately, the research studies reported in the literature have attempted to generalize the validity of the Big Five across a wide array of occupational settings using broad job performance criteria measures. The authors of this text argue that high scores on such factors as extraversion and intellect would be even more predictive of success in the quality setting than in organizations operating under a more traditional model.

Some of the tests or inventories that measure, at least in part, the Big Five personality factors include

- The California Psychological Inventory (CPI)[4]
- Adjective Checklist[5]
- MMPI[6]
- Edwards Personal Preference Schedule[7]
- Gordon Personal Profile Inventory[8]
- 16PF®[9]
- Prevue Assessment Inventory[10]

Figure 8.2 shows an example of an interpretive report from the 16PF, one of the more widely used inventories. Another example of a summary report from the Prevue Assessment Inventory is shown in Figure 8.3. Note that the Prevue instrument also provides interest and ability data for the client (see chapter 7).

Measuring Personality in the Quality Setting

While most personality measures have been developed for use in a wide array of organizational settings, we believe at least five instruments have a direct link to performance in quality settings.

PDI's CSI.[11] Developed by PDI, this 64-item test measures a test taker's customer service orientation. The CSI is described as "a screening tool that identifies those job applicants most likely to exhibit helpful and positive service behaviors as they interact with customers and co-workers." Individuals scoring high on the test are reported to be "more likely to be pleasant, helpful, customer-oriented employees." The CSI is considered appropriate for positions requiring substantial contact with customers or where the job requires attributes measured by the CSI (for example, friendliness, courtesy, open-mindedness, practicality, and competence).

We selected the CSI for discussion because it best exemplifies a professionally developed test that can be used to improve performance on an important quality-related attribute—customer service. The CSI was developed using job analysis, as well as a thorough understanding of personality measurement and the theoretical underpinnings of the concept of customer service. Test item selection was accomplished using a sophisticated process of cross-validation and double cross-validation. The final instrument was then evaluated using a completely independent sample. Subsequent studies using the CSI across a wide range of organizations and jobs show predictive validity coefficients in the .11 to .33 range for overall customer service performance ratings and .07 to .26 for rehireability (yes or no). The test-retest reliability for the CSI is .86. Additionally, the test publishers reported that no disparate impact against minorities or females was found in any of the organizations studied.[12]

Used in conjunction with other pertinent information, the CSI shows a great deal of promise for selection in positions requiring high degrees of customer service. Figure 8.4 provides score interpretation guidelines for the CSI.

Figure 8.2. An example of an interpretive report from the 16PF.

Basic Interpretive Report   NAME: Mark Sample
Global Factors   DATE: January 24, 1995

For each profile below, several 16 primary scales combine to determine the global factor score. Sometimes a low score on a primary scale contributes to a high score on a global factor, and vice versa. Occasionally, a primary scale score does not fall in the direction expected, based upon the overall global factor score. These unusual factor combinations or conflicting scores can be revealing; it may be useful to explore the ways in which the test taker's behavior reflects such combinations.

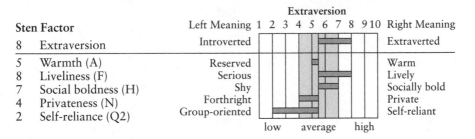

Mr. Sample's personality is highly extraverted. He shows a strong preference for social contact and probably enjoys interacting with others. Because his attention is directed toward other people, he may be uncomfortable when alone.

- His style of expression is often enthusiastic and playful. He may prefer a lively or active social environment.
- Because this person tends to be socially bold, he is unlikely to feel intimidated in group settings.
- When Mr. Sample chooses to reveal personal matters to others, he tends to be forthright and genuine.
- Mr. Sample prefers to do things and make plans with others. Additionally, he may avoid situations that require working alone.

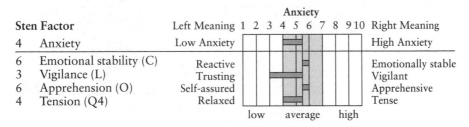

At the present time, Mr. Sample presents himself as somewhat less anxious than most people.

- He readily trusts other people. Because he is so accepting of others, he may not think to examine the motivation(s) behind their actions or behaviors.
- Most times Mr. Sample is relaxed and composed, and has few feelings of frustration.

Figure 8.3. An example of a summary report from the Prevue Assessment Inventory.

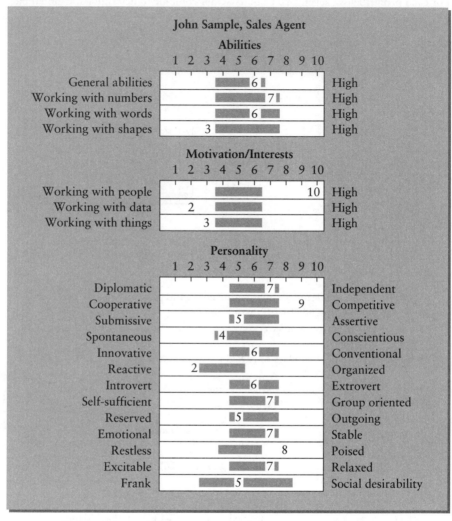

John Sample, Sales Agent

Abilities

1 2 3 4 5 6 7 8 9 10

General abilities — 6 — High
Working with numbers — 7 — High
Working with words — 6 — High
Working with shapes — 3 — High

Motivation/Interests

1 2 3 4 5 6 7 8 9 10

Working with people — 10 — High
Working with data — 2 — High
Working with things — 3 — High

Personality

1 2 3 4 5 6 7 8 9 10

Diplomatic — 7 — Independent
Cooperative — 9 — Competitive
Submissive — 5 — Assertive
Spontaneous — 4 — Conscientious
Innovative — 6 — Conventional
Reactive — 2 — Organized
Introvert — 6 — Extrovert
Self-sufficient — 7 — Group oriented
Reserved — 5 — Outgoing
Emotional — 7 — Stable
Restless — 8 — Poised
Excitable — 7 — Relaxed
Frank — 5 — Social desirability

Source: Profiles International, Inc., Waco, Tex., 1995. Used with permission.

The CSI's companion instrument titled the *PDI Employment Inventory* also shows high potential for use in quality settings. The EI is used to help identify dependable, reliable (conscientious) employees and helps reduce turnover.[13] Examples of the potential utility (ROI) for both of these instruments are presented in chapter 3.

ServiceFirst.[14] ServiceFirst, much like the CSI, is a test that measures customer service potential. Items on the test were designed to measure four dimensions of customer service.

Figure 8.4. Score interpretation guidelines for the CSI.

Customer Service Scale
Higher customer service scores suggest more competent, responsive, and courteous service behavior

Recommend Rejection bottom 25%	Caution lower 25%	Recommend Hire top 50%
0 57	58 64	65 86
Are more likely to be rude to customers; have a tendency to: • Act irritated at customers' requests • Argue with customers • Limit service for certain types of customers • Take too long processing customers' transactions	Are less likely to be responsive by: • Forgetting to give customers special information • Interrupting or failing to pay attention when customers speak • Socializing with a coworker while helping others • Mumbling when talking to customers	Are more likely to be competent and courteous on the job by: • Making good eye contact, smiling, and communicating effectively • Showing persistent enthusiasm in customer interactions • Tolerating rude customers calmly • Giving customers full attention • Putting aside other work to help customers • Finding solutions to customer problems • Remaining cheerful through a long, hard work day.

Source: George E. Paajanen, Timothy L. Hansen, and Richard A. McLellan, *PDI Employment Inventory and PDI Customer Service Inventory Manual* (Minneapolis, Minn.: PDI, 1993): 95. Used with permission.

1. *Active customer relations.* Seeks and acts on service/sales opportunities with customers.

2. *Polite customer relations.* Demonstrates courtesy, manners, and rapport in personal interactions with customers.

3. *Helpful customer relations.* Responds to customers' needs by taking extraordinary actions to assist them.

4. *Personalized customer relations.* Shows recognition of unique customer qualities; gets to know customers by name.

These four dimensions were identified as critical aspects of customer service orientation, based on a thorough review of the organizational, marketing, psychological, and management literatures. A complete description of those dimensions is shown in Exhibit 8.1.

ServiceFirst contains 50 test items and each of the four dimensions of customer service is measured by 10 items. The remaining 10 items are used to detect faking among respondents. The test items were

Exhibit 8.1. Understanding scale scores for the ServiceFirst instrument.

Active Customer Relations. This scale measures potential to seek and act on service and sales opportunities with customers.	
Individuals *high* on Active Customer Relations: • Perform tasks quickly and productively • Work with liveliness and vitality • Can work on more than one thing at a time • Do not tire easily • Enjoy a fast work pace	Individuals *low* on Active Customer Relations: • Perform tasks slowly and unproductively • Work lethargically • Have trouble working on more than one thing at a time • Tire easily • Do not enjoy a fast work pace
Polite Customer Relations. This scale measures potential to demonstrate courtesy, manners, and rapport in personal interactions with customers.	
Individuals *high* on Polite Customer Relations: • Frequently use phrases such as *please, thank you, excuse me,* etc. • Smile at customers often • Are courteous to rude customers • Easily establish rapport with customers • Get along well with employees and customers	Individuals *low* on Polite Customer Relations: • Infrequently use phrases such as *please, thank you, excuse me,* etc. • Rarely smile at customers • Are not courteous to rude customers • Have difficulty establishing rapport with customers • Do not get along well with employees and customers
Helpful Customer Relations. This scale measures potential to respond to customer needs by taking extraordinary actions to assist them.	
Individuals *high* on Helpful Customer Relations: • Show customers where things are rather than telling them • Offer extra assistance to customers when needed • Go out of their way to satisfy customer need • Get personal satisfaction out of helping people • Enjoy having responsibility for other people	Individuals *low* on Helpful Customer Relations: • Tell customers where things are rather than showing them • Offer little extra assistance to customers when needed • Do not go out of their way to satisfy customer need • Do not get personal satisfaction out of helping people • Would rather not have much responsibility for other people
Personalized Customer Relations. This scale measures potential to show recognition of unique customer qualities.	
Individuals *high* on Personalized Customer Relations: • Get to know customers by name • Address customers by name when known • Take an interest in customers' specific requests/needs • Enjoy socializing with customers • Listen attentively to customers	Individuals *low* on Personalized Customer Relations: • Do not get to know customers by name • Do not address customers by name when known • Do not take an interest in customers' specific requests/needs • Do not enjoy socializing with customers • Do not listen attentively to customers

Source: ServiceFirst™ Test Manual (Pleasant Hill, Calif.: CORE Corporation, 1995). Reprinted by permission.

written in two formats. Thirty-six of the items are behavior description questions that ask the respondent to read several statements and to indicate how well each of the statements describes him/her. The respondent's ratings are made on a five-point scale with a rating of "1" indicating that the statement is not at all like him/her and a rating of "5" indicating that the statement is exactly like him/her. The remaining items are situational judgment questions that ask the respondent to read several situations and a corresponding action that could be taken in each. The respondent is then asked to rate the likelihood that he/she would do what is described in each situation. The respondent's ratings are made on a five-point scale with "1" indicating that the respondent definitely would do what is described in the situation and a "5" indicating that the respondent definitely would not do what is described in the situation.

Numerous criterion-related validation studies have been conducted on ServiceFirst and, based on these studies, ServiceFirst has been found to be a valid, reliable predictor of customer service job performance in six industries, 12 different jobs, and with almost 2000 individuals.[15]

Hogan Personality Inventory (HPI).[16] While the HPI was not developed specifically for quality settings, it does, more than any other general measure of personality we could find, reflect the attributes considered important in the quality setting and the new workplace. The HPI is one of the few normal range personality instruments designed specifically for use in occupational settings. Quickly administered and reliable, the HPI consists of 206 true/false items. Easily generated reports help determine whether a person is suited for a particular occupation, will benefit from further education and training, should modify interpersonal style in order to be successful, or fits his or her current occupation. In particular, the HPI includes two occupational scales of interest: service orientation and reliability.

- *Service orientation.* Persons scoring high are courteous, attentive, and helpful when dealing with customers, clients, and coworkers.

- *Reliability.* Individuals with high scores are reliable, conscientious, careful, and easy to supervise.

Service orientation, for example, has been shown to discriminate between employees who are rude, tactless, and socially inept and those who are pleasant, tactful, and socially competent in a number of service-oriented settings including health care, insurance, and transportation.[17]

In addition to the two occupational scales, the HPI provides information on seven primary scales measuring different personality characteristics. Four of those scales relate directly to identified quality attributes and are as follows:

1. *Sociability.* High scorers are extraverted, are gregarious, need social interaction, and are successful in sales and promotional work.

2. *Likability.* High scorers are warm, charming, tactful, and successful in sales, management, or social service.

3. *Intellectance.* High-scoring persons are imaginative, curious, and creative.

4. *School success.* High scorers enjoy learning and are easily trained.

The HPI also measures *adjustment, ambition,* and *prudence.*[18]

Quality Consciousness Scale (QCS). The QCS is an 18-item psychological inventory designed to measure an individual's quality-oriented traits and attitudes (quality consciousness). The items were derived from the quality literature and knowledge experts. The QCS covers four dominant areas of an individual's quality consciousness.

1. *Quality locus of control.* The degree to which the individual takes responsibility for providing quality products and services.

2. *Error avoidance.* The extent to which the individual is committed to detecting and avoiding errors in his/her work.

3. *Quality skills.* The extent to which the individual engages in work habits and behaviors that ensure a high level of quality and excellence in all of his/her pursuits.

4. *Continuous improvement.* How much the individual strives to continually improve his/her products and service offerings.

The QCS is of particular interest because it represents a systematic effort at designing quality-oriented test scales that are directly tied to success in quality settings. Research findings indicate that the

QCS is predictive of both supervisory and self-evaluations of quality performance. One study also found a positive relationship between QCS scores and quality awards received.[19] While still in the research stage of development, the QCS shows a great deal of promise and hopefully portends things to come in the area of personality and quality test development.

The Quality Orientation Inventory (QOI). While it appears that several of the previously discussed personality measures hold promise for staffing in a quality environment, generally speaking they have been developed and validated in traditional settings. With the exception of the Quality Consciousness Scale, none of the instruments was designed specifically for selecting individuals in a quality-oriented setting. So, given the lack of quality-related personality measures and the relative importance of such attributes in quality settings, the authors of this book have developed the QOI.[20] The QOI measures six quality-related personality traits generally considered to be important for success in the quality-oriented organization.

1. *Customer orientation.* Individuals scoring high on this dimension enjoy helping others and are attentive to the needs of both external and internal customers. They are typically described as being courteous, good-natured, friendly, and empathetic.

2. *Teamwork orientation.* Persons scoring high on this trait enjoy and are effective working in group or team settings. Described as cooperative and collaborative, these individuals are supportive of group members, acknowledge and praise others for their good work, and take pride in the group's accomplishments.

3. *Flexibility/adaptability.* An individual scoring high on this trait is open to change and is willing to try new or innovative methods or approaches. Often described as accommodating, accepting, and able to adjust, these people have the ability to incorporate new information, adapt to changing circumstances, and work beyond narrow job descriptions.

4. *Openness to learning.* High-scoring individuals on this dimension derive satisfaction from continuous learning and skill development. They seek out education, training, and development opportunities for themselves and see constant learning as part of the job. They are typically described as curious, broad-minded, well educated, and open to experience.

5. *Creative thinking.* Persons scoring high on this trait enjoy experimenting with new ideas and applying novel approaches to solving current problems. These individuals can deal with ambiguity and are independent thinkers. They are often described as being nonconformists in their thinking and as being imaginative, innovative, daydreamers, and visionaries.

6. *Conscientiousness.* High-scoring persons on this trait are thorough, responsible, and hardworking. They show enthusiasm for their work and communicate the feeling, "I do make a difference." They are described as being results oriented, persevering, conscientious, and self-starters.

The QOI can be administered in individual or group settings and takes approximately 25 minutes to complete. This instrument is still in the development and validation stage but early research results indicate that the QOI reliably measures the six critical quality attributes previously described. It also successfully predicts job behavior and performance consistent with the quality-oriented organization. Easy-to-interpret graphic profiles are used to provide candidate results (see Figure 8.5).

Projective Techniques

Earlier we stated that personality tests were divided into two categories. Most personality inventories are self-report, but some projective tests are used in organizations. Projective personality measures ask the test taker to respond to some kind of intentionally ambiguous stimulus such as a picture or an ink blot. How respondents project themselves into such stimuli provides insight to the personality makeup of the individual. For example, most readers are familiar with the Rorshach Ink Blot Test where the respondent makes free, unstructured responses to a set of ink blots. These responses are considered to be projections of the needs, drives, and thoughts of the test taker. Another widely described projective technique is the **Thematic Apperception Test (TAT)**. Instead of ink blots, respondents are told to look at a set of pictures one at a time and then write a story based on what the pictures suggest. These stories are scored in terms of the various themes expressed by the test taker. David C. McClelland of the Harvard Business School has used TAT-type pictures in a number of research settings to measure such business-re-

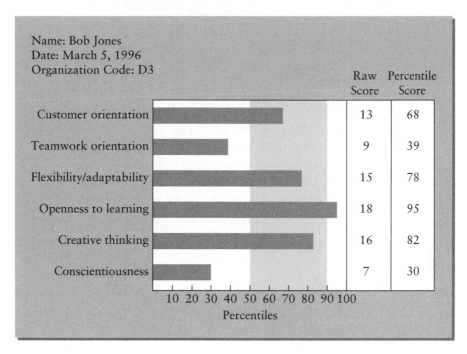

Name: Bob Jones
Date: March 5, 1996
Organization Code: D3

	Raw Score	Percentile Score
Customer orientation	13	68
Teamwork orientation	9	39
Flexibility/adaptability	15	78
Openness to learning	18	95
Creative thinking	16	82
Conscientiousness	7	30

10 20 30 40 50 60 70 80 90 100
Percentiles

Figure 8.5. Quality Orientation Inventory (QOI) example.

lated motives as need for achievement, need for power, and need for affiliation.[21]

Due to their subjectivity and lack of demonstrated validity, projective personality tests are not used very often in organizational settings. One notable exception is the **Miner Sentence Completion Scale (MSCS)** which was specifically designed for use in employment settings.[22] The MSCS consists of 40 incomplete sentences, such as "What annoys me is ____," "I wish ____," and "I like people who are ____." The candidate is instructed to complete each of the sentences with whatever comes to mind. How the test taker projects him/herself into these sentences supposedly reflects the person's motivation in seven job-related areas.

1. Capacity to deal with authority figures

2. Dealing with competitive games

3. Handling competitive situations

4. Assertiveness

5. Motivation to direct others

6. Motivation to stand out in a group

7. Desire to perform day-to-day administrative tasks

Readers are cautioned to be very careful when using such projective instruments in organizational settings. Reasons for concern include the lack of consistent predictive validity, the reluctance of candidates to take such tests, and the very traditional nature of the dimensions measured. One could easily hypothesize after reviewing the seven dimensions listed here that a low score on these factors may be more predictive of performance in a quality setting than a high score.

Summary

We believe that personality measures show a great deal of promise for predicting success in the quality setting. Given the increased emphasis on personality-related attributes in the total quality setting, these measures make sense and we argue for their increased use. Particularly when used in conjunction with other assessment tools, personality tests can be expected to add utility to the employment decision. We make this point because of the low reported use of personality measures in the ASQC sustaining member survey (see Figure 8.6). It

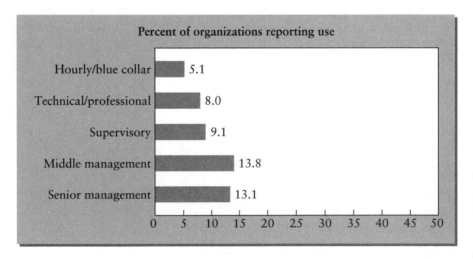

Figure 8.6. Use of standardized personality measures for selection and promotion.

would appear from these results that very few quality-oriented firms are making use of these potentially valuable tools.

Interest Inventories

Similar to self-report personality tests, interest inventories provide the respondent with information concerning the similarity between the test taker's preferences or interests and those individuals engaged in various occupations or occupational categories. For example, a high score on the Veterinarian scale tells the respondent that he/she has the same interests and preferences as those individuals employed in that occupation. Research indicates that such high scores are predictive of occupational satisfaction and that the person is likely to gravitate to that, or a similar, occupation. Two of the more popular interest or occupational inventories are the **Strong-Campbell Interest Inventory** and the **Kuder Preference Record.**[23]

As a rule, interest inventories are much more useful for vocational guidance and counseling than for selection purposes. Some notable exceptions are Sears and the U.S. military.[24] Sears uses interest inventories along with a battery of other measures to predict management success. The U.S. armed forces uses interest tests for determining assignments to military occupational training.

Most promising, however, are their use in helping individuals make career choice and career change decisions. Many firms provide interest testing and career counseling services for their employees. For example, an employee working in the financial function of the organization may be unhappy with his/her job or may simply want a career change. Feedback scores from such inventories might show that the person would likely be more satisfied in sales or as part of the HR function. Similarly, interest inventories are a valuable tool for outplacement counseling when the organization is forced to downsize its operations.

Simulations and Assessment Centers

Despite their demonstrated utility in personnel selection, many of the previously discussed will-do measures have their limitations in terms of predictive validity, test-taker acceptance, and possible litigation. In contrast, many experts advocate the use of performance or situational measures for predicting job performance.[25] They argue that samples of actual or simulated job behavior or tasks are more likely to be predictive of subsequent on-the-job behavior than are signs or predispositions (for example, personality tests) of that behavior. Simply put, the more closely the predictor measure resembles the job behavior in question, the more likely that measure is to make meaningful predictions. If the ability to work in a team environment is the critical job performance variable, then the obvious selection measure would be an exercise or simulation that reflects that teamwork orientation setting. And the closer that exercise mirrors the team environment in question, the more likely it is to be truly predictive.

The use of samples as predictors does not mean that biographical information, tests, and other selection procedures such as the employment interview should not be used. It does strongly suggest that, where possible, such measures should be behaviorally consistent with job performance criteria. This point will be discussed further in chapter 9 when we discuss the development of employment interview content.

We concur wholeheartedly with this behaviorally consistent use of samples when attempting to measure various quality-related attributes. A test or any other assessment tool is merely a sample of behavior used to make inferences about a larger performance domain. As such, the closer that link, the better. Laurence Siegel and Irving M. Lane make this point clear using the analogy of betting on how a particular horse will finish in a race.

> *A prediction can be made from information about the horse's characteristics (bloodline, temperament, physical condition). A more accurate prediction could probably be made from the horse's record of past performance under track and weather conditions like those expected for the upcoming race.*[26]

Work Samples and Simulations

Work sample or simulation exercises measure job skills and behavior under realistic conditions. These work samples or simulations can be used to measure everything from motor or technical skills (for example, reading a blueprint or constructing a Pareto chart), to assessing verbal or cognitive attributes (for example, problem solving, presentation skills, and interpersonal skills). Some of the quality-related attributes that lend themselves to being measured by work samples or simulations include the following:

- Skill in facilitating teams

- Skill in problem solving

- Customer orientation

- Teamwork orientation

- Flexibility/adaptability

- Skill in coaching others

- Knowledge (and application) of quality tools, experimental design, applied statistics, and so on

Anyone reading this book could easily select an attribute from this listing and quickly envision a simulation or work sample exercise that could be used to elicit the relevant behaviors. While the actual development of such exercises is obviously not that simple, the basic concept is. In practice, the key to developing a valid simulation or work sample is to carefully analyze the critical job tasks, behaviors, and KSAPs, and then develop exercises that truly reflect those work conditions and attributes. Care also needs to be taken to ensure the exercises possess required psychometric properties and adhere to the standards outlined in chapter 3 (reliability, standardized conditions, fairness, and so on).

The authors of this text have developed simulations in a number of contexts and find them to be particularly useful for measuring both can do and will do factors of performance. If, for example, stand-up presentation skills are important, then an exercise requiring the candidate to prepare and deliver a presentation makes sense. If telephone or customer contact skills are critical, then having the candidate role play or react to a number of relevant situations can be used to assess those skills. If you want to know how well the applicant can deal with interpersonal conflict, then put him or her in a situation that elicits that conflict resolution behavior.

In our 3M Canada cohesion case, those applicants who performed well on the skills and ability tests were invited to participate in the next phase of the selection process—*group assessment*. For proprietary reasons, we cannot describe those exercises, but we will provide a brief overview of two simulations used in similar circumstances.

Exercise 1: Productivity Improvement. In this exercise, participants are asked to work in a group with three others to discuss ways to improve the productivity of a fictitious manufacturing process. Each participant is given a simplified layout of the manufacturing process, a description of the various operator functions, and relevant production information. Participants are told to review the material and prepare for a group meeting. The group's task is to suggest improvements to increase the productivity of the operation. Trained assessors observe group and individual behavior and evaluate each candidate's performance using behavioral checklists describing highly effective, effective, and ineffective behaviors (see Exhibit 8.2).

Exercise 2: Gear Assembly. In this simulation, applicants are required to put together the parts of a gear assembly (see Exhibit 8.3). Candidates are provided assembly instructions by the assessor and then given time to practice putting the parts together. Next, they have a set period of time to assemble as many gears as possible while at the same time examining each piece for any defective parts. At the end of time period one, applicants are given time to discuss the work process and make suggestions for improving the process. This discussion is followed by setup time and then a second period where applicants assemble the gears. Finally, candidates end the simulation by discussing the process and making final recommendations. Once again, applicants are observed and evaluated by trained assessors. Attributes assessed in the two simulations include

- Communication with others
- Teamwork
- Work orientation
- Problem solving
- Active listening
- Adaptability
- Interpersonal interaction
- Judgment
- Inspection

Assessment Centers

"An assessment center is a comprehensive, standardized procedure in which multiple assessment techniques such as situational exercises and job simulations (i.e., business games, discussion groups, reports,

Exhibit 8.2. Behavioral checklist for evaluating teamwork attribute on simulation.

Teamwork

Contributing effectively as a team member, as in interacting with others effectively; creating and maintaining cooperative relationships; involving others in discussions and decisions; and putting the team's objectives ahead of personal agenda.

Behavioral Checklist

Assessor: Check all behaviors associated with this success factor demonstrated by the candidate.

Highly Effective Behaviors

1. ☐ Quickly and effectively established rapport with others; spoke in terms of "we."
2. ☐ Always involved others in discussion.
3. ☐ Asked questions to clarify others' input.
4. ☐ Gave credit to or praised others for their ideas; discussed others' ideas without "evaluating" them.
5. ☐ Changed positions if a better idea was presented.
6. ☐ Supported the group's decision once consensus was reached.

Effective Behaviors

7. ☐ Attempted to establish rapport with others.
8. ☐ Contributed suggestions or comments to the discussion.
9. ☐ Spoke to others in the group and participated in decision making.
10. ☐ Listened when others were speaking.
11. ☐ Added to the ideas of others; listened to others' ideas openly.
12. ☐ Disagreed with others tactfully.
13. ☐ Listened to criticism of own ideas openly.
14. ☐ Accepted the group's consensus decision.

Ineffective Behaviors

15. ☐ Did not establish rapport with others; remained quiet or aloof; always spoke in terms of "I," not "we."
16. ☐ Ignored others' comments; attempted to force his/her point of view on the group.
17. ☐ Made assertions as to the best recommendation without inviting discussion; made declarative statements (for example, "We should go with voice mail").
18. ☐ Spoke only when directly addressed.
19. ☐ Repeatedly interrupted others; did not apologize for interrupting.
20. ☐ Made negative comments about others or their ideas; insisted on taking credit for good ideas.
21. ☐ Rigidly held to own viewpoint when presented with better ideas.
22. ☐ Reacted defensively or withdrew from discussion when suggestions were criticized.
23. ☐ Refused to accept the group's decision.

Overall Success Factor Evaluation

Assessor: Based on your observations, notes, and checklist ratings, provide (circle) your evaluation of the candidate's overall qualifications in the area of Teamwork

Ineffective			Effective			Highly Effective		
1	2	3	4	5	6	7	8	9

Source: Reprinted by permission of HRStrategies, Grosse Pointe, Mich.

Exhibit 8.3. Gear assembly simulation layout.

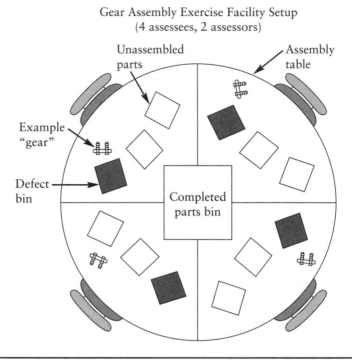

Gear Assembly Exercise Facility Setup
(4 assessees, 2 assessors)

Unassembled parts

Assembly table

Example "gear"

Defect bin

Completed parts bin

Reprinted by permission of HRStrategies, Grosse Pointe, Mich.

and presentations) are used to evaluate individual employees for various purposes."[27] Assessment center methodology is characterized by, among other things,

1. The delineation of multiple job-related performance dimensions

2. Inclusion of multiple assessment techniques to elicit behavior relevant to the performance dimensions

3. The use of multiple assessors who are trained to observe, record, and categorize candidate behavior for purposes of evaluating candidates independently, and in a consensus group session with other assessors

A wide variety of exercises are used in assessment centers depending on the attributes identified during job and work analysis. Thus, the decision to include a particular test or exercise should be based on that assessment tool's ability to elicit relevant job behaviors. Some of the more common assessment exercises are discussed next.

In-Basket. Not surprising, the in-basket exercise gets its name from the fact that candidates are asked to respond to a wide variety of materials of varying importance, urgency, and priority that might appear in the typical manager's in-basket. In most cases, the applicant is instructed that a previous manager has vacated the position several weeks prior to the time of the exercise and that a number of documents (letters, memos, requests, reports) have accumulated and must be addressed. Candidates are given background information on the department or unit and then required to deal, in writing, with the materials in a set period of time (for example, two hours). In some cases, the applicant is then interviewed by an assessor who asks the person to justify or explain the actions taken. In-basket exercises are particularly useful for measuring such attributes as planning, organizing, written and oral communication, decisiveness, and initiative. While the authors are not aware of any in-basket exercises developed specifically for the quality-oriented setting, we are convinced that in-baskets could be easily developed that would measure such quality-related attributes as customer orientation, process improvement (versus tampering or blaming the worker for process problems), openness to change, and skill in involving and empowering others.

Exhibit 8.4 profiles a managerial skills in-basket. The simulation was designed to evaluate the problem analysis and customer-orientation skills of candidates for an area manager position in the fast food industry. Candidates were given 90 minutes to work through the stack of 46 items. Candidate actions (memos, calls, to-do lists) were evaluated against a scoring key derived from input by senior executives of the company.

Leaderless Group Discussion (LGD). In these exercises, applicants are placed in small, leaderless groups and asked to reach consensus on some issue or problem such as making a promotion decision or allocating limited budgets or resources. In most instances, they are provided with some background information prior to meeting with other participants (for example, positive and negative information about each of the candidates or budget figures and alternatives for allocation). The productivity improvement exercise previously described is an example of an LGD. Attributes assessed include oral communication skills, persuasiveness, initiative, and leadership. LGDs have been used successfully to measure such quality-related attributes as problem solving, listening skills, process improvement, and flexibility.

Exhibit 8.4. An example of a managerial skills in-basket.

The Situation

For the next 90 minutes you are to play the role of Lee Baldwin, the new Area Director for Annie's, a nationwide chain of fast food restaurants. You recently joined Annie's in another division of the company. This is your first assignment in company operations.

Today is Saturday, February 17, 1996, and you have just arrived at your new office. You were appointed on very short notice because your predecessor, Sam Evans, quit suddenly while on out-of-town business. Mr. Evans' staff learned of his leaving on Friday, late in the day. Although the secretary was notified of your arrival, you have yet to meet any of your new staff.

It is early in the morning, and you are alone in your new office, without access to the files because they are locked. You cannot use the telephone. You have come in to take care of any matters which require your attention. You must leave in exactly 90 minutes for a previous engagement. You will not be able to return to this office until Wednesday, February 23, and prior commitments prevent you from taking any work with you.

In your desk you have found the attached materials which have been gathered by your new secretary, Lynn Reynolds. Included are: a job description of the position you have just stepped into (the Area Director position), descriptions of your staff members and their responsibilities, an organization chart, a copy of the 1995 (last year's) budget, and a three-month calendar. Attached to this background information are the items that have accumulated in Sam Evans' in-basket since his departure.

Instructions

In the next 90 minutes you are to deal with the items in any manner you feel is appropriate. You can prepare letters or memos, leave notes to staff members, schedule meetings, etc. Any action you take or propose to take should be indicated in writing or on the items themselves, as appropriate.

Remember:

- You are playing the role of Lee Baldwin, newly appointed Area Director.
- Today is Saturday, February 17, 1996, and you have only 90 minutes to deal with the items.
- The files are locked and the phone is not available.
- You will leave immediately and be out of town until Wednesday, February 21.

Exhibit 8.4. Continued.

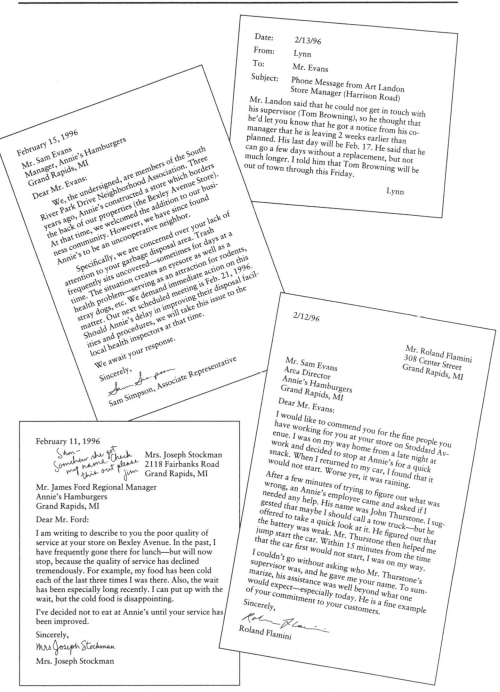

Date: 2/13/96
From: Lynn
To: Mr. Evans
Subject: Phone Message from Art Landon
Store Manager (Harrison Road)

Mr. Landon said that he could not get in touch with his supervisor (Tom Browning), so he thought that he'd let you know that he got a notice from his co-manager that he is leaving 2 weeks earlier than planned. His last day will be Feb. 17. He said that he can go a few days without a replacement, but not much longer. I told him that Tom Browning will be out of town through this Friday.

Lynn

February 15, 1996
Mr. Sam Evans
Manager, Annie's Hamburgers
Grand Rapids, MI

Dear Mr. Evans:

We, the undersigned, are members of the South River Park Drive Neighborhood Association. Three years ago, Annie's constructed a store which borders the back of our properties (the Bexley Avenue Store). At that time, we welcomed the addition to our business community. However, we have since found Annie's to be an uncooperative neighbor.

Specifically, we are concerned over your lack of attention to your garbage disposal area. Trash frequently sits uncovered—sometimes for days at a time. The situation creates an eyesore as well as a health problem—serving as an attraction for rodents, stray dogs, etc. We demand immediate action on this matter. Our next scheduled meeting is Feb. 21, 1996. Should Annie's delay in improving their disposal facilities and procedures, we will take this issue to the local health inspectors at that time.

We await your response.

Sincerely,

Sam Simpson, Associate Representative

2/12/96

Mr. Roland Flamini
308 Center Street
Grand Rapids, MI

Mr. Sam Evans
Area Director
Annie's Hamburgers
Grand Rapids, MI

Dear Mr. Evans:

I would like to commend you for the fine people you have working for you at your store on Stoddard Avenue. I was on my way home from a late night at work and decided to stop at Annie's for a quick snack. When I returned to my car, I found that it would not start. Worse yet, it was raining.

After a few minutes of trying to figure out what was wrong, an Annie's employee came and asked if I needed any help. His name was John Thurstone. I suggested that maybe I should call a tow truck—but he offered to take a quick look at it. He figured out that the battery was weak. Mr. Thurstone then helped me jump start the car. Within 15 minutes from the time that the car first would not start, I was on my way.

I couldn't go without asking who Mr. Thurstone's supervisor was, and he gave me your name. To summarize, his assistance was well beyond what one would expect—especially today. He is a fine example of your commitment to your customers.

Sincerely,

Roland Flamini

February 11, 1996

Sam—
Somehow she got my name. Check this out please Jim

Mrs. Joseph Stockman
2118 Fairbanks Road
Grand Rapids, MI

Mr. James Ford Regional Manager
Annie's Hamburgers
Grand Rapids, MI

Dear Mr. Ford:

I am writing to describe to you the poor quality of service at your store on Bexley Avenue. In the past, I have frequently gone there for lunch—but will now stop, because the quality of service has declined tremendously. For example, my food has been cold each of the last three times I was there. Also, the wait has been especially long recently. I can put up with the wait, but the cold food is disappointing.

I've decided not to eat at Annie's until your service has been improved.

Sincerely,

Mrs. Joseph Stockman

Mrs. Joseph Stockman

Source: Ronald B. Morgan, *Development of a Managerial Skills In-Basket,* technical report. Organizational Research and Development, Columbus, Ohio, 1983.

Oral Presentation. Here, applicants are allowed time to plan, organize, and prepare a presentation on an assigned topic. Assessors typically play the role of audience (client, customer, management) and ask questions following the presentation. Attributes measured include selling ability, persuasiveness, self-confidence, interpersonal skills, and customer awareness and responsiveness. As with other assessment center exercises, the reader is reminded that such exercises should be used only when they represent relevant work tasks and measure the attributes identified during job and work analysis.

Role-Play Exercise. In this exercise, the applicant is asked to assume the role of the incumbent for the target position. Typically, he or she is given background information about a situation and then deals with some problem or issue. For example, the applicant may be required to respond to an irate customer played by an assessor or asked to administer an oral disciplinary action against a subordinate (again played by the assessor). Interpersonal skills, oral communication, decisiveness, customer orientation, problem solving, and coaching are attributes that can be measured using role plays.

Other Exercises. Other tools used in assessment centers include business games, paper-and-pencil tests, background interviews, and analysis exercises.

Advantages of Work Samples and Assessment Centers

As the reader can easily surmise from our discussion of these assessment tools, we are highly in favor of their use in organizational settings. In particular, we feel that such exercises lend themselves nicely to the systematic assessment of important quality-related attributes. Work samples and assessment centers have at least four distinct advantages worth considering.

1. If for no other reason, these assessment devices warrant serious consideration based upon their accumulated validity evidence (see Table 8.1). Their track record (back to the horse race analogy) as predictors of performance is impressive.

2. They are viewed positively by job applicants. Candidates see them as job-related and fair.

3. Studies indicate that, unlike some tests, work samples and assessment centers show little or no disparate impact against women or minority groups.[28]

Table 8.1. Validity coefficients as a function of type of predictor.

Predictor	Number of validity studies	Average validity coefficient
General mental ability	53	.248
Special aptitude	31	.268
Physical ability	22	.315
Work sample	18	.378
Assessment center	21	.407

Source: N. Schmitt, R. Z. Gooding, R. A. Noe, and M. Kirsch, "Meta-Analysis of Validity Studies Published Between 1964 and 1982 and the Investigation of Study Characteristics," *Personnel Psychology* (1984): 415.

4. These exercises can also serve as an RJP for applicants. If done correctly, work samples and assessment centers place candidates in exercises that realistically resemble job tasks or activities. Designed to accurately portray certain aspects of the job itself, such exercises provide applicants with a preview of the characteristics and demands of the position (see Exhibit 8.5 for a discussion of Ford Motor Company's Regional Selection Program[29]).

Now, for the bad news. Despite their numerous advantages, our survey of ASQC sustaining members found that very few firms use either simulations or assessment centers for selecting and promoting their employees (see Figure 8.7). Given these findings, the obvious question becomes: Why, if these measures have such high utility for both the organization and the individual, do organizations avoid their use and rely on less valid assessment tools? While we can't answer this question, we do suggest a remedy for the discrepancy. Readers should begin to seriously consider the use of these performance measures as part of their selection and promotion systems. When correctly developed and administered, these powerful tools can do much to improve the ROI of staffing decisions. However, a word of caution is in order. The development of simulations and assessment centers, particularly full-blown assessment centers, is a relatively complex process requiring professional expertise. To ensure that the various standards of test development and validation are met, we suggest the involvement of an industrial and organizational psychologist or some other qualified professional with the necessary education and experience to oversee such an effort.

Exhibit 8.5. Ford Motor Company's regional selection program.

The Regional Selection Program was initiated by the Ford Parts and Service Division of the Ford Motor Company as an innovative approach to choosing college graduates for field sales and service positions. The primary objectives of the program were defined as: (1) to identify people who will be successful field managers, some of whom will eventually move ahead to fill key sales management positions, and (2) to reduce immediate voluntary turnover by providing candidates with a realistic preview of the field manager's position. Each of the four assessment exercises, along with the question and answer (Q&A) session, is briefly described below.

Track Record Interview. Prior to the assessment center, applicants are provided with a description of the field manager's work environment and results expected on the job. Applicants also receive a description of the performance dimensions used to evaluate college hires for the program. Applicants are asked to read the material provided and prepare for the interview by completing three Track Record Incident forms. These incidents describe selected past experiences relevant to the field manager performance dimensions. (This type of interview questioning will be discussed more fully in chapter 9.) Immediately before the interview, the assessor reviews the incident forms. The interview is structured with a set of standard questions asked of each recipient.

In-Basket Exercise. Like most in-baskets, this exercise is a collection of memos, letters, and other information that closely simulates the administrative demands of the field manager's position. It also contains a map of the zone that the prospective field manager must cover. Within a 90-minute time limit, the candidate must read through the materials, identify high-priority problems, and schedule a one-week itinerary.

Group Discussion. This exercise is an LGD where groups of four applicants argue the advantages and disadvantages of alternative university expenditures. Each candidate determines how he or she would allocate the funds, yet the group's task is to reach agreement on a single proposal.

Role Play. The fourth exercise included in the center is a role play where the assessor is an angry customer with a warranty problem. The participant's interpersonal skills and performance under pressure are tested as the interaction with the assessor is intense.

Q&A Session. After completing the exercises, applicants have the opportunity to ask questions both in a group setting with a job incumbent and in a one-on-one wrap-up session with an assessor.

In summary, the Regional Selection Program includes three major components that strengthen the role of the assessment center as a realistic preview of the position of Zone Manager. The components include: (1) a pre-assessment center package containing information about the work environment, results expected of Zone Managers, and the performance dimensions used to evaluate college hires for the position; (2) assessment center exercises, especially the in-basket and role play, which closely reflect the content and demands of the position; (3) the opportunity for applicants to ask questions of people knowledgeable of the job and organization.

Exhibit 8.5. Continued.

Qualitative Results:

Perception of program as a realistic preview (*n* = 322)

Compared with other hiring processes I've experienced, The Regional Selection Program:	Agree or strongly agree	Neither agree nor disagree	Disagree or strongly disagree
Gave me a better look at the position to be filled.	91%	7%	2%
Answered more of my questions about the job.	91%	7%	2%
Raised more questions in my mind about whether I'd like the job.	51%	26%	23%

Comments:

Provide content analysis examples from The Regional Selection Program.

"I learned a lot about Ford and about the job itself. It was a very thorough program and very enlightening."

"I believe that it was by far the best interviewing process I have encountered. It provided me with an excellent idea of the Zone Manager's responsibilities."

"The regional assessment program was the most interesting interview process I have experienced. It answered all my questions about the job and gave me a chance to experience what it might be like."

"Very challenging, and I think it showed the interviewee just what the job is about."

"I found it to be a very thorough procedure in the fact that assessors were judging our skills and abilities and we also were subjected to some of the actual rigors of the position."

"Gave me some background as to what the position will be like if I meet the standards and am hired."

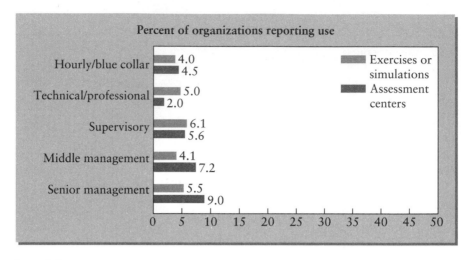

Figure 8.7. Use of exercises or simulations and assessment centers for selection and promotion.

Performance Appraisals

To some of the quality purists reading this book, the inclusion of performance appraisals as a tool for selecting and promoting quality-oriented employees may appear as somewhat of a contradiction. Many quality experts, including Deming, Scherkenbach, and Moen, view performance appraisals as anathemas and argue vehemently against their use in organizational settings.[30] Others have suggested that, if done correctly, appraisals can have a meaningful role in the quality organization.[31] However, the purpose of this section is not to argue either for or against the use of performance appraisals. Rather, we take the stance that appraisals remain a fact of life in the majority of organizational settings and will likely remain so for some time to come. Given that reality, the question becomes: How can we use that information most effectively in the staffing process?

Figure 8.8 shows our survey findings regarding the use of performance appraisal data for the selection and promotion of internal candidates. Obviously, the vast majority of ASQC member organizations continue to use performance appraisal information as input into their selection and promotion procedures. Based on that data, we assume that most organizations will continue to use some form of performance appraisal as input into their internal staffing decisions. We will also argue that the use of such data warrants consideration.

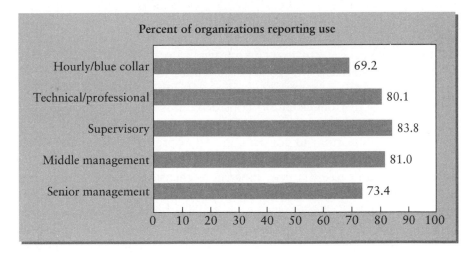

Figure 8.8. Use of internal performance appraisal data for selection and promotion.

For starters, the use of performance appraisal information is consistent with our ongoing exhortation that the best predictor of future behavior and performance is past behavior and performance in similar situations. Employees who have consistently performed their jobs in an exemplary fashion in the past are, in all likelihood, going to perform in a similar fashion in future situations. Conversely, individuals who in the past have behaved inadequately are not likely to change their future behavior in any appreciable manner. While there are always exceptions to this behavioral axiom, it is not where the smart money is bet.

Using performance appraisal information is also consistent with one of the arguments previously presented for promotion from within. While the potential of an external candidate is always somewhat of a question mark, the availability of performance data (formal and informal) on internal candidates provides us with at least some level of comfort that we know what we're getting.

Using Performance Appraisal for Staffing Purposes

So, how can the organization make the best use of performance appraisal information in its staffing decisions? We would suggest that, for performance appraisals to be effective as a staffing tool, three conditions must be met. First, the appraisal instrument and process must be relevant (valid). Second, individuals involved in making the appraisals must understand the appraisal process and how to make sound judgments or evaluations of employee behavior and performance. Finally, the performance appraisal information collected must be used in a systematic way to provide input into staffing decisions.

The key to ensuring a relevant appraisal is the systematic identification of those performance factors considered important to the success of the quality-oriented organization. The necessity for some kind of job analysis is as important in constructing an appraisal instrument as it is in developing any other assessment tool. As such, the appraisal will be effective to the degree that the dimensions measured reflect the quality orientation of the organization. Traditional supervisory and managerial dimensions such as directing and controlling must give way to, or at least be augmented with, the rating of dimensions that are consistent with the organization's quality philosophy and strategic direction. Too often, dimensions from the existing appraisal process are incompatible with the new work and culture of the organization. Under those circumstances, the use of the data may be unwarranted. In fact, those organizations that have made tremendous progress in revamping their culture may well find that success, as defined by the traditional performance appraisal process, is inversely related to success in the new culture.

Possible quality-related managerial dimensions might include involving and empowering employees, coaching and developing employees, or improving processes. Similarly, employee appraisal forms should reflect the organization's quality orientation. Thus, the evaluation of employees might include such performance factors as customer service, teamwork, or learning and skill development. While it is true that performance in the past is a prologue to future behavior, to be predictive of quality-oriented behavior, that measurement of past behavior must be similar and consistent with the quality imperative. The more similar the performance dimensions are to that imperative, the more predictive they will be of future behavior.

The second condition leading to the effective use of appraisal information relates to the appraisal or judgment skills of the individuals doing the appraisal. Detractors of performance appraisal (and they are not limited to quality advocates) often point to the inability of management personnel to make sound observations about employee performance. And they are right. Under the best of circumstances, a great deal of bias and error creeps into the evaluation process. While that contamination can never be completely eliminated, it can be substantially reduced by educating raters in the purpose and use of the process and through proper training in making accurate judgments about employee performance.[32] To be effective, supervisors and managers must be trained in both the why and how of performance appraisals.

The final condition of effective appraisal is the systematic use of the appraisal information in making staffing decisions. The performance data available need to be introduced into the staffing equation. While this may sound simple and obvious, it often does not happen in practice. The fact is that internal staffing decisions are frequently made without any reference to the performance appraisal data available. Either because the appraisal information is simply overlooked or because of a basic mistrust of such evaluations, managers often fail to include this information when making staffing decisions. However, if the first two conditions have been met (a relevant appraisal instrument is completed by trained and competent evaluators), then failure to use this valuable information would be a mistake.

A Note to the Quality Purist

To those readers who bristle at the thought of using performance appraisals, we would argue that it is virtually impossible to avoid some form of judgmental appraisal when making selection and promotion decisions regarding internal candidates. Even if every vestige of a formal appraisal procedure has been discarded by the organization, some kind of informal appraisal will, no doubt, happen during the selection decision process. Place three managers in a room making a promotion decision, and some discussion of the relative merits of the candidates will occur, like it or not. And when that happens, those managers would be well advised to keep the previous discussion of performance appraisals firmly in mind. In particular, they should identify those quality-related attributes important for success in the target position and then systematically evaluate each candidate against those success criteria. Has the candidate developed his/her staff? Has the candidate systematically improved processes in his/her present position? Is the individual a customer and quality advocate? These are the attributes that must be considered, performance appraisal form or not.

Performance Appraisal and the Law

Before leaving the topic of appraisal, a word of caution is in order. If performance appraisal information is used for making selection, promotion, or termination decisions, then appraisals are viewed in matters of EEO litigation as tests. As such, they are judged using the same standards as other tests or psychometric devices in terms of relevance and fairness. Although no performance appraisal system is completely safe from litigation, the following steps can be taken to improve the likelihood that the procedure can be successfully defended in a court of law. Additionally, these steps and considerations constitute sound theory and practice in the appraisal of employee performance.

1. Role of Job Analysis. Systematically analyze the job(s) and organization culture to ascertain those attributes (critical dimensions) important to successful job performance (see chapter 4). The courts have repeatedly reinforced the need for appraisal instruments that have been developed from a systematic analysis of the job and organization.

2. Prior Knowledge of Critical Elements. Performance standards, important job dimensions, and/or critical behaviors should be communicated to employees prior to appraisal. Employees should have advance knowledge of the criteria against which they will be evaluated.

3. Written Instructions. Specific written instructions should be provided to supervisors on completing the appraisals. Guidelines should generally include the following:

- The purpose of the appraisal and how it will be used
- How and when to complete the appraisal form
- Cautions against certain kinds of systematic bias and prejudice
- Written criteria upon which raters are to base their judgments

4. Supervisory Training. Ideally, written instructions should be supplemented with training that prepares the supervisor for this important responsibility. Without evaluation guidelines, it is difficult to determine whether employees are being judged by the same criteria. In addition to explaining the why and how of appraisal, sessions can be used to train supervisors in reducing rating contamination and conducting appraisal sessions that are more positive and developmental in nature.

5. Feedback of Results. The supervisor should review the results of the appraisal with the employee. Discussion of the evaluation with the employee helps demonstrate the above-board nature of the appraisal procedure.

6. Role of Documentation. Reasons for personnel evaluations and subsequent actions should be properly recorded in writing. Specific in-

stances of good and poor performance can act as documentation for evaluation rating.

7. Participation in Development. Ideally, the performance appraisal system should be developed using input from the supervisors and employees who will be using the procedure. Active involvement of individuals with a vested interest in the system is consistent with the quality imperative, enhances the quality of the product, and increases commitment to, and understanding of, the system.

8. Monitoring the Appraisal System. Some kind of review process should be instituted to assure the reliability and relevance of the appraisal system. Monitoring procedures may include any or all of the following:

- Some kind of mechanism for updating the system to reflect changes in job responsibilities or organization strategy

- An appeal process that employees can use to question perceived unfair ratings

- Wherever possible, the use of multiple raters or some kind of evaluation review process

9. Frequent Administration. Appraisals should be administered on a regular basis (at least once a year), and should be done even more frequently when an employee's performance is less than acceptable.[33]

Honesty and Integrity Inventories

One of the fastest growing areas of testing in the United States is the use of honesty or integrity tests. In an effort to curtail employee theft, many firms use these paper-and-pencil inventories to, hopefully, screen out applicants with a propensity for dishonesty and theft. Prior to its prohibition in 1989, most organizations relied on the polygraph test to screen applicants in terms of honesty and likelihood of theft.

Polygraph Examinations

The polygraph or lie detector is a mechanical device that measures an individual's galvanic skin response, breathing rate, and heart rate. In theory, the polygraph detects responses that have been falsified and records them on the machine's graphing mechanism. In the past, many firms, particularly those where employees had easy access to cash or merchandise (for example, retail stores, fast food chains, warehousing businesses), used polygraph testing to screen applicants for honesty. The polygraph had the added advantage of intimidating employees who might consider stealing money or merchandise. Some firms periodically tested employees or used the polygraph when theft occurred. However, serious questions were raised about the polygraph and its use in terms of reliability and the invasion of privacy of those examined.

Congress banned the use of the polygraph effective in 1989 (Employee Polygraph Protection Act of 1988). The act prohibits polygraph use for pre-employment screening purposes by most employers. Exempted from the law are certain private-sector employers such as security and pharmaceutical firms. Employers are allowed to use polygraphs internally for cases of theft or loss, but only if the employee voluntarily complies with the procedure.

Honesty and Integrity Testing

With the prohibition of the polygraph, a growing number of companies are using honesty or integrity tests to screen their job candidates. It is estimated that more than five million job applicants are tested each year using honesty and integrity tests.[34] These self-report tests contain items that have been empirically keyed to dishonest conduct. Sample questions might include the following:

- Should a person be fired if caught stealing $5?

- Would you tell your boss if you knew of another employee stealing from the company?

- Have you ever stolen change from your mother's purse?

While the validity evidence for such tests is fairly strong, critics of honesty tests point to the questionable methodologies of those studies.[35] Their concerns point to the fact that most of the validity studies have been conducted by the test publishers themselves and not by the firms using them. Other issues include the relevance of the criteria used during validation (self-report theft behavior) and the likelihood of misclassifying an individual. In addition, the concern over invasion of privacy, as with polygraph exams, is being raised by many individuals, with some states already restricting their use.[36]

Until further research is available on their validity, we suggest that honesty tests be used only as broad screening devices in conjunction with other staffing tools. We also wonder whether making an organization truly quality driven (drive out fear, remove barriers that rob people of pride in workmanship, and so on) would reduce the need for such tests.[37]

Handwriting Analysis (Graphology)

One very controversial staffing device used to measure personality is handwriting analysis or graphology. Graphology is widely used in Europe, Israel, and, to a lesser extent, in the United States. Handwriting analysts make the claim that a myriad of personality or character traits (such as extraversion, introversion, ambition, and creativity) can be assessed by examining a sample of the candidate's handwriting.

We strongly caution against the use of graphology as a staffing technique. We do so for three reasons. First, there is no research evidence that supports the validity of handwriting analysis. Indeed, a number of well-controlled studies show that the results of such analyses are not predictive of performance in organizational settings.[38] The only thing that can be consistently predicted using graphology is the sex of the respondent. And as one pundit once pointed out: "There are better, and more interesting, ways of determining those differences." A second reason for avoiding the use of handwriting analysis is the reaction of candidates to such techniques. Applicants understand and tolerate the use of selection techniques that they view as being job related, but they bristle when subjected to assessment devices where no such link is perceived. Studies show that candidates do not view the analysis of their handwriting as being relevant to their qualifications for a position. Applicants legitimately ask the question: "What does this have to do with whether or not I can perform the job?"

The final argument against using graphology has to do with the issue of litigation. As discussed in chapter 3, organizations often find themselves in the position of defending their selection procedures. We suggest that the reader imagine him/herself explaining to a government investigative agency or to some judge or jury that someone in their organization was not promoted because the candidate crossed his or her t's too low on the stem or lacked sufficient slope in lettering.

In summary, graphology as an assessment device has about the same validity and legitimacy as reading tea leaves or tarot cards. Stick to the use of job-related instruments and avoid any temptation to use handwriting analysis or any other related approaches.

Summary

In chapters 7 and 8 we have attempted to educate you about the wide array of assessment tools available for use in staffing. Many of those tools have a better track record for predicting job performance than the traditional and relied-upon employment interview. As organizations move toward a more complex and demanding work environment, these tools can play a valuable role in the improvement of the staffing process. While the employment interview will, no doubt, remain the mainstay for making employment decisions, we urge the reader to seriously consider adding some of these instruments to his or her staffing tool box. For those readers interested in improving their employment interview process, we now turn to that important topic.

Notes

1. S. R. Hathaway, J. C. McKinley, and James N. Butcher, *Minnesota Multiphasic Personality Inventory* (Minneapolis, Minn.: University of Minnesota Press, 1990).

2. Murray R. Barrick and Michael K. Mount, "The Big Five Personality Dimensions and Job Performance: A Meta-Analysis," *Personnel Psychology* 44 (1991): 1–26; Robert P. Tett, Douglas N. Jackson, Mitchell Rothstein, and John R. Reddon, "Meta Analysis of Personality-Job Performance Relations: A Reply to Ones, Mount, Barrick, and Hunter (1993)," *Personnel Psychology* 47 (1994): 157–172; Robert P. Tett, Douglas N. Jackson, and Mitchell Rothstein, "Personality Measures as Predictors of Job Performance: A Meta-Analytic Review," *Personnel Psychology* 44 (1991): 703–742.

3. Barrick and Mount, "The Big Five Personality Dimensions and Job Performance: A Meta-Analysis."

4. Harrison G. Gough, *California Psychological Inventory (CPI)* (Palo Alto: Calif.: Consulting Psychologists Press, 1987).

5. Harrison G. Gough, *The Adjective Checklist* (Palo Alto: Calif.: Consulting Psychologists Press, 1983).

6. Hathaway, McKinley, and Butcher, *MMPI.*

7. Allen L. Edwards, *Edwards Personal Preference Schedule* (San Antonio, Tex.: The Psychological Corporation, 1959).

8. Leonard V. Gordon, *Gordon Personal Profile Inventory* (San Antonio, Tex.: The Psychological Corporation, 1959).

9. Raymond Cattell, *16PF,* 5th ed. (Champaign, Ill.: Institute for Personality and Ability Testing, 1994).

10. David Bartram, *Prevue Assessment* (Waco, Tex.: Profiles International, 1994).

11. Personnel Decisions, Inc., *PDI Customer Service Inventory* (San Antonio, Tex.: The Psychological Corporation, 1991).

12. George E. Paajanen, Timothy L. Hansen, and Richard A. McLellan, *PDI Employment Inventory and PDI Customer Service Inventory Manual* (Minneapolis, Minn.: Personnel Decisions, Inc., 1993).

13. Personnel Decisions, Inc., *PDI Employment Inventory* (San Antonio, Tex.: The Psychological Corporation, 1985).

14. CORE Corporation, *ServiceFirst* (Pleasant Hill: Calif.: CORE Corporation, 1995).

15. Regina Burch-Konda, "ServiceFirst Construct Validation," paper presented at the Tenth Annual Conference of the Society for Industrial and Organizational Psychology, Orlando, Fla., May 1995.

16. Robert Hogan and Joyce Hogan, *Hogan Personality Inventory,* 2nd ed. (San Antonio, Tex.: The Psychological Corporation, 1992).

17. Joyce Hogan, Robert Hogan, and Catherine M. Busch, "How to Measure Service Orientation," *Journal of Applied Psychology* 69, no. 1 (1984): 167–173.

18. Hogan and Hogan, *Hogan Personality Inventory.*

19. Jeffrey A. Jolton and John W. Jones, "The Validity of a Job-Related Attitudinal Measure of Quality Consciousness," paper presented at the Tenth Annual Conference of the Society for Industrial and Organizational Psychology, Orlando, Fla., May 20, 1995.

20. Jack E. Smith and Ronald B. Morgan, *Quality Orientation Inventory* (White Lake, Mich.: HR Processes, and Northville, Mich., Organization Solutions, 1995).

21. David C. McClelland, "Business Drive and National Achievement," *Harvard Business Review* (July–August 1962): 99–112.

22. John B. Miner, *Miner Sentence Completion Scale* (Chicago, Ill.: Organizational Measurement Systems Press, 1986).

23. Edward K. Strong, Jr., *Strong Interest Inventory of the Strong Vocational Interest Blanks* (Palo Alto, Calif.: Consulting Psychologists Press, 1994); G. Frederic Kuder, *Kuder Personal Interest Inventory* (Chicago, Ill.: Science Research Associates).

24. V. Jon Bentz, "Executive Selection at Sears: An Update," paper presented at the Fourth Annual Conference on Frontiers of Industrial Psychology, Virginia Polytechnic Institute, August 1983.

25. Paul F. Wernimont and John P. Campbell, "Signs, Samples, and Criteria," *Journal of Applied Psychology* 52 (1968): 372–376.

26. Laurence Siegel and Irving M. Lane, *Personnel and Organizational Psychology,* 2nd ed. (Homewood, Ill.: Irwin, 1987), 197.

27. George C. Thornton III and William C. Byham, *Assessment Centers and Managerial Performance* (New York: Academic Press, 1982).

28. Ibid., 371–390.

29. Jack E. Smith and Douglas M. Garber, "The Assessment Center as a Realistic Job Preview," International Congress on the Assessment Center Method, Detroit, Mich., May 6, 1986.

30. W. Edwards Deming, *Out of the Crisis* (Cambridge, Mass.: MIT Center for Advanced Engineering Study, 1986); Ronald D. Moen, "The Performance Appraisal System: Deming's Deadly Disease," *Quality Progress* (November 1989): 62–66; William W. Scherkenbach, *Deming's Road to Continual Improvement* (Knoxville, Tenn: SPC Press, 1991).

31. Roger E. Breisch, Walter E. Breisch, and Jim M. Graber, "Performance Appraisal and Deming: A Misunderstanding?" *Quality Progress* (June 1992): 59–62.

32. Gary P. Latham, Kenneth N. Wexley, and E. D. Pursell, "Training Managers to Minimize Rating Errors in the Observation of Behavior," *Journal of Applied Psychology* 60 (1944): 550–555.

33. S. R. Burchett and K. P. DeMeuse, "Performance Appraisal and the Law," *Personnel* 62 (1985): 29–37; W. H. Holley and H. S. Field, "Will Your Performance Appraisal System Hold up in Court?" *Personnel* 59 (1982): 59–64; L. S. Kleiman and R. L. Durham, "Performance Appraisal, Promotion and the Courts: A Critical Review," *Personnel Psychology* 34 (1981): 103–121.

34. Mark L. Rieke and Stephen J. Guastello, "Unresolved Issues in Honesty and Integrity Testing," *American Psychology* (June 1995): 458.

35. Deniz S. Ones, Viswesvaran Chockalingam, and Frank L. Schmidt, "Comprehensive Meta-Analysis of Integrity Test Validities: Findings and Implications for Personnel Selection and Theories of Job Performance," *Journal of Applied Psychology* 78 (1993): 679–703.

36. Scott O. Lilienfield, George Alliger, and Krystin Mitchell, "Why Integrity Testing Remains Controversial," *American Psychologist* (June 1995): 257–258.

37. Deming, *Out of the Crisis.*

38. G. Ben-Shakhar, M. Bar-Hillel, Y. Bilu, E. Ben-Abba, and A. Flug, "Can Graphology Predict Occupational Success? Two Empirical Studies and Some Methodological Ruminations," *Journal of Applied Psychology* 71 (1986): 645–653; A. Rafaeli and R. J. Klimowski, "Predicting Sales Success Through Handwriting Analysis: An Evaluation of the Effects of Training and Handwriting Sample Content," *Journal of Applied Psychology* 68 (1983): 212–217.

The Employment Interview: Developing Structured Content

Overview

In this chapter, we provide the reader with an overview of the error and bias inherent in the employment interview, as typically conducted. Next, we provide a process for developing a structured and job-related interview that can substantially reduce that contamination and improve the employment decision process. We also show how one Baldrige Award-winning company, The Ritz-Carlton Hotel®, has used the interview to improve the quality of its services. Finally, we provide ROI results for a number of organizations using a structured interview process called Targeted Selection®.

Introduction

The authors feel safe in assuming that you know what the world's oldest profession is. But what you may not have known, prior to reading this book, is that selecting individuals for that career was accomplished using the employment interview. The use of the interview as a selection tool is ageless. Since individuals first started making selection decisions, they have wanted to look the prospect in the eye, ask a few questions, and attempt to size up the person in terms of potential for the position in question. Our own survey results confirm that popularity, and those results are consistent with previous studies that

Table 9.1. Frequency of interview use for hiring and promoting various employee position categories.

Positions	Extent of use
Hourly/blue collar	86.9%
Technical/professional	95.5%
Supervisory	93.4%
Middle management	92.8%
Senior management	93.0%

demonstrate the widespread use of the employment interview for the selection and promotion of employees (see Table 9.1). It can easily be described as the staffing tool of choice when making most employment decisions. However, despite the interview's longevity and wide use as a selection tool, the effectiveness of the selection interview is questionable. Research on the effectiveness of the interview goes back almost to the turn of the century.[1] Hundreds of studies have examined both the reliability and validity of the interview and, until recently, results of those studies have been disappointing and indicate that the employment interview, as usually conducted, is a poor predictor of subsequent job performance.[2] However, recent research indicates that the interview can be a reliable and valid predictor of performance when

1. A comprehensive listing of specific and job-related attributes has been identified for the target position (systematic job analysis).

2. Interview content (questions) focuses on measuring those identified attributes.

3. The interview is appropriately structured and interviewers adhere to established interview guidelines.

4. Interviewers have been trained to conduct the interview and evaluate information objectively.

5. Multiple interviewers assess the candidates and then meet to reach a consensus on those candidates considered most and least likely to succeed.[3]

In this chapter, we will begin by discussing some of the major reasons the employment interview often fails to measure up as the basis for making employment decisions. Next, we will focus on developing valid interview content.

Error and Bias in the Interview Process

As previously discussed, the employment interview as typically conducted has a poor track record as a predictor of job success. When scores derived from the interview are systematically correlated with job performance measures, the resulting relationships have been very low or nonexistent. Equally disappointing results have been reported for the reliability of the interview. When faced with the task of evaluating a number of applicants, interviewers seldom attain what is considered an acceptable level of agreement (interrater reliability). Historically, the research results have been so consistently disappointing that some researchers have suggested that we abandon the interview as a predictive tool. Milton M. Mandel of the U.S. Civil Service Commission put it best when he said: "The basic difficulty of the interview, as usually conducted, is that it involves making extensive inferences from limited data obtained in artificial situations, by unqualified observers."[4]

The abandonment of the interview will, of course, never happen in practice. Few, if any, organizations are prepared to rely on other predictive devices (such as tests, application blanks, historical data, and so on) and hire blind. As managers, we want to see our potential employees, "look 'em in the eye," and "get a feel" for their ability to successfully fit into our organization. In fact, most employment specialists and managers would summarily discount the research findings and argue that they can, in fact, obtain a valid measure of an individual's potential. Most interviewers honestly believe that they can determine a candidate's potential on the basis of information gleaned during that haphazard half-hour of interaction called *the interview*. Despite evidence to the contrary, the majority of interviewers maintain great faith and confidence in their own interviewing skills and decision-making abilities.

With these disappointing reliability and validity findings in hand and the fact that the interview is here to stay, some researchers began to examine the interview process. How is information collected? What kinds of interpersonal or psychological factors influence these interactions? When and how are decisions made? They theorized that understanding the dynamics of the interview process would help interviewers take steps to systematically improve the reliability and validity of the interview.

Dynamics of the Interview Process

Research examining interview dynamics began in earnest with a series of studies at McGill University in the mid 1960s. Those findings, along with subsequent research, have identified a plethora of errors and biases inherent in the interview process.[5] For purposes of this book, we will briefly discuss what we consider to be the major interview contaminants that have been identified and that the authors have observed in practice. As each of these problems is discussed, readers are encouraged to examine each issue in terms of their own experiences (meaning, does the shoe fit in terms of your own interviewing activities?). Awareness of these factors will help each reader confront sources of error in his or her use of the interview.

Cavalier Approach. The first source of error in the interview process is not recognizing the importance and difficulty of the task. Many interviewers approach the interview with a cavalier attitude. They fail to recognize the difficulty of what they are attempting to do. Think about it. The interviewer must

- Establish and maintain rapport.

- Question and probe for useful information.

- Record and remember information.

- Use the information to arrive at an evaluation of the applicant along a variety of knowledge, skill, and temperament dimensions.

In a sense, this process of collecting information and using it to make assessments is similar to what a counseling psychologist receives four years of graduate-level training to do. Many interviewers do not recognize the limits and challenges of conducting the process effectively and fail to invest the necessary time to effectively plan and conduct the interview.

Decisions Are Made Too Quickly. In theory, the typical interview may be 30, 45, or even 60 or more minutes in length. During that time, the interviewer is supposed to collect as much relevant information as possible. At the conclusion of the session, the interviewer is expected to systematically combine *all* of that information and make an informed and valid decision about the candidate. Again, this is in theory. In reality, studies show that the process is not quite that rational. Research findings show that early interview impressions greatly influence final accept/reject decisions. These early impressions, generally created during the first five minutes, can establish a bias that colors or influences subsequent interactions. Thus, the interview is basically of very short duration and not the lengthy process that we believe it to be.

Too Much Reliance Is Placed on Negative Information. Interviewers are influenced more by unfavorable than by favorable information. Again, in theory, the interviewer acts much like the scales of justice, collecting and weighing bits of positive and negative information about the candidate. In reality, the interview is often a search for negative information that can be critical to decision making. This is particularly true if that negative information occurs early in the interviewing process and/or if other information about the candidate is lacking. It has been suggested that this bias occurs because interviewers are all too often ill-prepared. Unstructured and ambiguous interviews leave the interviewer searching for something to hang a hat on. It provides an easy excuse for rejecting the candidate. Thus, we conclude that we *can't* hire anybody who

- Was fired from his or her last job
- Can't articulate his or her career goals
- Doesn't look you in the eye
- Has less then a 3.00 GPA
- Isn't sure where he or she wants to be in five years

Rather than evaluating applicants systematically on their relative strengths and weaknesses, interviewers reject otherwise qualified candidates because they mistakenly place too much weight on anything they view in a negative light.

Developing Stereotypes of a Good Applicant. Interviewers tend to develop their own stereotypes of a good applicant and then select or promote those individuals who match that stereotype. This stereotyping of the ideal applicant takes three forms. The first notion of a stereotype relates to what we typically refer to as a *conventional and oversimplified belief* *about a group of people.* Instead of examining each individual's unique capabilities, we ascribe competence or incompetence from stereotypes.

A second kind of stereotype is what we refer to as *implicit personality theories.* That is, we each have our own unique beliefs about which temperament/personality traits tend to go together. For example, the reader may believe that individuals who are outgoing are also intelligent, honest, and conscientious. When we meet someone who clearly possesses one trait, we infer that they also possess the others. The unique beliefs we each hold about what personality traits go together can mislead us in the subsequent evaluation of the applicant.

The third type of stereotyping is a little more subtle but equally pervasive. Here, the interviewer has an image of what the applicant should look and act like to be successful in a particular job. An oversimplified and exaggerated example might occur when hiring an accountant for our organization. One widely held stereotype for an accountant (bean counter) is that of a soft-spoken, frumpy, Casper Milquetoast person with horned-rimmed glasses who sits alone in a back office with stacks of papers and printouts and punches numbers into a calculator. When a six-foot-tall, physically fit, and gregarious candidate walks through the door in his Brooks Brothers suit and looks us in the eye while giving us a firm handshake, this obviously does not fit with our stereotype of what an accountant should be. And despite this person's qualifications, we reject him/her because the individual doesn't fit our stereotype of an accountant. While this example of stereotyping is exaggerated, it does demonstrate what can occur in the interview process. And what is the basis for this stereotype? Simple—it comes from perceptions of ourselves. The ideal applicants, it turns out, are individuals like ourselves. Through a mechanism sometimes called *cloning,* we look for people who reflect our personalities, philosophies, and attributes.

Not Enough Time Is Given to the Collection and Evaluation of Relevant Information. Once again, a major discrepancy exists between what should happen during the interview session and what actually occurs when the interview process is carefully examined. In theory, the interviewer should walk away from the session having garnered a great deal of useful information about the candidate. In fact, that seldom occurs. What does happen is that the time allotted for the interview is often abbreviated, with the interviewer dominating what little discussion does take place. And what is really frightening is that some research has shown that the more the interviewer talks (dominates the session), the more likely the candidate is viewed positively by the interviewer. The sad fact is that interviewers, as with most of us, like to hear themselves talk and welcome a good listener. The practiced or schooled candidate will often play to this fault by asking questions and then feigning attention and interest to the responses.

Why do interviewers fail to properly use the allotted time? Most likely it is because they are ill-prepared for the interview session. They have not spelled out the requirements for the position, nor have they put much thought into developing job-related interview questions. If they had, then they would use the time provided to make relevant inquiries instead of talking about the job, the organization, and whatever else comes to mind. Indeed, when properly prepared, interviewers often complain that they don't have enough time to adequately discuss all job-related aspects prior to making decisions. The interviewer should talk no more than 15–20 percent of the time allotted, using questions to get and keep the applicant talking.

The Selection Process Is Seldom Systematic. In chapter 3 we discussed the importance of standardization of the staffing process. Each candidate should go through exactly the same process and be given an equal opportunity to perform. But a review of the staffing process, particularly as it relates to interviewing, reveals that such a standardized process seldom occurs. Candidates being screened from a pool of applicants for a position are often interviewed by different individuals in different sequences and are frequently asked quite different questions.

Failure to Focus Interview Content on Job-Related Attributes. Individuals involved in interviewing do not obtain information on all the important aspects related to the job/candidate match, causing important information to be missed. This occurs because interviewers fail to fully spell out the requirements of the job. Even when very familiar with the target position, interviewers do not take the time to think through all pertinent responsibilities and related attributes. What specific KSAPs are related to success on the job? In short, interviewers fail to adequately analyze the job in question, which leads to interview sessions that are haphazard, irrelevant, and nonfocused.

When the job has not been analyzed, interviewers tend to rely on a set of standard or pet questions that act as filler for the interview sessions. They also begin to play the role of amateur psychologist instead of focusing on relevant information that can be systematically evaluated. In this situation, interviewers begin to ask questions such as

- "Why do you want to work at XYZ?"

- "What are your major strengths/weaknesses?"

- "Where do you want to be in five years?"

- "What did you like/dislike about your last boss?"

- "What are your long-term goals?"

These questions provide very little useful information and force the interviewer to evaluate competence based upon some kind of warm and fuzzy feeling about the candidate. And the questions often get worse. The authors have been exposed to scores of such irrelevant questions or inquiries. One interviewer, a VP of administration at a large financial institution, asks interviewees: "If you died, what would you want your epitaph to say?" Another interviewer informs the candidate that he wants to take him/her to lunch but that his car is being repaired. He asks the prospective employee to drive, and then uses the opportunity to examine how clean and orderly the candidate maintains his/her automobile. (Incidently, both of the authors would fail this little test.) We also know one manager who proudly announces that he doesn't even need to interview the candidate because he can assess the caliber of the person simply by shaking hands with the individual.

The interviewing horror stories are not unique to a few ill-prepared managers. Articles and books written on the topic of interviewing sometimes extol the virtues of asking such questions. For example, one how-to-interview article in a popular business magazine advocated the use of the interview question "Who are your heros?" to determine job fit.[6] The author argues that the interviewer can learn a lot about a candidate with such questions. What is interesting about the article was that the author pointed to the 1988 presidential debates between Michael Dukakis and George Bush where this question was asked by one of the commentators. The outcome was that Dukakis stumbled because he hadn't been coached for such a question. Also, he had to respond first, which gave Bush time to think through his response to the question, giving him the advantage of being better prepared to respond.

One of Bush's listed heros was Ronald Reagan. We ask, is the response "Ronald Reagan" to the question, "Who are your heros?" informative and useful when making a hiring decision? The authors would argue that this type of question and response is likely totally irrelevant to the selection process, and that any evaluation or judgment made says more about the interviewer's political preference than it does about the job fit of the candidate.

Interviewer Behavior Affects Candidate Performance. Interviewers can actually affect the performance of the applicant. As an interviewer, the reader must recognize that his or her mannerisms and behavior (including body language, posture, habits) have this result. An interviewer can demoralize and hinder the performance of an applicant through behaviors that signal inattentiveness or indifference (frowns, looking at his/her watch, and so on). Conversely, a reenergized interviewer can facilitate the performance of the next applicant. The impact that the interviewer has on the process is a major contributor to unreliability in interview judgments.[7]

Summary

While our list of interviewer errors and biases could continue, the previous discussion should alert the reader to some of the problematic aspects of the interview process. Hopefully, this awareness of the interview dynamics will help those involved in interviewing to understand and correct some of their own poor practices.

More importantly, we hope to reinforce the need for a structured and job-related interview process that objectively evaluates each candidate with reference to the requirements of the job. When the interview is done correctly, typical errors and biases are greatly reduced. Interviewers no longer approach the task in a cavalier manner. Snap decisions are less likely because many more job-related questions need to be answered before an evaluation can occur. Interviewers spend less time talking (filling time) because they have valuable information to collect. Candidates are judged on their job-related merits rather than on misguided stereotypes, and so on.

The remainder of our discussion will focus on how to develop and administer such job-related interviews.

Planning and Developing Structured Interview Content

Assuming that a systematic job analysis has been conducted and the critical KSAPs have been identified, the next step is to translate these attributes into job-related interview questions. That link should be direct and comprehensive in terms of measuring all KSAPs. In doing so, we advocate a highly structured, patterned interview where each candidate is asked basically the same questions. This approach starts with a standard set of questions, but does allow the interviewer to ask follow-up questions and probe in areas deemed necessary.

It is a well-established principle that highly structured interviews produce more effective judgments.[8] Consistency among interviewers is increased, meaning that a more uniform set of standards is being applied across various settings in the organization. Evaluations derived from a highly structured interview are generally more accurate (valid) than those produced from unstructured interviews. The unstructured or shoot-from-the-hip approach to interviewing is fraught with many of the errors and biases previously discussed, such as stereotyping, quick decisions, poor use of time, and so on. The job-related, structured interview forces the interviewer to ask meaningful questions, avoid early decisions, cover all important aspects of the job, avoid stereotyping, and so on. Highly structured and job-related interviews have an additional advantage in that they project a more organized and professional image of the organization. A well-executed interview will send important messages: The interviewer appears prepared, and the organization cares enough about the selection process to invest the necessary effort. This is an important consideration in efforts to attract a quality-oriented workforce. If the organization claims to value attentiveness to quality and seeks to convey that value to applicants, it will look somewhat hypocritical if the all-too-typical, nonfocused, rambling, and wasteful interview is conducted. Remember, the interview is one of the initial stages in which the organization will be defining itself. In effect, the focus on quality in the interview can serve as an RJP alerting applicants to the fact that the organization is serious about quality. By conducting a planned, relevant interview, the organization will convey to applicants its focus on quality.

Question Formats

Interviewers often miss opportunities to gather relevant information from candidates by limiting the variety of questioning techniques they use to collect information. In reality, there are a number of useful formats that can be used to gather information.[9] These include

1. Factual education and training questions

2. Factual work experience questions (including success history)

3. Specific knowledge questions

4. Hypothetical situation questions

5. Behavioral consistency questions

6. Self-appraisal and analysis questions

7. Probing or follow-up questions

While there are advantages and limitations associated with each question format, they might all be relevant in certain situations. The key is that, when this varied information is collected and combined, it can provide an excellent profile of the candidate's readiness for the job and organization. Following are descriptions of the seven questioning techniques and examples of questions designed to evaluate specific attributes and behaviors critical to quality settings.

Factual Education and Training Questions. One of the most common questioning techniques is designed to gather additional factual information about the applicant's educational background. These questions should build on and clarify, but not repeat, details provided in other materials (resumes, applications, or transcripts). Each question should focus on a specific attribute identified in the job analysis. In the sample questions that follow, possible probe or follow-up questions are listed and the specific attribute being evaluated appears in parentheses.

Q. Please describe any statistics courses you have taken or seminars you have attended (Knowledge of statistical quality control). Probes might include

- What topics were covered?

- What things did you learn that might help you on the job?

- What value do you see in using statistics in the workplace?

Q. Describe any courses or seminars that dealt with W. Edwards Deming's (or some other type of) philosophy (Knowledge of quality improvement models).

Probes might include

- How do you think those principles can be applied in the workplace?

- What struck you as most important about those ideas?

- Do you take issue with any of those concepts?

Q. Describe the SPC course you attended at ABC University (Knowledge of SPC).
Probes might include

- What topics were addressed?

- How have you used these tools in your workplace?

- How might you apply the use of control charts on your job?

Factual Work Experience Questions. Perhaps the most common format, these questions focus on the experiences or activities of the candidate.

Q. Without describing any proprietary information, what general models or procedures did you use at XYZ Corporation to ensure quality products and services? (Knowledge of quality improvement models)
Probes might include

- What exact measures did you use?

- How well did they work?

- How could they have been improved?

Q. Describe your experience with a quality or process improvement team or task force (Group problem-solving techniques).
Probes might include

- How successful was the group in meeting its objectives?

- Why was the group successful or unsuccessful?

- What steps could have been taken to improve the group's effectiveness?

Q. Describe your experience as the group leader for your company's customer service task force (Group facilitation skills).
Probes might include

- What steps did you take to keep the group on track? To participate?

- How successful was that group?

- What did you learn? What would you do differently?

Q. Whom do you consider to be your customers in your present job? (Awareness of internal and external customers)

Probes might include

- What do you do to meet their needs?

- How do you measure customer satisfaction?

- How do you encourage others?

When collecting and evaluating work experience questions, it is important to focus on the nature of the candidate's experience rather than the amount of such experience. The interviewer should determine the exact level of involvement and success of the experience rather than assuming that simply because it was done, it was done well. Five years of supervisory experience tells us little about the quality of that supervision.

Interviewers should pay close attention to the success history of the candidate. The most fundamental adage in employee selection is that the best predictor of future behavior or performance is past behavior or performance in similar circumstances. When trying to determine which candidates will embrace and foster the organization's quality efforts, the best bet is always those persons with a history of involvement in, and commitment to, quality values and practices. Thus, questioning should focus on the level of involvement and success of the candidate's quality efforts. What specific changes has the person made to improve quality? What was the role of the person on the quality improvement team? Does the candidate have a continuous improvement mind-set?

Specific Knowledge Questions. Knowledge questions are formulated to verify the applicant's mastery of specific bodies of information. The new quality orientation of business will require a greater variety and depth of technical knowledge in the workforce. When constructing job-knowledge questions, the challenge is to focus them at the correct level and to identify those facts or principles that differentiate applicants who have sufficient mastery from those who do not. The following are examples of job knowledge questions.

Q. Describe the basic ground rules for brainstorming (Knowledge of group problem-solving techniques and brainstorming). Probes might include

- When is brainstorming most likely to be effective?

- Have you used this technique? Was it effective?

- What do you do when someone is not contributing?

Q. What is a Pareto chart? (Knowledge of problem-cause identification techniques and Pareto charts)
Probes might include

- When would you use a Pareto chart?

- What steps would you take to develop such a chart to determine, for example, causes of eye injury or types of customer complaints?

- Have you ever constructed such a chart? Please explain.

Q. Please differentiate between common and special causes of variation in performance (Knowledge of SPC and control charts).
Probes might include

- What is meant by the term tampering?

- What are some of the rules for deciding if you have special cause variation?

- What steps do you take if you find special cause (or common cause) variation?

Hypothetical Situation Questions. This type of question presents applicants with descriptions about specific work-related situations and asks them to describe how they would respond in those situations.

Q. If an irate customer told you that she had been poorly treated and was going to take her business elsewhere, how would you deal with the problem? (Listening skills and conflict management skills)
Probes might include

- What if she was a poor customer anyway?

- Why is one unhappy customer such a big deal?

- What steps do you think can be taken to win back dissatisfied customers?

Q. Suppose you are facilitating a problem-solving meeting and the group continually gets off track. What steps would you take to ensure that the group stays on track? (Team leadership skills and group facilitation skills)
Probes might include

- What if they raise legitimate issues that have nothing to do with the task at hand?

- What if the group wants to talk about another issue?

- What does it mean to stay on track in terms of content/process?

Q. Suppose that an employee comes to you with a suggestion for reducing your delivery time. How would you respond if the idea seemed to have some merit but was poorly thought out and researched? (Interpersonal skills and oral communication skills) Probes might include

- How would you reinforce the effort?

- What exact guidance would you give to the person?

- What if the person didn't want to follow through on the idea?

The critical incident job analysis technique discussed in chapter 4 is particularly useful for developing situational questions and ensuring that those situations are job related. You may recall that the CI technique asks the individual to think of job incidents in which a worker's behavior resulted in either highly effective or highly ineffective performance. The incidents we collect tell us a lot about what kinds of behavior differentiate effective from ineffective employees. We can, therefore, nicely translate those CIs into interview questions, requiring the applicant to describe how he or she would perform. Exhibit 9.1 provides such an example using one of the CIs from chapter 4.

Behavioral Consistency Questions. Behavioral consistency questions ask the candidate to describe how he or she behaved in previous relevant situations. Because past behavior in these situations can be considered the best predictor of future behavior in the same kinds of situations, these questions are particularly helpful. Behavioral consistency questions are most useful when they probe for specific details about how an applicant behaved in previous situations.

Q. Sometimes a specific individual will dominate the group discussion, cut others off, and generally reduce the effectiveness of the group. Describe the most difficult situation in which you had to deal with such an individual (Team leadership and group facilitation skills).

Exhibit 9.1. Using critical incidents to generate behavioral questions.

Critical incident:

Setting. A new agent and sales manager were performing joint fieldwork. The agent discussed with the client the possibility of replacing a permanent life policy held with another company.

Behavior. After the meeting, the sales manager discussed the situation with the agent and showed how replacement was not in the client's best interest. Although it would have been as easy sale, the agent returned and explained the issues surrounding the policy.

Result. The sale was not made, but the client later expressed appreciation for the honesty and service received.

Hypothetical situation question:

Suppose that a client is interested in replacing a large life policy held at another company with one of your policies. You are pretty sure that you can make the sale but realize that replacing the policy may not be in the client's best interest. What would you do?

- Why would you do it that way?
- What if they were basically equal?
- What if your supervisor told you to make the sale?

Behavioral consistency question:

Tell me about the last time you had an opportunity to close a sale with a client but decided against it.

- Do you have any regrets?
- Do you have any other similar examples?
- What criteria do you use to make such decisions?

Specific probes might include

- What did you do?
- Did you confront him or her?
- What did you say? How did he or she respond?
- Was it successful?
- How would you handle the situation differently today?

Q. Describe the time you had to respond to the most difficult or dissatisfied customer you've ever encountered (Judgment and discretion, listening skills, and conflict management skills).

Specific probes might include

- What did you do?

- How did it work?

- What did you learn?

- What would you do differently?

Q. Describe a time when you worked on a quality or process problem with a group of peers (or subordinates) (Team leadership and group facilitation skills).
Specific probes might include

- What was your approach?

- What specific steps did you take?

- What worked?

- What didn't work?

- How successful was the group?

Behavioral consistency questions are based on the premise, once again, that the best predictor of future behavior and performance is past behavior and performance in similar situations. Candidate responses to these questions are rich with examples of how the applicant actually performed or behaved in similar job-related situations. As with hypothetical situation questions (see Exhibit 9.1), the transition from CIs to the formulation of behavioral consistency questions is relatively straightforward.

It is probably safe to say that these behavioral consistency (or behavioral description) questions are the basis for most of the state-of-the-art interviewing going on in the benchmark staffing organizations described in this book, such as The Ritz-Carlton Hotel®, 3M, Toyota, Motorola, Corning, and so on. Behavioral consistency questions were used in the selection process for team members in our 3M cohesion case. Exhibit 9.2 provides some examples of questions similar to those used at 3M Canada to measure the quality attributes *problem solving* and *teamwork*.

Behavioral interviewing, particularly the behavioral consistency format, has an excellent track record in terms of predicting performance.[10] We strongly encourage anyone engaged in the interview process to begin incorporating such questions into his or her structured interviews. To the reader interested in learning more about this

Exhibit 9.2. Behavioral consistency questions/examples.

Problem solving

> Describe a time when you were given the task to implement a new process or procedure.

1. How did you decide how the new process should be implemented?

    _____ Considered various methods and chose the one that provided the greatest benefit with the least cost.

    _____ Asked coworkers and supervisors to provide input on how to implement the process.

    _____ Tried the method that seemed to be the easiest.

    _____ Asked someone else to help decide how the process should be implemented.

2. What was the result of your action?

    _____ The new process or procedure was implemented quickly and easily.

    _____ There were some minor problems, but the process was implemented within the expected time frame.

    _____ The new method was implemented after various problems were resolved, but the implementation took longer than expected.

    _____ The new method was put into place, but only after some major problems were resolved.

> Describe a time when you were responsible for completing a very difficult project within a certain time frame.

1. How did you plan out the project steps?

    _____ Identified and prioritized tasks, identified needed resources.

    _____ Identified and prioritized tasks.

    _____ Made a list of important tasks.

    _____ Asked a supervisor or coworker how the tasks should be completed.

Exhibit 9.2. Continued.

Teamwork

Describe a time when you worked in a group with someone who was difficult to get along with.

1. How did you resolve the situation?

_____ Met with this person to identify and discuss any problems.

_____ Kept working with the individual and ignored differences.

_____ Asked the supervisor to intervene.

_____ Asked to be reassigned to a new group.

Sometimes technologists must give information to other employees about job performance. Describe a situation where you gave constructive criticism to someone.

1. How did you go about providing feedback?

_____ Drew on specific observations, used nonconfrontational language, and attempted to get the person involved in identifying improvements.

_____ Gave specific examples and used nonconfrontational language, gave instructions on how to improve.

_____ Gave vague feedback in a nonconfrontational manner; did not establish goals for improvement.

_____ Told the person they were doing it wrong and to do it right the next time.

2. What was the reaction?

_____ The individual accepted the feedback and worked to establish goals for improvement.

_____ The individual accepted the feedback and said he or she would try to follow instructions next time.

_____ The individual became defensive.

_____ The individual became angry, demanded more information, and complained to the supervisor.

Source: HRStrategies, Grosse Pointe, Michigan. Reprinted by permission.

approach to interviewing, we suggest the very informative and readable book, *Behavior Description Interviewing.*[11]

Self-Appraisal and Analysis Questions. Self-appraisal questions ask the candidate to step back and evaluate a personal attribute. These questions can be most useful at probing the individual's level of self-awareness. Some examples are

> Q. Describe your level of skill in using cause-and-effect analysis to diagnose production problems. (Knowledge of problem identification techniques)
> Probes might include
>
> - What tools or methods do you use?
>
> - When have you analyzed or troubleshot a problem?
>
> - What is meant by root cause analysis?
>
> Q. Describe your level of skill in leading a problem-solving group. Which behaviors do you feel are strong and which need further development and practice? (Group problem-solving skills)
> Probes might include
>
> - Why do you feel you are strong (or weak) in those areas?
>
> - What steps have you taken to overcome those shortcomings?
>
> - Do you have any plans for improving in this area?
>
> Q. Describe your level of skill in training others. What do you do well and what are you working on improving? (Training or group facilitation skills)
> Probes might include
>
> - Why do you feel you are strong (or weak) in those areas?
>
> - Exactly what have you done to improve your skills in this area?

The interviewer should avoid general questions like "What are your major strengths (or weaknesses)?" and focus on the candidate's self-appraisal of specific attributes. The more specific the question, the more likely the interviewer is to obtain accurate and useful information. Also, self-appraisal questions are most effective when used to assess specific can do attributes (knowledge and skills) rather than softer abilities and personal characteristics (personality traits). The interviewer is more likely to obtain a valid self-assessment for "skill in reading blueprints" than for "ability to get along with others."

Probing or Follow-Up Questions. In addition to developing a consistent pattern of questions, the effective interviewer should give some thought to how follow-up information to those questions can be collected. Outlining a set of probing questions to follow up initial inquiries will improve the effectiveness of the interview process. Many of the previous questions included follow-up probes. Here are some generic probing statements.

- Why did you do it that way?
- What did you learn from that situation?
- Explain exactly what steps you took.
- If given the opportunity, what would you do differently?

Each of the alternative question formats has the potential to make a unique contribution to the information gathered about the candidate. Combining this diverse information will increase the accuracy of the picture of the candidate's potential.

Resumes

The interviewer should review each applicant's resume before the interview. Although the typical resume is too brief and general to obtain much specific information, it can provide valuable background information that can help the interviewer during the interview session (areas in which detailed probing will be important). It is important that the review of the resume be organized around the specific KSAPs identified in the job analysis. The following resume categories will produce preliminary information about the applicant's quality readiness.

- Professional affiliations, such as ASQC or the American Society for Training and Development (ASTD)
- Level of involvement in relevant organizations, such as attendance at programs and conferences, committee activity, leadership positions
- Previous employment at organizations with strong quality and service orientations
- Education, training, and certification, such as statistics courses, group problem solving, or certification as a quality engineer, a reliability engineer, or a quality auditor

- Indicators of improvements in processes and customer satisfaction (versus the more typical references to level of responsibility and budgets)

The Attribute/Question Format Matrix

One useful approach for ensuring a direct link between job-related attributes and the development of interview questions is to fashion an attribute/question format matrix. Figure 9.1 illustrates such a matrix. KSAPs identified during job analysis are placed along the horizontal axis while the various questioning formats are listed on the vertical axis. The task of the interviewer is to decide which of the questioning formats lends itself best to measuring the specific job-related attribute. Thus, *knowledge of SPC* might best be measured during an interview using education and training, work experience, specific knowledge, and self-appraisal questions. In addition to the interview, an SPC knowledge test might be developed to measure the attribute. Other questioning formats, such as hypothetical situation or behavioral consistency questions may be more effective for measuring *team facilitation skills* or *customer orientation*. Thus, the matrix helps the interviewer focus the interview content on those questions most likely to elicit the information desired. Exhibits 9.3 and 9.4 demonstrate the end product of such an effort and show the reader what a structured, content-valid interview might resemble.

Selection at The Ritz-Carlton Hotel®

Called the quality selection process (QSP), the employment interview is the basic tool used by The Ritz-Carlton Hotel® Company, L.L.C. in its staffing efforts. Applicants for jobs with Ritz must survive four interviews before being hired. The QSP provides talent-based (behavioral) information that directly correlates with the future performance of candidates selected. More than 100 individuals in The Ritz-Carlton Hotel® system have been trained in how to conduct these interview sessions. Examples of the questions asked and how responses are interpreted (conceptual match) are shown in Exhibit 9.5. The measurable impact of The Ritz-Carlton Hotel® Company's collective quality efforts, including both selection and training, has resulted in a significant reduction in turnover, increased customer satisfaction, and a decrease in customer complaints. In 1991, for example, 25 percent of customers experienced some kind of defect while staying in a Ritz-Carlton Hotel® (for example, the key may not have fit in the door or

	Knowledge of SPC	Knowledge of process improvement	Team facilitation skills	Customer orientation	Openness to learning
Education and training	x	x			x
Work experience	x	x	x	x	x
Specific knowledge	x	x			
Hypothetical situation			x	x	
Behavioral consistency			x	x	x
Self-appraisal and analysis	x				x
Probing or follow-up questions					x
Other (tests, simulation, work samples)	x	x	x		

Figure 9.1. Attribute/question format matrix.

Exhibit 9.3. Structured interview rating form for the attribute *skill in developing and facilitating teams.*

Job attribute:	Skill in developing and facilitating teams. Includes keeping the group on track, training members in problem-solving skills, encouraging the active involvement of all group members, and protecting minority opinion.

Questions/inquiries:

1. Describe your experiences working with quality or process improvement teams or groups.

   _____ How successful was the team in meeting its objectives?

   _____ Why was the group successful or unsuccessful?

   _____ What was your role as a group member?

   _____ What would you do (have done) to make the group more effective?

2. How do you (would you) get people to participate or be involved in a group situation?

   _____ What tools or techniques would you use to generate ideas or suggestions?

   _____ How do you (would you) get members to stay on track?

3. All of us have been involved in team situations where one or more group members fail to complete assignments and do their fair share of the work. Please describe your most difficult experience in which you had to deal with such a person.

   _____ What specific steps did you take in dealing with the individual?

   _____ Did you confront him or her? What did you say?

   _____ How did he or she respond?

   _____ How effective were your efforts? Why? Why not?

   _____ What did you learn from the experience?

   _____ What would you do differently?

4. Suppose you're working on a team project to reduce department costs and all members, except one person, agree on a list of budget cuts. The one individual raises her hand and states that she is strenuously opposed to one of the cuts. What would you do? How would you deal with this person? What would you say to her?

   _____ Why would you do it that way?

   _____ Suppose that didn't work?

Exhibit 9.4. Structured interview rating form for the attribute *knowledge of SPC*.

Job attribute:	Knowledge of SPC includes awareness of system variation, causes of variation, and the use of control charts and tools for measuring and reducing variation.

Questions/inquiries:

1. Briefly describe what quality gurus refer to as *system* or *process variation*.
   - Differentiate between the concepts of common and special causes of variation.
   - What is meant by the term *tampering?*
2. When constructing a control chart, when is it appropriate to use $\bar{X}$ and R charts? When is it appropriate to use a p chart?
3. What are some of the factors used to determine if a process is out of control?
   - What steps should be taken when a process is out of control?
4. Have you ever used a run chart or a control chart to measure the performance of a process? Please describe.
   - What did you find?
   - How was the information used to improve the process?
5. Show the applicant a typical control chart used in your work situation and ask him/her to interpret the data.

Exhibit 9.5. Sample questions and ideal responses for interview questions used by The Ritz-Carlton Hotel®.

Question asked	Conceptual match
Q. Can you get other people to help or support you?	Yes
	and
(If yes) Please illustrate a time when you got others to help you.	Provides a specific successful example of gaining the help and support of others
Q. How important is it to you to be a part of a winning team?	Superlative (for example, "critical," or "an absolute must")
	and
So, tell me about a time when you were part of winning team and the role you played.	Provides a specific example of being part of a winning team (including specific achievement)
	Indicates being an integral part of the team's success

Source: Adapted by permission from Talent+ and The Ritz-Carlton Hotel® Company, L.L.C.

Figure 9.2 Pre- and post-QSP defect rate at The Ritz Carlton Hotel®.

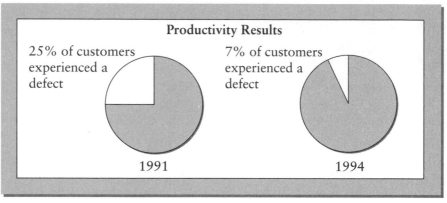

the bookmarker was not on the right page). This was prior to implementation of the QSP. By 1994, that defect rate was 7 percent and still improving (see Figure 9.2). Obviously, leaders at The Ritz-Carlton Hotel® know what they're talking about when they say that "quality starts with the selection of employees."

Structured Behavioral Interviewing and Return on Investment

At the beginning of this chapter we pointed out that the all-too-typical, shoot-from-the-hip interview has a poor track record for predicting performance. But what types of results can be expected if you use an interview process that reflects the principles espoused throughout this chapter and book? How effective is an interview process that is job related, structured, and behavior based? To help answer this question, we present some ROI data from three organizational settings in which such an approach was used. These examples of effectiveness are based on using one widely used interviewing method called Targeted Selection®. Targeted Selection is a proven, comprehensive system for hiring and promoting people based on specific job requirements and organizational skills. It was developed to provide interviewers with the skill and confidence they need to make accurate selection decisions. The system also helps organizations hire within legal guidelines, enhance their image, reduce turnover, and improve organizational performance. The three case studies demonstrate its use. (Copyright © Developmental Dimensions International, Inc., MCMXCV. All rights reserved. Used with permission.)

Case 1: Retail

Method. Targeted Selection was implemented in house by the retailer's staff. The organizations used the program to determine the requirements critical to success in the job by talking with incumbents and their managers, establishing a consistent approach to recruiting (for example, evaluating all candidates by the same criteria within the same system), and training interviewers and campus recruiters to make effective selection decisions.

To evaluate the Targeted Selection system, two groups were formed for comparison. One group comprised people hired through conventional methods; the other comprised people selected using the Targeted Selection process. Trainees participating in the study were tracked for 30 months.

Results. Turnover decreased significantly for the Targeted Selection group compared to trainees hired through conventional methods. Two groups of particular interest—women and minorities—showed large decreases in turnover, with an overall turnover decrease of approximately 50 percent among all trainees hired using Targeted Selection (see Figure 9.3).

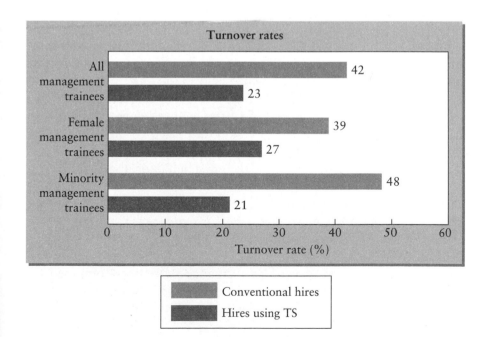

Figure 9.3. Turnover rates.

Trainee performance was also tracked for the 30-month period. Those hired using Targeted Selection received higher performance ratings and were ready for promotion sooner than were trainees hired through conventional means.

The decrease in turnover among management trainees hired using Targeted Selection and their rapid advancement show that Targeted Selection helped the organization to identify better performers. Not only did the organization select higher-caliber trainees, but interviewers reported that they were more confident and satisfied with their selection decisions. As a direct result of using the Targeted Selection system, the organization estimates that it saved $6 million in expenses over a three-year period.

Case 2: Baked Goods Production

Method. A baked goods plant was expanding its production operation into a new-high-technology facility. The goal was to staff the new facility with team members who could learn and operate the new, high-tech equipment and work effectively in empowered work teams. The plant leaders were determined to ensure a valid and objective selection process. Wanting proof that its selection system process would meet the high standards of the new plant, the bakery chose first to evaluate the effectiveness of Targeted Selection in its current facility.

Targeted Selection administrators at the plant conducted a thorough job analysis to identify dimensions—knowledge, behaviors, and motivations—needed for successful performance at the new facility. They then created Targeted Selection interview guides and trained a team of interviewers to assess 125 of the facility's current employees. Candidates were evaluated on five key dimensions: initiative, attention to detail, motivational fit, teamwork, and communication.

At the same time, the bakery developed behaviorally anchored rating scales to assess the job performance of the same sample of associates. A different team of managers was trained to use the performance appraisal measure. Each associate's performance was rated against the standards set for the new facility.

Ratings from both teams (interviewers and performance appraisers) were analyzed, and an overall performance score was computed for each associate. The overall performance score was then compared with each of the dimension ratings obtained through the interview process.

Results. Targeted Selection ratings in each of the five dimensions were significantly and positively correlated with the overall per-

Table 9.2. Correlation between targeted selection interview ratings and job performance.

Dimension	Overall performance score
Initiative	.22*
Attention to detail	.19*
Motivational fit	.28**
Teamwork	.27**
Communication	.20*

*Signigicant <.05   **Significant <.01   (I-tailed rest)

formance score (see Table 9.2). Candidates with higher Targeted Selection ratings tended to have higher job performance scores, confirming the selection system's effectiveness in predicting actual job performance.

An average interview rating—*more than acceptable, acceptable,* or *less than acceptable*—was calculated for each associate. The top 20 percent and bottom 20 percent of performers were identified, based on their overall performance score. Two outcome predictions were made: (1) the top performing group would have a larger proportion of *acceptable* or *more than acceptable* interview ratings; and (2) the bottom group would have a larger proportion of *less than acceptable ratings*. Both predictions were confirmed (see Figure 9.4).

Based on the results of the study, the baked goods plant concluded that using Targeted Selection facilitated valid, objective, and fair hiring decisions. Thus, the company decided to use the Targeted Selection system to staff the new facility.

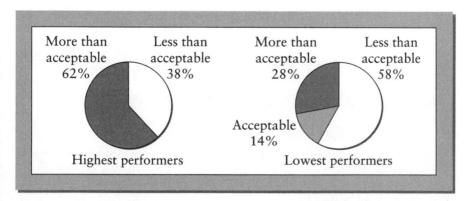

Figure 9.4. Distribution of interview ratings at two performance levels.

Case 3: Food Service

Method. Targeted Selection was implemented in one of the largest fast-food chains in the United States to help reduce turnover among management trainees. The company measured turnover before and after Targeted Selection was used. It also measured perceptions of the new selection system versus traditional systems from the viewpoint of both interviews and candidates.

Results. In terms of the interviewers' perceptions, 91 percent of hiring managers said that the Targeted Selection hiring process was an improvement over their old system. Also, 75 percent said they believed that their interviewing skills had improved.

The program also made a better impression on the management trainee candidates, who were asked to compare Targeted Selection to other traditional programs encountered at other companies.

	Targeted Selection same	Targeted Selection better
Depth of interviewing	25%	75%
Professionalism	42%	58%

Turnover, the most important criterion for the company, was reduced by nearly one-third after implementing Targeted Selection (see Figure 9.5).

What These Results Tell Us

These significant performance improvements and turnover reductions provide the payoff and ROI that organizations seek but do not always know how to attain. Note also that the candidate views such an ap-

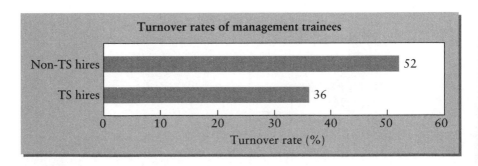

Figure 9.5. Turnover rates of management trainees.

proach more favorably than traditional approaches. Adhering to the guidelines presented in this chapter and in chapter 10 can benefit firms that are willing to invest the time and resources necessary to improve their interviewing process.

Summary

Avoiding many of the errors and biases inherent in the interview process can be accomplished by developing a structured and job-related set of questions and inquiries. Valid decisions are possible with the interview, but such decisions can be made only when considerable time and effort goes into developing interview content. While somewhat time-consuming and difficult to do early on, subsequent efforts are likely to be much easier and improve with time. Most importantly, the effort expended will pay dividends for years to come in terms of a quality workforce.

Notes

1. Robert F. Wagner, "The Employment Interview: A Critical Summary," *Personnel Psychology* (1949): 17–46. This article describes experiments on the consistency of interviews conducted by Walter D. Scott and by Scott, Bingham, and Whipple in 1917.

2. John E. Hunter and Rhonda E. Hunter, "Validity and Utility of Alternative Predictors of Job Performance," *Psychological Bulletin* 96 (1984): 72–98.

3. Allen I. Huffcutt and Winfred Arthur, "Hunter and Hunter (1984) Revisited: Interview Validity for Entry-Level Jobs," *Journal of Applied Psychology* (April 1994): 184–190. See also Michael A. Campion, James E. Campion, and J. Peter Hudson, Jr., "Structured Interviewing: A Note on Incremental Validity and Alternative Question Types," *Journal of Applied Psychology* (1994): 998–1002; Wayne F. Cascio, *Managing Human Resources,* 4th ed. (New York: McGraw-Hill, 1995), 209.

4. Milton M. Mandel, presentation given at the International Congress on the Assessment Center Method, Washington, D.C.

5. Edward C. Webster, *Decision Making in the Employment Interview* (Montreal, Quebec: The Eagle Publishing Co., 1964). See also H. John Bernardin and Joyce E. A. Russell, *Human Resource Management: An Experiential Approach* (New York: McGraw-Hill, 1993), 266–267.

6. Ed Papazian. "Who Are Your Heroes? It's Not a Silly Question." *Working Women* (March 1989): 28.

7. For additional discussion of the sources of error in the interview and how structured interviewing reduces those errors, see Ronald B. Morgan, "The Selection Interview," in *The Handbook of Engineering Management,* John E. Ullmann, ed.

(New York: John Wiley, 1986). For an example of a structured interview, see Ronald B. Morgan, "Preparing for and Conducting the Interview," in *The Handbook of Engineering Management,* John E. Ullmann, ed. (New York: John Wiley, 1986).

8. Huffcutt and Arthur, "Hunter and Hunter (1984) Revisited."

9. Ronald B. Morgan and Jack E. Smith, "A New Era in Manufacturing and Service," *Quality Progress* (July 1993): 83–89.

10. Michael A. Campion, James E. Campion, and J. Peter Hudson, Jr., "Structured Interviewing"; Cynthia Searcy, Patty Nio Woods, Robert D. Gatewood, and Charles F. Lance, "The Structured Interview: A Meta-Analytic Search for Moderators," paper presented at the Society for Industrial and Organizational Psychology, San Francisco, Calif., 1993; Willi H. Wiesner and Steven F. Cronshaw, "A Meta-Analytic Investigation of the Impact of Interview Format and Degree of Structure on the Validity of the Employment Interview," *Journal of Applied Psychology* 79, no. 6 (1988): 275–290.

11. Tom Janz, Lowell Hellervik, and David C. Gilmore, *Behavior Description Interviewing* (Boston, Mass.: Allyn and Bacon, 1986).

The Employment Interview: Conducting the Interview Session

Overview

To this point, we have attempted to orient the reader to the steps needed for developing a structured and content-valid interview. In this chapter, we will discuss the interpersonal skills associated with effective interviewing, the steps involved in actually conducting a professional interview session, and how to use the interview data along with other assessment information collected to make valid employment decisions.

Introduction

We apologize in advance for the almost checklist-like nature of this chapter, but this approach was necessary to provide a comprehensive overview of the critical skills involved in conducting a successful interview session. We ask the reader to think of these guidelines as quality standards for interview administration. Adherence to these standards will do much to ensure an interview process that is reliable, valid, and fair. It will also substantially increase the positive perceptions of the process by the candidate.

In addition, we will briefly discuss the final decision-making process. This discussion incorporates the use of recruiting and assessment tools discussed in previous chapters.

Interviewer Skills

There are at least four skills that are important when conducting the interview session. They include note-taking skills, listening skills, probing and follow-up skills, and controlling the interview.

Understanding the importance of these skills and then applying and practicing them will do much to improve the accuracy and perceived fairness of the interview.

Taking Notes

Interviewers often question the necessity of taking notes during the interview session. Many view it as disruptive or impolite. However, research clearly shows that taking notes during the session improves interviewer recall of relevant information when making employment decisions.[1]

The purpose of note taking is to have an accurate record of as much information as possible. Your role during the interview process is twofold: (1) to gather relevant information by asking questions, probing, listening, and observing, and to take notes that describe, rather than judge or evaluate, the candidate's responses; (2) to categorize and evaluate the information. This should only take place following the interview session (see Figure 10.1).

Complete and accurate notes increase the probability of making reliable and valid judgments about the candidate. The following hints should help the interviewer improve note-taking skills.

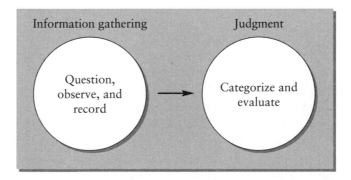

Figure 10.1. Dual roles in the employment interview.

1.   Because the human memory is fallible, note taking should be as complete and accurate as possible. Interviewers who fail to document completely and accurately are more likely to exhibit many interviewing errors such as halo, early decisions, and contrast effects. If necessary, slow the pace of the interview for note taking.

2.   Use key words or phrases rather than attempting to keep a verbatim transcript of the interview session.

- Took 2-day course in SPC
- Devlpd c-chart for delivery errors
- QC group couldn't even agree on prob to tackle
- Knew diff between spec and comm cause variation
- Said "Had it out with 2 group members"
- Says prefers working alone

3.   Avoid judgment or evaluative comments when taking notes. Writing that the person demonstrates "good interpersonal skills" or shows "poor planning and organizing" should be avoided. Suspend judgments until after the interview.

4.   Focus your efforts on observing and recording the responses and behavior of the candidate. Your notes should focus on what the person said or did during the interview. To help ensure your understanding of the difference between recording behavior and making evaluative comments when taking notes, try completing the quiz shown in Exhibit 10.1. Focusing on behavior instead of making evaluations or judgments helps the interviewer avoid the errors discussed in the previous chapter. It provides relevant information that can then be categorized and evaluated at the end of the session.

5.   Once the interview is completed, notes should be reviewed, edited, and then placed in the appropriate category/dimension for justifying ratings. These behavioral notes are documentation of your rationale for evaluating the candidate the way you did. Perhaps the best self-test of your skills as an interviewer comes when you are able to support your judgments with a complete set of behavioral notes. You will know you have arrived as a skilled interviewer when you are prepared to justify your ratings based on what the candidate said or did during the interview session.

Exhibit 10.1. Behavioral note-taking quiz.

Examine each of the following interviewer notes and determine whether or not the comments are behavioral.

Notes	Behavioral?	
	Yes	No
1. Demonstrated good communication skills	—	—
2. Rubbed hands together while talking	—	—
3. Attended advanced SPC course	—	—
4. Conscientious at work	—	—
5. Stated that "didn't like to work overtime"	—	—
6. Motivated worker	—	—
7. Practiced speech in front of mirror	—	—
8. Reviewed program with boss before finalizing	—	—
9. Poor work attitude	—	—
10. Said "ya know" several times	—	—
11. Called back to make sure customer's complaint was resolved	—	—
12. Reduced report generation cycle time by 50%	—	—

Answers: No, Yes, Yes, No, Yes, No, Yes, Yes, No, Yes, Yes, Yes

Listening Skills

Remember that failure to actively listen is one of the major interviewer errors. Use the time allotted for the interview sessions as wisely as possible to collect (and provide) meaningful information. Save your war stories and pet peeves for another time and place. Key points for improving listening skills include

1. Actively listen to the candidate and demonstrate interest and concern using both verbal and nonverbal communication.

2. Use short, neutral statements ("uh-huh," "I see," "I understand," "that's interesting") and nonverbal gestures (nodding your head, leaning forward) to encourage discussion without providing clues as to the appropriateness of the response.

3. Reinforce positive accomplishments by the candidate. This not only encourages open communication but leaves the person with a good feeling about you and the company.

4. Downplay negative information as much as possible. The goal is to create an atmosphere where the applicant feels comfortable sharing not only positive but negative information. Also remember that overweighing negative information is a major interviewer error. For example, suppose the applicant indicates that his/her previous job ended unfavorably. Rather than accentuating the negative with a reply like, "So, you were fired," you are more likely to learn the details of the situation by saying something like, "So, it appears that the job wasn't for you."

5. Don't be afraid of silence or long pauses during the interview. Interviewers often feel uncomfortable with such lapses and want to jump in and help the person by rephrasing the questions, moving to another topic, or even answering their own questions. Resist the urge to end silent periods in the discussion.

Probing and Follow-Up

The major objective of the interview is to determine whether a good match exists between the candidate and the specified job and organizational qualifications. Obtaining complete and accurate information about the candidate requires a great deal of skill on the part of the interviewer. Following are some suggestions for obtaining such information.

The key to eliciting in-depth information about the candidate is advance preparation on the part of the interviewer. Two elements of this preparation are critical. First, the interviewer must have a clear understanding of the attributes that he/she is attempting to measure. Second, the interviewer must have thought through how he/she can best extract that information from the candidate. Pre-developed questions and follow-up questions help the interviewer focus the discussion and obtain relevant information. As with initial questions, probes should avoid closed-ended and leading questions.

Poor questions

- "Did you follow up to make sure the task was accomplished?"

- "Will you continue your education?"

- "Would you require some kind of accountability when making those assignments?"

Probes should focus on the use of open-ended and indirect questioning.

- What, Where, When, Who, How, Why
- Explain
- Give an example
- Tell me more

Better questions

- "Give me an example of how you went about doing that."
- "Who had responsibility for the success of the project?"
- "Why did you do it that way?"
- "Tell me more about how you dealt with that client."
- "What did you learn from that situation?"

Controlling the Interview

The interview process requires the collection of a great deal of information within a limited time frame (typically 30 minutes to one hour in length). Therefore, it is imperative that the interviewer use the time available wisely by maintaining control and keeping the interview on track.

1. The first step in controlling the interview is to inform the candidate of the purpose, structure, and time limitations of the interview. Discussing this outline of the interview procedure at the beginning of the session allows the interviewer to easily bring a meandering interview back on track.

Example: "That's very interesting, but we only have about ten minutes left, and I'd like to know more about why you decided to leave XYZ Corporation."

2. Continually refocusing the interview on the match between the candidate and the work also helps the interviewer maintain control.

Example: "We've discussed your education and experience at length, but now I'd like to shift gears and ask how you might handle some situations we often encounter around here. What would you do if . . ."

3. When dealing with a particularly talkative candidate, don't be afraid to interrupt the discussion to refocus the content or to remind the candidate of the time constraints. This can be accomplished in a polite manner with minimal disruption of the session.

Example: "I'm sorry to interrupt, but I'm particularly interested in your specific responsibilities when you were the team leader. Could you tell me more about . . ."

4. What happens if you run out of time and still feel you have not collected all of the necessary information needed to make a decision? First, don't go over the allotted time if it will disrupt the interviewing schedule or impinge on someone else's time. If this is not a problem, ask the candidate if he/she would mind continuing for a little while longer. If it will interfere, attempt to collect the information at another time (during lunch or after other interviewers are finished). If necessary, invite the candidate back for a second interview when feasible. It is important for you to make every attempt to obtain the information necessary to make a sound decision. You and the organization are likely to be affected by the decision for years to come.

Conducting the Session: A Checklist

While the development of a structured and job-related interview is the primary consideration in ensuring content validity, the actual execution of the interview session is also important. It is, of course, during this all-important session that information about the applicant is collected, concerns and questions are dealt with by both parties, and the interviewer and candidate assess job and organizational fit.

Administration Checklist

As an aid to helping the interviewer, we have listed the key considerations that the interviewer should keep in mind at each step of the interview session process (see Figure 10.2). We suggest that you think of these points as a checklist that should be reviewed prior to beginning the session.

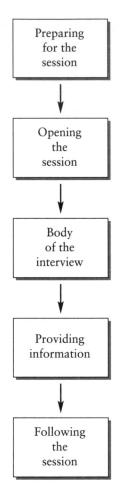

Figure 10.2. Steps in the interview session process.

Preparing for the Interview Session

1. Thoroughly review candidate materials (application, resume, personnel history record, transcripts, performance appraisal forms). Pay special attention to such information as education and experience, quality-related activities, and efforts at self-development such as coursework and professional affiliations. Also, carefully examine evidence of progression and career direction as well as changes in (or lack of) responsibility (success history). Always remember that the best predictor of future behavior and performance is past behavior and performance.

2. When using multiple interviews, agree on the time schedule and who will do what during the interviewing process in advance. This reduces down-time, helps interviewers schedule their activities, and presents the candidate with a positive, professional image of the organization and those conducting the interview sessions. An interview schedule should be developed and disseminated to all interested parties, including the candidate.

3. Review the structured interview format previously developed. A quick review of your questions and probes will help keep the session on track and ensure that all relevant areas are addressed.

4. Prepare the physical setting for the session. Clearing your desk or work area, setting up a nonthreatening seating arrangement, and allowing for privacy (shut the door and hold phone calls) help to create a positive and productive climate for the session.

5. Establish a positive frame of mind. Interviewers need to be upbeat and view the session as an important activity that can, if done correctly, have significant impact on the long-term success of the organization. It should not be viewed as an encumbrance that interferes with daily work activities. Maintaining a positive attitude is particularly critical when the interviewer is required to do extensive interviewing. Staffing personnel, line managers doing campus interviewing, and individuals involved in large-scale hiring initiatives must continually remind themselves of this point.

Opening the Interview Session

6. Begin the interview on a positive, nonthreatening note. Smile, stand and shake hands, take the candidate's coat, get him/her a cup of coffee, or do whatever will establish a positive tone for the session. Be sure to pronounce the person's name correctly. If necessary, ask the candidate for the correct pronunciation and how he/she prefers to be addressed.

7. Introduce yourself and explain your position within the organization.

My name is Cheryl Jones, and I am the Assistant Sales Manager for Retail. The person who fills the position of Internal Sales Representative will report directly to me.

One very useful approach for introducing yourself and how you fit into the scheme of things is to use an organization chart. Candidates appreciate knowing with whom they are interacting and the person's position in the organization.

8. Briefly explain the purpose of the interview session, general topics to be discussed, interview length, and subsequent interaction with other organization personnel.

> *The purpose of today's session is to provide you with an overview of our organization and the position in question. More importantly, we want to use the time available to determine if there is a match between your qualifications and the position of Internal Sales Representative. I will be asking you questions concerning your education, background, work experience, and specific job-related skills. We'll also spend some time discussing the responsibilities of the position and the company's quality-philosophy and expectations. We will be meeting for the next hour, until 11:00, at which time you will be interviewed by Rick Hagopian, my counterpart on the wholesale side of sales. Do you have any questions before we begin?*

A brief outline of the purpose and direction of the interview is beneficial for a number of reasons. First, it gives you control over the interview by establishing the preset pattern and order of topics. This makes it easier to guide the interview and keep it on course. Second, outlining the interview is a courtesy to the applicant. This gives the person an idea of where the interview is going. Third, it conveys the message that the interview has been planned, that you take it seriously, and that it is important to you. It assures the applicant that you have a genuine interest in him or her. Finally, it gives the impression of professionalism. It is clear that you, the interviewer, know what you are doing. If you have ever suffered through a rambling interview, with no idea of what topics were to be covered by the interviewer, you can appreciate the benefits to the applicant a clearly defined outline provides.

9. Inform the candidate that you will be taking notes during the session.

> *As we go through the interview, I will be jotting down a few notes. They will help me make sure that I get all of the important facts correct. We will be interviewing several candidates,*

and I want to make sure I don't forget any of the things we discuss during our session.

10. If it has not previously been communicated, provide the candidate with a brief overview of the position in question and solicit his/her candor and cooperation. This should not be a detailed description of all duties and tasks but rather a simple overview of the job.

As you may know, Jim, the position we're interviewing for is Internal Sales Representative. This is our entry-level sales position. Basically, you would be one of our counter persons dealing with retail sales.

11. Don't spend a lot of time engaged in nonrelevant small talk. Interviewers are often told that they should spend the first several minutes of the interview putting the person at ease. Most of the popular literature on interviewing actually supports the notion of engaging in this form of casual conversation. It is suggested that this process of exchanging pleasantries helps develop rapport and set the stage for a more effective interview. Some even suggest that the interviewer go into the session with a couple of these small-talk topics already in mind. While intuitively appealing, these "How did you spend your summer vacation?" discussions have at least three problems. First, valuable time is wasted that could be spent collecting relevant information. Only a limited amount of time is available for the body or assessment component of the interview. Using that time for small talk is a waste of valuable time. Next, these little chitchats compound an already existing interviewer error. Remember that decisions are typically made very early in the interview session. This tendency toward making early decisions becomes particularly disconcerting when based on discussions of the weather, the success or failure of the local sports team, or the fact that you both have the same alma mater. Finally, this effort at building rapport inherently places the interviewer in the role of playing amateur psychologist. Both parties know the purpose of the interview session, so why not cut to the chase and start sharing and collecting useful information that improves the decision process? We don't spend 10 minutes giving an applicant for a clerical position a back rub prior to administering a keyboard (typing) test, so why waste precious time attempting to relax the person through meaningless gab before asking relevant questions? The relaxation is easily accomplished through the demeanor of the interviewer.

This admonition to get on with the interview does not imply that the interviewer should be curt or impolite. We have already said that the interviewer should be positive and upbeat and address all of the social amenities associated with having a guest (customer) enter your domain. What it does imply is that the time available should be used judiciously for the intended purpose.

The Body of the Interview

12. Follow the patterned interview format previously developed. The key to a valid interview session is adherence to a structured, job-related format. Everything else is secondary. Don't be afraid to continually refer to the structured format as the interview progresses. Some interviewers mistakenly feel that the interview session should be a freewheeling and spontaneous affair. Systematically progressing through an established set of job-related questions is the most important thing an interviewer can do to ensure the reliability and validity of the interview process.

In terms of sticking to the structured format, one question frequently asked by interviewers is: "What should I do if it becomes obvious that the candidate is a poor fit and obviously unqualified early in the session? Can I cut the session short?" An abbreviated session is generally not a good idea. This is particularly true when the possibility of litigation (charges of unfair discrimination) exists. Having a standardized process that affords each candidate a fair and equal examination becomes critical in such cases. One way to avoid such a predicament is to improve the rigor of the screening process (initial phone interview, resume reviews, and so on).

13. Begin the interview session with a comprehensive but job-related question.

- *Why don't we start by your telling me about the responsibilities on your last job?*

- *Why don't we start by your telling me about your last four years at _____ University?*

These questions are a comfortable start for the interviewee and do more to relax the person than the irrelevant small talk previously discussed. This type of opening also makes it easy for the interviewer to make the transition to very specific questions concerning the candidate's experience, education, and so on.

14. Take copious notes. We have already discussed the importance of note taking during the interview session but it warrants repeating. Interviewers should get in the habit of documenting all responses. If necessary, slow the pace of the session to allow for note taking. The goal should be to have collected a complete set of relevant information about the candidate to present in the consensus session for making the selection decision. Ideally, each interviewer should be prepared to justify his/her ratings of various attributes with specific examples of what the candidate said or did during the interview session. A complete set of notes becomes the basis for that justification.

15. Throughout the session, attempt to positively reinforce the candidate's cooperation and help.

- *I appreciate your honesty.*

- *That gives me a much better picture of your experience working in team situations.*

- *It must have been difficult to get such grades while working full time.*

Providing Information

16. Provide the applicant with a realistic preview of the job and the organization. As previously discussed, this RJP should include both the positive and negative aspects of the position or job. A frank discussion of the quality expectations and demands of the job should also be included at this point.

- *Individuals in this position are expected to travel to our other plants once or twice each month. Trips generally take a couple of days and require staying overnight.*

- *During peak work times, our employees often work considerable overtime. Work weeks of 60 or more hours become the norm. While this usually occurs two or three times a year, everyone is expected to contribute to the effort.*

- *We absolutely demand that our employees do everything possible to make our customers happy.*

- *We strongly believe in teamwork and cooperation between various units and functional areas. We view other depart-*

ments and areas as our internal customers, and treat them
with the same enthusiasm and care as we do our external
customers.

- We expect employees to stay current in their fields and be
open to training and development opportunities. We expect
that you would avail yourself of our internal training programs, and we encourage professional development both
inside and outside the organization.

17. Allow the candidate the opportunity to ask questions and provide additional information.

- Before we conclude, do you have any questions or concerns
about the job or the organization?

- Is there anything you would like to add concerning your
qualifications or experience that you think we've missed or
that might help us in our decision process?

18. Initiate the closing by determining the candidate's interest in
further discussion and consideration. Some interviewers mistakenly
assume that the candidate will automatically want to continue the
process. But selection is a two-way process and, quite possibly, the individual may want to remove him/herself from further consideration.
This is particularly true if the session includes a thorough RJP.

19. Clearly communicate the remaining steps in the selection
process (subsequent interviews and assessments, decision time line,
who will contact him/her and in what time period). Don't leave applicants guessing as to what happens next and when they can expect
to know something about his/her application status. End the session
on a positive note and thank the candidate for his/her interest and
cooperation.

Well, Mary Beth, that concludes the interview session. Our
discussion has been very enlightening, and I've appreciated
your honesty and cooperation. We still have three or four candidates who will be interviewed for the position, but we hope
to complete those sessions and make a decision within two
weeks. Either I or someone from our Human Resource Department will call you at that time regarding our decision.
Thank you again for your interest in our company.

If the process takes longer than expected (for example, hiring freeze, additional interviews), contact the person and inform him/her of the status of the selection process. Always remember that the candidate is a customer and should be treated accordingly.

Following the Interview Session

20. Immediately following the interview session, the interviewer should review and edit notes and categorize information into dimensions (KSAPs). Even when following a structured interview format, relevant information concerning a specific attribute can come at any time during the session. Supporting information, positive or negative, should be pulled from the interview notes and placed in the appropriate category—the sooner, the better. Following is an example of such notes for the attribute *team facilitation skills*.

Team Facilitation Skills
Notes:

- *Has worked on several team projects in work situation*

- *Was the team leader for a process improvement team assigned to reduce billing errors (team only met a couple of times and then disbanded due to lack of interest and time)*

- *Took a two-day ASQC course on group problem solving*

- *Knew the rules to brainstorming and gave examples of using brainstorming techniques to get people involved (uses flip-charts for generating ideas and solutions)*

- *Said that he "had a hard time keeping the group on track" when he was the team leader*

- *Failed to protect minority opinion on the hypothetical question—said he would "go with the majority opinion" without considering the individual's rationale*

21. Once you have categorized it, compare the information collected with the established criteria and evaluate the candidate on each of the specified KSAP dimensions. Document those judgments and evaluations by noting behaviors that support your conclusions. Exhibit 10.2 shows what an actual interview form, including notes and summary rating, might look like for the dimension *team facilitation skills*.

Exhibit 10.2. Interview rating form for "teamwork"—an example.

Job Qualification: Team Facilitation Skills: Working in situations that require a great deal of group interaction, cooperation, and problem solving.

Questions/inquiries:

Q. Beginning with your most recent experiences, tell me about your participation in group or team situations.
- How effective? Why or why not?
- Your role?
- Like/Dislike?
- How would you (did you) improve the effectiveness of the group?

Q. How do you (would you) get people to participate or be involved in a group situation?
- Get them to generate ideas?
- Keep on track?
- Tackle a difficult and complex problem (such as process improvement)?

Q. Tell me about a time when you had to work most closely with other individuals on a major group or team project.
- Your role?
- Leader effectiveness? Why? Why not?
- Involvement of participants
- Problem-solving steps?
- Results or effectiveness?

Q. What kinds of training or support do you feel is needed by problem-solving groups? What makes them effective or ineffective?
- Specific tools or methods helpful?
- Organization or management support needed?

Q. What kinds of people would (do you) look for when putting together a broad process improvement effort?
- Group dynamic skills?
- Group problem-solving skills?
- Technical skills?

Q. Suppose you're working on a group project and someone isn't doing his or her fair share—what would you do?
- Why that way?
- Suppose that didn't work—what then?

Exhibit 10.2. Continued.

Evaluation guidelines:

- Varied, widespread, and successful experience working in team situations including group facilitation
- Knowledge of group problem-solving tools (e.g., brainstorming, cause-and-effect diagrams, force field analysis)
- Understands basics of keeping the group on track in terms of both content and process.
- Understands and uses systematic problem-solving and process improvement models (such as scientific method, PDCA, process improvement)
- Understands importance of participation and uses facilitation skills to encourage involvement
- Genuine enthusiasm for employee involvement and teamwork.

Notes:

Wkd. on several team projects. Doesn't like inds who jump in & take control. Understands & uses brainstorming techniques to get people involved—uses flip charts for generating ideas & solutions. Has been trained in Kepner-Tregoe. Says he always has an agenda.

Summary rating:

Unacceptable	Somewhat less than acceptable	Acceptable	More than acceptable	Outstanding
1	2	3	4	5

22. Do not communicate your impressions and evaluations with other interviewers until they have had an unbiased opportunity to interview and evaluate the candidate. Enough bias (early impressions, halo) is inherent within the interview process without adding to it by contaminating another interviewer's perspective.

23. Inform the candidate of any decision made and leave the person with a positive image of the organization. As we have consistently pointed out, candidates are customers and should be treated as such. Don't leave them hanging in regards to the firm's hiring decision.

Summary

To be most effective, this checklist should be reviewed prior to conducting your next interview session. Also, feel free to pass these guidelines on to other members of the interview team. After a couple of reviews, adherence to these guidelines will become second nature, and you will become a skilled interviewer. Equally important, candidates will view you as professional and the organization in a favorable light.

Evaluating Candidates

The final stage of the interview process is actually making the hiring decision. This involves the difficult task of deciding who should be accepted, who should be given an offer, and who should be rejected. Figure 10.3 graphically displays the key steps in that process.

Interview Team

To reduce rater bias and maximize the reliability of results, the interview team should ideally consist of between three and five individuals. Using three to five interviewers maximizes the reliability of the process and ensures a balanced perspective. Interviewers should be knowledgeable concerning the target position and bring different points of view to the interview process. Ideally, varying perspectives should reflect differences in age, gender, and race. Not only will this help pro-

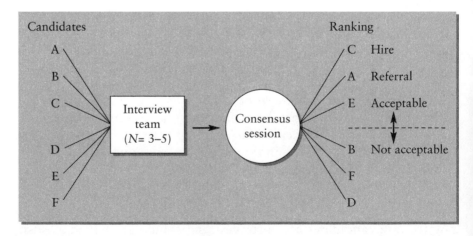

Figure 10.3. Steps in the interview process.

tect against interviewer errors such as stereotyping, but it will be seen as a fair process by candidates. But remember, all interviewers should adhere to the same structured interview content.

Consensus Session

The purpose of the consensus session is to meet as a group and make final evaluations. This is accomplished by pooling and discussing observations made during the interviews. Agreement is reached on the strength and weaknesses of the candidates, and a final judgment (rating, ranking, pass–fail, hire–no hire, promote–don't promote) is made. Consensus differs from a simple summing up of scores in that a general agreement for the final score is reached through group discussions on the various individual interviewer ratings for each category or dimension. Table 10.1 show what the results of such a session might resemble.

Each interviewer comes to the session with his or her individual ratings of candidates completed. The critical attributes or KSAPs are listed vertically (usually on a flip chart), and then the ratings of each

Table 10.1. Example of consensus session output.

Candidate: *Jacob Smith*

Dimensions	Rick	Cheryl	Mary Beth	Bob	Consensus rating
SPC	4	4	3	4	4
Knowledge of process improvement	3	2	3	2	2.5
Team facilitation skills	1	2	3	2	2
Customer orientation	2	3	2	4	4
Openness to learning	3	4	5	3	4
Technical skill A	4	4	5	4	4
Technical skill B	3	4	3	3	3
				Total:	23.5

Rating scale:
5 = Excellent
4 = Above average
3 = Average
2 = Below average
1 = Unacceptable

interviewer are posted. The task of the group is to systematically arrive at a consensus rating on each of the attributes for the candidate.

The major strength of consensus sessions is that interviewers are forced to reconcile differences and to justify their evaluations using specific observations rather than resorting to making decisions based upon their warm and fuzzy feelings about the candidate. Thus, the key to an effective consensus meeting is the documentation (notes) that the interviewer brings to the session. Note, for example, that Bob, in the illustration, was able to convince other members of the interview team that Jacob Smith should receive a final rating of "4" on "customer orientation." This was accomplished despite the low ratings by other group members. This, no doubt, occurred because Bob had asked several customer orientation questions and collected a complete set of notes demonstrating Jacob's competence in this area.

In some cases, the interview team may want to increase the sophistication of the evaluation process. For example, the team may want to assign weights to the various attributes. If SPC is considered much more important than other KSAPs, then a higher weight might be given to that attribute:

$$4 \quad \times \quad 1.5 \quad = \quad 6$$

(Rating) (Weight) (Weighted rating)

Similarly, some groups will designate certain attributes as knock-out factors. That is, the team determines that an attribute (or attributes) is so critical to performance that the candidate must possess an acceptable level of the KSAP (average rating) or the person is excluded from consideration. As such, high scores on other attributes will not compensate for a low score on one of these knock-out factors. Consequently, a score of "2" for Jacob Smith may prevent him from being accepted for the position despite his other relatively high scores. If weights are assigned or knock-out factors are used, they should be consistent with the results of the job analysis (high ratings in terms of the attributes related to job performance).

Ideally, the consensus session should be held after all of the candidates have been interviewed. However, this should only occur if all of the prospective candidates are interviewed within a reasonable time period (one week, with a maximum of two weeks). Greater time periods will necessitate meetings following each candidate's interview.

Combining Interview Data with Other Assessment Information

Throughout this book we have advocated that the total quality organization should broaden its use of assessment tools beyond the typical application form and employment interview. Performance in the new workplace is complex and requires the use of multiple assessment tools to assess all relevant attributes. Predictor measures such as tests, biographical information, and work simulations all have demonstrated validity in a wide variety of quality settings. These tools can do much to improve the utility (ROI) of our staffing decisions. As such, it is typically desirable to use a battery of assessment tools rather than a single measure of performance. Exhibit 10.3 shows a selection procedure design matrix for a team member in a plant setting. In practice, there are basically two methods for combining information when using such batteries: the multiple-hurdle method and the composite score method.

Multiple-Hurdle. Sometimes called the multiple-cutoff or funnel method, this approach involves the administration of assessment tools sequentially with the elimination of candidates at each stage who do not score at a satisfactory level. Our 3M Canada cohesion case exemplifies this approach and is shown in Figure 10.4. For example, all applicants complete an application form and skills inventory, with low-scoring applicants being eliminated from the pool. Those successful candidates who remain are then required to take the various skill and ability tests (reading comprehension, graphic arithmetic, mechanical comprehension) with further screening taking place, and so on.

The multiple-hurdle approach is particularly appealing in those situations where a large application pool exists for a relatively small number of openings (low SR). It is simply too costly and time-consuming to run everyone through the full assessment battery. Generally speaking, we want to put those tools at the beginning which validly screen a large number of applicants at a relatively low cost to the organization. Applications, skill inventories, and paper and pencil tests are all good for that purpose. While it is not always true, these measures typically focus on the can do factors previously described. Tools that are costly and time-consuming to administer, such as simulations and interviews, are usually placed near the bottom to make final cuts. Also, the reader should be reminded that all measurement devices used as part of the multiple-hurdle process should adhere to the reliability, validity, fairness, and utility standards laid out in chapter 3.

Exhibit 10.3. An example of a selection procedure design matrix for a team member.

Selection procedure design matrix
Team member

Skill category	Important skill	Selection procedure*			
		Test battery	Group assessment	Interview	Medical examination
Learning and analytic skills	Procedures learning	I	I	I	
	Applied learning	I	I	I	
	Planning and organizing		I	D	
	Classifying	I			
	Judgment	I	D	D	
	Troubleshooting	D		D	
Language skills	Applied reading skills	D			
	Reading Comprehension	D			
	Referencing written materials	D			
	Forms completion	D			
Perceptual skills	Checking	D			
	Inspection		D	I	
	Monitoring	D			
	Spatial visualization				

Math skills	Arithmetic computation	D		
	Arithmetic reasoning	D		
	Measurement			
Interaction skills	Active listening		I	D
	Communicating with others		D	D
	Interpersonal interaction		D	D
	Teamwork		D	D
Technological literacy	Diagram and blueprint reading	D	D	D
	Table and graph comprehension	D	D	D
	Instrumentation		D	D
	Mechanical comprehension			D
Personal characteristics	Work orientation		D	D
	Adaptability		D	D
	Stress tolerance		I	D
Physical characteristics	Strength			D
	Stamina			D
	Physical flexibility			D
	Manual dexterity			I
	Arm/hand steadiness			I
	Hearing			I
	Visual acuity			I

"D" means the skill is directly assessed by the procedure.
"I" means the skill is indirectly assessed by the procedure and it is very unlikely a person could perform well in the selection procedure without an acceptable level of competence in the skill.

Source: HRStrategies, Grosse Pointe, Mich. Reprinted with permission.

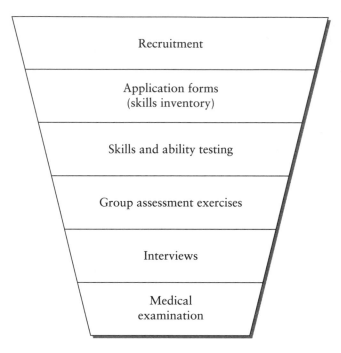

Figure 10.4. Multiple-hurdle (funnel) selection process at 3M Canada.

Source: 3M Canada and HRStrategies, Grosse Pointe, Mich. Reprinted by permission.

Composite Score. These scores are derived by having all candidates complete the entire assessment battery and then combining each person's results for decision-making purposes. This can be accomplished in several ways, but we will limit our discussion to three approaches in terms of different levels of sophistication. The first and least complex approach is to simply sum the raw test scores to derive a total score that becomes the basis for decision making. Table 10.2 shows the results for a hypothetical person on a team leader selection battery developed by one of the authors for a small manufacturing firm. The battery consisted of six components and was administered to those internal candidates that qualified (satisfactory attendance and discipline record). While the adding of raw scores is simple and straightforward, it can produce total scores that are distorted or improperly weighted. This is particularly true when the mean and variance of the subscores vary substantially (note the differences in "total score possible" shown in Table 10.2).

The next level of sophistication is meant to overcome the problem of differing subscore variabilities. Raw scores are converted to some form of standard scores before they are added. While a discussion of

Table 10.2. Summing raw test scores to obtain a total score for making selection decisions.

Candidate: *Jake Smith*

Assessment tool	Raw score	Total score possible
Work performance	13	(25)
Education and experience	15	(20)
Job knowledge (e.g., shop math, blueprint reading, ISO 9000 standards)	54	(99)
Mechanical comprehension	38	(68)
Scheduling simulation	45	(56)
Work sample	51	(130)
Total	216	(398)

standard scores and normal distribution theory is beyond the scope of this book, a simplified variation of this concept will be presented for the team leader position previously introduced. Here, converted scores for any subtest ranged from one (1) to five (5) and were derived by dividing the percentile ranks into approximately five equal sections (see Table 10.3). Thus, those individuals with percentile ranks ranging from 0–19 on the scheduling simulation subtest were given a converted score of one (1), individuals with percentile ranks of 20–39 were given a two (2), and so on. Converted scores have several advantages: they allow for direct comparisons of subtests, they simplify the combining of test scores, and they improve the ease in which test scores can be communicated to candidates. Another plus is that subtests can be easily weighted in terms of their importance to overall performance. While more elaborate standard score conversion score methodologies exist (z-scores, T-scores) and are suggested where feasible, hopefully the example makes the point.

The final and most sophisticated approach for combining various battery subtests is the use of multiple correlation or multiple regression weights to establish a best-fit prediction of job performance. Previously described in chapter 3, this mathematically based methodology assigns a weight to each subtest based on its statistical relationship with job performance and its relationship with other battery measures (see Figure 10.5). Of course, this approach assumes that a criterion-related validation study has been conducted and that each

Table 10.3. Recommended converted scores for team leader selection procedure.

Work performance		Education and experience	
Raw	Converted	Raw	Converted
21–25	5	18–20	5
18–20	4	15–17	4
14–17	3	12–14	3
11–13	2	9–11	2
5–10	1	4–8	1

Job knowledge		Mechanical comprehension	
Raw	Converted	Raw	Converted
80–99	5	51–68	5
70–79	4	46–50	4
60–69	3	41–45	3
50–59	2	36–40	2
0–49	1	0–35	1

Scheduling simulation		Work sample	
Raw	Converted	Raw	Converted
48–56	5	120–130	5
40–47	4	108–119	4
30–39	3	90–107	3
20–29	2	50–89	2
0–19	1	0–49	1

candidate completes all components of the battery. While ideal, these prerequisites are seldom met in the typical employment setting. For example, the team leader position discussed earlier did not have a large enough sample size to conduct a criterion-related study. A content validity strategy was used to determine the job relatedness of various assessment tools.

Ranking of Candidates

The statistical relationship between a valid assessment tool and job performance is typically linear. Therefore, it is suggested that candi-

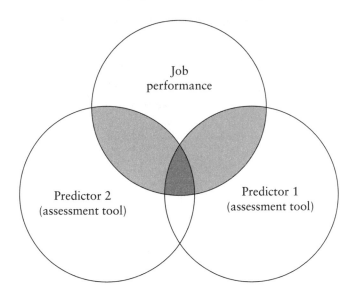

Figure 10.5. Using a multiple regression approach to establish a best-fit prediction of job performance.

dates be rated or ranked with selection decisions (offers) made starting with the top (highest rated or ranked) candidate and then working down the list. This approach maximizes utility and is preferred over methods such as picking anyone above some minimum cutoff or selecting from a list of the top three (or four or five) candidates. However, cutoff points are useful in terms of deciding a minimal acceptable level below which offers will not be made. They are also necessary when a multiple cutoff approach is used.

Summary

At the beginning of chapter 9, we made the point that the employment interview can be a reliable and valid predictor of job performance when certain conditions are met (for example, measuring job-related attributes using a structured format, using trained interviewers, and so on). Chapters 9 and 10 have provided a point-by-point discussion of those conditions. Applied properly, these guidelines can help ensure that your organization selects and promotes those employees prepared to function in the new workplace. We believe strongly that adherence to these recommendations will pay huge dividends in the long term and do much to ensure the success of the organization.

Note

1. Life Insurance Marketing and Research Association, *Face to Face* (Hartford, Conn.: LIMRA, 1974). See also Allen J. Schuh, "Effects of Early Interruption and Note Taking on Listening Accuracy and Decision Making in the Interview," *Bulletin of the Psychonomic Society* 13 (1980): 263–264.

chapter 11

Developing a Quality-Oriented Workforce

Overview

The viewpoint taken in this chapter is that staffing in the total quality organization is a continuous process. It does not end with the decision to hire and place the individual on a job. Rather, it is a dynamic, ongoing series of activities and decisions that meets the needs of both the organization and individual. Content focuses on the broader concept of development rather than on training per se. We provide some general guidelines for career and leadership development along with a discussion of some of the more frequently used tools and methods in total quality settings.

Introduction

No discussion of the staffing process would be complete without addressing the issue of career development. In today's ever-changing job market, few employees will be hired to then spend the rest of their working lives doing the same jobs. Rather, they are likely to change both jobs and companies many times throughout their work careers. Thus, career development programs have been established in many organizations to match individual career needs and aspirations with organizational workforce demands. The idea of career development makes a lot of sense if the organization wants to attract, retain, and motivate good employees while simultaneously ensuring that its own

HR requirements are being met. If done correctly, career development can truly be a win-win activity that enhances the satisfaction of employees while at the same time improving organizational effectiveness.

In practice, career development programs vary significantly in terms of both formality and success. Some organizations have instituted very structured and deliberate programs for career planning and career management including

- Career development workshops

- Career counseling

- Performance appraisal and judgment of potential

- Career planning workbooks (for example, identifying career-related goals, career opportunities, self-assessment, and force-field analysis)

- Mentoring programs

- Various interest and value tests

Firms known for their successful career development systems include 3M, Kodak, AT&T, Boeing, Corning, General Electric, American Express, Motorola, and Ford Motor Company.[1] These benchmark organizations all have extensive programs that actively involve employees and provide a number of formal support mechanisms such as those previously listed.

Many other career development programs vary in terms of their sophistication, acceptance, and success. Poorly designed systems, unrealistic expectations on the part of many employees, limits on employment and upward mobility, and the reality of internal politics all affect employees' skeptical views of some programs. For example, it becomes difficult for employees to get very excited about a career development workshop when their organization is systematically flattening its organizational structure and downsizing its ranks. Concerns like "Will I have a job next week?" take precedence over embracing career development programs.

Guidelines for Career and Leadership Development

Following is a brief overview of some of the key elements that make for a successful career and leadership development system. For a more extensive discussion of these and other guidelines as well as discussions of benchmark organizations, we recommend the books *Organizational Career Development*, *Corporate Quality Universities*, and *Developing Human Resources*.[2]

Development as Strategy

Throughout this book, we have discussed the importance of strategy as it relates to quality. To be successful, the firm must incorporate employee development into its business strategy. Make the statement "employees are our most important resource" more than just words on a mission or values statement. Link development efforts with the strategic quality initiative of the firm. Unfortunately, our experience with many firms is that they fail to see the connection between their management and employee development efforts and the organization's quality initiative. The primary reason for this is that these efforts are being sponsored and championed by different corporate entities (a quality office versus the firm's HR training and development unit). To be successful, these functional entities must work closely to achieve quality. For example, the quality-oriented organization should develop and reinforce a set of employee and leadership skills or competencies consistent with the quality initiative (coaching, facilitating, empowering, customer orientation). Developmental assignments should include working in or facilitating problem-solving groups. Education and training efforts should focus on programs and seminars that teach and reinforce quality (such as corporate quality values, problem solving, statistics, quality certification such as CQE, and so on).

It is also important to back development efforts with strong chief executive officer (CEO) and senior executive support. Managers and employees at all levels take their cues from top management. If senior managers truly believe in the development initiative and practice what they preach, then others will likely fall in line. Make sure the system has some champions at the top.

Finally, focus on developing the person to help meet organizational and individual goals and not on promotion per se. Every attempt should be made to align employee and organizational needs and then provide developmental activities to meet those needs.

Development as a System

Successful quality-oriented firms understand that employee development is a process not a technique, event, or program, and that development never ends. Learning in the quality organization is a lifelong endeavor. The simple fact is that every organization is engaged in employee development. It is just that some are doing a good job, while others do it in a rather haphazard and poor manner. Viewing development as a process allows us to systematically analyze the various components, and then make ongoing improvements in development efforts. Those improvement efforts should begin with careful selection. As previously discussed, development is much more likely to be successful if it is done with a workforce that is conscientious, open to learning, flexible, and technically competent. Likewise, leadership potential should be identified early on so that necessary developmental experiences can be provided. Entry-level candidates should be informed via an RJP that continuous learning is a requirement for admission to the firm. And that message should be reinforced throughout the selection and orientation process.

It is important to create an organizationwide infrastructure for career development using a variety of developmental tools and methods (see Exhibit 11.1). Those tools and methods typically should be linked into an overall system of development. However, the actual implementation of that process typically should be left to individual business units, divisions, or sites. Each should be allowed to tailor development efforts to its own needs and capabilities. Also, every attempt should be made to give high visibility to the career development initiative.

Finally, as with any process, it is important to evaluate and continually revise and improve the career development effort. Include feedback from both participants and line managers. Wherever possible, evaluation measures should include behavior changes and bottom-line results as well as learning and reaction to the process.

The Role of Line Management in Development

To be successful, line managers must be involved in all facets of development. In the quality organization, development must be seen as an integral part of managers' jobs. Every effort must be made to train and prepare them for this important role. Ask them what they need and then provide them with as much support as possible, but hold them accountable for their actions. Most importantly, reinforce managers through promotion, recognition, and pay for being coaches, counselors, and developers of their employees. The best means for developing important skills and behaviors is through actual work experience, and managers are in the best position to provide that experience.

Exhibit 11.1. Some possible career developmental tools and methods.

- Career development workshops
- Career counseling
- Developmental performance appraisal
- Career planning workbooks and aids
- Job rotation
- Special developmental assignments
- Mentoring programs
- Networking opportunities
- Internal education and training programs (courses, workshops, brown bag lunches)
- External education and training programs (tuition reimbursement, seminars and workshops, professional conferences)
- Individual developmental assessment and feedback (assessment centers, 360-degree feedback, self-assessment inventories)
- Succession planning
- Dual-career ladders
- Job posting
- Career resource information
- Skills inventories
- Job enrichment and job redesign
- Management training in career development and coaching.

Perhaps the most difficult career development guideline to implement is the recommendation to unclog career channels by moving marginal individuals to make room for high potential (quality-oriented) employees. In today's flattened and lean organization, fewer and fewer opportunities exist for advancement to higher levels. And those limited opportunities that do exist cannot be blocked with individuals that either fail to embrace quality or who have long ago "pulled their oars into the boat." More will be said about this topic in subsequent chapters on leadership and downsizing.

The Role of the Participant in Development

Every employee must understand that the primary responsibility for development lies with the individual. While the organization should create both a positive climate and appropriate support mechanisms, it is the individual employee that must take charge of his/her own development activities. That is why it is so important to select individuals with the propensity to grow and develop.

The quality–oriented organization must encourage the development of all employees and not just "fast-trackers." While special efforts should be made to develop high-potential employees (with developmental assignments, special mentoring, and counseling), career development needs to be encouraged for all employees. Also, employees should be encouraged and reinforced for developing a full range of technical, quality, and managerial skills. Such development may not necessarily lead to promotion, but it will improve the effectiveness and job security of the employee.

Finally, the participants of training and development should not be limited to employees. Jeanne C. Meister in her book, *Corporate Quality Universities,* points out that

> *State-of-the-art training extends beyond the corporation to include key constituencies in a company's customer/supply chain. Corporate Quality Universities are reaching out to form educational partnerships with customers, suppliers, and, in some cases, the universities and even elementary schools that supply the organization with its human talent.*[3]

Career Development in the Quality Organization

It is our contention that organizations that embrace total quality may very well do more for enhancing real career development than most organizations that are forced to introduce a formal career development program into their planning and development systems. The quality-oriented organization affords many developmental opportunities not available in more traditional settings. Traditional organizations, with their pyramidal structures, functional demarcations, divisions of labor, control mechanisms, and formal chain-of-command relationships, do little to support true employee development. In such organizations, career development programs are typically contrived and artificial, with much of the effort aimed at overcoming organizational barriers to development. Activities focus on educating employees about other functional areas and opportunities within the company, using instruments to assess employee strengths and areas for improvement (euphemism for weakness), developing formal mentoring programs, and so on.

Total quality organizations, on the other hand, offer the individual a wide range of naturally occurring developmental opportunities. No longer does the employee need to attend a workshop to learn what employees do in Department B. Viewing the organization as a system with interconnecting processes and belonging to a cross-functional process improvement or reengineering team will teach the employee more about how the organization operates than any half-day workshop. Formal mentoring programs become passé when employees and managers work closely together to solve meaningful, work-related problems. Conventional assessment devices lose much of their additive predictive and feedback usefulness when employees actively participate on a regular basis in team problem-solving sessions.

Adele Scheele, in her popular career development book, *Skills for Success,* identifies six critical career competencies that enable employees to pursue opportunities for themselves while helping the organization become more effective.[4] They include the following:

1. **To experience doing** means building a wardrobe of behaviors from a number of diverse activities and projects, career related or not. Only in this way can you extend the boundaries of your self-imposed and limited circle of possibility and ability.

2. **To risk linking** is the skill of combining risk-taking and connecting to people, to organizations, and to ideas. This skill builds on the human use of human beings, on starting associations, and on sharing networks and resources.

3. **To show belonging** is the skill of enhancing your own organization by paying attention to it, caring for it, supporting it, and creating a more productive and interactive department or division.

4. **To exhibit specializing** is the skill of demonstrating your worth to your organization, apart from just doing your job well. It includes figuring out not only what you're particularly good at in your job but also what others who work with you need you for, apart from your specific work-related responsibilities.

5. **To use catapulting** is the skill of using your business associates or job-related contacts and sometimes your friends to connect you to others who can be of help to you in your career.

6. **To magnify accomplishing** is the supreme skill, the culmination and synthesis of all the foregoing ones. It is the displaying of your work and ideas before many publics. It involves active participation in your organization, taking on leadership in professional associations, speaking and moderating panels before community and other business groups, and writing articles in trade journals.

A review of Scheele's career development skills list shows that much of what she refers to as *career development* becomes inherent in the environment created by a total quality organization. In short, the true practice of TQM will likely do more for career development than anything the organization can contrive.

Tools and Methods

While a full discussion of the various components of career development interventions is beyond the scope of this book, we will briefly address a few of the programs and tools used in career development along with their implications in a total quality organization.

Skills Inventories

Many organizations have developed computerized *skills inventories* of their current workforces. These databases contain comprehensive records of the firms' employees, including

- Knowledge, skills, and abilities ratings
- Previous work experience
- Education degrees and major fields of study
- Work histories and accomplishments
- Training completed
- Geographical preferences
- Career aspirations and objectives
- Anticipated retirement dates

Skills inventories are maintained to help firms understand the make-up of their workforces. Information is used for making transfer and promotion decisions, developing needed skills training, and improving the recruitment and selection process. These inventories can also benefit employees in terms of their own career aspirations. For example, General Motors now has a very sophisticated skills inventory system where employees interested in job openings call an 800 number and listen to the various job openings in the corporation. If they choose to apply for a position, they simply enter their social security number, and the system pulls their job history and skills inventory from the skill inventory database. While not as sophisticated as the General Motors system, a number of software packages are available commercially at a reasonable price.

We strongly believe that the need for such inventories will steadily increase in future organizations. Two significant trends are likely to force organizations to maintain some kind of inventory of their employees' skills. The first is the tendency for jobs to require a greater number of, as well as more complex, skills. Keeping track of who has these skills will be a must for making internal staffing decisions. The second trend will be thoroughly discussed in chapter 14, and has to do with the changing dynamics of the workplace. Workers will no longer be hired to perform a job. Rather, they are likely to perform a wide range of tasks or jobs, belong to several project teams, and be moved about the organization, or from organization to organization, based on needs. Thus, staffing decisions will occur much more frequently and require skill information for determining who goes where.

The trends toward higher skill levels and more frequent staffing decisions should increase the need for skills inventories. Just imagine that your firm is going to build a state-of-the-art manufacturing plant in Mexico, and that you have been asked to coordinate much of that effort. Wouldn't it be nice to go to a terminal and start generating a list of your possible team members who can speak Spanish, have knowledge and experience in agile and lean manufacturing, would be willing to relocate, and so on? Such capabilities are likely to make the development and use of skills inventories much more cost-effective.

Consistent with our previous themes, we also strongly believe that these inventories should reflect the quality orientation of the firm by emphasizing quality-related skills, training, and experience. Knowledge of SPC and experimental design, ASQC certification (such as CQE, CRE, and so on), and experience working in process improvement or reengineering teams are just a few of the quality characteristics that should be inventoried.

AMP in Waynesboro, Pennsylvania, uses a computerized job skills system that tracks and matches employees' job skills with emerging technologies at AMP.[5] The tracking system reportedly promotes quality, efficiency, and teamwork at AMP's Waynesboro plant. AMP had recently switched from specialized units each producing a part to a team approach using multiskilled specialists, working together to produce a complete subassembly. Its manufacturing skills inventory system (MSIS) became an essential part of its new team-based manufacturing system, which requires that employees be more highly skilled.

Using the MSIS, Waynesboro supervisors and employees were able to identify every skill required to manufacture a complete applicator subassembly. Each employee then received a list of all necessary skill requirements and performed a self-assessment of his or her own skill level, which the company entered into the database.[6]

AMP uses this information to assign workers and furnish strategic training that maximizes employee potential. This team approach coupled with the MSIS has reduced production setup time by 60 percent and cut work-in-process and finished-goods-inventory levels by 86 percent. Lead time between receipt of a work order and completion of the finished product is now one day (versus 75 days prior to the new system), and quality problems are nonexistent.

Dual-Career Ladders

One interesting outgrowth of quality and the new leaner and flatter organization has been a renewed interest in the practice of providing dual-career ladders for employees. First popularized in the 1970s, dual-career ladders provide both technical and managerial employees with equal but separate tracks for advancement in the organization (see Figure 11.1).

Historically, the primary purpose for these dual tracks was to increase satisfaction and reduce the turnover of technical employees. Prior to the introduction of dual-career ladders, many technical employees in such areas as engineering and R&D were faced with very difficult career dilemmas. Should they stay with their chosen professions and continue to engage in the kind of work they enjoy doing, or should they make the career choice of moving into management to advance their careers?

Figure 11.1. A model dual-career ladder.

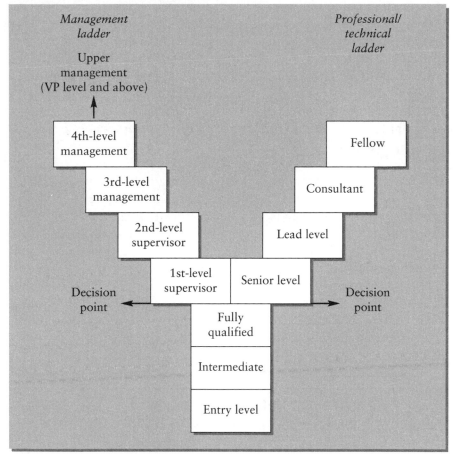

Source: Hewitt Associates' Dual Career Ladders, 1992. Reprinted by permission.

The result of such choices was often negative from both an employee and employer perspective. Employees who did not wish to move into management watched in frustration as their colleagues advanced into supervision and management with increases in compensation and prestige. The dissatisfaction created from this situation often led to high rates of turnover among technical employees as they looked to other organizations for reward and recognition. Conversely, many technically oriented employees felt like fish out of water in management roles and longed for the good old days when they were able to apply their trades.

In an effort to retain talented technical employees, many organizations instituted dual-career ladder programs. However, efforts to institute such programs have met with mixed results. While many organizations extol the virtues of dual-career programs, surveys of employees often fail to support such enthusiasm.[7] The majority of technical employees continue to believe that the management ladder is the best avenue for advancing their careers, and many organizations have abandoned their efforts to institute dual-career ladders. Even best practices companies such as 3M, Ford, IBM, and TI have had mixed results with their dual-track programs. For example, the master of business administration (MBA) management track is still the most sought-after postgraduate degree for many engineers who see it as the best way to advance their careers.

Why the resurgence of interest in dual-career ladders? Because dual-track career paths make a lot of sense in light of changes occurring in today's organizations. Lean organizations with their flatter structures and wider spans of control for managers will result in fewer opportunities for advancement into the management ranks. Also, the clear demarcation between employees and levels of management (chain of command) inherent in traditional organizations is often blurred in the new organizational setting. For example, self-directed work groups, product development teams, and process improvement and reengineering teams typically operate quite effectively without the traditional boss to direct and control the group's efforts.

In such a changing environment, creative career development systems need to be employed. Technical as well as other employees in the organization need to be challenged and rewarded to keep them from leaving. Dual-career ladders provide one such avenue for motivating and retaining competent employees. Fortunately, through a certain amount of trial and error, we've learned a lot about why many career ladder programs have failed in the past and what steps can be taken to help ensure their success. Following is a brief discussion of some of the issues involved.

First, the technical or professional track must be perceived by employees as a viable and equitable alternative to the management track. Remember that, when you institute alternative tracks, you are paddling upstream to the traditional notion of career advancement. Employees must view the technical ladder as desirable and believe that they will be equitably compensated for choosing that track.

A second related issue is the need to clearly define and lay out the alternative tracks. Employees fully understand the traditional management track with its clearly defined organization levels, compensation grades, and accompanying pay and perks. The same clearly defined paths must be established for technical ladders if they are to be successful.

The third consideration focuses on the issue of selectivity and prestige. Many dual-career ladder programs failed because the technical track is viewed as a dumping ground for incompetent managers or individuals viewed as having little or no management potential. To be successful, entrance and upward mobility in the technical track must be based on true merit. In the spirit of this book, movement from level to level through the technical track should be based on clearly established criteria, with established promotion procedures. These criteria and procedures should be increasingly rigorous. Advancement in technical and professional tracks should progress at approximately the same rate as movement through the management track—only a select few should attain the level and status of "fellow." The previously discussed issues of planning, valid selection, and fairness are as applicable with dual-career tracks as they are with other areas of staffing.

Finally, training and development of technical track employees is just as important as it is for individuals wishing to succeed in management, and that training and development should not be exclusively in the technical areas. Interpersonal skills, group problem solving, teamwork, and group facilitation are important skills for everyone, including those on the technical track.

Before leaving the topic of dual-career ladders, two additional points should be made. First, discussions of dual-career tracks or ladders have typically focused on the improved satisfaction and retention of technical employees. Few of the writings point out that a dual-track approach allows the organization to better utilize its talent. A single path to the top forces everyone who wants to move up the ladder to consider only that option, whether or not everyone is able and willing to be successful managers. Many a good engineer, scientist, or other professional has been pressed into management service, resulting in the discovery that the organization has lost a good technical employee and gained a lousy manager. Career alternatives that play to the strengths of different employees make good business sense.

The final issue relates to becoming more creative with career pathing alternatives. The previous discussion of dual-career ladders assumes that employees will follow either a technical/professional track or a managerial track. Once the selection has been made, the employee is basically locked into that career path. Why put such constraints on an individual's career? A different view of career pathing, dubbed *spiral paths,* is described in *Industry Week.*

A different view is offered by Hay Group's Mr. Bratkovitch, who describes spiral career paths that create opportunities for some employees to switch regularly among management, professional, and entrepreneurial positions within a company. People in this situation take on different responsibilities, depending on the juncture of their careers. The key here is also flexibility because the employees shift between vastly different opportunities.[8]

One engineering/architecture firm familiar to the authors has instituted a tri-career path model that allows engineers to follow any one of three ladders—line management, project management, or technical specialist. This need to be more creative is reflected in the newest buzzword in career development: *lattice careers*—the interlacing of career experience and development across a myriad of cross-functional and cross-project activities. The new organization with emphasis on rapid change, teamwork, and servicing the customer must downplay the old notion of hierarchical and bureaucratic career pathing. Innovative approaches are needed that truly utilize and develop the potential of the workforce.

Fast-Track Employees

Whether done formally or informally, most organizations attempt to identify individuals with high potential and place them on a fast track for career progression. These stars or water walkers are provided with special and intensive development opportunities that prepare them for ever-increasing responsibilities and advancement. Historically, these individuals have been identified early in their careers and have been given special opportunities, such as frequent and broad-based job changes, more challenging job assignments, extensive counseling and feedback, assigned mentors, and additional training.

If these employees are to be the leaders of tomorrow, then we strongly encourage organizations to systematically integrate quality into the development activities of these individuals. Examples might include

- Having them act as team leaders for problem-solving or process improvement teams
- Assigning them to positions that include direct contact with external customers

- Requiring them to attend both internal and external training programs on quality and quality management

- Having them train other employees in the principles of quality and quality management

Success, or lack thereof, in such activities should then be used to decide whether or not such star status is warranted.

Development Assessment Tools

Formal career development efforts typically begin with some kind of assessment of the individual's strengths and weaknesses (areas for improvement). Having a clear understanding of one's deficiencies becomes a prerequisite for devising a development plan. A number of such assessment tools are used for this purpose and are briefly outlined in Exhibit 11.2. One of those tools, 360-degree feedback, warrants further discussion.

360-Degree Feedback

The most popular approach to leadership development in recent years has no doubt been the use of 360-degree feedback instruments.[9] The 360-degree process of leadership development gets its name from the fact that an individual receives feedback on his/her behavior from multiple sources and multiple perspectives. Managers, supervisors, peers, subordinates, and sometimes even customers, evaluate the person on job-relevant behavior (see Figure 11.2). Organizations such as Hewlett-Packard, Boeing, Microsoft, Ford, Texaco, Shell, State Farm, Prudential, and the U.S. Postal Service, just to mention a few, are using 360-degree processes for developing their management personnel. And some of those firms have extended its use to evaluation as input into making organizational decisions (performance appraisal, disciplinary counseling, pay, succession planning, and promotion).

The 360-degree methodology is particularly appealing in total quality settings because of the increased emphasis on customer satisfaction (customer feedback), cross-functional cooperation, teamwork (peer feedback), and the need to involve and develop subordinates (direct report feedback). Thus, multirater feedback helps shift the emphasis away from the traditional *quid pro quo* relationship between employee and boss and extends it to include other important con-

Exhibit 11.2. Developmental assessment tools.

Career-planning workbooks

Workbooks or career development guides are used by many organizations such as General Electric and General Motors to help individual employees systematically assess their strengths or abilities, interests, and career aspirations and then generate personal development plans.

Self-help books and tools

A number of self-help career workbooks exist that help the individual through the process of self-assessment and career planning. *Where Do I Go from Here with My Life?* by John Crystal and Richard N. Bolles and *Self-Directed Search* by John Holland are two examples of such tools.

Self- and associate-assessment inventories

These structured assessment inventories typically ask the individual or some associate (e.g., immediate supervisor) to complete a set of questions describing the individual in terms of job-related skills). For example, the PRISM instruments and associated development tools have been used by a number of organizations including Ford Motor Company for its management development program. This package contains both self-assessment and associate assessment instruments that measure strengths and weaknesses on eight factors or roles.

- Innovator
- Broker
- Producer
- Director
- Coordinator
- Monitor
- Facilitator
- Mentor

Development performance appraisal

In addition to its role in making administrative decisions (e.g., pay, promotion), performance appraisal information can also be used as a developmental tool. Appraisal can be used to define effective performance, identify strengths and weaknesses, and use the information to establish developmental objectives. Thus, appraisal sessions become the basis for diagnosing and coaching employee performance.

360-degree feedback

In the typical 360-degree feedback format, a standardized instrument is compared by the participating manager's supervisors, peers, and subordinates, evaluating the manager's performance on a variety of skills and behaviors linked to dimensions of managerial performance. Typically, these multiperspective evaluations are then organized into a graphic feedback format that the manager uses as a standalone development guide or as part of a management development program. This 360-degree feedback has proven to be a powerful and popular management development tool.

Developmental assessment centers

The assessment center is a comprehensive, standardized procedure where candidates participate in a series of assessment exercises such as tests, interviews, and simulations. Individual behavior and performance is evaluated by trained assessors and fed back to the employee as a development tool. As previously discussed, assessment centers are also used for selection and promotion purposes.

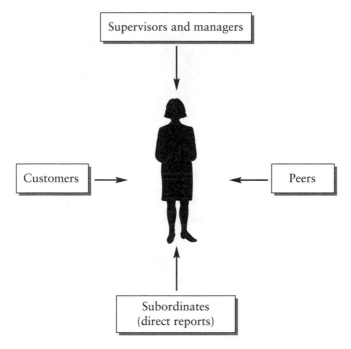

Figure 11.2. Multirater feedback sources.

stituencies. Now, instead of just pleasing the boss (the first rule of thumb for the upward aspiring manager) (see Figure 11.3), the individual is expected to satisfy or please peers, subordinates, and the all-important customer.

While intuitively appealing, 360-degree feedback is not without its pitfalls. The use of these instruments raises a host of issues and questions, some of which include

- What should be the content of the instrument (what types of behaviors should the instrument measure)?

- How should the individuals who complete the instruments be selected?

- How should the instruments be disseminated, collected, and analyzed?

- Who should be privy to the results? (employee? boss? organization?)

- What kind of rater training or directions are needed?

Figure 11.3. The traditional feedback relationship.

- What kind of training or support is needed by the ratee to help interpret and use the information?

- Will the information be confidential and used for developmental purposes or will others be privy to the feedback data and use it for purposes of evaluation?

- Does the purpose (developmental versus administrative) change the way people are rated?

These are just a few of the critical issues that must be addressed prior to instituting a 360-degree feedback process. That is the bad news. The good news is that these instruments appear to be very powerful developmental tools and are likely to remain the rage for some time to come. We also feel strongly that 360-degree instruments have great potential for reinforcing the quality-oriented culture discussed throughout this book. Here are a few suggestions for getting a 360-degree process started and increasing the probability of its success.

Get Some Help. Our first suggestion is to obtain the expertise required to embark on such an ambitious endeavor. Most firms will not have the internal capabilities to develop and administer such a program. So look for a consulting firm with both the professional credentials and experience to help you through the process. But be careful. Because it is the latest and hottest thing going, everybody is doing 360-degree feedback. Take a page from total quality and develop a close working relationship with a quality consulting firm. A good consultant should be able to help you systematically answer all of the questions previously posed.

Tie Content to the Strategic Quality Initiative. Design of the 360-degree process instrument content, training, and action planning should all be linked to the quality initiative of the organization. If, for example, the organization's quality program focuses on using teams to engage in systematic process improvement efforts, then survey items should reflect that behavior.

But herein lies one of the major dilemmas associated with instituting a 360-degree process. That is, should the organization avail itself of one of the commercially available 360-degree systems or develop its own tailored instrument? Highly reputable consulting firms such as Development Dimensions International (DDI), Personnel Decisions, Inc. (PDI), and The Center for Creative Leadership have excellent 360-degree systems developed and available. Similar instruments like the one accompanying the competing values model (the *PRISM®*), devised by Robert F. Quinn, are also available.[10]

The major advantages of using these commercially available 360-degree systems include the fact that they are likely to be more extensively researched, norm data exist, and, most importantly, they all have substantial customized training and development support material.[11] For example, PDI provides the *Successful Manager's Handbook* for participants to be used in conjunction with its 360-degree instrument, *The PROFILOR®* (see Figure 11.4). Its handbook is organized around the nine factors and 39 management skills of its management model. The handbook provides suggestions and tips on how to improve each of the management skills as well as suggested readings and possible training or workshops. Both DDI's *Synchrony®* and the *PRISM* provide similar developmental support.

The major disadvantage of these commercial 360-degree systems is that they may not accurately portray your own organization's core leadership competencies and management skills. While based on sound theory and practice, these systems are generic in nature and use terminology that fits most organizations, quality oriented or not. Because of this, some firms choose to develop their own tailored instruments that reflect the unique leadership factors, skills, and jargon of the organization.

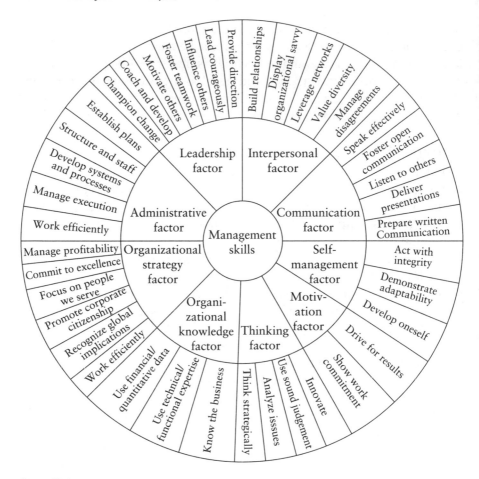

Figure 11.4. Profilor for management.

Source: Personnel Decisions, Inc., Minneapolis, Minn. © Personnel Decisions, Inc. 1991. Used with permission.

In defense of the three instruments discussed, all have been used successfully as part of a larger quality initiative and all contain some factors and skills consistent with the quality paradigm. Ford, for example, has used the *PRISM* and competing values model as part of its LEAD program for developing middle managers and has also used it for increasing involvement at the plant level.[12] Also, the staff at PDI reports that approximately half of their 360-degree business is now done with tailored instruments and that much of that effort is with total quality organizations.

One notable 360-degree feedback instrument is the Personal Quality Orientation Audit (PQOA) developed by Attitude Resources in conjunction with the authors.[13] The PQOA was developed from the ground up based on much of the same research findings addressed in this book. The instrument uses 150 behavioral items to provide feedback on 20 skills specifically related to quality. Those skills, along with representative items, and are graphically portrayed in Figure 11.5 and are listed in Exhibit 11.3.

The PQOA is the only 360-degree feedback instrument that we are aware of that focuses exclusively on quality-oriented factors or competencies. Instrument content (factors and items) can be tailored to meet the specific needs of the organization, and both training and developmental support materials are available. The PQOA has the dual advantage of focusing directly on total quality processes and objectives while improving the buy-in of participants through tailoring of the instrumentation to better reflect the values and priorities of the specific organization.

In summary, the 360-degree system should reflect your firm's total quality effort. This is a relatively straightforward process if you use a tailored approach, but if the decision is to go outside and use an existing system, then carefully select one that generally ties to your compe-

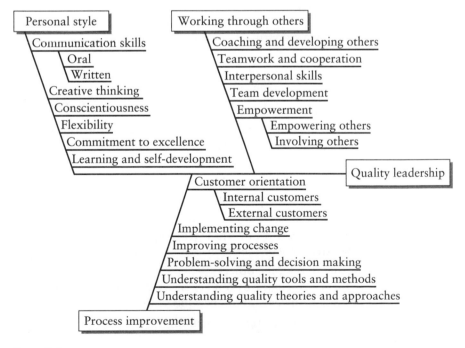

Figure 11.5. PQOA general competencies and skills.

Source: Attitude Resources, Morristown, N.J., 1995.

Exhibit 11.3. PQOA skills and representative items.

1. Conscientiousness
   • Can be relied on to do what it takes to get the job done
   • Has a high energy level
2. Commitment to excellence
   • Has high personal work standards
   • Creates a work climate that encourages excellence
3. Flexibility
   • Readily accepts the need for change
   • Is willing to try new approaches
4. Learning and self-development
   • Is willing to learn new things
   • Actively pursues self-development opportunities
5. Communication skills (oral and written)
   • Listens carefully to others
   • Speaks effectively in front of groups
6. Creative thinking
   • Works effectively in ambiguous situations
   • Generates innovative and creative solutions
7. Team development
   • Encourages teamwork among associates
   • Recognizes and rewards good team effort
8. Involving others
   • Asks for input and suggestions before making decisions
   • Listens to others' ideas and suggestions
9. Empowering others
   • Encourages others to handle job-related problems themselves
   • Cuts through red tape so that others can change things
10. Interpersonal skills
    • Treats others consistently and fairly
    • Will not tolerate unethical behavior
11. Teamwork and cooperation
    • Develops effective work relations with other departments/units
    • Develops effective work relations with subordinates
12. Coaching and developing others
    • Gives others challenging assignments to aid their development
    • Coaches others in developing their job skills
13. Internal and external customer orientation
    A. General
       • Willingly helps others
       • Is friendly in dealings with others

Exhibit 11.3. Continued.

  B. Internal customers
   • Encourages others to do the job right the first time
   • Recognizes and rewards high quality service to internal customers.
  C. External customers
   • Works to meet the needs of external customers
   • Recognizes and rewards high quality service to external customers

14. Improving processes
  • Develops new or better ways of doing things

15. Understanding of quality theories and approaches
  • Reads books and articles on quality and process improvement
  • Takes courses or workshops on quality and/or customer service

16. Understanding of quality tools and methods
  • Uses charts and other visual tools to plan and monitor work
  • Applies statistical methods

17. Problem solving and decision making
  • Seeks information needed for making effective decisions
  • Systematically approaches problems

18. Implementing change
  • Actively involves other in the change process
  • Identifies and addresses barriers to change

Source: Attitude Resources, Inc., Morristown, N.J. Reprinted by permission.

tency model or that can be modified (many can) to mirror your needs. And in some cases a hybrid approach may be warranted. One of the authors has successfully used one of the aforementioned instruments in conjunction with a tailored instrument as part of a leadership development program.

Develop Support Mechanisms. Development and administration of the 360-degree feedback instrument is only the first step in the development process. To be effective, the 360-degree system must include a number of components aimed at using the feedback for making constructive change. The instrument itself is only a springboard for action. Help in interpreting and internalizing feedback results, action planning, career counseling, skills training, supervisory/mentor training, organization support mechanisms (networking, job posting, tuition reimbursement, developmental assignments) and follow up are just a few of the issues that require attention for a 360-degree program to work effectively. Giving the participant a computerized feedback report, along with the admonition to use the information to improve behavior, undermines the potential of the program. Put as much or more thought and effort into what follows the feedback as into the development and administration of the instrument.

Summary

Staffing as we have described it in this book is a continuous process. It is not merely a series of major decision points (hire/don't hire or promote/don't promote) affecting a person's career. Providing an individual with a developmental assignment, sending a person to training, or placing a person on a problem-solving team are all examples of staffing-related decisions. As such, development should be carefully tied to the total quality strategy of the firm. When done correctly, the quality setting can, and should, become the foundation for all developmental initiatives. Total quality provides the ideal climate for nurturing and developing employees.

Notes

1. Thomas G. Gutteridge, Zandy B. Leibowitz, and Jane E. Shore, *Organizational Career Development* (San Francisco: Jossey-Bass, 1993). See also Jeanne C. Meister, *Corporate Quality Universities: Lessons in Building a World-Class Work Force* (Alexandria, Va.: American Society for Training and Development; and Burr Ridge, Ill.: Irwin, 1994).

2. Gutteridge, Leibowitz, and Shore, *Organizational Career Development;* Meister, *Corporate Quality Universities;* Kenneth N. Wexley, ed., *Developing Human Resources* (Washington, D.C.: The Bureau of National Affairs, 1991).

3. Meister, *Corporate Quality Universities.*

4. Adele Scheele, *Skills for Success* (New York: Ballantine, 1987).

5. Dennis E. Guessford, Albert B. Boynton, Jr., Robert Laudeman, and Joseph P. Giusti, "Tracking Job Skills Improves Performance," *Personnel Journal* (June 1993): 109–114.

6. Ibid., 112.

7. Zandy B. Leibowitz, Beverly L. Kaye, and Caela Farren, "Multiple Career Paths," *Training and Development* (October 1992): 31–35.

8. Mark L. Goldstein, "Dual-Career Ladders: Still Shaky But Getting Better," *Industry Week* (January 4, 1988): 57–60.

9. David W. Bracken, "Straight Talk about Multirater Feedback," *Training and Development* (September 1994): 44–51.

10. Robert E. Quinn, *Beyond Rational Management: Mastering the Paradoxes and Competing Demands of High Performance* (San Francisco: Jossey-Bass, 1988).

11. Brian L. Davis, Carol J. Skube, Lowell W. Hellervik, Susan H. Gebelein, and James L. Sheard, *Successful Manager's Handbook* (Minneapolis, Minn.: Personnel Decisions, Inc., 1992). See also Robert E. Quinn, Sue R. Faerman, Michael P. Thompson, and Michael R. McGrath, *Becoming a Master Manager: A Competency Framework* (New York: John Wiley, 1990).

12. Rodney B. McGraw, "Union-Management Interface: Using the Competing Values Framework as a Diagnostic Tool to Bring Increased Involvement at the Plant Level," *Human Resource Management* 32 (1993): 51–73.

13. The personal quality orientation audit (PQOA) system is distributed by Attitude Resources, Morristown, N.J.

Selecting and Promoting Leaders

Overview

In this chapter we reinforce the importance of leadership in total quality and the critical role that selection and promotion of quality leaders plays in reaching the goal of total quality. We also argue that, while a new set of leadership attributes is required in the new workplace, many organizations, including some that profess quality, fail to systematically select and promote quality-oriented managers.

Introduction

Nowhere in our discussion of staffing for quality is the valid selection and promotion of personnel more important than in the management arena. Virtually every quality expert agrees that the success, or failure, of a firm's quality initiative can be traced to the executive suite and to acceptance by middle management. Witness the following quotes.

> A leader, instead of being a judge, will be a colleague, counseling and leading his people on a day-to-day basis, learning from them and with them. Everybody must be on a team to work for improvement of quality.
> —W. Edwards Deming[1]

> Process teams, consisting of one person or many, don't need bosses; they need coaches. Teams ask coaches for advice. Coaches help teams solve problems.—Managers have to

switch from supervisory roles to acting as facilitators, as enablers, and as people whose jobs are the development of people and their skills so that those people will be able to perform value-adding processes themselves.
—*Michael Hammer and James Champy*[2]

It is the manager's ability to communicate job requirements and the organization's needs that will energize the Quality Improvement Process. The manager makes improvement happen.
—*Philip Crosby*[3]

Top managers become critical because they provide the vision and direction for the quality effort. These senior managers are the ones who must make the strategic decision to embrace the new quality paradigm and then develop the framework for ensuring success. Middle managers are also crucial because they are the ones that make quality improvement happen. They are the caretakers of the various organizational processes. Without their buy-in and support, meaningful quality improvement, particularly employee-focused, incremental improvement, is highly unlikely.

Finally, both middle and top managers serve as models for the quality effort. Employees are more likely to respond to the actions they see than to the vision or rhetoric they hear. If the actions of top and middle management are not supportive of the quality effort, the effort will be greatly diminished.

Why is this new way of managing accepted and applied successfully in one setting but a failure in another? While many factors contribute to the success or failure of quality initiatives, quality professionals agree that one key factor is support (or lack thereof) from top and middle management. So, how do we generate such acceptance and persuade managers to embrace the new way of doing business? Perhaps the following account from one of the authors will provide some insight.

Some years ago, in the role of consultant, one of the authors was asked by a large organization to train the managers in one of the hot management theories of the day. The author has long since forgotten which training fad he was presenting (those attending the sessions have no doubt done the same). But the experience was not a total loss because, in addition to getting paid, he was introduced to the Wave Ducker Principle by one of the more astute and candid managers attending the sessions. Part way through the training, this manager confided that the managers in the room were not likely to change their behavior in any appreciable manner because of these training efforts, no matter how rational or well presented the material. He explained that those in attendance had been through many such programs through the years and had seen each new approach come and go only to be replaced by the next fad on how to manage. He further explained that, with each new training wave, managers had learned to simply hold their noses (feign acceptance), duck down, and wait for the fad to pass, and then bounce up and go on with work as usual until required to attend the next program to come down the pike. He had dubbed this process of periodically holding one's nose and ducking while the latest fad rolls on, the Wave Ducker Principle.

The Wave Ducker Principle

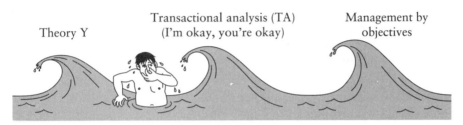

Theory Y   Transactional analysis (TA)   Management by
            (I'm okay, you're okay)   objectives

How many managers in your organization are wave duckers? How many pay lip service to quality while changing their behavior very little? How many talk about employee involvement and empowerment but still make all the decisions? How many have added the terms *change*, *empowerment*, and *risk* to their management jargon but hold to the status quo and punish those who try to do anything differently? How many make the pronouncement that the "customer is king" but make decisions based upon their own self-interests?

The question then becomes: How can we convince managers and employees that quality is not just the latest fad and that they should get on the bandwagon? One sure way is to change the performance measurement and reward structure of the organization. It is true that what is measured and rewarded becomes what is perceived as important in the organization. Managers quickly learn what is rewarded in the organization. Consequently, the criteria for hiring and promoting those individuals must reflect the new values and job requirements consistent with quality initiatives. As we have shown, the behaviors and attributes required of managers in the new quality-oriented manufacturing and service settings differ significantly from those required of managers in traditional settings. The day we start hiring and promoting managers who are both willing and able to embrace the new philosophy is the day real progress will occur. As Tom Peters argues, we should "focus less on measures such as budget variance and profitability and more on the explicit question: 'What, exactly, have you changed lately?'"[4] Thus, we should walk the talk by hiring and promoting those individuals who truly empower their employees, learn and apply the various quality and problem-solving tools, make systematic changes in their work process, and most importantly, measure and meet their customers' needs and expectations.

The simple fact is that organizations are not likely to become truly quality driven until top and middle managers' efforts are reinforced for integrating and exhibiting basic quality values and principles, such as Deming's 14 points. And one of the primary reinforcers of management behavior is what they believe will lead to advancement and promotion. The basic question that all managers ask themselves (or others) is: "What must I do to get ahead in this organization?" Unfortunately, the answers are often not consistent with the notion of quality.

Risk and noble failure (Motorola motto) are encouraged, but it is the behavior of those who play it by the book that is reinforced. Employees are told to be creative and innovative and occasionally go out on a limb, but in most cases, it is the trunk huggers of the world that are rewarded, and those who fail or fall flat on their faces are shunned. As one organization pundit put it: "We're so conservative and careful around here that if you become a manager, you have to wear both a belt and suspenders."

As quality professionals, we espouse the virtues of customer service and preach that the organization's primary goal is to meet or exceed the needs and expectations of the customer. But promotions are most likely to come to those individuals who keep their bosses, not the customers, happy. The first rule for climbing the corporate ladder is to make the boss look good. We talk the talk in terms of teamwork and cooperation and argue that different functional areas should work more closely together for the common good of the organization. But when it comes time to select, developmentally move, or promote a manager, we are likely to examine the individual accomplishments of the person and not those of the team. If you doubt this contention, review any stack of management resumes or listen in on an interview with a management hopeful. What you will find is reference after reference to "my" responsibilities and what "I" accomplished in the position (versus "our" and "we").

Likewise, *empowerment*, for the great majority of individuals in leadership positions, is simply a new word for inclusion in the management vocabulary. In practice, it has little to do with the way many managers relate to their employees. Even those managers who embrace the concept of empowerment have a very difficult time putting it into practice in the workplace. They do not bestow greater responsibility and authority on their subordinates. And they do not increase the autonomy of employees or their decision-making authority.

While a full discussion of the issue of empowerment is beyond the scope of this book, anyone wondering why some managers fail to fully involve and empower their employees should read the Center for Creative Leadership's report entitled "Why Managers Have Trouble Empowering."[5] This very enlightening discussion on the topic of empowerment contends that the managerial strengths that organizations reward have little to do with the notion of sharing power with others. Real empowerment, the report argues, is not likely to occur until radical changes are made in how the organization is structured, how the management learning process takes place, and until the reward system is modified to reinforce power sharing.

In summary, most organizations rely on education and persuasion to obtain management support for quality. The firm attempts to sell the concept and the need for embracing the quality paradigm. While quality should be an easy sell because it does make good business sense, the realities of large-scale organizational change are much more complex and difficult than most realize. For quality to work, it requires dramatic changes in management understanding, values, commitment, and behavior. One way of obtaining these changes is to reinforce those managers who truly accept and practice quality. And one of the best ways to do that is to change the way we select and promote our management personnel.

Who Assesses?

Quality and HR professionals not only have to reexamine what is measured but also how and by whom that assessment takes place. Historically, management promotion decisions have been made by those individuals situated at higher levels in the organizational hierarchy. Thus, the boss and the boss's boss are given the responsibility of determining who will be promoted. Typically, this is accomplished using formal and informal references, internal performance information (performance appraisals), and some kind of interview process. But within the quality organization, this traditional approach is likely to prove inadequate.

For example, if you really want to know about the individual's customer orientation and focus, then it only makes sense to ask the customer (external and internal) for input on the individual's behavior and performance. Does the managerial candidate truly put the customer first? And when problems do occur, are they dealt with quickly and positively? Only the customer is in a position to provide a complete picture of the person's customer orientation. This can be done indirectly through conversation with customers or through more formal means such as surveys of customer satisfaction. Companies such as Taco Bell, Prudential Insurance Company, and Xerox use customer satisfaction data as input into their evaluation and reward process for field managers.[6] While it is not reported, we hope these firms are using that same customer satisfaction as input into their promotion decisions.

Similarly, if teamwork and cross-functional cooperation are important factors in the organizational setting, then peers and suppliers become valuable resources for input. How well does the candidate relate to other functional areas? Does the individual see the big picture and work for the good of the organization, or is his or her view myopic and parochial in nature? Has the person developed a close working relationship with vendors and suppliers, or is that connection removed and antagonistic? These are questions best answered by peers and suppliers, not managers two levels up in the hierarchy.

Finally, if the critical attributes identified relate to such factors as employee involvement, empowerment, employee development, and employee trust, then subordinates are in the best position to judge the effectiveness and potential of the candidate. Trust, in particular, is a very personal quality that is difficult to assess by anyone removed from that interpersonal context. In a truly quality-driven organization, employee input should be a key part of the promotion selection process. From the subordinates' perspective, the questions become: Does this person actively involve us in decisions that affect our work? Does he or she empower us with the responsibility and authority to carry out our work duties? Can we place our confidence in the integrity of this individual's words and actions? Has the candidate made an honest effort to train and develop us to our potential? These are all questions that are worthy of serious consideration when making promotion decisions in a quality organization. The best source for answering these questions is the individuals presently reporting to that person.

In chapter 11, we discussed the use of 360-degree feedback instruments as a management development tool. We believe that the 360-degree instrument has potential for use in making management promotion decisions. A formal procedure could be developed to collect performance information from various meaningful sources (subordinates, peers, customers, and supervisors). That data, along with other promotion criteria, would become the basis for making promotion decisions. Two examples of using 360-degree instruments for promotion are Boeing and SSOE. Boeing has been faced with the challenge of changing the behaviors of approximately 12,000 managers. In the past, Boeing, like most organizations, has relied on a command and control management style for running its organization. But faced with increasing competition in a global environment, Boeing is presently instituting and reinforcing a systemwide culture change that promotes teamwork, empowerment, and innovation. As such, it has identified 10 key attributes important for leadership in the new workplace (for example, quality, customer focus, promoting teamwork, empowering people). Boeing has developed its own 360-degree feedback instrument based on these 10 attributes and uses it as a component of its leadership development effort. While the first round of 360-degree feedback has been used for developmental purposes only, subsequent administrations of the 360-degree tool will also be used as input into making promotion decisions. Change agents at Boeing feel strongly that managers are more likely to accept their new roles if positive change is reinforced in the form of advancement.[7]

Similarly, SSOE, an engineering and architectural firm headquartered in Toledo, Ohio, has extended its use of 360-degree instruments beyond the developmental role. SSOE has embraced total quality and uses a 360-degree tool as the basis for its leadership development program. Attributes such as innovation, customer orientation, process improvement, team building, and use of quality methods and tools are measured and fed back to participants. SSOE, like Boeing, is implementing a phase-in approach to using their 360-degree instrument as an evaluation tool. First-time results are completely confidential (accessible only to the program participants) and used for development. While action plans are shared and mutually refined by participants and their superiors, only the participants are privy to specific feedback data. Phase two requires participants to share their feedback data with their bosses and mutually develop action plans. The focus remains developmental. In the final phase, 360-degree feedback data, along with supervisor judgments of developmental effort (implementation of action plans), is used in conjunction with other performance indicators as input into the succession planning process.[8]

It should be pointed out that the use of 360-degree instruments for evaluation or performance appraisal purposes is somewhat controversial. When used to make organizational decisions such as pay, promotion, and retention, issues such as acceptance, rater bias, and reprisal become important considerations. Many practitioners argue that multirater feedback instruments are more likely to be successful and change behavior if feedback remains confidential and used for developmental purposes only.[9] In addition, all of the issues of reliability, validity, and fairness covered in chapter 3 become important when using 360-degree tools for evaluation. While the jury is still out on this issue, we believe that these instruments show promise for providing input into promotion and developmental move decisions. We hypothesize that those managers most resistant and threatened by peer and subordinate evaluation are likely the same managers who have failed to embrace the new paradigm. If, as a manager, I am truly empowering and developing my subordinates, I should welcome their input into those decisions that affect my career. Similarly, customer-oriented managers should not feel threatened by input from those sources.

At a minimum, we strongly suggest that management decision makers actively solicit input from others when deciding who should be promoted. If the organization truly believes that the role of management should be that of empowering employees, developing trust and teamwork, and coaching and training employees, then subordinates should have an active voice in who indeed meets those criteria. Quality professionals have long espoused employee involvement in solving problems and making decisions. They argue that the employee is often in the best position to make meaningful suggestions concerning how the work gets done. We are simply suggesting that such involvement be extended to the promotion arena, where employees also are in an ideal position to provide useful input.

Likewise, if customer orientation is critical, then customer input should be solicited. If cross-functional cooperation is important, then peer recommendations make sense, and so on.

Selecting for Quality Leadership

To this point, we have agreed with the various quality professionals who state that leadership is absolutely critical to the success of any total quality initiative. We have also argued that traditional management staffing efforts are typically deficient, and that the vast majority of organizations fail to put enough thought and effort into this important area. The quality literature is replete with admonitions to recognize and reinforce quality-related behavior, but it seldom makes the link to the number one management reinforcer—-promotion. In our efforts at researching and preparing for this book, we were pleasantly surprised by the number of firms engaged in the systematic selection of quality-oriented employees at the entry level (3M, Motorola, Corning, Saturn, Toyota, and Pepsi). Locating specific examples of promoting managers for total quality was much more difficult. The question we were forced to ask ourselves was: "Do organizations make as concerted an effort in systematically promoting for quality as they do in entry-level selection?" What concerns us most is that some so-called quality-oriented organizations may be hiring and promoting managers based on attributes more closely aligned with the traditional organization. Such a situation was created during the late 1980s at the Flat Rock, Michigan, plant of Mazda (now AutoAlliance International, a 50-50 joint venture of Mazda and Ford). A special report in *The Detroit News and Free Press* describes how Mazda Flat Rock workers were carefully selected for their high skill and intelligence levels, as well as their positive attitudes, flexibility, initiative, and willingness to participate in decision making.[10] But workers soon learned that the management style at Mazda was not conducive to the qualities said to be important and used in selection. Managers failed to involve and listen to employees and were inflexible in their policies and practices. To quote the article

> *The lesson, according to scholars who have studied the Mazda situation, was even clearer: You can hire a completely different kind of worker, but if you don't treat that worker differently, your results won't be good. "Teamwork and worker empowerment were definitely oversold," says Steve Babson, a labor program specialist at Wayne State University's Labor Studies Center. Babson surveyed Mazda Flat Rock workers for the United Auto Workers union. "They were hired to participate in decision-making and were more than disappointed that the opportunity to act (on their suggestions) was not there."*

In all fairness, it should be pointed out that things are different now at the Mazda plant. With the advent of the joint venture with Ford, the new managers have become much more flexible and participative in their approach. Worker morale has increased substantially. However the Mazda example clearly points to the need to be truly committed to the quality paradigm before embarking on the staffing process outlined in this book. Don't staff your organization with quality-oriented employees who are then stifled by management in an existing traditional environment.

So, how can the organization go about improving its staffing process to ensure it has quality-oriented leadership? The answer is actually quite simple. The difficulty, as they say, is in the details. The solution is to follow the advice and steps previously outlined in this book. Begin by carefully specifying the quality attributes important for management success in your organization (that is, job analysis). Next, integrate the assessment of those quality needs into *all* facets of the planning, recruitment, selection, and development system (advertising, screening, testing, interviewing, socialization). And finally, assess those relevant quality attributes using multiple inputs such as peers, subordinates, customers.

The remainder of this chapter will demonstrate what this management selection process resembles in practice. The focus will be on those management attributes identified as important in our survey of ASQC sustaining member organizations. Since results from our survey show that the interview is the assessment tool of choice when making management selection decisions, we will also center our attention on the use of the employment interview in management selection.

Quality-Related Attributes for Managers

Table 12.1 presents a ranking of the top 10 important quality attributes for first-line, middle, and senior managers as determined in our survey of quality-oriented organizations. Some of those findings warrant a brief discussion. First, we were somewhat surprised to find that respondents considered the soft skills (flexibility, interpersonal relations, customer orientation, coaching) to be relatively more important than the more technical or hard KSAPs (for example, computer skills, SPC, applied statistics, experimental design, quality tools).

Next, it appears that the skills required of first-line and middle managers are very similar. While the rank order differs somewhat, both have identical top 10 attributes. We were also pleased to find that, overall, the top ranked attribute was customer orientation. This emphasis on the customer appears to be particularly important for both middle and senior management personnel. Not so surprising was the importance of implementing organizational change for senior management. This skill is viewed as an absolute must for those leading an organization's quality effort. And the acceptance of that change

Table 12.1. Quality attribute rankings for various levels of management.

Attribute	Management ranking		
	First line	Middle	Senior
Customer orientation	4	1	2
Flexibility/adaptability (openness to change)	2	2	4
Skill in relating to others	1	3	6
Skill in coaching others	3	4	10
Skill in oral communication	10	5	3
Skill in empowering others	9	6	5
Skill in involving others	7	9	9
Conscientiousness	5	7	—
Teamwork orientation	6	10	—
Openness to learning	8	8	—
Skill in implementing organizational change	—	—	1
Creative thinking	—	—	7
Skill in written communication	—	—	8

(openness to change) is the second most important attribute for both first-line and middle managers.

It should also be pointed out that, while our focus is on staffing, these findings have obvious implications for the training and development of managers as well as for other HR activities (for example, appraisal, compensation, performance management). Those individuals involved in a management development effort should pay close attention to attributes considered important to the successful implementation of quality improvement efforts.

Finally, readers should, once again, be cautioned to do their own analyses of what constitutes important attributes. Organization quality initiatives vary substantially from situation to situation and, even when they are similar, organizations are likely to be at different phases of quality implementation. Quality attributes considered critical in one setting may not be that important in another. Two examples of such lists of attributes or competencies are shown in Exhibits 12.1 and 12.2. The list of managerial competencies shown in Exhibit 12.1 was developed by the federal government's Office of Personnel Management (OPM) and represents the changing orientation of what Uncle Sam expects of managers. Exhibit 12.2 lists Corning's competencies for excellence. Corning uses these competencies as the basis for its performance-based interview process.[11]

Exhibit 12.1. Office of Personnel Management's 21 competencies for effective managers.

General competencies

- Written communication
- Oral communication
- Interpersonal skills
- Flexibility
- Decisiveness
- Leadership
- Self-direction
- Technical competence

Supervisory competencies

- Managing a diverse workforce
- Conflict management
- Influencing/negotiating
- Human resources management
- Team building

Managerial competencies

- Creative thinking
- Planning and evaluating
- Financial management
- Client orientation
- Technology management
- Internal controls and integrity

Executive competencies

- Vision
- External awareness

Source: Office of Personnel Management's *21 Competencies for Effective Managers*, 1995.

Assessing Quality Readiness

Our survey results indicate that the four most frequently used assessment devices for hiring and promoting managers are, in order of use, the employment interview, reference checks, internal performance appraisal data, and applications. While each of these assessment tools has been thoroughly described in previous chapters, we will briefly discuss each device as it relates to management staffing and provide examples of how those tools might be applied in practice. Because of

Exhibit 12.2. Corning's competencies for excellence

Key human traits
- Achievement orientation
- High self-confidence
- High commitment
- Initiative risk taking
- Persistence
- Flexibility
- Honesty and integrity

Leadership skills
- Accurate self-assessment
- Relationship building
- Information utilization
- People development
- Valuing diversity
- Networking
- Teambuilding
- Integration
- Change facilitation
- Innovation
- Strategic influence
- Strategic thinking
- Visioning

Operational attributes
- Market/customer orientation
- Planning and organizing
- Problem solving and decision making
- Priority setting
- Quality results orientation
- Technological curiosity

Source: Jeanne C. Meister, *Corporate Quality Universities: Lessons in Building a World-Class Work Force.* (Alexandria, Va.: American Society for Training and Development, and Burr Ridge, Ill.: Irwin, 1994), 57. Used with permission of Corning.

its demonstrated payoff in the selection, promotion, and development of management personnel, we will also discuss the use of simulations and assessment centers. But before discussing the various assessment devices, it might be helpful to briefly review some of the key staffing concepts previously discussed.

1. Begin staffing for quality at the recruitment stage of the process. Whatever the recruitment source (for example, ads, search firms, referrals, employment agencies), make it clear that your organization is quality oriented and that you are looking for managers who understand and apply quality principles.

2. Recruit widely (internally and/or externally) and strive for a selection ratio that maximizes the utility of your staffing process.

3. Because of the high cost of management selection, use a multiple–hurdle or funnel approach for screening applicants. Eliminating low-scoring applicants at each stage of the process reduces costs and ensures that only the most qualified candidates reach the final stage of the selection process.

4. Standardize the process such that each candidate is afforded the same opportunity at each stage to be considered for the position.

5. Generally speaking, the higher the management level, the more time and effort recruiting and selecting should be put into the selection process. Typically, the utility or payoff to the organization is higher for top management than for management at lower levels. The organization can compensate for a hiring mistake made at lower levels, but it can ill-afford poor selection decisions made at the top.

6. Remember that, as we move up the organizational hierarchy, increasing thought should be given to hiring from outside the organization boundaries. While the focus should remain on promoting from within, some thought should be given to the infusion of new ideas (new blood) and to filling some key management positions with external candidates. This is particularly important when a quality initiative is in its early stages. Having a few managers with experience in introducing a quality effort and who can champion the cause is a big plus and is likely to increase the probability of success.

7. Finally, management selection in a quality-oriented organization requires the use of multiple inputs into the decision process. That translates into the use of various selection and promotion tools (tests, interviews, performance information, assessment centers) and the use of multiple assessors that provide a complete picture of the candidate's quality-related qualifications (peers, subordinates, customers, suppliers). While the final selection decision will no doubt lie with a few senior managers, failure to obtain input from the various quality-related constituencies would be folly.

Having reviewed these basic staffing concepts, we turn our attention to illustrating how different selection devices (interviews, reference checks, performance appraisal data, and applications) can be used to assess managerial potential in a quality organization. As we discuss each of these tools, note that the primary assessment theme is the past performance of the candidate. Once again, the reader is reminded that the best predictor of future performance is past behavior and performance. The vast majority of managerial candidates have a fairly extensive track record that can provide the focus for assessing managerial potential. Even candidates for entry-level management have had quality-related experiences (team, customer, problem solving) that can provide insight into their possible competence as quality managers. If the individual has failed to embrace quality concepts and principles in the past, don't expect some kind of miraculous conversion to these ideas with the advent of the new position. The candidate's achievement history must be carefully examined as it relates to quality-specific activities. Hard work, intelligence, and superior technical skills are no longer sufficient. While necessary, these traditional attributes are not enough to justify advancement in the quality organization. The focus must become one of evaluating the success (or failures) of the applicant as those achievements relate to change and process improvement, teamwork, customer orientation, employee involvement, and so on.

Employment Interview

Exhibits 12.3 and 12.4 provide examples of what a structured interview might resemble in practice. We used the quality attributes *skill in implementing organizational change* and *customer orientation* to demonstrate what such an interview might include when assessing managerial potential. Possible interview questions for the remainder of the attributes presented in Table 12.1 are provided in appendix D.

In addition to the various questions and probes shown, we have provided a list of some of the key behaviors (evaluation guidelines) that the interviewer should use when evaluating the candidate. For example, when selecting a top manager that will be given responsibility for initiating or maintaining a company- or divisionwide quality initiative, the interviewer should look favorably on those candidates who have previously instituted similar large-scale organizational changes, know how to plan for such changes, and actively involve others in the change process. The reader should be reminded that ap-

Exhibit 12.3. Interview questions for assessing customer orientation.

Attribute: Customer orientation (meeting or exceeding customer needs and expectations)

Q. In your present job, who do you view as being your customer(s)?

- What steps do you take to determine customer needs? Customer satisfaction?
- What are those needs and expectations (be specific)?
- In what areas are you doing a good job? How do you know?
- In what areas do you have to improve? How do you know?
- What plans do you have for making those improvements in customer satisfaction?

Q. What does it mean to you to exceed customer expectations?

- What actions do you take to exceed the expectations of your customers?

Q. Please describe your most comprehensive effort at improving customer satisfaction.

- Why was the effort undertaken? That is, how did you know you had a problem?
- What specific actions were taken to improve customer satisfaction?
- How successful was the effort?
- What tools or methods were used to determine the effectiveness of the effort?

Q. Many organizations collect customer satisfaction information (surveys, customer complaints, focus groups) to aid in their efforts at meeting customer needs. Please describe any such measures that you've had experience using.

- How do you feel such information can be used most effectively to improve customer satisfaction?
- Who should receive such information?
- How can that data be used as a stimulus for action?

Q. Sooner or later, we all have to deal with a customer who is dissatisfied with the product or services he or she receives. Tell me about the most difficult customer you ever experienced.

- Exactly why was the customer dissatisfied?
- How did you respond to the customer's concerns?
- How effective were your efforts? Did you satisfy the customer?
- What did you learn from the interaction?
- What changes, if any, did you make in procedures or processes to prevent similar problems in the future?

Q. How would you judge your own performance in terms of being customer oriented? Why?

Exhibit 12.3. Continued.

- Give some examples of why you feel you are customer oriented.
- How familiar are you with various tools used to measure customer needs and satisfaction?
  —Surveys?
  —Focus groups?
  —Customer complaints?
- Have you ever used quality function deployment or any other systematic techniques for improving customer satisfaction?

Evaluation Guidelines:
- Does the candidate understand the link between what he/she does and customer satisfaction?
- Does the candidate understand that he/she has both external and internal customers?
- Does the candidate have experience systematically measuring customer needs and satisfaction?
- Did the candidate demonstrate efforts at systematically improving customer satisfaction? Has the condidate made changes in processes or procedures specifically aimed at improving customer satisfaction?

Exhibit 12.4. Interview questions for assessing skill in implementating organizational change.

Attribute: Skill in implementing organizational change (creating climate and direction for change)

Q. Thinking back on your last job, please describe your major efforts at instituting new or innovative changes in procedures or work processes.
  - How did the changes originate?
  - What was your role in making those changes?
  - Were others involved? How?
  - What difficulties or resistance did you run into when making those changes?
  - How did you handle that resistance?
  - How successful were those changes?
  - What about changes on previous jobs?

Q. As managers, we have all attempted to make fundamental changes in the way work gets done. Tell me about the most difficult change that you have undertaken.
  - How did the change originate?
  - Why was it so difficult?

Exhibit 12.4. Continued.

- What specific steps did you take to implement the change?
- What, if anything, would you do differently if you were making the change today?

Q. Describe a time when you attempted to make a change and it backfired.

- Exactly why did the change fail?
- What could you or should you have done differently?
- What did you learn from the experience?

Q. Suppose that you are a plant manager and have just attended a company-sponsored workshop on process improvement. Now you want to begin using problem-solving (process improvement, reengineering) teams at your plant (location, division, unit). Exactly what steps would you take to implement such groups at your site?

- What do you see as your role in getting such groups started?
- Who else would you involve in the change process? How would you use them?
- How would you ensure long-term success and continued enthusiasm?
- Suppose that the local union sees process improvement as another management ploy to get more work using fewer employees and asks members not to participate. What would you do?

Q. If you were teaching a seminar on large-scale change in organizations, what advice would you give to the participants? What are the key points that you would attempt to communicate?

- Why would you give that advice?
- What do you feel is the single most important consideration when implementing change?
- Can you give me a specific example of how you applied that concept?

Evaluation Guidelines:

- Does the candidate have varied experiences in large-scale change efforts?
- Were the changes made by the candidate quality driven (customer driven)?
- Did the candidate systematically plan for those changes?
- Did the candidate actively involve others in the changes process?
- Did the candidate demonstrate a clear vision of where he/she wanted to be (end result)?

proximately half of all quality initiatives fail, and those that are successful have experienced many mistakes along the way. We believe that such failures and mistakes could be greatly reduced with a cadre of top management personnel that have experienced and truly understand the principles and difficulties associated with large-scale organizational change, particularly as it relates to quality.

Reference Checks

References, both formal and informal, are frequently used as input into management promotion decisions. As previously discussed, such information is often biased and unreliable as typically collected. To improve the reliability and validity of reference information, we suggest the following.

1. Take control of the reference giving process. You, not the candidate, should decide both who should be a reference source and what information needs to be collected. Allowing the candidate to select reference sources or reference content is a mistake.

2. Focus on quality-related attributes when assessing the candidate's past performance. Reference questions and probes should systematically assess the individual's track record as it relates to quality.

3. Be prepared to ask specific questions related to the past behavior and performance of the management candidate. Think of the reference check much the same as you would a good structured interview. Prepare a set of specific job-related questions. Avoid general questions such as, "What do you think of John?" or "Do you think Mary would make a good supervisor?"

4. Broaden your scope of reference sources. In addition to the candidate's superiors, collect past performance information from peers, suppliers, customers, and subordinates.

Performance Appraisal Information

Our survey results show that the vast majority of ASQC sustaining member organizations currently use internal performance appraisal data for evaluating applicants for promotion: 83.8 percent for supervisory positions, 81.0 percent for middle management, and 73.4 percent for senior management positions.

At this point, it is not our role to debate the use of performance appraisal information in quality settings. We will, however, make a few suggestions on how that information can be the most relevant and useful. When using rating scale methods that focus on behavior, performance appraisal dimensions should reflect the firm's quality initiative. Performance factors such as *customer orientation, teamwork, coaching,* and *problem solving* should be used to appraise employee and management performance. Exhibit 12.5 provides some representative illustrations of such dimensions for one company's appraisal process along with behavioral examples of those dimensions in practice. If the appraisal system is oriented more toward assessing individual goal accomplishment or outcomes [for example, management by objectives (MBO)], then performance appraisal should focus on process improvement, customer satisfaction measures, and the development of subordinates.

Applications and Resumes

As typically used, neither applications nor resumes are particularly useful as selection tools. This is particularly true for resumes, given this age of resume-writing computer programs and professional resume services. If properly constructed, application blanks can be useful for screening purposes and as input into interview content (follow ups and probes) but should not be a major input into the selection decision. Remember that it is quality of experience that predicts performance and not quantity. Also, review the application and/or resume with an eye to progression and success history.

Where applications can be predictive is when items have been statistically keyed (WABs and BIBs discussed in chapter 7). One review of studies examining the relationship of personal history data with management success found the average validity to be .38. When broken down by category, the data were able to predict sales success at .50 and success in science and engineering at .41.[12] While we are not aware of any studies relating personal history data to quality-related leadership attributes, WABs and BIBs are likely to be predictive.

Other Measures of Leadership Success

One of the surprising findings from the sustaining member survey was the limited use of tests and assessment centers/simulations for making

Exhibit 12.5. Quality-oriented management performance dimensions and behavioral examples.

Leads continuous quality improvement focused on customer satisfaction

- Measures and tracks organization performance and process improvements using a customer input
- Challenges work processes to better meet customer needs
- Uses facts and statistical analysis to improve customer satisfaction
- Works cross-functional issues to address customer needs; doesn't "throw problems over the fence"

Removes barrier, promotes teamwork, and empowers people to improve business performance

- Spends time in the work area; is available to direct reports on a regular basis
- Persists in working to resolve issues within and between work groups
- Charters teams, sets guidelines, and then follows through by using recommendations
- Promotes team-related work and provides time for team meetings
- Uses expertise of others inside or outside the work group to get the job done
- Involves affected parties in problem solving and decision making
- Encourages direct reports to determine the details of how they do their work (doesn't micro-manage)
- Includes SMEs in meetings with management

Demonstrates innovation and seeks to improve technical and business competence

- Repeatedly takes risks in the support of new ideas and improvements
- Takes practical steps to transform creative ideas into reality
- Rejects "This is the way we've always done it" approach
- Encourages others to come up with new ways to continuously improve competence

Coaches people to develop their capabilities

- Provides individuals with honest, timely feedback on their performance
- Encourages direct reports in their learning and development
- Provides challenging job assignments based on individual skill levels
- Communicates challenging expectations and a belief in direct reports' ability to succeed

---

hire and promotion decisions for management positions. This is particularly disconcerting given the fact that cognitive ability tests and assessment centers both have excellent track records for predicting managerial success across most jobs and settings. Indeed, most reviews of the literature show measures of intellectual ability to be the best predictor of success as a manager, with simulations a close second.[13]

Personality measures also appear to hold considerable potential for predicting managerial success in total quality settings. Measures of conscientiousness, agreeableness, and emotional stability in particular seem to show promise for predicting performance.[14]

In summary, we strongly recommend that quality-oriented organizations broaden their horizons in terms of the tools they use to assess leadership effectiveness. In addition to references, performance appraisal information, and the interview, firms should seriously consider using cognitive ability tests, simulations, personality inventories, and multirater instruments such as 360-degree evaluations to assess leadership potential. A number of studies have concluded that the base rate of managerial incompetence is somewhere between 50 percent and 70 percent.[15] If that is true in traditional settings, then how high must the failure rate be in quality-oriented organizations where leadership becomes so much more complex and critical? While we can't answer that question, we have provided the reader with a methodology and some valid assessment tools that can be used to improve the managerial success rate in his or her organization.

A Letter to Deming and a Response

In the fall of 1991, one of the authors attended a three-day seminar given by Deming in conjunction with the Ford Motor Company. Throughout the seminar, the author was struck by the number of times participants questioned Deming concerning rewarding and promoting people in organizations. They obviously had difficulty reconciling Deming's admonition not to equate the evaluation of individual performance (performance appraisal) with the very real need to make promotional decisions in the workplace. They also were obviously not satisfied with Deming's response because the issue continued to surface throughout the sessions. Addressing the issue of management promotion, the author wrote Deming a letter which included the following excerpt.

I also have a thought concerning the issue of promotion in organizational settings. Several participants in our seminar raised the question of how promotional decisions should be made (alluding to the issue of merit and promotion based on performance). At the risk of being somewhat presumptuous, I have an idea for an appropriate response. Given the importance of management's role in quality and productivity improvement and the fact that best efforts are not enough, perhaps the major criteria for promotion, assuming appropriate technical competence, should be:

1. *an understanding and appreciation of "profound knowledge," and*
2. *demonstrated success in systematically improving systems (processes) versus tampering, using numerical goals, pay for performance, etc.*

    In short, perhaps we should hire and promote managers who have the "know how" and "willingness" to apply the 14 Points that you espouse.

    I would be very interested in your response to these suggested criteria for hiring and promoting managers. Thank you again for a very enjoyable and stimulating learning experience.[16]

As the letter states, the author was very interested in knowing how Deming would respond to such a suggestion. The author also admits to a bit of uneasiness concerning Deming's reaction to the idea of promotion based on some kind of merit, albeit quality-oriented merit. As anyone who has attended a Deming seminar can attest, Deming was not particularly known for sugar coating his responses to questions.

But the author's fears were unwarranted, given the reply from Deming shown in Exhibit 12.6.

Obviously Deming provided some credence to our notion that systematically selecting and promoting quality-oriented managers makes a great deal of business sense.

Summary

If your organization is truly committed to quality, then no individual should gain entrance into the management ranks without demonstrating both a competence and commitment to quality. Now is the time for action. Begin by spelling out the critical management quality skills for your organization, and then start screening management candidates based on the assessment of those quality attributes. Doing so

Exhibit 12.6.   A letter from W. Edwards Deming.

W. EDWARDS DEMING, PH.D.
CONSULTANT IN STATISTICAL STUDIES

WASHINGTON 20016
4924 BUTTERWORTH PLACE
———
TEL. (202) 363-8552
FAX (202) 363.3501

21   December   1991

Dear Dr. Smith,

I thank you for your letter of 27 November 1991. Your suggestions for criteria for promotion please me. I may incorporate them into my seminars and into a book, with a reference to the source. I remain with best greetings

Sincerely yours,

W. Edwards Deming

To Dr. Jack E. Smith
34770 Whittaker Court
Farmington, Michigan
48024

---

will accomplish two important quality outcomes. First, it will provide the organization with quality-oriented managers that are customer oriented, understand the change process, and involve and develop employees. Second, it sends a very profound message to other management personnel concerning what is important. Begin to seriously hire and promote quality-conscious managers, and then stand back and watch your management workforce scramble to climb on board the quality bandwagon. Communicate to your managers that the quality wave is much more than the latest fad, and that they'll likely drown if they attempt to duck this critical strategic initiative.

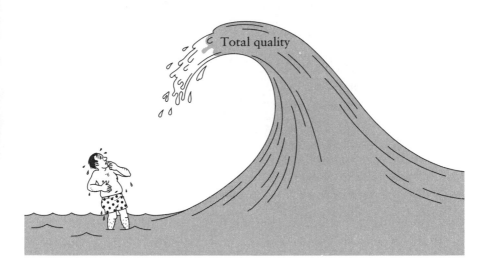

Notes

1. W. Edwards Deming, *Out of the Crisis* (Cambridge, Mass.: MIT Center for Advanced Engineering Study, 1986).

2. Michael Hammer and James Champy, *Reengineering the Corporation* (New York: Harper Business, 1993).

3. Philip Crosby, *Quality Improvement Through Defect Prevention* (Winter Park, Fla.: Philip Crosby Associates, 1985), 191–192.

4. Tom Peters, *The Promises* (Palo Alto, Calif.: Excel, 1986), 89.

5. Wilfred H. Drath, "Why Managers Have Trouble Empowering: A Theoretical Perspective Based on Concepts of Adult Development," A Center for Creative Leadership publication, Report 155, Greensboro, N.C., 1993.

6. James L. Heskett, Thomas O. Jones, Gary W. Loveman, W. Earl Sasser, Jr., and Leonard A. Schlesinger, "Putting the Service/Profit Chain to Work," *Harvard Business Review* (March-April 1994): 169. See also John A. Pearce, II, and Richard B. Robinson, Jr., *Strategic Management: Formulation, Implementation, and Control* (Burr Ridge, Ill.: Irwin, 1994), 42.

7. Lise Saari, "Management Development of Boeing: Struggling with Success and Established Management Practices," presentation at the Tenth Annual Conference of the Society for Industrial and Organizational Psychology, Orlando, Fla., May 19–21, 1995.

8. SSOE, personal communication with the author. Reprinted by permission.

9. Maxine Dalton, "Tampering with the Conditions for Change: 360 Feedback," presentation at the Tenth Annual Conference of the Society for Industrial and Organizational Psychology, Orlando, Fla., May 19–21, 1995.

10. Mike Casey, "Auto Workers of the 21st Century," *The Detroit News* (June 11, 1995): 1D and 3D.

11. Jeanne C. Meister, *Corporate Quality Universities: Lessons in Building a World-Class Work Force* (Alexandria, Va.: American Society for Training and Development, and Burr Ridge, Ill.: Irwin, 1994), 57.

12. Richard R. Reilly and Georgia T. Chao, "Validity and Fairness of Some Alternative Employee Selection Procedures, *Personnel Psychology* 35 (1982): 1–62.

13. John E. Hunter and Rhonda E. Hunter, "Validity and Utility of Alternative Predictors of Job Performance," *Psychological Bulletin* 96 (1984): 72–98; Barbara B. Gangler, Douglas B. Rosenthal, George C. Thornton, III, and C. Bentson, "Meta-Analysis of Assessment Center Validity," *Journal of Applied Psychology* 72:493–511; see also George C. Thornton, III, and William C. Byham, *Assessment Centers and Managerial Performance* (New York: Academic Press, 1982); Wayne F. Cascio, *Managing Human Resources,* 4th ed. (New York: McGraw-Hill, 1995), 217.

14. Murray R. Barrick and Frank L. Schmidt, "Personality and Personnel Selection: Views from Personality and I-O Psychology," panel discussion at the Tenth Annual Conference of the Society for Industrial and Organizational Psychology, Orlando, Fla., May 19–21, 1995. See also Robert Hogan, Gordon J. Curphy, and Joyce Hogan, "What We Know about Leadership: Effectiveness and Personality," *American Psychologist* (June 1994): 1–12.

15. Hogan, Curphy, and Hogan, "What We Know about Leadership: Effectiveness and Personality," 2.

16. Jack E. Smith, personal correspondence with W. Edwards Deming, 1991.

chapter **13**

Staffing Teams

Overview

This chapter examines the importance of team and teamwork staffing to the total quality organization. We also discuss the staffing process as it relates to different types of teams and different organizational constraints when staffing for teams.

Introduction

Fortune magazine named Rubbermaid as "America's Most Admired Company" for 1994. Described as the "master of the mundane and a champion innovator," Rubbermaid was voted the best-of-the-best by 10,000 senior executives, outside directors, and financial analysts surveyed by *Fortune*. In beating out perennial winners IBM and Merck, Rubbermaid was praised for its creativity and success rate in introducing more than 365 new products a year. What was the secret to Rubbermaid's success? According to Richard Gates, head of business development at Rubbermaid, much of the credit goes to the use of cross-functional, product development teams. To quote *Fortune,*

> *Most ideas for products flow from a single source: teams. Twenty teams, each made up of five to seven people (one each from marketing, manufacturing, R&D, finance, and other departments), focus on specific product lines, such as bathroom accessories. So successful has been the team approach to innovation that Dick Gates fears to contemplate a world with-*

out it. *"If we weren't organized that way,"* he says, a look of concern spreading over his face, *"who would be thinking about ice cube trays? Who would be thinking about johnny mops?"*[1]

Rubbermaid is not alone in its belief in, and use of, teams to improve organizational effectiveness. Indeed, the list of companies that have embraced the team concept reads like a "Who's Who" of American industry—Ford, Eastman-Kodak, Motorola, 3M, Federal Express, General Electric, Corning, AT&T, Met Life, and IBM. The 1993 ASQC/Gallup survey previously discussed attests to the number of companies that have team activities and the frequency of employee involvement in team-based activities. Results from our own survey found that 96 percent of the companies reported having teams of one kind or another.

Obviously, the use of teams is an integral part of most quality-related initiatives. And much has been written on how to make such teams effective. But, once again, an important ingredient to successful team performance is often overlooked or addressed haphazardly. In previous chapters, we have discussed the "train 'em" mentality that pervades the quality literature. Over and over, we are reminded that "to be effective, team leaders and team members need to be thoroughly trained." And while we agree wholeheartedly with that dictum, we argue that, if the team member selection process is carried out correctly, the organization may very well reduce the need for such extensive and costly training and do much to improve the probability of team success.

We will begin with a general discussion of team selection and then focus our attention on two general types of teams: *problem-solving teams* and *self-directed teams*. Each presents its own unique issues related to selection, and each will be discussed separately.

Building a Team Success Profile

At this point, the reader is well aware of the importance of generating a complete and specific listing of the attributes needed to function in a particular setting. The same holds true for selection and/or placement decisions in a team setting. Exactly what do we mean when we ask for an employee who is team oriented or who values teamwork? What is the success profile of an individual who performs well in a team environment? As discussed in chapter 4, the better job we do of identifying and defining teamwork attributes, the more likely we are to make good staffing decisions.

While much of the discussion of *teamwork orientation* has been very general and platitudinous in nature, some specific attributes are beginning to emerge from both practice and research. The Interpersonal Skill Dimensions identified in chapter 4, along with the KSA Requirements for Teamwork in chapter 7, provide an excellent starting point for identifying specific, team-oriented attributes.[2] Other attributes that could easily be added to the list include openness to learning, creativity, conscientiousness, knowledge of various quality tools and methods, broader and higher-order technical skills, and a host of leadership-related skills historically considered the exclusive province of management (planning, scheduling, assigning work, and so on). Thus, a fairly comprehensive list of team-oriented attributes or skills begins to emerge (Exhibit 13.1).

While this general listing or taxonomy of team orientation attributes is possible, wide differences can be expected in terms of inclusion or emphasis depending upon the particular setting. Thus, we encourage readers to develop their own attribute profile based upon their specific situation. Such a profile is likely to be influenced by a number of factors including type of team, maturity of the team, and the organization's philosophy and values.

Type of Team. The first issue has to do with the type of team in question. For example, an attribute profile for a problem-solving team setting may emphasize skills related to reengineering, process improvement, quality tools and methods, customer orientation, and creative thinking. On the other hand, the profile for a self-directed team would likely stress responsibility and accountability (self-starter), ability to learn new and varied tasks, sensitivity to others, and the skill (or even willingness) to take on what has typically been the purview of management (planning and scheduling, performance feedback, troubleshoot problems and equipment). This concept will be explored further later in the chapter.

Team Maturity. The second consideration is the maturity of the team. Maturity is defined not in terms of how long teams have been in place, but rather the extent to which they have developed and taken on greater responsibility.[3] For example, in one of the organizations where the authors consult, problem-solving groups have taken major strides in their process improvement efforts during the last three

Exhibit 13.1. Possible attributes of the concept of teamwork.

Teamwork attributes

Michael J. Stevens and Michael A. Campion (Teamwork KSA requirements)

1. Conflict resolution
2. Collaborative problem solving
3. Communication
4. Goal setting and performance management
5. Planning and task coordination

Joyce Hogan (Interpersonal skills)

6. Sensitivity to others
7. Flexibility
8. Leading
9. Trust and confidence
10. Consistency
11. Responsibility and accountability
12. Communication

Others

13. Openness to learning
14. Creative thinking
15. Customer orientation
16. Conscientiousness
17. Knowledge of quality methods and tools

---

years. Starting with very small and easy projects (for example, making a form more user-friendly), they now engage in major reengineering efforts requiring rather sophisticated skills in technology, process mapping, and experimental design. Similarly, as self-directed teams mature, they are likely to take on increased responsibility such as budgeting, team member selection, and even counseling and disciplining team members.

Philosophy and Values. Finally, each organization differs in terms of its total quality values and philosophy. As previously discussed, no two total quality efforts are the same, and those differences should be reflected in your team attributes profile.

Selection Versus Placement Versus Volunteers

The topic of team staffing is also somewhat clouded by the realities of the situation in terms of the sources or input for team membership. Can we truly select individuals for team membership or are we constrained in terms of team make-up by factors beyond our control? Witness the following three scenarios.

Scenario One: True Selection. This scenario represents the ideal in terms of a clean slate for staffing. Here the organization is starting from the ground floor and is able to select those individuals most likely to function effectively in a team setting. The best example of this would be a startup plant in a new location using self-directed work teams as the basic work unit. Our 3M cohesion case provides such an example.

Scenario Two: Placement. In this situation, the organization has determined it should pilot self-directed work teams for a particular unit, or it has decided to begin using large-scale process improvement or reengineering teams. In both these cases, the firm can still systematically screen individuals for team membership, but it is constrained in terms of placing individuals from their present workforce.

Scenario Three: Volunteers. This scenario represents the far end of the continuum in terms of staffing for teams. Here, the organization has determined that it wants to reinforce the concept of teamwork in the organization and begin using employee involvement or problem-solving groups to improve its processes and customer satisfaction. Everyone is given the opportunity to participate (training). Problem-solving groups are typically comprised of volunteers.

While the possible listing of such scenarios is endless, they do point to many of the constraints associated with team selection. However, none of the possible scenarios diminishes the need for careful and systematic team staffing. Indeed, we would argue that each situation offers its own unique opportunity to improve staffing decisions. For example, if you are opening a new store, building a new plant, or relocating your business, use that opportunity to select a team-oriented workforce. Don't hire your employees and then hope to shape them into a cohesive team.

Scenario two also offers considerable potential for improving success. The self-directed work group pilot example is much more likely to be successful if team membership is based on systematic selection.

Most of the self-directed, work team failures that we are aware of made no effort to systematically select team members. Their assumption was that the transition could easily be made with existing employees. Similarly, the make-up of large-scale process improvement or reengineering teams can benefit from a more carefully thought-out screening process. The right mix of technical and personality characteristics can do much to ensure the success of such teams.

Even scenario three has implications for staffing. The organization embarking on the total quality voyage with the increased use of teams needs to closely examine its entry-level staffing practices and begin using tools to screen for team-oriented employees. If your organization espouses teamwork and group problem solving but does nothing to select for team-related attributes, then you are missing the point of this book.

Selection Tools

Because previous chapters have dealt with complete descriptions of the various selection instruments or tools, this section will briefly summarize the instruments most frequently used for hiring in team-oriented environments.

The Big Three

What staffing tools are used by quality-oriented organizations to select team members? To answer that question, we examined several books and articles on teams, as well as our own knowledge of such selection procedures (for example, consulting, professional conferences, open-ended survey comments). In particular, we carefully reviewed the 20 selection processes described in the book, *Inside Teams*.[4] Results of that review clearly showed that three tools were used by the majority of benchmark firms. They included job-specific knowledge and aptitude tests (such as math, reading, and mechanical comprehension); team-oriented simulations; and behavioral interviews. While these tools have been discussed previously, we will illustrate their applications at the end of the chapter by describing selection procedures used at the Toyota Manufacturing plant in Georgetown, Kentucky.

Other results of our review included the finding that selection processes typically took a day or more to complete (some as many as three days), and most used a multiple-hurdle or funnel approach beginning with tests and ending with a behavioral interview. Additionally, many of the examined firms used RJPs as an integral part of their staffing processes and skills inventories to screen down the applicant pool.

Realistic Job Previews

RJPs in particular show promise for use in team settings. Requirements often change dramatically in team settings and not everyone is prepared to function effectively in those situations. This is particularly true for self-directed work teams where members are expected to broaden their technical skills considerably (perform multiple tasks) and take on responsibilities for many of the duties previously performed by management.

For example, the Cambridge plant of the Colgate-Palmolive Company instituted an RJP when it found that some team members had unrealistic expectations concerning advancement opportunities at the plant.[5] Sprint–United Telephone also uses RJPs as part of its staffing process. Sprint is piloting the use of RJPs at one of its Ohio locations. Sprint is particularly interesting because it incorporates its RJPs into the interview process where interview teams include peer members. It is during these peer interviews that RJP information is communicated to the candidate. Sprint feels that RJP information will have more impact on the candidate if it is communicated by an individual engaged in the same work the applicant will be expected to perform if hired. Sprint prepares peers for this task by training them in the interview process. Sprint also requires an interview and RJP role play before allowing peers to conduct interviews.[6]

Knowledge of Teamwork

In chapter 7 we briefly discussed a knowledge of teamwork test developed by researchers Campion and Stevens for measuring the five teamwork requirements outlined in Exhibit 13.1. Exhibit 13.2 provides example items from that test. Campion and Stevens have conducted two studies investigating the reliability and criterion-related validity of the test. One study was conducted in a startup of a southeastern pulp mill designed around self-managed work teams. Participants in the study ($n = 70$) were current employees applying for jobs in the new facility. The teamwork KSA test correlated .44 with ratings

Exhibit 13.2. Sample items from the teamwork KSA test.

---

1. Suppose that you find yourself in an argument with several coworkers about who should do a very disagreeable but routine task. Which of the following would likely be the most effective way to resolve this situation?
   a. Have your supervisor decide, because this would avoid any personal bias.
   *b. Arrange for a rotating schedule so everyone shares the chore.
   c. Let the workers who show up earliest choose on a first-come, first-served basis.
   d. Randomly assign a person to do the task and don't change it.

2. Your team wants to improve the quality and flow of the conversations among its members. Your team should:
   *a. Use comments that build upon and connect to what others have said.
   b. Set up a specific order for everyone to speak and then follow it.
   c. Let team members with more to say determine the direction and topic of conversation.
   d. Do all of the above.

3. Suppose you are presented with the following types of goals. You are asked to pick one for your team to work on. Which would you choose?
   a. An easy goal to ensure the team reaches it, thus creating a feeling of success.
   b. A goal of average difficulty so the team will be somewhat challenged, but successful without too much effort.
   *c. A difficult and challenging goal that will stretch the team to perform at a high level, but attainable so that effort will not be seen as futile.
   d. A very difficult, or even impossible goal so that even if the team falls short, it will at least have a very high target to aim for.

Source: Michael J. Stevens, "Teamwork-KSA Test," 1993. Reprinted by permission.

---

of subsequent on-the-job teamwork performance ($p < .05$); with ratings of on-the-job technical performance ($r = .56$, $p < .05$) and with ratings of overall job performance ($r = .53$, $p < .05$). A second study conducted in two northeastern cardboard box plants ($n = 72$) believed to be "farther along in the transition from an individual to a team-based system," replicated the positive relationship between the test and ratings of job performance. In that study, the teamwork KSA test was correlated with subsequent teamwork ratings provided by supervisors ($r = .21$, $p < .05$) and ratings by peers ($r = .23$, $p < .05$).[7] The teamwork KSA test provides one more example of the quality-related assessment tools emerging in the professional literature and available to improve staffing decisions.

Types of Teams

To this point, we have addressed the topic of teams and teamwork in general terms. We will now turn our attention to discussing two types of teams and what that means in terms of staffing.

Problem-Solving Teams

Problem-solving or project teams are what many of us think of when discussing teams in a quality setting. These are groups brought together for a particular purpose, such as a process improvement team, quality action team, cross-functional team, reengineering team, or a quality control circle team. Generally speaking, these teams devote only a relatively minor portion of their time to team activities and usually disband or reconfigure once a project has concluded. Exceptions do exist, however, and include some quality control circles that function for years, dealing with different issues, problems, or reengineering efforts where team members are required to devote full or near full time to reengineering initiatives.

At least four important roles emerge when discussing problem-solving teams. Each should be carefully examined when discussing selection.

- **Team leader:** One who manages the team, facilitates group sessions, and acts as a liaison with other parties.

- **Team members:** Those who attend group sessions, learn new quality-related skills, and become actively involved in improving quality.

- **Quality consultant:** One who provides the quality-related technical skills to advise and support group efforts.

- **Support personnel:** Those who provide the managerial and organizational support necessary to ensure team success.

Exhibit 13.3 presents some of the general criteria for effective team leadership. Both the tasks/duties and attributes of effective team leaders are provided. The lists for Exhibit 13.3 and subsequent figures were taken from, or inferred from, a review of a number of books and articles on quality teams, as well as our own experiences with such teams.[8] The tasks/duties and attributes listed are not meant to be all-inclusive nor do they apply to all organizations or team leader roles. For example, some teams distinguish between the role of leader and the role of facilitator. Also, the role of team leader in a reengi-

Exhibit 13.3. Team leader job description and specifications (attributes).

Tasks or duties associated with being a team leader.	Attributes associated with success of team leaders.
<ul><li>Manages or runs the team</li><li>Develops agendas for meetings</li><li>Coordinates and schedules meetings</li><li>Facilitates team sessions</li><li>Handles logistical details</li><li>Keeps the group on track (both content and process)</li><li>Orchestrates all team activities</li><li>Handles or assigns administrative details</li><li>Mediates conflicts</li><li>Is liaison with other departments, steering committees, sponsors, and so on</li></ul>	<ul><li>Knowledge of quality concepts and theories</li><li>Cares about people and respects them as individuals</li><li>Skill in facilitating teams</li><li>Skill in written and oral communication such as negotiation, persuasion, presentations</li><li>Knowledge of systematic problem-solving techniques and quality tools</li><li>Willing to seek out education, training, and development opportunities for team members and self</li><li>Ability to work effectively with people in other departments and at higher levels in the organization</li><li>Skill in resolving interpersonal conflicts</li><li>Time available to successfully manage team activities.</li></ul>

neering effort is more likely to be one of comember rather than leader.

The purpose of Exhibit 13.3 is to show that success as a team leader depends on a number of tasks/duties and associated leader attributes. The probability of team success is directly related to the degree that the leader possesses these important attributes. And selection, as well as training, can contribute to that success. In fact, while some of the attributes are easily trained, many are not, and some have nothing to do with training. How do you train somebody to "have enough authority to make changes" or ensure that individuals "have the time available necessary to devote to the team effort."

The reader is also reminded that CIs can be used to describe important team behavior and provide the basis for developing job-related interview questions (see Exhibit 13.4).

Similarly, Exhibit 13.5 describes the role of the team member along with the attributes associated with being a successful member of the team. Take, for example, the listed attributes *conscientiousness* and *dependability.* Anyone familiar with problem-solving groups knows that much of the real work of teams occurs outside the group setting. Data need to be collected and analyzed, possible problem causes need to be investigated, benchmark studies need to be conducted, and so on. Without group members willing and able to carry out such activities on a timely basis, groups flounder and eventually fail.

We contend that many groups fail to meet expectations because members have been assigned to these groups with little thought being given to the success attributes described in Exhibit 13.5. Who would not argue that some serious thought should be given to the make-up of problem-solving teams? Careful selection of both the group leader and group members can do much to improve the effectiveness of such groups. Attempts at systematic selection are particularly important for initial or pilot efforts used as demonstration projects. Lack of success stories in the beginning stages of a quality initiative will most likely dampen the enthusiasm of others being introduced to the new way of doing things.

Quality professionals and managers involved in the formation of problem-solving groups need to pay greater attention to the make-up of such groups. They need to apply the concepts discussed in this book to identify the necessary quality attributes of team leaders, team members, and quality consultants (see Exhibit 13.6) and then use that information to systematically select or assign group membership.

Exhibit 13.4. CIs and alternate question formats for the attribute team leadership skills.

CIs	Alternate question formats	Follow-up questions and probes
Setting: The group was wrestling with a problem for which there was no clear solution. One of the members suggested a unique—but costly—idea. **Behavior:** The team leader said, "Let's not toss that idea aside. Instead, let's say we could get the necessary funds. How would this solve the problem?" **Result:** The group continued to work on the idea and eventually pulled out a workable solution from what was originally an impractical idea. **Setting:** A critical product defect was being discussed in a team meeting. A member of the team kept getting the group off track. **Behavior:** The team leader walked over the posted agenda and said, "Bill, I think we agree with you that we should take that question on—and we will later—for now we must deal with the issue we've posted on the agenda." **Result:** Bill agreed and the meeting got back on track.	**Education and training** Please describe any seminars or workshops that you have taken in team building, group problem solving, or related topics. **Work experience** Describe your experiences working in a work team or task force situation. **Specific knowledge questions** Describe the basic ground rules for brainstorming in a group situation. **Hypothetical situation question** Suppose you are facilitating a problem-solving meeting and the group continually gets off track. What steps would you take to assure that the group stays on track? **Behavioral consistency question** Sometimes a specific individual will dominate a group discussion, cut others off, and generally reduce the effectiveness of the group. Tell me about the most difficult situation where you had to deal with such a person. **Self-appraisal analysis** Describe your level of skill in leading a problem-solving group. **References** Please tell me about _____'s role on your quality task force.	• Tell me more about how it dealt with (specific topic). • What are some of the main points that you have found useful? • How have you applied what you learned in work situations? • Which groups were effective? Why? • What was your role in these groups? • Describe a situation in which you used the brainstorming technique. How did it work? • How would you describe that to the group? • What reaction would you expect? • What if someone continued to take the discussion off track? • What did you do? Did you confront the person? • How well did your strategy work? • How did the person respond? • What did you learn from the situation? • What, if anything, would you do differently if faced with a similar situation? • Which positive behaviors do you have? • Which need further development and practice? • Tell me more about the kind of roles she took on in the task force. • What skills should she work on?

Exhibit 13.5. Team member job description and specifications (attributes).

Tasks or duties associated with being a team member.	Attributes associated with success of team members.
• Attend team sessions • Actively participate and contribute • Learn new skills (such as quality concepts, problem solving, quality tools) • Carry out assignments between meetings	• Knowledge of job and operations (understand present processes) • Ability to work comfortably in a team setting (identify with group, active involvement) • Dependability (willing and able to attend sessions, complete assignments) • Basic math and reading skills • Openness to learning, development, and retraining • Creative (imaginative, broadminded) • Skill in oral communication • Conscientiousness (thorough, responsible, hardworking) • Flexible/adaptable (open to change) • Credible with coworkers • Active listening

Exhibit 13.6. Quality consultant job description and specifications (attributes).

Tasks or duties associated with being a quality consultant.	Attributes associated with success of a quality consultant.
• Trains group leaders (and sometimes group members) in the basics of quality, group problem solving, quality tools, and so on. • Acts as a resource person for the group	• Knowledge of quality principles • Knowledge of various quality tools and methods • Understanding of group dynamics • Ability to develop and administer training

Self-Directed Teams

Unlike a problem-solving team that meets occasionally to work on a task or problem, the self-directed work team is an intact and ongoing work group that essentially manages itself with very little, if any, direct supervision. These groups are responsible for the planning, directing, controlling, and "doing" activities of their own work process. As such, they are responsible for the allocation of work, quality control, product and process improvement, and dealing with day-to-day problems and issues. Many self-directed groups help screen and select applicants to fill team vacancies and some groups are even given responsibility for counseling or disciplining team members when required. In short, these teams epitomize the concept of empowerment in the workplace.

The modern version of self-directed work teams has its roots in the job redesign and sociotechnical theories of the 1950s. A series of studies undertaken in British coal mines from 1948 to 1958 and later experiments in Sweden by the Volvo Corporation demonstrated the need to view jobs in the context of the individual's needs and social work systems.[9] Since those early studies, a number of firms, including 3M, General Motors (Saturn), Pitney Bowes, Procter & Gamble, Corning, Kodak, Steelcase, General Electric, and Federal Express, have instituted some form of self-directed work teams. In a recent survey of 476 *Fortune* 1000 companies, published by the American Quality and Productivity Center, results showed that about 7 percent of the current workplace was organized into self-directed teams, and 50 percent of the companies questioned said they would be utilizing this concept in the years ahead.[10] Will this trend continue? More than likely, because the bottom line results have, for the most part, been very positive and include cost savings from reduced headcounts; increased levels of employee satisfaction and morale; improvements in productivity, quality, and customer service; improved participation and communication; and higher levels of problem solving and innovation.

It should also be mentioned that much of the impetus for using such teams has come from the quality movement. The use of self-directed work teams, as well as problem-solving teams, is totally consistent with the concept of total quality. Indeed, teamwork, along with the basic principles of customer focus and continuous improvement, is the foundation of most total quality initiatives. The use of self-directed work teams becomes a natural step for many organizations that adopt a total quality philosophy.

Before discussing the staffing issues associated with using such teams, we would like to point out that any firm seriously considering the formation of self-directed work groups should begin its study of the concept by reading the book *Empowered Teams*.[11] The book provides practical hands-on advice on what makes self-directed work teams successful and how to implement them in an organizational setting. It also contains the results from a survey of more than 500 organizations using self-directed teams. The book is particularly impressive from our viewpoint because of its coverage of staffing-related issues. The book's authors conclude, and we agree, that the attributes required for success as a self-directed team member differ substantially from those traditionally needed. Failure to match the individual with the team environment is a mistake. We also recommend the book *Inside Teams* for a description of how 20 benchmark firms are using teams to improve quality and performance.[12]

Exhibit 13.7 presents some of the primary tasks or duties associated with being a self-directed team member, along with a list of attributes considered critical for team success. Additional tasks typically

Exhibit 13.7. Self-directed team member job description and specifications (attributes).

Tasks or duties associated with being a team member	Attributes associated with success of team members
• Carry out day-to-day work tasks and assignments	• Flexibility/adaptability (openness to change)
• Learn a number of tasks and skills	• Teamwork orientation (group identification involvement)
• Improve work processes and procedures	• Skill in relating to others (listening to others, developing cooperative relationships, and dealing with conflict)
• Troubleshoot problems	
• Develop work schedules and assignments	
• Train other team members	• Conscientiousness (thorough, responsible, hardworking)
• Select new team members	• Openness to learning, development, and retraining
• Provide performance feedback information	• Skill in problem solving
• Meet scheduling and work demands	• Planning and organizing
	• Oral communication
• Interact with others outside the group (suppliers, internal and external customers, other functions or units)	• Reading comprehension
	• Technical/professional proficiency
	• Judgment

done by team leaders include preparing and managing cost budgets, making compensation decisions, handling performance appraisals, and dealing with individual performance problems.[13] However, because the team leader is typically selected from the group or handled on a rotating basis, we have not created a description for that position.

Of particular interest on the list of attributes are the characteristics flexibility/adaptability and teamwork orientation. Research on team effectiveness has shown that these two member attributes are positively correlated with team effectiveness.[14] In particular, "flexibility" was found to be related to manager judgments of effectiveness and teamwork ("preference for group work") related to employee satisfaction.

Case Study

Selecting the Right People at Toyota

One of the largest and most celebrated examples of staffing in a team-oriented setting was carried out at the Toyota Motor Manufacturing plant in Georgetown, Kentucky.[15] Toyota was faced with the challenge of hiring more than 2000 employees at its startup factory to fill three job categories—team member, team leader, and group leader—for both production and skilled jobs. Toyota wanted a selection system that would identify individuals with a unique combination of quality-oriented attributes that reflected Toyota's *Kaizen* philosophy (flexibility, diligence and perseverance, problem solving, initiative, oral communication).

The selection system used at Toyota was developed by Development Dimensions International (DDI) and included several phases or steps, each of which narrowed the applicant pool. These stages included

- **Phase 1: Advertising and recruitment.** Jobs were advertised at all 28 employment offices in Kentucky.

- **Phase 2: Orientation and application process.** Applicants completed application forms and were given a fact sheet describing Toyota's values and expectations. Candidates also viewed an orientation video explaining Toyota's management philosophy (Kaizen) and an overview of the selection process. More than 60,000 applications were completed.

- **Phase 3: Technical skills assessment.** Every applicant took a battery of written tests including the General Aptitude Test Battery (GATB), a job fit inventory, and tests that measured specific technical skills. Approximately 90 percent of the applicants were screened out at this point.

- **Phase 4: Interpersonal assessment center.** Candidates next went through eight hours of assessment by participating in four different simulations designed to elicit behavior related to such attributes as decision making, interpersonal communication, problem solving, and process improvement. Top performers moved on to the next phase.

- **Phase 5: Leadership assessment center (LAC).** Remaining applicants participated in three exercise simulations (in-basket, employee development, and scheduling) used to measure their decision-making and interpersonal skills unique to leadership.

- **Phase 6: Targeted selection interviewing.** The final phase was comprised of interviews conducted by a team of Toyota human resources and line managers using a special targeted selection interviewing technique similar to the behavioral interviewing approach previously described. Those individuals passing this final phase were given a physical exam including a test for substance abuse. Recommendations for hire were made at this point. An applicant's view of this demanding process is shown in Exhibit 13.8.

The Toyota case exemplifies many of the key concepts discussed throughout the book. That includes highly favorable SRs, staffing based upon identified critical attributes, and the use of varied screening and selection tools in a sequential fashion. The results have been very positive in terms of both low turnover and absenteeism rates, as well as high productivity and quality.

Summary

The use of teams is integral to most total quality initiatives. And the success of those teams depends to a large extent on the attributes members bring to the team setting. The time spent systematically selecting leaders, members, and support personnel will pay high dividends in terms of the effectiveness of those groups.

Exhibit 13.8. Applicant's perception of Toyota's selection process.

AN INSIDER'S VIEW:
Going Through the System

I was part of the first group that went through the selection process. I have to tell you, at times I wondered if it would ever end!

But a funny thing happened along the way. I noticed how there were fewer and fewer people as I went through the process. I began to feel a real sense of accomplishment. I recognized that Toyota was taking its work force seriously, that the company was going to end up with high caliber, motivated people . . . that if I was hired I'd be part of a group that was "beyond the ordinary."

Some of the process was downright fun. I got to know many of the other applicants. Over time we developed a real sense of camaraderie. And I enjoyed many of the simulations, especially the ones that were "hands on." They taught me a lot about myself and gave me a clear sense of what the company was looking for.

What impressed me the most about the process was its fairness. Everywhere you looked, the treatment was equal. Everyone experienced the same challenge.

I'm glad I persisted. Now I'm working with a group of people who really participate and engage in creative action. Without question, the quality of our people is unmatched.

—Bill Constantino, group leader
  Plastics Section
  Toyota Motor Manufacturing, U.S.A.

Reprinted with the permission of *HRMagazine,* published by the Society for Human Resource Management, Alexandria, Va.

Notes

1. Alan Farnham, "America's Most Admired Company," *Fortune* (February 7, 1994): 52.

2. Joyce Hogan and Jared Lock, "A Taxonomy of Interpersonal Skills for Business Interactions," presentation at the Tenth Annual Conference of the Society for Industrial and Organizational Psychology, Orlando, Fla., May 19–21, 1995; Michael J. Stevens and Michael A. Campion, "The Knowledge, Skill, and Ability Requirements for Teamwork: Implications for Human Resource Management," *Journal of Management* 20, no. 2 (1994): 503–530.

3. Richard S. Wellins, William C. Byham, and George R. Dixon, *Inside Teams: How 20 World-Class Organizations Are Winning Through Teamwork* (San Francisco: Jossey-Bass, 1994), 15.

4. Ibid.

5. Ibid., 167, 177.

6. Leora Schmiat, Sprint–United Telephone, personal communication, described with permission.

7. Stevens and Campion, "The Knowledge, Skill, and Ability Requirements for Teamwork."

8. P. R. Scholtes, *The Team Handbook* (Madison, Wis.: Joiner and Associates, 1988); Michael Doyle and David Straus, *How to Make Meetings Work* (New York: Berkley, 1976); Michael Hammer and James Champy, *Reengineering the Corporation* (New York: Harper Business, 1993); Jon R. Katzenbach and Douglas K. Smith, *The Wisdom of Teams* (New York: Harper Business, 1993); D. Keith Denton, "Building a Team," *Quality Progress* (October 1992): 87–91. See also Michael A. Campion, Gina J. Medsker, and A. Catherine Higgs, "Relations Between Work Group Characteristics and Effectiveness: Implications for Designing Effective Work Groups," *Personnel Psychology* 46 (1993): 823–847.

9. Eric Trist, "The Evolution of Sociotechnical Systems," occasional paper, Ontario Quality of Working Life Centre, June 1981; D. Katz and R. L. Kahn, *The Social Psychology of Organization,* 2nd ed. (New York: Wiley, 1978).

10. Ibid.

11. Richard S. Wellins, William C. Byham, and Jeanne M. Wilson, *Empowered Teams* (San Francisco: Jossey-Bass, 1991).

12. Wellins, Byham, and Dixon, *Inside Teams: How 20 World-Class Organizations Are Winning Through Teamwork.*

13. Wellins, Byham, and Wilson, *Empowered Teams.*

14. Campion, Medsker, and Higgs, "Relations Between Work Group Characteristics and Effectiveness: Implications for Designing Effective Work Groups."

15. Chuck Consention, John Allen, and Richard Wellins, "Choosing the Right People," HR Magazine (March 1990).

chapter **14**

Emerging Issues: Downsizing and the Contingent Workforce

Overview

This chapter will address two of the primary staffing issues facing the new organization: downsizing the organization and the contingent workforce. In particular, we will discuss how these issues affect quality and then provide some recommendations for downsizing the operations of a quality organization and how to most effectively utilize contingent workers.

Introduction

The Engineering Services Group (ESG) is a full-service engineering consulting firm that provides project engineering services and support personnel for a number of organizations, primarily automotive related. Due in part to the recent upswing in auto sales, ESG has experienced substantial growth and was recently listed as one of the fastest growing privately owned companies in Michigan! As such, ESG reflects a growing segment of the workforce—contingent workers. ESG is an interesting case, not because it provides contract engineers to the auto industry, and not because it is experiencing growth, but rather because it has begun to acquire its own cadre of contingent workers. ESG, like many firms, needs personnel to handle large projects and meet its customers' needs. But it realizes that the cyclical nature of the automotive industry may necessitate the need to downsize its own workforce. In an effort to address this eventuality, ESG has begun to develop a list of retirees and independent personnel who are willing to work for short periods on an as-needed basis.

This need for a contingent workforce firm to develop its own contingent workforce illustrates rather dramatically the changes that are occurring in the way organizations manage their staffing needs. In the words of the old rock song, "Times, they are a changin'." As the previously discussed *Fortune* article in chapter 4 points out, "Today's organization is rapidly being transformed from a structure built on jobs into a field of work needing to be done."[1] The future will no doubt bring some rather strange configurations of internal and external workers who come together for some task or project, and then disband only to be reconfigured for another purpose. These comings and goings of workers, along with the rightsizing of the organization, will create a number of unique and challenging problems for the quality organization. The management expert Peter F. Drucker clearly makes this point by stating, "businesses will undergo more and more radical restructuring in the 1990s than at any time since the modern corporate organization first evolved in the 1920s."[2]

Downsizing in the Context of Quality Improvement

Q. Does quality improvement lead to downsizing?
A. Upper management needs to face this reality head-on because it does happen.
—Joseph M. Juran[3]

A company must make it clear that no one will lose his job because of improvement in productivity.
—W. Edwards Deming[4]

While not always the case, quality interventions such as process improvement, reengineering, and lean management are likely to result in workforce reductions in the affected areas. In addition, changes in the marketplace, downswings in the economy, and other competitive and economic factors can create the need for downsized operations. Preparing for that likelihood should be a critical component of the staffing process. Deciding how the workforce reduction will be accomplished—who should be retained, and how displaced workers as well as remaining employees should be dealt with—is a critical staffing issue that increasingly needs to be addressed.

Our survey results show that 63.9 percent of the respondents have downsized their workforces in the last five years. While these results are significant, they are somewhat lower than data that indicate more than 85 percent of *Fortune* 1000 firms downsized their white-collar workforces between 1987 and 1992.[5] And despite recent record profits, companies continue to lay off employees. Witness the number of U.S. jobs that were eliminated each year from 1990 through 1994.

- 1990   (recession year)   315,000
- 1991   (recession year)   555,000
- 1992   (recession year)   275,000
- 1993   625,000
- 1994   515,000[6]

The onset of the recession in 1990 gave fresh urgency to the drive to limit labor costs and boost efficiency. The downsizing movement hit its stride. General Motors was one of the more dramatic examples of downsizing with 74,000 jobs and 21 plants (one-fifth of General Motors' North American holdings) being eliminated. Other companies followed suit: Boeing cut 30,000 jobs; Sears 50,000; AT&T 83,000; and IBM 85,000. Many of these companies had previously had a no-layoff policy.[7]

Today, profitable companies are still in the midst of major layoffs. Mobil, Procter & Gamble, Xerox, Sara Lee, US Air, Martin Marietta, Cigna, American Airlines, R. J. Reynolds Tobacco, Dow Chemical, and Banc One, among others, have announced layoffs in the last year or so. Procter & Gamble, for example, plans to drop 13,000 jobs and 30 plants over a four-year period. Xerox, despite its profitability, has laid out plans to cut 10,000 jobs within four years.[8]

While many of those reductions can be attributed to companies experiencing hard times or efforts to reduce costs, a significant portion of the downsizing efforts has direct ties to what we generally refer to as quality improvement. For example, the five-year MIT study that resulted in the book *The Machine That Changed the World* describes in detail the need for manufacturing companies to embrace what they refer to as *lean production*.

Lean production is lean because it uses less of everything compared with mass production—half the human effort in the factory *[authors' emphasis], half the manufacturing space, half the investment in tools, half the engineering hours to develop a new product in half the time.*[9]

In addition to lean production, Hammer and Champy, in their much touted book, *Reengineering the Corporation,* provide the reader with example after example of reductions in the workforce as a result of reengineering efforts.[10] They describe how IBM's Credit Operation replaced its specialists with generalists resulting in one generalist doing the job previously done by four specialists. They also report that Ford Motor Company now has 125 people involved in vendor payment instead of the 500 who previously performed that process. Finally, they describe how, in 1988, Taco Bell had approximately 350 area supervisors controlling 1800 restaurants. That has changed to just over 100 market managers responsible for almost 2300 company-owned restaurants.

The quality literature is laden with such examples of improved operations and processes with the admonition to *do more with less.* However, these improvements often create an HR management and staffing dilemma. On one hand, we ask managers and employees to actively participate and embrace the new quality paradigm. We encourage them to systematically look for ways to improve the efficiency and effectiveness of the organization by standardizing, error proofing, and streamlining their work processes. But in so doing, managers often eliminate the need for certain jobs or positions, at times even their own. So, how do we deal with this unpleasant situation? How can downsizing be done most effectively? Following are some of the things we have learned about downsizing an organization.

Expected Outcomes

For starters, it helps to understand why organizations downsize their workforces and the envisioned benefits they hope to receive as a result. Some of the frequently given expected outcomes include

- Lower overhead and reduced expenses
- Less bureaucracy
- A more empowered workforce
- Faster and more effective decision making

- Smoother, less distorted communication

- Greater entrepreneurship

- Quicker response to competitors' actions

- Quicker diffusion of new ideas

- Greater interdepartmental cooperation

- Increased quality and productivity

- An organization that adapts quickly to changes in the external environment

Who can argue with efforts aimed at achieving these outcomes, especially when the reality is that, to survive in today's global and competitive environment, the organization must be lean and adaptive? Even that giant bureaucratic monolith we call *government* is beginning to see the light. Based on the "Gore Report on Reinventing Government," the federal government has plans to eliminate 252,000 jobs (or 12 percent) from its 2.2 million employee payroll.[11] Layer after layer of corporate fat and nonvalue-added employees can no longer be tolerated. Employees must be truly empowered to make decisions and satisfy their customers. This cannot be accomplished when a manager's span of control is four or five employees. A lean organization can facilitate and encourage employees to accept greater responsibility and ownership. It also allows the organization to be increasingly flexible in an ever-changing environment.

Actual Outcomes

While the intended outcomes of downsizing are laudable, the actual results are not always so positive. A 1991 survey of 1005 firms conducted by the Wyatt consulting firm found that the majority of restructuring efforts fail to achieve their intended goals. For example, 71 percent of the firms surveyed gave increased productivity as one of their objectives but only 22 percent of those firms felt that the goal had been accomplished.[12] Another study conducted by the Society for Human Resource Management found that more than half of the 1468 downsizing firms indicated that productivity had deteriorated as a result of downsizing.[13] Polls conducted by Right Associates and the American Management Association (AMA)[14] have found similar reasons for concern when downsizing. The AMA study found that approximately half of the firms were poorly prepared for the downsizing initiative and the myriad problems created by dismantling the organization. The Right Associates poll found that the great majority of senior managers in these firms felt that morale, trust, and productivity had deteriorated as a result of downsizing. Thus, the actual outcomes often include the following:

- Declines in worker productivity

- Low morale and motivation

- Unquenchable thirst for information

- Employees that become narrow-minded, self-absorbed, and risk aversive

- The loss of critical employees

- Diminished public image and relations

- Lawsuits by disgruntled ex-employees

- Decreased quality and customer service

Additionally, the initial savings from headcount reduction are often negated as the firm is forced to meet work demands by hiring new employees, using contingent workers, or, in some cases, bringing back downsized workers as consultants or contract workers. Finally, many firms that have downsized find themselves having to downsize again. A number of companies that trimmed their workforces not only failed to see a rebound in earnings, but found their ability to compete eroded even further. These negative side effects of downsizing diminish the organization's ability to compete in the marketplace and create a downward spiral that is difficult to recover from.

These less than sterling results have led some researchers and practitioners to paint a picture of gloom and doom for firms that engage in downsizing efforts. However, the fact is that many firms are doing an excellent job of streamlining their operations and reducing headcount. Ford Motor Company's effort to cut the fat in the 1980s helps explain the company's record profits in recent years. TRW, Pepsi, and Eastman-Kodak are other examples of firms that have experienced positive results from their efforts to stay competitive with fewer people. The question then becomes, "What practices separate those firms that have successfully downsized from those who have experienced negative results?"

The How, When, Where, and Who of Downsizing

To this point, we have discussed the need for a lean and flexible organization that adapts quickly to changes in the external environment (customer needs, competition, market conditions, and so on). We have also pointed out that the downsizing experience for many firms has not been positive. Efforts aimed at reducing overhead and cutting fat have not always led to the intended outcomes. So what is it that separates firms that have experienced positive outcomes from those that obtained questionable results or regretted their downsizing initiative? Following are some of the primary lessons learned from those organizations that have effectively downsized their workforces.

Lesson 1: Process Improvement Is the Key. The good news in terms of downsizing is that, as quality professionals, we are on the right track (at least in theory) in terms of our approach to eliminating positions. Experts almost unanimously agree that downsizing is most effective in terms of employee acceptance and positive economic benefits when it is the result of systematic process improvement efforts (doing more with less).

> *For long-term, sustained improvements in efficiency, reductions in headcount need to be viewed as part of a process of continuous improvement that includes organization redesign, along with broad, systematic changes designed to eliminate redundancies, waste, and inefficiency.*[15]

> *The most effective firms [in terms of downsizing], however, engaged in surgical procedures. That is, they identified precisely where redundancy, excess cost, and inefficiencies existed, and they attacked those areas specifically.*[16]

While in theory we are doing things right, the realities of practice are not quite so positive. In our survey of ASQC sustaining members, we asked those who had downsized the question: "To what degree was that reduction in headcount a result of a systematic continuous improvement effort?" Results of that question are presented in Table 14.1 and show that there is much room for improvement. Only 13.5 percent of respondents indicated that the downsizing was mostly or exclusively a result of process improvement, and 57.1 percent reported that reductions in headcount were mostly or exclusively a result of across-the-board headcount. Obviously, much room for improvement exists in the quality community.

Table 14.1. Downsizing as a result of process improvement.

Survey question: To what degree was that reduction in headcount a result of a systematic continuous improvement effort (process changes designed to eliminate redundancies, waste, and inefficiency versus simply a reduction in headcount)?

Response	Percent
Exclusively a result of process improvement	3.2
Mostly a result of process improvement	10.3
Mix of process and across-the-board headcount	29.4
Mostly across-the-board headcount	34.1
Exclusively across-the-board headcount	23.0

$N = 132$

Despite these somewhat discouraging findings, the key remains to systematically improve processes and eliminate those positions that fail to add value to organizational outcomes. The goal becomes one of streamlining, reorganizing, or reengineering the organization so that no position or person is either under- or overutilized. Do not make a 10 percent, across-the-board cut in the workforce and then hope to see the envisioned outcomes materialize. The result will be a lot of frustrated employees trying to do the same amount of work with fewer people. Also, review any proposed reduction in the workforce to ensure that it will not adversely affect the quality of the products or services sold to the customer. In some cases, as previously stated, firms address the increased work load by hiring back the same people they terminated or other individuals (contingent workers) to perform those same duties.

Downsizing should be carried out selectively and over time as a direct result of continuous process improvement and not vice versa. The quality organization should be constantly looking for ways to become lean, but it should be doing so systematically. Exhibit 14.1 provides a starting point for analyzing the fat in your organization.

Lesson 2: Carefully Examine Who Goes and Who Stays. When selecting into the organization, the decision process is, at least in theory, fairly straightforward. Select the best person for the job and organization, and tell the remainder of the candidates, "Thanks but no thanks." These entry-level decisions can get away with paying little attention to the needs and feelings of those rejected ("Don't call us, we'll call you"). But the process of *selection-out* is much more complex. Here, the firm must

Exhibit 14.1. How lean is your company?

It's hard to find a major corporation that hasn't downsized in recent years. But simple reductions in staffing don't make for lean management. Here's a checklist, developed from interviews with executives and consultants, that may tell you if your company needs a diet.

Company characteristic	Analysis
1. Layers of management between CEO and the shop floor	Some companies, such as Ameritech, now have as few as four or five where as many as 12 had been common. More than six is most likely too many.
2. Number of employees managed by the typical executive	At lean companies, spans of control range up to one manager to 30 staffers. A ratio of lower than 1:10 is a warning of arterial sclerosis.
3. Amount of work cut out by your downsizing	Eliminating jobs without cutting out work can bring disaster. Downsizing should be accompanied by at least a 25% reduction in the number of tasks performed. Some lean companies have hit 50%.
4. Skill levels of the surviving management group	Managers must learn to accept more responsibility and to eliminate unneeded work. Have you taught them how?
5. Size of your largest profit center by number of employees	Break down large operating units into smaller profit centers—less than 500 employees is a popular cutoff—to gain the economies of entrepreneurship and offset the burdens of scale.
6. Post-downsizing size of staff at corporate headquarters	The largest layoffs, on a percentage basis, should be at corporate headquarters. It is often the most overstaffed—and the most removed from customers.

Source: John A. Byrne, "Management Belt Tightening the Smart Way," *Business Week/Enterprise* (1993), 35. Reprinted by permission.

balance the sometimes conflicting needs of the organization with those of the employees involved. Issues of fairness, equity, humanity, and even contractual obligations come into play. For example, the fairness or contractual criteria for making decisions might include a policy for a last hired, first fired approach to downsizing. But if that means losing some of the firm's best and brightest, the organization suffers and such criteria become questionable. Conversely, strictly performance-based criteria for retention can lead to extreme levels of dissatisfaction among those who remain, as well as those terminated. Those who keep their jobs become less trusting and loyal, while those terminated may respond with "We'll see you in court."

So how can the firm go about making good selection-out decisions while maintaining some reasonable level of justice? For starters, we contend that much more thought and effort should be put into making systematic and valid selection-out decisions. Every effort should be made to retain those individuals who are able and willing to embrace the quality paradigm. If the purpose of downsizing is to improve the efficiency and effectiveness of the organization, then it becomes self-defeating to keep those employees who add little or no value to organization outcomes.

The literature on downsizing is replete with ways for making downsizing decisions easier and more palatable (early retirement, buyouts, sabbaticals, voluntary terminations, split jobs, and so on). While these approaches definitely have their place, they all fail to address the needs of the organization in terms of retaining a qualified workforce. If, for example, a major league team downsized its operations from a 40-person roster to 30 players in order to become more profitable, would the coach offer an early buyout to an aging pitcher with a 2.50 ERA? Would management allow the team's only .340 hitter to go on some kind of sabbatical? We doubt it, and yet that appears to be the thinking of many organizations that downsize.

Previously in this chapter, we discussed the fact that many efforts at downsizing fail to meet their anticipated outcomes in terms of improved efficiency and cost savings. We contend that one primary reason why these benefits fail to materialize is that poor decisions have been made by the organization in terms of who goes and who stays. Many skilled and knowledgeable employees are lost during downsizing. Is it possible that many of those employees who accept an early buyout are marketable individuals who feel they can easily go elsewhere? Could it be that the person who agrees to split a job with another employee does so with the thought in mind of starting his/her own business (as your new competitor)?

Throughout this book, we have discussed the importance of making good selection and promotion decisions and the payoff associated with such valid decisions. The same holds true for selection-out. In fact, we could easily argue that downsizing and selection-out decisions are even more important than those made upon entry. Given the years of experience and developmental investment, decisions concerning whom to keep become critical to the survival of the firm, particularly if it hopes to operate successfully as a leaner and meaner organization. Employees can no longer be viewed as replaceable parts in the organizational machinery. They need to be viewed as the valuable assets they are.

So, when deciding who goes and who stays, it is back to the basics. Identify those quality attributes considered important to the organization's success, and then make retention decisions based upon those criteria. View each employee's tenure as an extended job trial test where the person is systematically assessed against those quality attributes deemed critical to success. While, ideally, both employees and managers will have embraced the new paradigm, the reality is that many do not. Some fail to develop and broaden their skills. Some employees refuse to join or be involved in problem-solving groups or to make suggestions for improvement. Some are inflexible and resist change of any kind. The downsized and quality-oriented organization cannot afford to retain such employees at the expense of losing individuals who have developed their skills, are flexible, and who are team oriented.

Likewise, managers who fail to accept and practice quality principles are not good bets for retention. In chapter 12, we discussed the Wave Ducker Principle as it applies to leadership and the quality wave. While a little healthy skepticism is acceptable, managers who continue to resist the change to quality should not be rewarded with continued employment. The wave duckers of the organization should be at the top of the "who goes" list.

Lesson 3: Pay Special Attention to Those Employees Who Have Lost Their Jobs. The loss of a job is one of life's major stressors.[17] Only the death of a loved one or failure of a marriage causes more mental tension. The quality organization should recognize that fact and take responsibility for helping the employee adapt to the circumstances created by the loss of employment. Every effort should be made to provide attractive severance packages (pay and benefits) and to make available complete outplacement services (counseling, job search training and support, retirement planning, and so on).

The organization should also carefully examine alternatives to terminating experienced and loyal employees. For example, Hewlett-Packard used a rather creative approach to downsizing one of its operations. Faced with a surplus of 400 employees at its Loveland, Colorado, division, Hewlett-Packard used a relocation, loan, and reclassification strategy to place the majority of its downsized employees. Workers were given the opportunity to choose from the following alternatives.

- *Regional redistribution* where surplus employees moved to other divisions within the region.

- *Relocation* where eligible employees were given priority employment opportunities over nonsurplus employees at other Hewlett-Packard locations.

- *Loan program* where volunteers were loaned to other divisions where a short-term need existed.

- *Reclassification* for those employees who preferred to stay put but were willing to be reclassified, sometimes at lower pay levels.

- *Employee draft* for those highly skilled individuals who could not be easily placed. These individuals became part of a pool for filling available jobs in the region.

- *Voluntary terminations* where Hewlett-Packard implemented voluntary termination incentive packages to those employees interested."[18]

This combination of creative alternatives allowed Hewlett-Packard to successfully place 376 of the 400 displaced workers. In so doing, they were able to meet many personnel shortages in other areas of the firm. Efforts such as these are not only consistent with the quality philosophy but do much to negate the bad press and tarnished corporate image associated with downsizing. Planned downsizing over an extended time period opens up many possibilities for reducing staff without layoffs.

Lesson 4: Successful Downsizers Consider Those Who Remain with the Firm. While the impact of downsizing is more traumatic for the displaced employees, those remaining do not escape the consequences of downsizing. Survivors often experience increased workloads, pay decreases (or no increases), and anxiety about their own future with the firm (waiting for the ax to fall on them). They typically experience decreased loyalty to the firm and often begin updating their resumes and looking for employment elsewhere. In addition, many experience guilt feelings regarding their displaced coworkers. This feeling of self-reproach is so pervasive among employees of downsized organizations that it has been dubbed *survivor's syndrome*. This syndrome presents a great risk because it can cause the employer/employee contract to be weakened and greatly reduce feelings of trust, loyalty, and commitment.

To be effective, the quality organization must recognize that special effort is needed in dealing with those employees who remain. These efforts begin with ongoing and open communication. Survivors should be thoroughly informed as to why the downsizing is necessary and what steps are being taken to become lean and competitive. They should be provided with sound business reasons for the layoffs. "They [executives] should talk to employees as if they were an audience of Wall Street analysts, selling them on the business rationale for the downsizing and convincing them of the business opportunities available once the firm becomes a lean warrior."[19] Extensive communication by top management is necessary to help employees cope with the changes occurring. This often means making employees privy to information previously considered privileged, but it is this kind of information that helps win back their trust and commitment. Finally, that information must be forthright and honest. The rumor mill will run rampant during this transition period. Managers should actively listen for those rumors and be prepared to respond appropriately. While management should remain upbeat and positive, keep in mind that trust will further erode if the organization is not totally honest in its communication. It is not the time to announce that no more layoffs are anticipated when another round of cuts is inevitable.

A second consideration when dealing with survivors is the issue of fairness. While the notion of fairness, much like beauty, is no doubt very much in the eye of the beholder, those who remain must view the downsizing effort as fair and above board. We contend that the key to perceived fairness is the systematic application of lessons 1 and 2. The downsizing effort should be surgical in nature and aimed at streamlining processes and removing fat. Most quality-oriented employees can see the logic of such efforts. Next, employees should understand that decisions concerning who goes and who stays are not arbitrary. When survivors ask the question "Why me?", the answer should be that it is because of their commitment to quality and performance and willingness to contribute to the goals of the organization.

Finally, acceptance of the new organizational structure requires the active participation of those remaining. Survivors must feel that they are active contributors to the new organization and not simply view themselves as victims. Involving employees at all levels in the formulation and implementation of process improvement and competitive positioning efforts will do much to rebuild many of the bridges damaged during downsizing. Work extra hard at communicating and reinforcing successes that do occur.

Lesson 5: Develop Systems That Allow the Organization to Retain Good Employees. Projections are that the United States will experience a severe labor shortage by the year 2000. A number of factors, including declining birth rates and a beleaguered education system, have created the need for skilled workers. The organization of the future can ill-afford the skilled and dedicated workers going out one door while searching for similar employees to come in another. The organization of the future will need to develop more creative mechanisms for retaining skilled and quality-oriented employees. Providing reeducation opportunities, developing skill inventories, establishing dual-career ladders, and providing valued benefits are just a few of the ways that an organization can improve its retention of good employees. The previously described efforts at Hewlett-Packard demonstrate such a creative effort. Similarly, a recent study of firms' family-friendly policies (parental leave, flexible schedules, and child-care assistance) increase the organizational attachment of parents but also increase that attachment for nonparents.[20]

Lesson 6: Carefully Review Those Leaving Versus Those Remaining in Terms of Disparate Impact. The technical and legal standards discussed in chapter 3 should be carefully considered when downsizing. Headcount reductions that cause a disparate impact against a protected group (minority, female, over forty), can result in charges of discrimination. This is particularly true in terms of age discrimination, where management sometimes makes the decision, mistakenly, to rid itself of older, more expensive employees to make room for younger workers. And, if that disparate impact is established or shown, then the burden of proof shifts to the employer who must demonstrate the business necessity or job relatedness of that disparity. The action of downsizing the workforce is viewed in the same way as any other employment practice (selection) and is subject to the same scrutiny by EEO agencies and the courts. The number of firms, including several *Fortune* 500 companies, that have experienced such charges of discrimination point to the need for carefully examining such a possibility.

Summary

Eliminating redundancies and streamlining processes should be the unending goal of every organization. When done correctly, downsizing is not at odds with quality. Rather, it becomes a by-product of the quality initiative. Improving processes and the resultant reduction of staff should become a way of life for the quality organization. As such, the term *rightsizing* becomes more than just a euphemism for *downsizing*. It becomes a way of thinking about how the organization should be staffed. Management should not wait until it is required to downsize in order to survive. The firm of the future must learn to re-define its strategic goals and to restructure itself and its workforce daily, weekly, and monthly, not every three to five years. Indeed, one common criticism of downsizing action is that it should have been taken sooner.

The good news is that those organizations that focus on quality and remain lean and competitive will continue to thrive and require an ongoing influx of new qualified employees. Much like Deming's quality chain reaction, improved quality will lead to a more competitive organization that captures market share and provides jobs.[21] Our own survey results would appear to support that contention. As previously discussed, ASQC sustaining member organizations appear to be doing less downsizing than many other organizations (63.9 percent in the last five years compared to 85 percent for *Fortune* 500 companies). Survey results also indicate that member organizations are less likely to reduce their workforce in the next five years (see Table 14.2). Only 38.8 percent see downsizing as likely. Similarly, those employees and

Table 14.2. Likelihood of downsizing in the future.

Survey question:	How likely is it that your organization will reduce its workforce in the next five years?

Response	Percent
Very likely	23.8
Somewhat likely	15.0
Possibly	19.7
Somewhat unlikely	17.1
Very unlikely	24.4

$N = 206$

managers who embrace quality and continue to grow and develop will do much to help ensure their own job security. There is no question that the workplace is changing. Organizations that adapt to those changes will, however, survive and prosper.

Contingent Workforce

By most estimates, one out of four employed Americans is a contingent worker, and every indication is that the trend toward using such workers will steadily increase. Some analysts predict that, by the year 2000, approximately one-third to one-half of all employees will be contingent workers. The contingent workforce takes many different forms, which include part timers, temps, leased workers, contract employees, students, retired employees, consultants, and volunteers. In some cases, organizations have contracted out entire business functions such as payroll, janitorial, and cafeteria services. These outside firms are viewed as being more capable of performing certain services and doing so at a more reasonable cost to the organization.

Obviously, this trend toward using contingent workers has profound implications for quality efforts and staffing the organization. Does the use of such workers negatively affect quality or can it have a positive effect on quality initiatives? Can these outside employees be expected to fully contribute to the quality initiatives of the organization or is it naive to expect that kind of commitment?

Quality Organizations and the Use of Contingent Workers

Results from our survey indicate that the use of contingent workers is prevalent among quality-oriented organizations. An overwhelming 97.5 percent of the respondents indicated that they use some kind of contingent workers in their organizations. The breakdown of contingent worker usage is shown in Table 14.3. In particular, the use of temps, part-time employees, and students is prevalent. Our survey results also confirm that the trend toward using contingent workers will likely continue (see Table 14.4). Roughly 54 percent of respondents stated that they have increased their use of contingent workers over the last five years, while only 9.5 percent have used fewer contingent workers. And 93 percent expect that trend to remain either the same or actually increase in the next five years. Only 7 percent see a reverse in the trend toward using contingent workers.

Table 14.3. Percent of organizations using each contingent worker category.

Contingent worker category	Use
Part-time employees	74.2
Temporary workers	82.8
Leased workers	19.2
Contract laborers	47.5
Students (such as interns, co-ops, summer hires)	76.8
Retired employees	37.4
Other (such as volunteers, consultants)	5.6

These results are consistent with a recent *Fortune* CEO poll among *Fortune* 500 companies.[22] Executives queried in this survey reported a 44 percent increase in the use of contingent workers compared with 1988 levels, and 88 percent expect that trend to continue.

Impact of the Contingent Workforce on Quality

In a recent *Quality Progress* editorial, Brad Stratton discussed the trend toward using contingent workers and concluded that, "The increasing use of contingent workers is the next big issue in quality."[23] His concern focused on the long-term effects of the contingent workforce on the quality of goods and services and the organization's ability to be truly quality driven. The obvious implication of the Stratton commentary is that the contingent workforce will negatively affect quality improvement efforts. At first blush, that would appear to be true. How can individuals with minimal organization knowledge, little quality-related training, and virtually no loyalty to the firm be expected to positively affect the quality initiatives of the organization?

Table 14.4. The trend of using contingent workers.

	Compared to five years ago, our use of contingent workers has:	In the next five years, our use of contingent workers will likely have:
Increased	54.3	33.8 ⎱ 93
Remained the same	36.2	59.2 ⎰
Decreased	9.5	7

However, the fact that contingent workforces do indeed lower costs, increase flexibility, and provide access to specialized expertise suggests that there is also a very positive side to the use of such workers.

In an effort to shed some light on this important issue, we queried ASQC sustaining member organizations concerning the impact of the contingent workforce on quality. While we expected a negative reaction, the results of the survey were surprising, showing mixed reactions in regards to the use of contingent workers (see Table 14.5). The majority of respondents (55.8 percent) took the middle ground on the use of contingent workers, and that feeling was reflected in a number of comments.

- "It has impacted our quality both negatively and positively. Temporary/contract and part-time employees who are happy with their status impact positively once trained but movement among this group causes quality problems."

- "Positive because we need their capability; negative because of continuous training efforts and turnover."

- "Negative—if used for inspection. Positive—if used to help supplement resources for projects."

- "Depends on our situation, cafeteria workers and janitorial virtually no impact. Consultants are used when we do not have qualified people or 'management takes action' to 'fix' things."

- "Retired employees tend to have a positive impact while temps, part-timers, and students have a more neutral or negative impact due to young age and inexperience."

Table 14.5. Impact of the contingent workforce on quality.

	In what way does the use of a contingent workforce impact your quality effort?
A strong positive impact	2.0 percent
A strong impact	17.1 percent
No impact, positive or negative	55.8 percent
A negative impact	23.6 percent
A strong negative impact	1.5 percent

However, a number of those queried had more polar views related to the use of contingent workers. With these differing views in mind, we will attempt to provide the reader with both the positive and negative sides of the contingent workforce equation.

Positive Side Effects of Using Contingent Workers

Almost 20 percent (19.1 percent) of those responding to the survey saw the use of contingent workers as having a positive impact on quality. The major reasons are as follows.

1. *Flexibility.* One of the most often cited reasons for using contingent workers is flexibility. Short-term needs of the organization, fluctuations in the economy, and natural business cycles make the use of contingent employees particularly inviting. Survey comments such as, "Provides greater flexibility and responsiveness to short-term needs" and "It buffers our permanent workforce from unexpected layoffs and gives us more flexibility" reflect respondent's positive attitudes toward the use of contingent workers.

2. *Specialized expertise.* Several respondents stated that many contingent employees, particularly contract laborers, improve quality because they are highly specialized in their particular area of expertise. "Allows us to bring in specialized skills that help improve internal systems and practices," "Professionals hired as contingent workers are usually hired because of their expertise, therefore, quality of work is high," and "Typically, contracted laborers improve quality efforts because they specialize in what they're doing" are all comments that support this positive side of contingent workers. Outsiders can bring knowledge and skills to an organization that may not be presently available.

3. *Cost.* At the top of most lists for using contingent workers is cost considerations. Contingent workers are usually paid less and almost never receive benefits. Organizational attempts at becoming lean (cost cutting, downsizing, process improvement) have made the use of contingent workers particularly enticing. Contingent workers cost an estimated 20 percent to 40 percent less than full-time regular status employees.[24] However, while nobody can fault the organization for cost containment and its impact on low-cost products and services, cost cutting per se is often a two-edged sword when it comes to quality. As one respondent commented, "Management uses temps to hold down overhead at the expense of quality."

4. *Selection tool.* Several survey comments pointed out that the firm's pool of contingent workers provided an excellent source for the selection of full-time, regular status employees. In previous chapters, we discussed various selection and promotion procedures (tests, interviews, and so on). We also pointed out that those tools are simply samples of behavior that are used to make inferences about the individuals likelihood of success in the target position. As such, it is probable that none of the previously discussed instruments will be as predictive of success as will the natural screening process inherent in using contingent workers. In many ways, this approach represents the ideal selection tool because the firm is able to observe the person actually working over an extended period of time. This large sample of behavior provides the organization with excellent information concerning the individual's potential. As a selection tool, some representative survey comments include: "Contingent workers offer the opportunity to choose the very best" and "Use of interns provides foundation for future hiring." With the increasing use of contingent workers by most organizations, these job tryouts will likely become the staffing tool of choice for many firms. In the future, it is very likely that for many employment hopefuls, full-status employment will only occur following a trial period as a contingent worker.

5. *New ideas.* Another interesting argument for the use of contingent workers is the infusion of new blood and new ideas into the organization. Contract employees, temps, and consultants in particular have worked for other organizations and have varied experiences that can be used to improve processes and procedures. Survey comments such as, "They bring in new ideas and a different perspective" and "I believe we can learn a lot from outside workers," reinforce the new ideas proposition.

6. *Avoidance of laws.* One seldom discussed reason for using contingent workers is the avoidance of certain EEO and labor laws. While they may not admit to it, many organizations feel that they can avoid compliance with these laws by transferring the burden to the contract or temporary agency, or by claiming that these workers are independent contractors.[25] In short, the attitude becomes one of letting someone else deal with the headaches associated with compliance.

Negative Consequences of Using Contingent Workers

While using contingent workers provides the organization with certain benefits such as flexibility and apparent bottom-line cost savings, there is also a downside to using such workers. Approximately 25 percent of the survey respondents felt that the contingent workforce has a negative impact on their quality effort. Most of the negatives take the form of indirect or hidden costs that are not so easily quantified as payroll and benefit savings. Negative consequences include the following.

1. *Training.* One of the most often discussed negative consequences of using contingent workers is the issue of training. The constant coming and going of such workers means an ongoing training effort to get these outside workers to even a minimum performance level. In addition, this emphasis on learning the job leaves little time for other kinds of quality and development training. Typical survey comments include: "Temporary workers present many problems; the most common is having to train and re-train to our system each day" and "Training problems using part-time/temporary employees due to short employment times."

2. *Turnover.* Several survey comments focused on the issue of turnover as a major problem when using contingent workers: "Add to cost of quality effort—too much turnover" and "The contingent workforce requires more training as new workers join the workforce and come and go." Turnover affects quality in at least two important ways. The first is the direct costs (orientation and training) associated with replacing the worker. The second negative is a little more subtle but even more important in terms of quality—the issue of experienced workers. Robert E. Cole, in a provocative article, points out that much of what we call quality resides in the organizational memory of its employees. No matter how precise the procedures or thorough the documentation it cannot always replace the know-how of an experienced employee. As Cole points out, "There are particular situations and points of contact in which customers form their opinions about a company and a process associated with those occasions. These are what Jan Carlzon of SAS called 'moments of truth.'" He points to the role of flight attendants and check-in and reservation clerks in the airline business. What happens if the process that delivers service or products at these occasions is staffed by personnel who regularly turn over? Similarly, what happens if the customer has his or her transaction with the organization at a time just after a loyal and knowledgeable long-term employee has left? In both cases, there is a greatly increased probability of quality failure and customer defection.[26]

3. *Productivity.* For a lot of reasons (including commitment, lack of training, and experience), many contingent workers do not produce

at the same level as their full-time counterparts. This feeling of lower productivity is exemplified in the succinct comment of one survey respondent who stated "The contingent workforce doesn't work as hard." That attitude is not without some empirical support. One study of data-entry operators found that the contingent workers' output was 8 percent less than their counterparts', while their compensation was only 6 percent less than regular status workers. In addition, the company needed to provide contingent workers 200 hours of training.[27]

4. *Pay dissatisfaction and conflict.* As any compensation specialist can attest, individuals can deal with a certain amount of external inequity when it comes to pay, but their tolerance is extremely low when it comes to confronting the reality of internal inequity. Contingent and full-time employees working side by side performing the same job, but receiving vastly different pay creates a climate for dissatisfaction and conflict. Witness the experience of Kolmar Laboratories as described in Fortune.[28] Roughly half of its assembly-line workers were temps who earned $5.60 per hour with no benefits while the remainder of the workers were permanent employees who received up to $9 per hour plus benefits for doing the same work. The result was extreme dissatisfaction on the part of temps and dissension between the two factions to the point of physical confrontation. Today, Kolmar no longer uses temps as assemblers because of its bad experience. As Bill Brooks, Kolmar's general manager explained: "It was a wash . . . . What we saved on hourly rates we paid for in rework, recruiting costs, and training."[29]

5. *Low commitment and loyalty.* The overriding theme throughout this discussion of negative consequences is the low commitment and loyalty engendered as a result of the second-class status afforded contingent workers. On the one hand, we expect these individuals to work hard and do a good job. On the other, we put less value on their contribution (pay them less) and let them know that if things get tough, they'll be the first to go. It should not be surprising that this lowly status creates low attachment, high turnover, and low involvement on the part of these individuals.

6. *Loss of technological and operational edge.* While contingent workers may bring new ideas and approaches to the organization, they also transfer their newly acquired knowledge and experiences to the next employment site. Because everybody knows what everybody else is doing, the notion of industrial espionage is rapidly becoming passe. A revolving door of engineers, scientists, and consultants provides a flow of information across organizations and creates a leveling effect which may negatively affect the cutting edge or best-in-class firms.

7. *Lack of inclusion in quality efforts.* One final concern associated with using contingent workers is their exclusion from quality training and quality initiatives. While difficult to generalize, many of those surveyed stated that they do not involve contingent workers in their quality effort: "We do not train contingent workers in quality principles/practices, nor do we include them in our quality efforts." Does this mean that, on average, 25 percent of the organization's workers are not included in attempts to become a quality-driven firm? Given the trend toward using contingent workers, if the answer is yes, then the truly quality-driven organization has reason to be concerned.

Using Contingent Workers in the Quality Organization

To this point, we have attempted to present a balanced look at the use of contingent workers in the quality organization and concluded that, like most complex issues, there is both an upside and a downside to employing such workers. In which direction does the pendulum swing?

Our conclusion is that the truly quality-driven firm should be very careful when jumping on the contingent workforce bandwagon. As quality professionals, we are continuously cautioned to avoid a short-term and line item mentality to running our businesses and, instead, to focus on providing quality goods and services that meet our customers' needs. In many ways, the decision to use contingent workers is a throwback to the more traditional model of running the organization. As such, cost considerations, not quality, become the driver for making decisions. A person is hired to do a narrowly defined job and not contribute to the overall effectiveness of the firm. Further, the worker is viewed as an expendable commodity, not the most important resource in our organization that we attest to in our quality-related mission statements. Thus, while cost and flexibility are important considerations in HRP, the overriding criteria for making decisions should be the impact of using contingent workers on the quality of products and services. At the minimum, it should most certainly be factored into the decision equation.

An additional reason for questioning the use of contingent workers is the true cost-effectiveness of such decisions. Recent research indicates that the cost savings envisioned may not always materialize when all factors are considered. In their forthcoming book on the contingent workforce, Stanley Nollen and Helen Axel argue that organizations should be very careful when assuming that cost savings will result from using such workers.[30] Nollen and Axel discuss many of the direct and indirect costs (such as increased training, higher turnover, and lower productivity) associated with using contingent workers. Of particular interest is their contention that work unit performance may be hampered in those settings where teamwork is important (the quality setting). Contingent workers tend to join and leave work units frequently, resent pay differentials, have lower commitment, and often bring less knowledge and skills to the table.

In another report written for *New Ways to Work,* Nollen provides a methodology for measuring the cost-effectiveness of using contingent labor.[31] He examined the cost-effectiveness of contingent labor in three firms and concludes that, for two of those companies, the expected savings were not realized. In short, results indicate that supposed cost savings can quickly disappear when doing a careful cost/benefit analysis.

Our *caveat* aside, the fact remains that the trend toward using contingent workers is on the upswing and will likely continue. Even our survey of quality-oriented organizations reinforces that tendency. Results indicate that more than 50 percent of the firms have increased their use of contingent workers over the last five years, and that 93 percent plan to continue or increase that practice. Because the contingent workforce is a fact of life in today's organizations, we will attempt to provide the reader with a model for deciding the appropriate use of such workers in the context of a quality organization.

The Stable Core/Flexible Ring Concept

One particularly useful approach for conceptualizing the relationship of contingent workers with the organization is the stable core/flexible ring design advocated by Joel R. DeLuca. Here, the organization establishes a stable core of permanent employees and a flexible ring of contingent personnel that come and go on an as-needed basis (see Figure 14.1).

In DeLuca's own words,

> *The organization would establish a stable core of personnel whose long-term careers would be in the company and a flexible ring of personnel whose overall careers would include time in the company but extend to include other companies as well. The stable core would have some form of employment stability. Their employment would not be threatened by the constantly changing structure and fluctuating size of the corporation. The flexible ring would be professionals and others in jobs with designated time spans, say two to five years, who would predictably and knowingly leave the organization at the end of that period.*[32]

Figure 14.1. Stable core/flexible ring design.

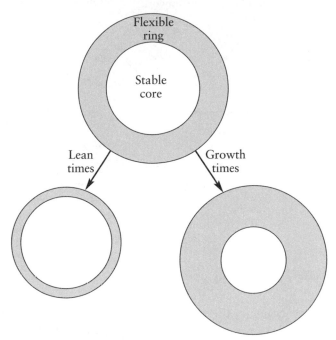

Source: Joel R. Deluca, "Strategic Career Management in Non-Growing Volatile Business Environment." Reprinted with permission from *Human Resource Planning*, Vol. 11, No. 1 (1988), p. 57. Copyright 1988 by The Human Resource Planning Society.

This design allows for the much needed flexibility that organizations increasingly require, while at the same time providing a stable core of career employees that would be the foundation for all quality and process improvement activities. In a quality setting, stable core employees would likely be the process experts and engage in multiple tasks and activities. The organization would invest heavily in the training and development of these employees and rely on this group to provide long-term direction and leadership for the firm.

Make-Up of the Flexible Ring

While a great deal has been written on the proliferation of the contingent workforce, little discussion has focused on the ideal make-up and use of that flexible ring of workers. If, as we've discussed, there are both positives and negatives to using contingent workers, then when does it make sense to use contingent workers and when should the firm avoid reliance on such a workforce? Questions such as whom to use, when to use, where to use, and how to use contingent workers

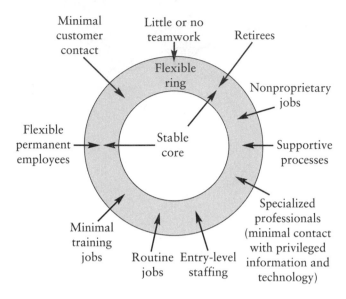

Figure 14.2. Make-up of the flexible ring.

warrant serious consideration. We believe that the theory and practice of quality provides an excellent framework for that kind of analysis and discussion. Using quality principles, survey comments regarding the use of contingent workers, and a little bit of our own experience as HR practitioners, we have identified 10 types of employees or situations that lend themselves to being part of the flexible ring in a quality organization (see Figure 14.2).

1. *Supportive vs. primary processes.* One useful consideration for deciding where to use contingent workers is the distinction between primary and supportive processes in a system. **Primary processes** are the series of activities that are essential for producing an output. They should add value. **Supporting processes** are the activities that allow a primary process to become more effective or efficient. (Neglect of supporting processes may ultimately result in a failure of a primary process or maintenance.)[33]

Thus, primary processes can be viewed as those activities directly linked with providing a product or service (what the organization is in business for). Providing fast food at McDonald's, producing cars and trucks at Chrysler, and changing oil at the Jiffy Lube are all examples of primary processes at different firms. However, to carry out those activities, certain supporting processes must be in place. To be effective, McDonald's requires an efficient delivery process and a cleaning and maintenance system that upholds the McDonald image (great place to stop and use the bathroom). Chrysler also must have supportive processes such as training (both job specific and quality) and the moving of parts and material between plants (just-in-time inventory). Even the neighborhood Jiffy Lube requires processes for compensating employees, marketing its services, and computerizing its system ("Our records show that it has been three months since your last service").

This distinction between primary and supporting processes provides us with the first rule of thumb for deciding where to use contingent workers. That principle is, if you're going to use contingent workers, look to the supporting processes in the system and avoid those processes considered as primary. Thus, maintenance, housekeeping, compensation administration, transportation, marketing, and training are all processes that warrant consideration for inclusion in the flexible ring. Conversely, line workers in a plant, counter people at McDonald's and maintenance workers at the Jiffy Lube should be part of a stable core.

2. *Highly specialized professionals.* As previously discussed, respondents to our survey were quick to point out the quality-related positives of using highly specialized professionals to augment their workforces. As organizations and the world of work become increasingly complex, the need for such professionals will no doubt increase. These contingent workers may be hired for a special project, placed on a retainer, or, in some cases, contracted to do certain work depending on the specific needs of the organization. For example, both the authors of this text are part of that contingent workforce. We consult in the fields of HR management and quality (staffing, compensation, EEO compliance, quality training) and are adjunct professors in business schools at local universities, both on an as-needed basis that provides the organizations with highly specialized professionals. As such, we might be asked to help the firm set up a staffing process (do a job analysis, develop selection or promotion instruments, ensure EEO compliance) or develop a compensation system (conduct a job evaluation, do a salary survey, set up a compensation structure). Once the assignment is completed and in place, we turn the new process over to appropriate internal personnel for administration.

Most firms cannot afford the luxury of having specialized professionals that meet every need. And those who try usually wish they hadn't when rough times hit the organization. Thus, the use of highly specialized professionals as part of the contingent workforce is intuitively appealing. Systems and computer specialists, quality training professionals, marketing research specialists, and, in some cases, research and engineering professionals with specific expertise are excellent candidates for the flexible ring.

3. *Flexible permanent employees.* Several years ago, one of the authors was giving a lecture in his HR management class on the topics of work schedule and compensation alternatives. Included in the lecture was a discussions of both flextime work schedules and cafeteria benefit packages. It was an evening MBA class (students worked full time during the day) and most of the class was fighting to stay awake while the author droned on about the benefits of being creative when implementing HR practices. However, one student, the director of nursing at a local hospital, was intently listening to every word and taking copious notes on the lecture. After class, the young woman had a number of questions related to the topics covered in class. As it turned out, her hospital was experiencing difficulty staffing and scheduling nursing personnel for the weekend shifts. Unable to persuade present nursing staff to work on the weekends or to hire personnel for those shifts, the hospital was forced to rely on the use of temporary agencies to meet its weekend staffing needs. Not only was this costly (in excess of a million dollars per year), but the quality of patient care suffered as a result of using inexperienced nursing personnel that changed from week to week.

Using the innovative staffing concepts discussed in class and her own creative instincts, the nursing director devised a package entitled "$2 \times 12 = 40$" (work a 12-hour shift both Saturday and Sunday and receive 40 hours' worth of pay with no benefits), placed an ad in the paper, and watched as hundreds of qualified nurses applied for the weekend positions. As it turned out, there were many qualified individuals (students and women who had left nursing to raise a family) for whom the $2 \times 12 = 40$ package met their financial and scheduling needs. Thus, the director was able to save the hospital literally hundreds of thousands of dollars in costs and improve the quality of patient care by looking at some creative alternatives to traditional staffing.

So what is the point of this little story? Simply that flexibility can be accomplished internally as well as externally when meeting organizational needs. The temptation to always go outside the organization to meet flexibility needs should be tempered by an awareness of the hidden costs (training, high turnover, lower quality) associated with using contingent workers. Often, creative alternatives such as split jobs, flexible scheduling, and flexible staffing with current employees can avoid many of those hidden costs.

Paul Rupert, past director of New Ways to Work's Equiflex Project and presently manager, Flexibility Consulting Practice for Rodgers and

Associates, encourages organizations to design integrative flexibility programs that combine employee needs for flexible work options with organizational needs for flexibility.[34] He argues that, in most cases, it is better to design flexibility internally rather than going outside with part-time, temporary, and contract workers. Rupert also provides examples of firms that have successfully used such an approach including the Joy Cone Company, a producer of ice cream cones for Hardees, McDonald's, Baskin-Robbins, and Nabisco, among others. The cyclical nature of Joy Cone's business along with its rigid, low-paying environment create a situation where the use of contingent workers appears ideal. But Joy Cone has chosen instead to incorporate an employee-centered, flexible scheduling procedure that allows employees to request, within limits, an individualized work schedule every week. Employees love it and it works, says Rupert. "The quality organization should be more creative and look for flexibility within its core employees before looking to the outside for meeting its needs."[35]

4. *Retirees.* Consistent with the previous discussion of internally flexible employees, one set of viable candidates for the flexible ring is retirees. A review of our discussion of pluses and minuses of using contingent workers reveals that retirees possess virtually all of the positives (highly flexible, low cost, high organizational knowledge, EEO compliance) and few, if any, of the negatives (little training, likely to leave, unproductive, low commitment and loyalty, and no potential for inclusion in quality efforts).

Labor statistics clearly show that the workforce is aging and that the over-60 generation will be an increasing segment of our population. The forward-looking quality-oriented organization will keep this trend in mind and begin to make better utilization of these retired employees. If the organization wants low-cost flexibility, while at the same time it desires a trained and committed workforce, then creative use of retirees will become a must.

5. *Minimal customer contact.* Given the quality dictum that the customer is king (or queen for the politically correct), one criterion for flexible ring inclusion would be the amount of customer contact the contingent workers will encounter on the job. High customer contact jobs (for example, sales people, cashiers, and flight attendants) are, generally speaking, poor candidates for inclusion in the flexible ring. These front-line employees need to be committed, demonstrate positive attitudes, and possess the organizational knowledge necessary to deal with customer problems and concerns. The last thing the organization wants its customers to hear is "That's not my job" or "I don't know, you'll have to ask somebody else," when the customers have a question or concern.

While perhaps not quite as critical, customer contact is also important when considering the degree of internal customer relationships. Workers involved in processes with numerous and complex internal constituencies should be part of the stable core and not the flexible ring.

6. *Routine and highly standardized jobs.* Another set of viable candidates for inclusion in the flexible ring are those individuals placed in highly routine and standardized jobs. If the positions require little idiosyncratic behavior and knowledge of the organization, then the use of contingent workers is likely to have potential. This would be particularly true if the firm ensures that ample policies, procedures, and controls are in place.

7. *Jobs requiring minimal training.* Obvious from our previous discussions is the issue of training when making contingent workforce decisions. Generally speaking, the less training required, the more potential for inclusion in the flexible ring. Cost of training, frequency of training (turnover), and performance learning curves should all be factored into the firm's cost accounting and human resource planning decisions.

8. *Proprietary or cutting-edge technology or processes.* Many firms, particularly those engaged in heavy R&D efforts, are rethinking their use of contract professionals in many settings. Combine the comings and goings of these individuals with their lack of organizational loyalties, and the potential for problems is obvious. Engineers, scientists, and other professionals who are privy to the firm's technology and process innovations may be poor risks for the flexible ring.

9. *Situations requiring considerable teamwork.* As previously discussed, the more team oriented the work situation, the less likely contingent workers are to be effective. Research shows that the more stable and long-lasting the team, the more effective it becomes.[36] The high turnover and lower commitment of contingent workers is not likely to be conducive to those situations requiring high levels of cooperation and teamwork.

10. *Entry-level staffing.* The flexible ring provides firms with a potentially powerful selection tool for screening individuals who wish to enter the stable core. Serving a trial period as a contingent worker will become commonplace before achieving full-status employment in the firm of the future. Hopefully that selection process will adhere to the concepts presented in this book.

Summary

The effective organizations of the future will no doubt begin more closely to examine their use of contingent workers and be selective in terms of flexible ring membership. We encourage our readers to carefully think through their decisions to use such workers and to place quality and customer service at the top of their decision-making criteria.

Suppliers of Contingent Labor

In chapter 6 we discussed the importance of viewing recruitment sources as suppliers, and the need to develop close working relationships with those entities that provide input into our staffing process. Just-in-time staffing, to be effective, requires the same viewpoint. As such, improvements in the contingent workforce staffing process should focus on the following two interrelated considerations.

Plan Ahead. The starting point for the effective utilization of contingent workers is the forecasting of the HR needs of the organization. In best practices companies, the HR staff works closely with line managers to determine expected workloads and where contingent workers might address expected needs. The up-front determination of when these workers will be needed, how many will be required, and the skills needed allows HR to better meet the needs of the organization. Failure to plan ahead leaves the organization in a position of scrambling to find warm bodies to fill the void. Witness the following quote from Ron English, president of McDonnell Douglas Technical Services (MDTS) company.

> *Contingency workers fail when they're hired as a last-ditch effort rather than being used as a planned, integrated resource. All too frequently, a manager will discover he or she is behind three months in production, panic, and call HR for some bodies to throw at the problem. This isn't only detrimental to core employees, but the complementary workers hired to help are destined to fail. When this happens, human resources wants to blame the failure on engineering or manufacturing, when in reality, if everyone worked together to anticipate the upcoming workload, they could have avoided problems altogether.*[37]

Work Closely with Suppliers. Developing a close working relationship with agencies is a must. Ideally, such agencies should become an extension of the HR function and be encouraged to closely align their services with the needs of the organization. By working closely with an agency, the firm can clearly communicate expectations and provide ongoing feedback regarding the quality of services provided. For example, Aligned Fiber Composites (AFC) in Chatfield, Minnesota, works closely with the local office of Express Personnel to ensure that job candidates possess the necessary reading and math skills needed for its firm. Cheryl Nelson, HR Manager at AFC, states

> *Our plant is involved in continuous improvement and statistical process control, so our employees need to have a certain level of math skills. We don't have satisfactory means of testing employees in-house, so we turned to Express. I avoid some major headaches by allowing them to screen and select the candidates for us.*[38]

This is particularly important because AFC uses temps as a way to prescreen employees for permanent positions. While not all temps at AFC are offered full-time positions, all recent hires have gone through the temporary-employment process.

Another example of working closely with suppliers is found in a large manufacturing organization for which one of the authors consults. Because of the large, growing number of contract workers being used, the firm established a subsidiary that acts as an intermediary with the agencies providing contract labor. All of the firm's contract labor needs are addressed by the subsidiary, which acts as a type of HR department for contract labor. One advantage of such an arrangement is the opportunity for the subsidiary to develop close working relationships with the agencies and to evaluate, through an annual survey of user satisfaction, the quality of personnel and service those agencies provide. Managers who use contract labor are asked to describe their satisfaction with both the contract laborer (skill level, performance, dependability, and so on) and the agency (training, orientation, timeliness, support, and so on). Information collected is used to improve relationships with the supplier agencies or, when necessary, to justify dropping an agency from the accepted supplier list.

The Human Side of Using Contingent Workers

As previously discussed, both of the authors would be labeled as contingent workers. We fall into this category both in terms of our consulting practice and as adjuncts to several local universities teaching courses in business labor and industrial relations and psychology. As such, we can talk from first-hand knowledge when discussing the personal side of being a contingent worker. For example, the universities where we teach vary considerably in how they use and treat adjunct faculty. Some schools have practices that demonstrate respect and consideration for the part-time instructors as valued contributors. They plan ahead and give ample time to adjust schedules and prepare for courses. Some even ask what days and/or times would be most convenient for us. A few of these institutions have orientation sessions for all adjunct faculty (for example, to meet the dean and faculty, and be provided with orientation material with information regarding clerical services, use of equipment, and so on), and actively involve adjunct faculty in some meetings and social gatherings. These practices go a long way to make us feel comfortable and a viable part of the institution. At the other end of the continuum are those schools that call a week before classes are to begin, giving us no latitude in selecting the schedule or textbook. In some cases, there is no contact with other faculty or administration, no office space, and no information on the use of equipment such as overhead projectors and computer labs. We are left to just come and go with no real sense of affirmation or belonging.

The point of this little true-life comparison is to demonstrate the differences in the way contingent workers can be, and are, treated. It is true that much of how people behave is related to how they are treated (the Pygmalion effect). Treat them as second-class citizens, and that's exactly what you will get. Given the situation that most contingent workers find themselves in, it is little wonder that firms get lower levels of loyalty and productivity along with higher turnover rates. Following are a few suggestions for improving the satisfaction and commitment of your contingent workforce.

Provide an RJP. First and foremost, be honest and forthright in your dealings with contingent workers. Provide them with an RJP that details the kind of work they will be doing, the likely length of the assignment, and realistic probabilities concerning the likelihood of permanent, full-time employment. Do not hold out full-time employment carrots where none exist.

Don't Use Contingent Workers as a Dumping Ground. Resist the temptation to give temps all of the least enjoyable work that core employees don't want to do. As Beverly Geber puts it in her excellent article on using contingent workers wisely and humanely,

Contingent employees are people, not dogs; they won't love you no matter how badly you treat them. If they feel exploited, it could dampen their enthusiasm to do a good job. In extreme cases, it could lead to sabotage.[39]

Involve Contingent Workers in Quality. One of the disconcerting findings from our survey was the exclusion of contingent workers from quality initiatives and training. While full participation may not be possible or desirable (possible co-employment litigation), we believe that some involvement is necessary to make contingent workers feel part of the organization. Participation in problem-solving groups and some training in corporate values and quality seem warranted. We doubt that contingent workers will lose their temporary status if they're asked for suggestions or are invited to the company picnic.

Train Managers. With the growing number of contingent workers, we suggest that some form of training be provided for leaders to help them with this new management role. Microsoft, for example, includes a module on "Managing the Contingent Workforce" as part of its frontline management training.[40]

Other suggestions made by Geber for dealing with the contingent workforce include providing some benefits (such as holiday pay), explaining your moves to use temps to your core employees, and clearly defining the different roles of contingent and core employees.[41]

Final Observation

One very interesting finding from our survey was the statistical relationship between the items "extent the organization has incorporated the philosophy and practices of TQM into their business" and "the likelihood of using contingent workers in the next five years." Results of correlation were significant and show that the more the organization has incorporated TQM into how it does business, the less likely it is to report plans for using contingent workers in the future. Hopefully, this finding indicates that the truly quality-driven organization is more aware of the quality-related downside to using contingent workers and is somewhat more cautious in its use of such workers.

Conclusion

We believe that the organization of the future is more likely to resemble chaos theory than the rigid, hierarchical structure envisioned by

Adam Smith, refined by management theorists and practitioners during this century and still taught in many of today's B-schools. The flexible organization of the future will be constantly changing directions to meet changes in the marketplace, with older divisions or functions continually giving way to the new. Strategic alliances with other firms, closer working relationships with tier-one suppliers, and the use of contingent workers will leave many of tomorrow's workers wondering at times exactly who they do work for. Work or project team members will be shuttled about the organization depending on need. And, if that is not enough, a steady stream of contingent workers will be flowing in and out of the organization on an as-needed basis. There is no doubt that the most overworked and frustrated employee in the firm of the future will be the individual responsible for updating the firm's organization chart.

To remain competitive in this changing environment, the quality organization must learn to do more with less, while continually revising its strategic direction, reorganizing and reconfiguring its structure, improving its processes, and maximizing the use of workers within the firm. Staffing will no longer be limited to organizational entry and promotion decisions. Managers at all levels will be required to make staffing decisions (selection, placement, transfer, group assignment, professional track, promotion, and so on) on an ongoing basis. Those decisions must be creative but always with an eye to the customer and the selection and retention of individuals who can function effectively in this dynamic environment.

Notes

1. William Bridges, "The End of the Job," *Fortune* (Sept. 19, 1994): 62–74.

2. Peter F. Drucker, *Managing for the Future* (New York: Truman Talley Books/Plume, 1993), 18.

3. Joseph M. Juran's response to a question, Last Word Tour, Milwaukee, Wis.

4. Mary Walton, *The Deming Management Method* (New York: Putnam Publishing, 1986), 84.

5. Jaclyn Fierman, "The Contingency Workforce," *Fortune* (January 24, 1994): 30–36.

6. Al Murray, "Amid Record Profits Companies Continue to Lay Off Employees." *The Wall Street Journal* (May 4, 1995): A1.

7. Ibid.

8. Caroline V. Clarke, "Downsizing Trounces Diversity 1994," *Black Enterprise* (February 1994): 269.

9. James P. Womack, Daniel T. Jones, and Daniel Roos. *The Machine That Changed the World* (New York: Rawson Associates, 1990), 30–36.

10. Michael Hammer and James Champy, *Reengineering the Corporation* (New York: Harper Business, 1993).

11. Gore Report on Reinventing Government.

12. Amanda Bennett, "Downsizing Doesn't Necessarily Bring an Upswing in Corporate Profitability." *The Wall Street Journal* (June 6, 1991): B1–B4.

13. Ronald Henkoff, "Cost Cutting: How to Do It Right," *Fortune* (April 9, 1990): 17–19.

14. Laura Rubach, "Downsizing: How Quality Is Affected as Companies Shrink," *Quality Progress* (April 1995): 23–28.

15. Wayne F. Cascio, "Downsizing: What Do We Know? What Have We Learned?" *Academy of Management Executive* 7, no. 1 (1993): 95–104.

16. Kim S. Cameron, Sarah J. Freeman, and Aneil K. Mishra, "Best Practices in White-Collar Downsizing: Managing Contradictions." *Academy of Management Executive* 5, no. 3 (1991): 57–73.

17. Thomas H. Holmes and R. H. Rahe. "The Social Readjustment Rating Scale," *Journal of Psychosomatic Research* 11, no. 4 (1967).

18. G. James Francis, John Mohr, and Kelly Anderson, "HR Balancing: Alternative Downsizing," *Personnel Journal* (January 1992): 71–78.

19. Editorial, *Personnel* (April 1991): 17; adapted from *Bulletin,* a publication of the New York-based consulting firm of William M. Mercer, a Marsh & McLennan Company.

20. Steven L. Grover and Karen J. Crooker, "Who Appreciates Family-Responsive Human Resource Policies: The Impact of Family-Friendly Policies on the Organizational Attachment of Parents and Non-Parents," *Personnel Psychology* 48 no. 2 (1995): 271–288.

21. W. Edwards Deming, *Out of the Crisis* (Cambridge, Mass.: MIT Center for Advanced Engineering Study, 1986), 3.

22. Jaclyn Fierman, "The Contingency Workforce."

23. Brad Stratton, "The Next Big Issue," *Quality Progress* (March 1994): 5.

24. Wayne F. Cascio. "Downsizing: What Do We Know? What Have We Learned?"

25. Robert E. Cole, "Learning From Learning Theory: Implications for Quality Improvement of Turnover, Use of Contingent Workers and Job Rotation Policies," *Quality Management Journal* (October 1993): 9–25.

26. Ibid.

27. Clare Ansberry, "Hired Out: Workers Are Forced to Take More Jobs With Few Benefits," *The Wall Street Journal* (March 11, 1993).

28. William Bridges, "The End of the Job," *Fortune* (Sept. 19, 1994): 62–74.

29. Ibid.

30. Stanley Nollen and Helen Axel, *Contingent Workforce* (New York: AMA-COM, 1995).

31. Stanley Nollen, "Exploding the Myth: Is Contingent Labor Cost-Effective?" *New Ways to Work: A Report* (San Francisco, Calif.: 1993).

32. Joel R. Deluca, "Strategic Career Management in Non-Growing Volatile Business Environments." *Human Resource Planning* 11 no. 1 (1988): 49–61.

33. Bryan J. Beasor, "How to Use Flow Charts to Streamlining Processes, Systems, and Procedures," Michigan State University seminar series, 9, ©1992 Qualstat Services.

34. Paul Rupert, "Flexible Work for Older Workers: A Competent vs. a Contingent Strategy," AARP Textbook Authors Conference, Washington, D.C., October 8, 1993, 23–27.

35. Ibid.

36. Warren Watson, Larry K. Michaelsen, and Walt Sharp, "Member Competence, Group Interaction, and Group Decision Making: A Longitudinal Study," *Journal of Applied Psychology* 76, no. 6 (1991): 803–809.

37. Shari Caudron, "Contingent Work Force Spurs HR Planning," *Personnel Journal* (July 1994): 58.

38. Ibid.

39. Beverly Geber, "The Flexible Work Force: Using Contingent Workers Wisely and Humanely," *Training* (December 1993): 23–30.

40. D. Douglas McKenna, Susan Crandall, Jeffrey J. McHenry, Andrea Umbach-Tevlin, and Janet Phillips, Microsoft Corporation, "Management Development at Microsoft: Struggling with Success and Growth," presentation at the Tenth Annual Conference of the Society for Industrial and Organizational Psychology, Orlando, Fla, May 19–21, 1995.

41. Beverly Geber, "The Flexible Work Force: Using Contingent Workers Wisely and Humanely."

chapter **15**

Staffing the New Workplace:
Best Practices and Recommendations

Overview

In this chapter we reflect on what appears to be a burgeoning interest in staffing for quality. We present what has emerged as a set of best practices for staffing and then present our summary of best practices for staffing in the unique context of the new workplace. We end the chapter with an invitation to engage in a dialogue on staffing for quality. Specifically, in the interest of continuous improvement, we ask you to send us descriptions of issues and examples of effective staffing practices for inclusion in future editions of this book.

Introduction

There is a phenomenon in psychology, in perception to be precise, termed *selective attention*. A hungry person will spot food that others may not notice. A mother will hear her infant cry well before others notice the sound, even if it is masked by other more prominent noise. The point is that we are sometimes attuned to perceive things around us that others may not notice. We use this concept to account for why it seems that virtually every book, journal, magazine, and billboard we have recently encountered seems to call out staffing for quality. Hey, we're immersed in research for a book. We're obsessed with the topic. It's us, our selective attention, and not the rest of the world that has now focused on staffing as a means for quality improvement. Well, we're not quite sure to what degree our selective attention has distorted our perception, but as we bring our research and writing of this book to a close, it does now seem that wherever we turn there is a new call for attention to staffing as a critical component of a systematic quality initiative.

Witness some of the examples we've noted in the past few months alone.

A recent cover story in *Business Week* entitled "Go-Go Goliaths: How 10 of the Best, Big Companies Keep Growth Sizzling" describes how firms such as Hewlett-Packard, Southwest Airlines, Nucor, and Motorola keep expanding.[1] The article draws six common lessons from these thriving giants including the admonition to "hire carefully: Sign up skilled people at all levels who demonstrate versatility and responsiveness."

In his recent book, *Reengineering Management*, James Champy recognizes the importance of staffing in the new, reengineered workplace, and devotes an entire chapter to the topic.[2] He cites seven points.

- Develop a profile of the technical and interpersonal skills that the new work requires.

- Remember that an ability to learn is one of the important capabilities you are looking for.

- Determine what formal testing procedures can tell you about the candidate.

- As much as possible, observe the candidate operating under real or simulated work conditions.

- Broaden the interviewing process to include team members with whom the candidate would be working.

- Don't limit your pool of candidates by requiring past experience—-it may not be relevant to the new work and it may eliminate talented candidates.

- Design the recruiting process to expose your culture to the candidate and treat him or her as a company member during the process. The candidate should clearly understand what it means to work for your company.

Champy's recommendations, in fact, are a nice outline of the major points on which the content of this book is based.

In her recent book, *Corporate Quality Universities* (essentially a book about training for quality), Jeanne C. Meister points out appropriately that the first priority should be to "hire smart."[3]

Increasingly, companies are beginning to realize that training employees in a set of CORE workplace competencies . . . on its own will not guarantee improvements in job performance. While employees can be trained to enhance their basic and interpersonal communication skills and to upgrade their technical skills, the effectiveness of such training depends as much on the aptitude of the employee as on the quality of the training. What is required are attention, planning, and resources targeted to ensure that the right individual is hired into the company so he or she can reap the fullest benefit from the extensive training programs. . . . Accordingly, progressive companies who have committed to the sophisticated training epitomized by Corporate Quality Universities are exercising greater scrutiny in the hiring practices for all levels of the work force.

A recent conference sponsored by the professional association for industrial/organizational psychologists had sessions entitled

- "Benchmarking Salaried Selection: Learnings from Ford, Bell Atlantic, Anheuser-Busch & Others"
- "Selecting Service-Oriented Employees with Biographical Data"
- "Construct Validity of the PDI Customer Service Inventory"
- "Measuring Service Orientation with Biodata and SOI"
- "Validity of a Job-Related Attitudinal Measure of Quality Consciousness"
- "Personality Correlates of Success in Total Quality Manufacturing"
- "Does HRM Walk the TQM Talk?"[4]

Even daily newspapers have published articles on the topic. A recent *Detroit Free Press* article, entitled "Assembling a New Generation of Autoworkers," detailed the use of new assessment tools (simulations) to measure new attributes in entry-level auto production jobs.[5]

Furthermore, there has been a number of senior executives who have reflected on the importance of staffing to the success of their organizations. For example, Herbert Kelleher, CEO of Southwest Airlines, notes that "hiring employees that have the right attitude is so important that the hiring process takes on a patina of spirituality."[6]

In short, everyone seems to be talking about the important role staffing must play in a strategic quality transformation!

Contrast the dialogue and consensus that seem to have now emerged with the state of affairs that existed when we began this project. In 1992 we published an article in *Quality Progress*, calling for increased attention to quality-oriented attributes in staffing TQM settings.[7] The literature search we did in preparation for that article failed to turn up a single piece that dealt with selection or promotion in those settings. We did, however, identify 162 articles that dealt with training for quality.

As we noted in our introductory chapter, it is easy to explain and account for the fact that the quality movement, in it's infancy, was focused on training. At that time, the installation of quality tools and processes required the training of the existing workforce. The tools and practices were new to virtually all employees. Consequently, the only path to initial implementation was training. Furthermore, there is no question that training and development is philosophically consistent with the values and culture of quality.

Only after the initial training, and some experience with the quality effort, did companies begin to revise their other HR processes. And, as we have argued throughout this book, it is only those companies that do reconfigure their HR practices that will endure in their quality transformation. There is now stronger evidence of the link between staffing and long-term success of the quality initiative. As we noted in the chapter 1, recent research suggests an association between commitment and success of the quality initiative, and organization efforts to revise staffing practices.[8] Whereas the initial quality push ran, in part, on the collective adrenaline of the new philosophy, an enduring change requires the support of all organizational practices and policies.

In addition to the new, very prominent call for attention to staffing, there is clear evidence that many organizations are making tangible changes in their staffing effort. Whereas the 1991 survey of the initial Baldrige Award winners revealed little change in staffing, subsequent surveys of broader organization populations show clear evidence of change.[9]

Because of the important contribution staffing can make to the quality initiative, and the fact that there is now an emerging recognition of the need to address the staffing process, we present one more look at best practices.

A Study of Best Practices

In early 1994, Ford Motor Company contracted with the consulting firm HRStrategies to identify and benchmark best practice companies in entry-level (professional/technical) exempt selection. The findings of that study were recently presented at the Annual Conference of the Society for Industrial and Organizational Psychology.[10] The results parallel much of the discussion of this book and the recommendations we've made throughout our presentation of each staffing activity. We think that the results nicely amplify the points we've made in the book. The specific best practices identified in the sample of 28 companies are described on the following page. Before doing so, one important point we must make is that few companies had actually adopted all nine of the practices. That is the bad news. In fact, consistent with our own findings and other research, there is much room for progress. To quote the author of the study, John D. Arnold, VP, HRStrategies, "One of the strongest findings of the benchmarking study was the extent to which even 'best practice' companies are continuing to rely on relatively traditional methods of selecting exempt employees." For almost every company participating in the study, the selection system includes

- Using interviews as the primary selection tool of choice

- Placing more effort and resources into sourcing and recruiting candidates than into selection of candidates

- Using some type of computer-aided resume tracking system as a central repository of candidate information

- Administering the selection system in a decentralized fashion (at the plant level), while maintaining minimal corporate oversight

- *Not* using a well-developed, validated, multiple measure selection model

The consultants presented their checklist of best practices, and we abstract them here.

1. **Competency models.** Identify the set of competencies (KSAPs) required for effective performance in each job family.

2. **Competency models integrated into all employee relations activities.** Base all HR decisions (selection, performance appraisal, training needs analysis, succession planning) on the identified competencies.

3. **Use multiple selection tools and methods.** These include paper and pencil tests, interviews, biographical predictors, and assessment exercises.

4. **Train test administrators, interviewers, and assessors.** To ensure consistency in the administration of selection tools and evaluation of candidates, all test administrators, assessors, and interviewers receive training, including training on attending to job-relevant examples of behavior.

5. **Validated selection tools.** Each component of the selection model is validated, using either a criterion-related or content strategy.

6. **Tracking and cost control of selection.** Costs of the overall selection system are being tracked and controlled by companies engaging in this best practice.

7. **Strategic design of the selection system.** Companies are making conscious strategic decisions to manage candidate passing rates, especially early in the system, to maximize the likelihood of identifying the most qualified candidates. Simultaneously, the least costly selection tools are being used at the selection stage where candidate volume is the greatest. These two approaches combine to screen in the top candidates instead of screening out the bottom ones (focus on getting the best, rather than avoiding the worst).

8. **Alternative assessment presentation media.** Alternative presentation media, including traditional paper and pencil, as well as computer- and video-administered assessments, are used.

9. **Full utilization of information technology.** Information technology is used to score assessments, to drive candidate consensus rating discussions, and to track candidates in a centralized database.

Best Practices in Quality Improvement Settings

The list presented by HRStrategies represents a hybrid of best practices across the 28 companies included in the study. On the basis of our research for this book, and our consulting in both quality improvement and staffing, we've assembled the following best practices in staffing for quality improvement.

View Staffing as a Process That Can Be Systematically Described, Measured, Analyzed, and Improved . . . and Then Improved Again.

In our experience, one of the greatest detractors from effective human resources, particularly in terms of the impact on quality, is the segmented way in which policies and practices are designed and implemented. Strategic planning, recruitment, assessment, selection, training, motivation, appraisal, and promotion policies and practices are sometimes conceived and conducted in virtual isolation. A process perspective leads to the recognition that these components are intricately tied together. Poorly conceived or executed practices upstream in the sequence place strain on the downstream components. For example, failure to specify and accurately assess basic math skills in entry-level technical hires increases training time and training costs, reduces overall job performance, and increases turnover.

The second result of a process view of staffing is that it, like all organization processes, can benefit markedly from the application of process improvement and reengineering. Cycle times can be decreased, the reliability and validity of judgments and decisions can be increased, and internal customer satisfaction can be increased. The University of Hartford case in chapter 6 illustrates how much can be accomplished by systematic improvement (PDSA) of the process.

Design the Staffing Process Around a Success Profile.

Systematically identify both the functional and quality attributes (competencies) necessary to succeed in jobs or career paths within the company. Doing so will focus the staffing process on those attributes needed to support the organization's mission in general, and the quality initiative in particular. Because of the implications downstream, the more attention you give to thinking through this success profile, the more credible each subsequent activity will be. If you focus the selection process on clearly defined, meaningful attributes (ones that really do make a difference in success), the design and choice of assessment tools will be a straightforward process, the recruitment of credible applicants will be easier, the outcomes of the process (the choices made) will be more valid, and the ROI will be greater. Look again at the massive savings experienced by the quick service restaurant chain discussed in chapter 3 because it was able to identify, measure, and select on specific attributes such as conscientiousness and customer orientation. Remember again the downstream effect. The more capable your new hires are in terms of critical attributes, the more effective and efficient your training efforts will be, the greater your retention rate will be, and the more effective your work process will run.

Cross-Functional Input to the Process. Include representatives from human resources, quality, and other functional areas in the key components of the staffing process. In particular, include these different perspectives in the development of the success profile and in serving as recruiters and interviews. Recall our discussion of process validity—-inclusion of these different perspectives will result in a more credible success profile. The issue of involvement in constructing the success profile is even more critical in the new workplace where the jobs are often new and often changing. Because of the dynamic nature, those performing the work may not fully understand, or be able to anticipate, what the envisioned work will look like. Human resources may not fully understand what the envisioned work will look like. The engineers who design the new technology may not fully understand what the envisioned work will look like. Together, though, these different perspectives will help you identify a realistic, accurate success profile for the future.

Develop Mutually Beneficial Relationships with HR Suppliers. The labor market for those attributes that will make a difference in the success of your organization will be tight and competitive. Begin now to build symbiotic relationships with relevant suppliers: high schools, colleges, professional associations, and temporary agencies. Specify the attributes you will need, and work closely to see that these agencies are working with and for your interests. If the local high schools are the source of your nonexempt workforce, get involved in a push to improve their focus on basic skills, workplace values, and the values and practices of quality improvement. If you use temporary agencies, establish measurable standards for the personnel supplied by these agencies.

Expand the Mix of Assessment Tools. Our experience in organizations, our survey of ASQC sustaining member organizations, and the benchmark study conducted by HRStrategies all suggest that organizations are overly reliant on the interview as the basis for assessment. The new workplace demands a variety of knowledge, skills, abilities, and personal characteristics—many of which are simply measured with greater reliability and validity by other tools. Do not misinterpret our point. We do not advocate that you dispense with the interview. Instead, improve it and use it as one source of data. Use additional tools (paper and pencil ability tests, work simulations, biographical inventories, skills inventories, and well-selected personality measures). In particular, as you broaden your mix of assessment tools, consider the important role measures of general and specific cognitive abilities can serve. The greater the complexity of the work, and the more your workforce must continue to learn and work with new information, the more appropriate it will be for you to include these measures. Combine them with well-chosen measures of quality-relevant aspects of temperament, and with specific measures of skills, and you will get a more complete picture of the whole person.

Improve the Interview. There has emerged a clear consensus that the reliability, validity, and utility of the interview can be dramatically increased by the methods we present in chapters 9 and 10. Specifically, develop a structured, behaviorally based interview, focused on specific, important KSAPs. Train interviewers in the effective use of the process. Conduct consensus discussions, and make decisions based on consensus ratings of applicants.

Use Validated Tools. To a large measure, validity must be designed into the staffing process. A content valid process is based on a demonstration that the content of the assessment process has a rational link to the work done on the job. If you've selected and designed the assessment tools around specific behaviors and KSAPs needed on the job, you've laid the basis for content validity. When feasible, conduct internal validations of your selection tools and processes, or, if you are a very small employer, consider participation in a multicompany validity study. Refer again to the concurrent validity study in the health care facility (chapter 3). Also, for many well-established standardized tests, the accumulated validity evidence can sometimes serve as the basis on which to use tests (a concept termed *validity generalization*). Finally, while you are only required to present validity evidence in the event that your selection process is shown to have disparate impact, an efficient, well-constructed validation can provide you with the reassurance that the process is, in fact, producing effective hiring decisions and can, in fact, be used to calculate ROI.

Remember That Systematic Staffing Extends Beyond Selecting Entry-Level Employees. Staffing decisions occur not only at hire, but in placement, in transfer, in promotion, in project assignment, and in selecting out. All of these decision points are subject to the same standards as the hiring decision. Make the decisions based on specific, important attributes. This also means integrating the core quality attributes into these career transition points. Doing so will make the choices more supportive of the quality initiative, and will reinforce the message that quality is a central value.

Finally, in the event that the organization is to undergo a downsizing effort, conduct it with the quality initiative in mind. Use a process-driven approach (reengineering, process improvement) rather than across-the-board, headcount strategies. By doing so, you will prevent the loss of strategic skills that typifies more shortsighted approaches to downsizing.

If You Use Contingent Workers, Do So with Appropriate Forethought. We're convinced that contingent workers can either serve to support the quality initiative, or become a critical strain on the development of a quality culture. If you do use contingent workers, examine their impact on your quality initiative. The guidelines we outlined in chapter 14 will help you make effective use of this flexible resource and do so in a manner supportive of the quality values of your company. Be cautious in contingent worker use.

Evaluate the Utility of Staffing Practices. Investigate the ROI associated with the tools you are currently using, and use the utility framework to evaluate the addition of new tools.

In conclusion, we believe that these best practices will lay the basis on which you can make your staffing effort a constructive, supportive factor in your organization's quality initiative, and in its success over the coming decade. Staffing the new workplace correctly can pay dividends to your quality initiative and to the long-term success and survival of the firm.

Staffing-for-Quality Network

In the spirit of continuous improvement, we encourage you to share with us your staffing-for-quality issues, initiatives, and experiences. Our intent is to compile additional cases and best-practice illustrations for future of this book. Contact us at the following addresses and phone numbers.

Ronald B. Morgan, Ph.D.
Industrial/Organizational
  Psychologist
Organization Solutions
20893 Woodland Glen Drive,
  #202
Northville, MI 48167-2436
Phone: 810-348-9386
Fax: 810-349-5425
E-mail: rbmorgan@mcimail.com

Jack E. Smith, Ph.D.
Industrial/Organizational
  Psychologist
HR Processes
6830 Highland Road, Suite 105
White Lake, MI 48383
Phone: 810-887-5465
Fax: 810-887-6744

One of the authors, Ronald B. Morgan, invites readers to receive updates on staffing and HR issues by reading the newsletter *Human Resources in the New Workplace*, published by the consulting firm Organizational Solutions. The publication will include profiles of new assessment devices, summaries of legislative changes that affect the staffing process, questions and answers on issues raised in this book, innovative ideas, and "war stories" from readers of this book. To receive the inaugural issue, contact Ronald B. Morgan (contact information provided above.)

Notes

1. Wendy Zellner, Robert D. Hof, Richard Brandt, Steven Baker, and David Greising, "Go-Go Goliaths: How 10 of the Best, Big Companies Keep Growth Sizzling," *Business Week*, February 13, 1995, 64–70.

2. James Champy, *Reengineering Management: The Mandate for New Leadership* (New York: Harper, 1995).

3. Jeanne C. Meister, *Corporate Quality Universities: Lessons in Building a World-Class Work Force* (Alexandria, Va.: American Society for Training and Development, and Burr Ridge, Ill.: Irwin, 1994).

4. Selected session titles from the Tenth Annual Conference of the Society for Industrial and Organizational Psychology, Orlando, Fla., May 19–21, 1995.

5. Greg Gardner, "Assembling a New Generation of Autoworkers," *Detroit Free Press* (April 10, 1995): 10F–12F.

6. James L. Heskett, Thomas O. Jones, Gary W. Loveman, W. Earl Sasser Jr., and Leonard A. Schlesinger, "Putting the Service/Profit Chain to Work," *Harvard Business Review* (March-April 1994): 165.

7. Ronald B. Morgan and Jack E. Smith, "A New Era in Manufacturing and Service," *Quality Progress* (July 1993): 83–89.

8. Richard Blackburn and Bensen Rosen, "Human Resource Management and Total Quality Management," in *Research in Quality Management,* D. Fedor and S. Ghosh, eds. (Greenwich, Conn.: JAI Press, in press).

9. Jack Smith and Ronald Morgan, "Staffing for Quality Improvement: A Survey of ASQC Sustaining Member Organizations," technical report (White Lake, Mich.: HRProcesses, and Northville, Mich.: Organization Solutions, 1994).

10. John D. Arnold, "Benchmarking Salaried Selection: Overview of Best Practices," paper presented at the Tenth Annual Conference of the Society for Industrial and Organizational Psychology, Orlando, Fla., May 20, 1995.

appendix A

Staffing for Quality Improvement: A Survey of ASQC Sustaining Member Organizations

STAFFING FOR QUALITY IMPROVEMENT:
A Survey of ASQC Sustaining Member Organizations

Instructions

The following sections ask about the experiences your organization has had in staffing for quality improvement. Please read each section carefully and respond in the manner you feel best characterizes your organization. In most cases we ask that you generalize about your organization. We ask you to do so even though the quality practices within your company may differ from division to division, or unit to unit.

USE A NO. 2 PENCIL ONLY

IMPROPER MARKS	**PROPER MARK**
⊘⊗⊖⊙	●

- Use only a No. 2 pencil
- Erase all changes cleanly and completely
- Do not make any stray marks on the form

Organizational Confidentiality

The survey items will ask about practices within your specific organization. However, the results of your individual organization's response will be held in strict confidentiality. Data will be summarized over all participating organizations. **Only aggregated data will be reported.**

Glossary

Throughout the survey, we use terms from both the quality and human resource disciplines. To facilitate understanding, we've attached a glossary of *least understood* terms at the end of the survey. Please refer to page 11 as needed.

General Questions about Quality Improvement in Your Organization

1. To what extent do you feel your organization has incorporated the philosophy and practices of a TQM organization in how it does business?
   - ○ Slight extent - quality practices in beginning stages
   - ○ Some extent
   - ○ A moderate extent - but there is still much to do
   - ○ A great extent
   - ○ Very great extent - the driving force for our organization

2. In some organizations, quality efforts are highly centralized (e.g., a few programs initiated, developed and implemented by headquarters). In others, quality improvement efforts are decentralized (e.g., initiated, developed locally). Which best characterizes the quality efforts in your organization?
   - ○ Very centralized
   - ○ Somewhat centralized
   - ○ Mixture: some centralized, some decentralized
   - ○ Somewhat decentralized
   - ○ Very decentralized

3. Which of the following characterizes the philosophical roots of your quality improvement efforts?
   Mark all that apply.
   - ○ Deming
   - ○ Juran
   - ○ Crosby
   - ○ Kaizen
   - ○ Other (please list) _____

Current Quality Improvement Practices

4. There are a variety of quality improvement philosophies, tools and processes. They may be used individually or in various combinations. Please indicate the extent to which these tools are used in your organization.

Identify the extent to which your organization does or does not use each practice.

Extent of Use

Extensive use
Considerable use
Some use
Limited use
None

Quality Improvement Practices

If needed, please describe your quality initiatives in greater detail:
_____
_____
_____

a. Comprehensive TQM Program ① ② ③ ④ ⑤
b. Benchmarking Programs ① ② ③ ④ ⑤
c. Statistical Quality Control (e.g., SPC) ① ② ③ ④ ⑤
d. Customer Service Programs ① ② ③ ④ ⑤
e. Process Improvement ① ② ③ ④ ⑤
f. Reengineering Programs (e.g., Hammer & Champy) ① ② ③ ④ ⑤
g. Team-based Programs
   1. Quality Circles or Problem Solving Teams ① ② ③ ④ ⑤
   2. Work Teams (not self-managed) ① ② ③ ④ ⑤
   3. Self-directed or Self-managed Teams ① ② ③ ④ ⑤
h. Quality Standards
   1. Malcolm Baldrige ① ② ③ ④ ⑤
   2. ISO 9000 ① ② ③ ④ ⑤
i. Other _____ ① ② ③ ④ ⑤
j. Other _____ ① ② ③ ④ ⑤

5. Some organizations have a short period of experience with systematic quality improvement programs, while others have a more extensive base of experience. How long have your quality improvement efforts been in place?

Estimate the duration in years for each of the following programs. If the time differs for various functions, record the interval for the function or unit with the longest history.

Mark the years next to each program. Leave blank those not being used.

Length of time quality improvement program has been in place (Years)

a. Comprehensive TQM Program ① ② ③ ④ ⑤ ⑥ ⑦ ⑧ ⑨ ⑩
b. Benchmarking Programs ① ② ③ ④ ⑤ ⑥ ⑦ ⑧ ⑨ ⑩
c. Statistical Quality Control (e.g., SPC) ① ② ③ ④ ⑤ ⑥ ⑦ ⑧ ⑨ ⑩
d. Customer Service Programs ① ② ③ ④ ⑤ ⑥ ⑦ ⑧ ⑨ ⑩
e. Process Improvement ① ② ③ ④ ⑤ ⑥ ⑦ ⑧ ⑨ ⑩
f. Reengineering Programs (e.g., Hammer & Champy) ① ② ③ ④ ⑤ ⑥ ⑦ ⑧ ⑨ ⑩
g. Team-based Programs
   1. Quality Circles or Problem Solving Teams ① ② ③ ④ ⑤ ⑥ ⑦ ⑧ ⑨ ⑩
   2. Work Teams (not self-managed) ① ② ③ ④ ⑤ ⑥ ⑦ ⑧ ⑨ ⑩
   3. Self-directed or Self-managed Teams ① ② ③ ④ ⑤ ⑥ ⑦ ⑧ ⑨ ⑩
h. Quality Standards
   1. Malcolm Baldrige ① ② ③ ④ ⑤ ⑥ ⑦ ⑧ ⑨ ⑩
   2. ISO 9000 ① ② ③ ④ ⑤ ⑥ ⑦ ⑧ ⑨ ⑩
i. Other _____ ① ② ③ ④ ⑤ ⑥ ⑦ ⑧ ⑨ ⑩
j. Other _____ ① ② ③ ④ ⑤ ⑥ ⑦ ⑧ ⑨ ⑩

Quality-related Attributes in the Non-Managerial Workforce

6. The following asks you to identify the importance of various quality attributes to the successful implementation of quality improvement efforts in your organization.

Because these attributes may be more important for some roles than for others, we ask you to think separately about two categories of employees, hourly/blue collar and professional/technical.

Read through the complete list of attributes. Then, think about hourly/blue collar employees in your organization. Complete the ratings of importance for hourly/blue collar employees. Repeat these judgements for professional/technical employees. Consider your organization culture and the nature of the quality interventions you are using when completing your rating.

Importance to Quality Effort

Rating scale for each: Unimportant (1), Slightly Important (2), Important (3), Very Important (4), Critical (5)

Attribute	Hourly/Blue Collar	Technical/Professional
a. Basic Reading Skills	①②③④⑤	①②③④⑤
b. Basic Math Skills	①②③④⑤	①②③④⑤
c. Basic Personal Computer Skills	①②③④⑤	①②③④⑤
d. Knowledge of Applied Statistics	①②③④⑤	①②③④⑤
e. Knowledge of Statistical Process Control	①②③④⑤	①②③④⑤
f. Knowledge of Experimental Design	①②③④⑤	①②③④⑤
g. Knowledge of Benchmarking	①②③④⑤	①②③④⑤
h. Knowledge of Process Improvement Techniques	①②③④⑤	①②③④⑤
i. Knowledge of Quality Theories and Approaches (e.g., Deming, Juran, Crosby)	①②③④⑤	①②③④⑤
j. Knowledge of Reengineering	①②③④⑤	①②③④⑤
k. Knowledge of Quality Tools (e.g., run charts, fishbone diagrams, Pareto charts, Brainstorming)	①②③④⑤	①②③④⑤
l. Knowledge of ISO 9000	①②③④⑤	①②③④⑤
m. Knowledge of Baldrige Criteria	①②③④⑤	①②③④⑤
n. Skills in Involving Others (e.g., encouraging input and participation)	①②③④⑤	①②③④⑤
o. Skill in Coaching Others (e.g., helping others to set and attain their personal best; supporting others)	①②③④⑤	①②③④⑤
p. Skill in Empowering Others (e.g., helping others assume responsibility and make decisions)	①②③④⑤	①②③④⑤
q. Skill in Relating to Others (e.g., listening to others, developing cooperative relationships, and dealing with conflict)	①②③④⑤	①②③④⑤
r. Skill in Oral Communication	①②③④⑤	①②③④⑤
s. Skill in Written Communication	①②③④⑤	①②③④⑤
t. Skill in Developing and Facilitating Teams (building cooperation, keeping on track, managing conflicts)	①②③④⑤	①②③④⑤
u. Skill in Problem Solving (using systematic methods such as PDCA cycle and scientific method to improve quality)	①②③④⑤	①②③④⑤
v. Skill in Implementing Organizational Change (e.g., creating climate and direction for change)	①②③④⑤	①②③④⑤
w. Customer Orientation (friendliness, agreeableness, empathetic)	①②③④⑤	①②③④⑤
x. Creative Thinking (imaginative, broad-minded)	①②③④⑤	①②③④⑤
y. Openness to Learning, Development and Retraining	①②③④⑤	①②③④⑤
z. Teamwork Orientation (group identification, involvement)	①②③④⑤	①②③④⑤
aa. Conscientiousness (thorough, responsible, hardworking)	①②③④⑤	①②③④⑤
bb. Flexibility/Adaptability (Openness to Change)	①②③④⑤	①②③④⑤

Quality-related Attributes in Managers

7. Some attributes are more important than others to the successful implementation of quality improvement efforts. Considering your organization's culture and the nature of the quality interventions you are using, indicate the importance of the following attributes to the roles of 1st Line, Middle and Top Management in your organization.

Read through the complete list of attributes. Then, begin by indicating the importance of each to your 1st line managers. Next, complete the ratings for middle managers, and last for Senior/Top management.

Importance to Quality Effort

Rating scale (for each of 1st Line Mgmt, Middle Mgmt, Senior Mgmt): Uninportant (1), Slightly important (2), Important (3), Very important (4), Critical (5)

Attribute	1st Line Mgmt	Middle Mgmt	Senior Mgmt
a. Basic Reading Skills	①②③④⑤	①②③④⑤	①②③④⑤
b. Basic Math Skills	①②③④⑤	①②③④⑤	①②③④⑤
c. Basic Personal Computer Skills	①②③④⑤	①②③④⑤	①②③④⑤
d. Knowledge of Applied Statistics	①②③④⑤	①②③④⑤	①②③④⑤
e. Knowledge of Statistical Process Control	①②③④⑤	①②③④⑤	①②③④⑤
f. Knowledge of Experimental Design	①②③④⑤	①②③④⑤	①②③④⑤
g. Knowledge of Benchmarking	①②③④⑤	①②③④⑤	①②③④⑤
h. Knowledge of Process Improvement Techniques	①②③④⑤	①②③④⑤	①②③④⑤
i. Knowledge of Quality Theories and Approaches (e.g., Deming, Juran, Crosby)	①②③④⑤	①②③④⑤	①②③④⑤
j. Knowledge of Reengineering	①②③④⑤	①②③④⑤	①②③④⑤
k. Knowledge of Quality Tools (e.g., run charts, fishbone diagrams, Pareto charts, Brainstorming)	①②③④⑤	①②③④⑤	①②③④⑤
l. Knowledge of ISO 9000	①②③④⑤	①②③④⑤	①②③④⑤
m. Knowledge of Baldrige Criteria	①②③④⑤	①②③④⑤	①②③④⑤
n. Skills in Involving Others (e.g., encouraging input and participation)	①②③④⑤	①②③④⑤	①②③④⑤
o. Skill in Coaching Others (e.g., helping others to set and attain their personal best; supporting others)	①②③④⑤	①②③④⑤	①②③④⑤
p. Skill in Empowering Others (e.g., helping others assume responsibility and make decisions)	①②③④⑤	①②③④⑤	①②③④⑤
q. Skill in Relating to Others (e.g., listening to others, developing cooperative relationships, and dealing with conflict)	①②③④⑤	①②③④⑤	①②③④⑤
r. Skill in Oral Communication	①②③④⑤	①②③④⑤	①②③④⑤
s. Skill in Written Communication	①②③④⑤	①②③④⑤	①②③④⑤
t. Skill in Developing and Facilitating Teams (building cooperation, keeping on track, managing conflicts)	①②③④⑤	①②③④⑤	①②③④⑤
u. Skill in Problem Solving (using systematic methods such as PDCA cycle and scientific method to improve quality)	①②③④⑤	①②③④⑤	①②③④⑤
v. Skill in Implementing Organizational Change (e.g., creating climate and direction for change)	①②③④⑤	①②③④⑤	①②③④⑤
w. Customer Orientation (friendliness, agreeableness, empathetic)	①②③④⑤	①②③④⑤	①②③④⑤
x. Creative Thinking (imaginative, broad-minded)	①②③④⑤	①②③④⑤	①②③④⑤
y. Openness to Learning, Development and Retraining	①②③④⑤	①②③④⑤	①②③④⑤
z. Teamwork Orientation (group identification, involvement)	①②③④⑤	①②③④⑤	①②③④⑤
aa. Conscientiousness (thorough, responsible, hardworking)	①②③④⑤	①②③④⑤	①②③④⑤
bb. Flexibility/Adaptability (Openness to Change)	①②③④⑤	①②③④⑤	①②③④⑤

Work Force Planning

8. Has your organization downsized its work force in the last five years?

   ○ Yes
   ○ No

If you answered "no" to item **8**, skip to item **11**.

9. Which part(s) of the work force was(were) downsized? Mark all that apply.

   ○ 1st Line Managers (supervisors)
   ○ Middle Managers
   ○ Senior Managers
   ○ Hourly/Blue Collar
   ○ Technical/Professional

10. To what degree was that reduction in headcount a result of a systematic continuous improvement effort (i.e., process changes designed to eliminate redundancies, waste, and inefficiency versus simply a reduction in headcount)?

    ○ Exclusively a result of process improvement
    ○ Mostly a result of process improvement
    ○ Mix of process and across the board headcount
    ○ Mostly across the board headcount
    ○ Exclusively across the board headcount

11. How likely is it that your organization will reduce its work force in the next five years?

    ○ Very likely
    ○ Somewhat likely
    ○ Possibly
    ○ Somewhat unlikely
    ○ Very unlikely

Comments: _____

_____

Use of Contingent Work Force

The following items deal with the use your organization makes of contingent workers (part-time employees, temporary workers, leased employees and contract laborers).

12. Does your organization use any of the following? Mark all that apply.

    ○ Part-time employees
    ○ Temporary workers
    ○ Leased workers
    ○ Contract laborers
    ○ Students (e.g., interns, co-ops, summer hires)
    ○ Retired Employees
    ○ Other_____

13. Compared to five years ago, our use of contingent workers has:

    ○ Increased
    ○ Remained the Same
    ○ Decreased

14. In the next five years, our use of contingent workers will likely:

    ○ Increase
    ○ Remain the Same
    ○ Decrease

15. In what way does the use of a contingent work force impact your quality effort?

    ○ A strong positive impact
    ○ A positive impact
    ○ No impact, positive or negative
    ○ A negative impact
    ○ A strong negative impact

Comments about the role and impact of your contingent work force on your quality effort: _____

_____

_____

Evaluating Applicants for Selection and Promotion

16. The following item concerns your selection and promotion practices. Each item asks that you evaluate the extent to which **quality-related attributes** (like those listed earlier) are evaluated when making selection and promotion decisions.

The first column asks about your **current** selection and promotion practices related to quality. The second column asks you to think back to your selection and promotion practices **five years ago**. Column three asks you to judge about the future, **five years from now**.

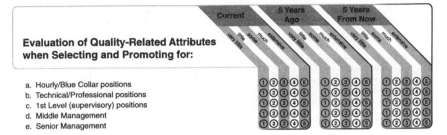

Evaluation of Quality-Related Attributes when Selecting and Promoting for:

	Current	5 Years Ago	5 Years From Now
a. Hourly/Blue Collar positions	①②③④⑤	①②③④⑤	①②③④⑤
b. Technical/Professional positions	①②③④⑤	①②③④⑤	①②③④⑤
c. 1st Level (supervisory) positions	①②③④⑤	①②③④⑤	①②③④⑤
d. Middle Management	①②③④⑤	①②③④⑤	①②③④⑤
e. Senior Management	①②③④⑤	①②③④⑤	①②③④⑤

Assessment Devices Currently Being Used in Your Company

17. The following item deals with the assessment practices currently being used within your company to evaluate the attributes and experiences of **applicants for hire and/or promotion**.

Complete for hourly/blue collar, then technical/professional, and so on.

Which of the following are currently used to assess applicants for...	Hourly/ Blue Collar Positions	Technical/ Professional Positions	Supervisory Positions	Middle Mgmt Positions	Senior Mgmt Positions
a. Interviews	○	○	○	○	○
b. Written <u>knowledge</u> test	○	○	○	○	○
c. Written aptitude/ability tests (such as basic skills, mechanical aptitude...)	○	○	○		○
d. Work sample tests	○	○	○	○	○
e. Exercises or simulations measuring team interaction skills	○	○	○	○	○
f. Standardized (paper and pencil) personality measures (such as Myers-Briggs or California Psychological Inventory)	○	○	○	○	○
g. Assessment Centers	○	○	○	○	○
h. Applications	○	○	○	○	○
i. Biographical Inventories	○	○	○	○	○
j. Reference Checks	○	○	○	○	○
k. Internal Performance Appraisal Data (for internal promotions)	○	○	○	○	○

Procedures Used to Assess Quality-related Knowledge, Skills, Temperament and Experience

18. In the previous section you identified various assessment procedures your organization uses in hiring and/or promotion decisions. Now, we'd like you to tell us if any of those tools are used to assess quality-related attributes and experience.

○ Yes, we use assessment procedures to evaluate specific quality-related attributes
○ No, we don't evaluate specific quality-related attributes

If yes, please identify the specific procedures used to assess quality attributes and experiences, the attributes they evaluate, and the types of jobs (hourly/blue collar, technical/professional, supervisory, middle management, senior management).

If necessary, refer back to the list of quality attributes (page 4) and to the list of assessment devices (page 6).

Procedure(s) Used to Evaluate Quality Attributes	Job Categories	Quality Attributes Assessed	Comments

General Comments: _____

_____

_____

_____

_____

_____

_____

PAGE 7

Recruiting Sources

19. Most organizations rely on a variety of recruiting sources. The following items ask for your evaluation of various sources of **external applicants for hourly/blue collar, technical/professional and managerial positions.**

Complete for hourly/blue collar, then technical/professional, then managerial.

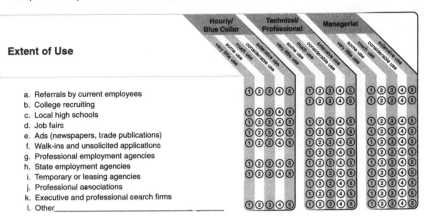

Extent of Use

a. Referrals by current employees
b. College recruiting
c. Local high schools
d. Job fairs
e. Ads (newspapers, trade publications)
f. Walk-ins and unsolicited applications
g. Professional employment agencies
h. State employment agencies
i. Temporary or leasing agencies
j. Professional associations
k. Executive and professional search firms
l. Other_____

Mix of Internal - External Recruiting

20. Organizations have different practices regarding their mix of internal/external recruitment. Excluding entry level positions, some organizations promote exclusively from within, others recruit outside the organization. Describe your organization's approach.

Mix of Internal/External Recruitment

a. Hourly/Blue Collar positions
b. Technical/Professional positions
c. 1st Level (supervisory) Management
d. Middle Management
e. Senior Management

Quality Related Competence of New Hires

21. This item asks you to evaluate the quality attributes and experiences of the new employees hired into your organization.

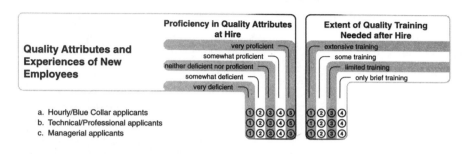

Quality Attributes and Experiences of New Employees	Proficiency in Quality Attributes at Hire	Extent of Quality Training Needed after Hire
	very proficient / somewhat proficient / neither deficient nor proficient / somewhat deficient / very deficient	extensive training / some training / limited training / only brief training
a. Hourly/Blue Collar applicants	① ② ③ ④ ⑤	① ② ③ ④
b. Technical/Professional applicants	① ② ③ ④ ⑤	① ② ③ ④
c. Managerial applicants	① ② ③ ④ ⑤	① ② ③ ④

About Your Organization

The following information will be used to look at trends across different types of industries and organizations.

22. **Industry Grouping:** Which industry grouping best characterizes your organization?

- Health Care
- Educational Institution
- Manufacturing
- Financial Services
- State, Local, Federal Government
- Construction
- Utility
- Transportation
- Telecommunications
- Computer Services
- Chemical & Pharmaceutical
- Mining & Petroleum
- Retailers, Wholesalers, Merchandise
- Consumer Products (e.g., Food/Beverage)
- Hospitality (e.g., Hotel, Restaurant)
- Other _____

23. **Organization Size:** Which of the following best characterizes your organization?

- <100
- 100-499
- 500-999
- 1,000-4,999
- 5,000-9,999
- 10,000+

24. **Function of Person Completing Survey:**

- Human Resources V.P. or Manager
- Staffing Specialist or Manager
- Quality Specialist or Manager
- General Manager (e.g., plant or facility manager)
- Other _____

Profile of Benchmark Staffing Organizations

25. If you would like to profile a staffing issue, incident, practice or technique in the ASQC Quality Press book, please provide a brief description below. We will then contact you for further discussion. If you have information that you believe would be of interest, but you would prefer that you and your organization remain anonymous, we will honor that request. We are very interested in finding out about your company's experiences, innovations and challenges.

_____

_____

_____

_____

Quality Staffing Network

26. If you would like to list yourself and/or your organization in the Quality Staffing Network, please note so below. The Quality Staffing Network will appear in the book, and will provide interested readers with a network of individuals to call for purposes of sharing innovations and experiences regarding various staffing issues. If you choose to, you can identify an issue of particular interest or expertise. This would identify you as a source to which others could turn for collegial discussion and networking.

Yes, I would like to include myself/my organization in the Quality Staffing Network.

Name of contact person _____

Organization _____

Address _____

Phone (___)_____

Issues/topics I would like listed with my name (e.g., downsizing, use of contingent workers, testing quality attributes):

_____

_____

Contact Person

27. Please identify the person who completed this survey.

Name _____

Title _____

Address _____

_____

Phone (___)_____

Quality Glossary

ASSESSMENT CENTER: Selection and development process where individuals are evaluated as they participate in a series of exercises or simulations which resemble what they might be called upon to handle on the job.

BALDRIGE AWARD AND CRITERIA: U.S. presidential citations awarded annually to recognize companies that excel in quality management and quality achievement. A specific set of award criteria are provided and can be used to provide a framework for quality initiatives.

BENCHMARKING: An improvement process in which a company measures its performance against that of best-in-class companies, determines how those companies achieved their performance levels, and uses the information to improve its own performance.

BIOGRAPHICAL INVENTORIES: Form used for predicting job success which utilizes biographical information of job applicants.

CROSBY, PHILIP: Prominent quality consultant known for his writings on "the cost of poor quality" and for originating the term "zero defects".

DEMING, W. EDWARDS: A prominent consultant, teacher, and author on the subject of quality. Known for his efforts in helping Japan recover from its wartime losses and for his 14 points for quality management.

EXPERIMENTAL DESIGN: A formal plan that details the specifics for conducting an experiment to determine cause and effect.

ISO 9000 SERIES STANDARDS: A set of five individual but related international standards on quality management and quality assurance developed to help companies effectively document the quality system elements to be implemented to maintain an efficient quality system.

JURAN, JOSEPH M.: Also a prominent consultant and author on the subject of quality. Known for his focus on managing for quality and his prolific writings on the topic of quality.

KAIZEN: A Japanese term that means gradual unending improvement by doing little things better and setting and achieving increasingly higher standards.

PLAN-DO-CHECK-ACT CYCLE (PDCA CYCLE): A four-step process for quality improvement including a plan to effect improvement is developed, the plan is carried out, the effects of the plan are observed, and the results are studied to determine what was learned.

QUALITY TOOLS: Tools that help organizations understand their processes in order to improve them. Other tools than those listed include check sheets, control charts, flowcharts, histograms, and scatter diagrams.

REENGINEERING: The fundamental rethinking and radical redesign of business processes to achieve dramatic improvements in critical, contemporary measures of performance (Hammer and Champy). It means "starting over" versus simply improving an existing process.

STATISTICAL PROCESS CONTROL (SPC): The application of statistical techniques to control a process. Often the term "statistical quality control" is used interchangeably with SPC.

TOTAL QUALITY MANAGEMENT (TQM): A comprehensive management approach to long-term success through customer satisfaction. TQM is based on the participation of all members of an organization in improving processes, products, services, and the culture they work in.

WORK SAMPLE TESTS: Tests that require the examinee to perform tasks that are actually a part of the work to be performed on the job.

PAGE 11

appendix **B**

The Quality Attributes Inventory

Quality Knowledge and Skills

Basic

1. Reading
2. Mathematics
3. Oral communication
4. Written communication
5. Personal computer (PC) skills
6. Presentation skills
7.
8.
9.

Quality Theories and Approaches

10. Deming, W. Edwards
11. Juran, Joseph M.
12. Crosby, Philip
13. Kaizen

14.

15.

Quality Tools: The Basic Seven

16. Pareto diagrams

17. Cause-and-effect (fishbone) diagrams

18. Histograms

19. Control charts

20. Scatter diagrams

21. Graphs (bar, line, circle, or pie)

22. Check sheets

Other Quality Tools and Methods

23. Run chart

24. Process flowchart

25. Affinity diagram

26. Interrelationship diagram

27. Tree diagram

28. Matrix diagram

29. Brainstorming

30. Nominal group technique

31. Force-field analysis

32. Suggestion systems

33. Arrow diagram

34. Root-cause analysis (five whys)

35. Gantt chart

36. Critical path chart

37. Decision matrix

38. Inspection
39. Supplier quality assurance

Basic Descriptive and Inferential Statistics

40. Central tendency measures (mean, median, mode)
41. Variability (standard deviation, range)
42. Sampling
43. Probability
44. Correlation
45. Regression
46. *T*-tests
47. Analysis of variance (ANOVA)
48.
49.
50.
51.
52.

Systematic Problem Solving

53. Scientific method
54. Process decision program chart (PDPC)
55. Seven-step quality improvement process
56. Experimental design (Taguchi methods)
57. Plan-do-check-act cycle (PDCA)
58. Process improvement
59. Reengineering
60.
61.
62.
63.

Quality Standards

64. Malcolm Baldrige National Quality Award criteria and award

65. ISO 9000 series standards

66. Benchmarking

67. Deming Prize

68. QS-9000 automotive quality standard

69.

70.

71.

Attitude and Satisfaction Measures

72. Customer satisfaction surveys

73. Focus groups and panels

74. Complaint measures

75. Employee attitude surveys

76. Quality function deployment (QFD)

77.

78.

79.

80.

Interpersonal and Group Skills

81. Group facilitation skills

82. Listening skills

83. Persuading others

84. Employee involvement skills (temperament)

85. Empowering skills (temperament)

86. Stand-up training skills

87.

88.

89.

90.

Personality and Temperament Traits

The Quality Six

91. Customer orientation (friendliness, agreeableness, empathy)

92. Creative thinking (imaginative, innovative, broad-minded)

93. Openness to learning, development, and retraining

94. Teamwork orientation (group identification, cooperation, involvement)

95. Conscientiousness (thorough, responsible, hard working)

96. Flexibility/adaptability (openness to change)

Other Quality-Related Traits

97. Quality consciousness

98. Interpersonal skills

99. Integrity/ethical

100.

101.

102.

Certification and Professional Affiliation

ASQC Certification

103. Certified Mechanical Inspector (CMI)

104. Certified Quality Auditor (CQA)

105. Certified Quality Engineer (CQE)

106. Certified Quality Technician (CQT)

107. Certified Reliability Engineer (CRE)

108. Quality Engineer in Training (QEIT)

109. Certified Quality Manager (CQM)

Professional Affiliation

110. American Society for Quality Control (ASQC)

111. American Society for Training and Development (ASTD)

112. American Management Association (AMA)

113. Society of Reliability Engineers

114. American Quality Forum

115. Engineering Society of America

116.

117.

118.

119.

Engineering and Quality Assurance

120. Just-in-time inventory

121. Kanban

122. Computer-assisted design (CAD)

123. Computer-assisted manufacturing (CAM)

124. Concurrent engineering

125. Agile manufacturing

126. MRP/MRPII

127. Nondestructive testing and evaluation (NDE and NDT)

128.

129.

130.

Firms Specializing in Recruiting in the Quality Setting

Company	Type of jobs	Specific industries	Geographical area	Fee schedule
J. N. Adams & Associates, Inc. 315 S. Allen St., Suite 222-B State College, PA 16801 (814) 234-0670 (814) 234-4361 fax	Quality and engineering professionals at management and director levels	Across industries	United States with the exception of the west coast	30% of first year's earnings
Advanced Performance Solutions, Inc. 4109 Leesburg Pike Falls Church, VA 22041 (800) 235-1999 (703) 418-3634 fax	Primarily executives with quality experience for socio or technical needs	Health care, manufacturing, government, service, airspace and defense	Continental United States	Negotiable
Advent Management Associates, Ltd. 1220 Ward Ave., Suite 350 West Chester, PA 19380 (215) 431-2196 (215) 431-2641 fax	Primarily senior executives, ISO coordinators, quality engineers, directors of quality, quality managers	Across industries	North America, Europe, and the Far East	30–35 percent of first year's earnings
American Newspaper Consultants Ltd. P.O. Box 08509 Milwaukee, WI 53208 (414) 272-6173 (414) 272-6173 fax	Middle and upper-level management	Newspaper	United States and Canada	Negotiable
Arctic Slope Inspection Services 301 Arctic Slope Ave. Anchorage, AK 99518-3035 (907) 349-5148 (907) 349-4213 fax	Inspectors for visual on-site mechanical and civil inspection	Petrochemical	United States	Negotiable

Company	Type of jobs	Specific industries	Geographical area	Fee schedule
Benchmark Technologies Corp. 1995 Tremainsville Rd. Toledo, OH 43613 (419) 474-6609 (419) 474-8655 fax	Quality inspectors, engineers, and managers at all levels	Manufacturing and service	United States	Negotiable
Corporate Resources Group 180 Belden Hill Rd. Wilton, CT 06897 (203) 761-9707 (203) 762-7947 fax	Middle and upper-level executives in public relations and marketing	Across industries	Mexico, Europe, and the United States with emphasis on the metro New York area	25–30 percent of first year's earnings
J. D. Cotter Search, Inc. Terri Rowe 2999 E. Dublin-Granville Rd., Suite 301 Columbus, OH 43231 (614) 895-2065	Quality directors, managers, engineers. All engineering positions, HR/training/OD positions	Across industries	Midwest	30 percent of first year's total compensation
Dunhill 9918 Coldwater Rd. Fort Wayne, IN 46825 (219) 489-5966 (219) 489-6120 fax	Quality engineers, quality managers, statisticians, reliability engineers, and various other quality professionals	Manufacturing and service	United States with an emphasis on the Midwest and Southeast	30 percent of starting salary or negotiable
F-O-R-T-U-N-E Personnel Consultants of Alabama 3311 Bob Wallace Ave., Suite 204 Huntsville, AL 35805 (205) 534-7282 (205) 534-7334 fax	Middle to upper-level quality engineers and managers	Manufacturing and engineering	United States	1/3 of first year's earnings

Company	Type of jobs	Specific industries	Geographical area	Fee schedule
F-O-R-T-U-N-E Personnel Consultants of Charleston, Inc. 389 Johnnie Dodds Blvd., Suite 201 Mount Pleasant, SC 29464 (803) 884-0505 (803) 884-9522 fax	All quality positions in management and engineering from the top of an organization to the bottom	Automotive	United States, Mexico and Canada	Negotiable
F-O-R-T-U-N-E Personnel Consultants of Columbia 108 Columbia Dr. N.E. Suite H Columbia, SC 29223 (803) 788-8877 (803) 788-1509 fax	Quality directors, managers, purchasers, vice presidents, engineers, supervisors, accounting and finance, and MIS personnel	Manufacturing	United States	Negotiable
F-O-R-T-U-N-E Personnel Consultants of Knoxville, Inc. 10339 Chapman Hwy., Suite 8 Seymour, TN 37865 (615) 577-1313 (615) 577-4370 fax	All quality positions from engineers to vice presidents	Automotive, chemical, electronic, plastic, medical device, and HV/AC	United States	1 percent per $1000 with a maximum of 35 percent of first year's earnings
F-O-R-T-U-N-E Personnel Consultants of Rockland County, Inc. 71 E. Eckerson Rd., Suite A Spring Valley, NY 10977 (914) 426-3200 (914) 426-3814 fax	All middle management and executive-level quality-related personnel	Mechanical and electromechanical	United States	Negotiable
F-O-R-T-U-N-E Personnel Consultants of Sarasota, Inc. 98 Sarasota Center Blvd., Suite C Sarasota, FL 34240-9770 (813) 378-5262 (813) 378-8833 f	Quality engineering, materials management, purchasing, and manufacturing operations	Manufacturing	Continental United States	Negotiable

Company	Type of jobs	Specific industries	Geographical area	Fee schedule
Grady & Associates 40 C Lake St. Winchester, MA 01890 (617) 721-5770	Middle and upper-level quality managers and engineers	Printing, publishing, paper, and allied	New England area	Negotiable
G. E. Hassell Associates 645 Main Place P.O. Box 471 Niles, OH 44446 (216) 652-5871 (216) 652-3683 fax	Quality and reliability directors, managers and engineers	Manufacturing and some service	United States	Negotiable
Jamohr USA Enterprises, Inc. P.O. Box 144 Jefferson, NY 12093 (800) 452-6647 (617) 652-3302 (617) 652-3302 fax	Provides individuals in procurement quality assurance services including supplier qualifications, audits, surveillances, source inspections, and product management	Power utility and manufacturing	International	Negotiable
Paul D. Krensky Associates, Inc. Adams Bldg., 9 Merriam St. Lexington, MA 02173 (617) 862-3003 (617) 862-3004 fax	Quality reliability, inspector, vice presidents, and middle to upper-level managers, engineers, and directors	Across industries	United States	Negotiable
Management Recruiters of New Bern 1319 S. Glenburnie Rd. New Bern, NC 28562-2605 (919) 633-1900 (919) 633-3121 fax	Middle and upper-level quality managers and engineers	Manufacturing and plant management	United States	30 percent of first year's earnings

Company	Type of jobs	Specific industries	Geographical area	Fee schedule
Moody-Tottrup International, Inc. 650 N. Sam Houston Parkway East, Suite 228 Houston, TX 77060 (713) 448-0700 (713) 448-1401 fax	Quality control positions from the shop floor to upper management	Oil, gas, chemical, power, and petrochemical	International	Negotiable
The Mulcahy Co., Inc. 140 S. Park St., Suite 200 Port Washington, WI 53074 (414) 284-1700 (414) 284-6220 fax	Middle and upper-level quality directors, managers, and engineers	Manufacturing and process industries	Midwest	30 percent of first year's earnings
Phelps Personnel Associates, Inc. P.O. Box 4177Q Greenville, SC 29608 (803) 232-8139 (803) 271-1426 fax	Middle to upper-level quality engineers and managers (must have degree)	Manufacturing with an emphasis on the automotive, electronic, and chemical industries	United States with an emphasis in the Southeast	Negotiable
Quality Control Recruiters P.O. Box 1900 Bristol, CT 06011-1900 (203) 582-0003 (203) 585-7395 fax	Quality control and reliability engineers, managers, and directors	Manufacturing and service	United States	Fixed rates
Resource Management Services 2422 Berton Southeast Grand Rapids, MI 49546 (616) 336-0200 (616) 336-0238 fax	Quality control engineers, middle and upper-level management, pharmacists, X-Ray technicians, and respiratory therapists	Technical and engineering-related industries, health care	Southeast Michigan	Negotiable

Company	Type of jobs	Specific industries	Geographical area	Fee schedule
Total Business Service Center P.O. Box 23436 Rochester, NY 14692-3436 (716) 385-7570 (716) 385-5662 fax	Middle to upper-level quality control managers and engineers	Research and design, government, hospital	United States	Negotiable
Warren Executive Services P.O. Box 1517 Lilburn (Atlanta), GA 30226 (404) 381-1175 (404) 279-7865 fax	Middle to upper-level quality and reliability engineers, managers, and supervisors	Manufacturing with an emphasis on the automotive, electronics, and computer industries	United States	Negotiable
Zenith Consulting Group, Inc. 17 Morgan CT. Hurricane, WV 25526 (304) 757-9379 (304) 757-8484 fax	Engineering positions ranging from junior engineers to assistant vice president	Manufacturing	300–500 mile radius	Negotiable

appendix **D**

Interview Questions for Key Managerial Attributes

Possible interview questions for those attributes considered important for managerial success in the quality setting. Attributes include the following:

- Flexibility/adaptability
- Skill in relating to others
- Skill in coaching others
- Skill in oral communication
- Skill in empowering others
- Skill in involving others
- Conscientiousness
- Teamwork orientation
- Openness to learning
- Creative thinking
- Skill in written communication

These questions are for illustration purposes only and are not meant to replace individual organization efforts at developing interview questions. They should be viewed as a starting point for developing a structured interview. We suggest that these questions be modified for local use and that additional questions and probes be developed.

Flexibility/Adaptability

Attribute: The individual is flexible and open to change.

Q. Despite our best efforts to keep operations running smoothly, inevitably there are occasions when some unexpected event disrupts the normal work routine. Thinking back on your last job, tell me about an incident when the normal work routine was disrupted.

- How did you respond?

- What actions did you take to restore order?

- How long did it take?

- How often did unexpected events such as this one occur?

- In retrospect, was there any way this disruption could have been avoided or minimized?

- What did you learn from the experience?

Q. Please describe a time when you had difficulty adapting to a new method of doing an aspect of your job.

- Why do you think you had difficulty adapting?

- Did other workers have trouble adapting to the new method?

- Were you trained in the new method?

- Did you finally learn the new method? If so, how long did it take?

- In the end, did you decide the new method was better or worse than the old method? In what ways?

- Can you think of something that would have made it easier for you to adapt to the new method?

Q. From time to time, most of us are called on to fill in for an absent co-worker. Please recall a time when you had to take a co-worker's place and do his or her work for a short time.

- Was the work you did for the co-worker significantly different from the type of work you normally do?

- Did you have to rely on notes or instructions left by the co-worker? If so, were the notes helpful?

- Were you working with your co-worker's established customers/clients? If so, how did they respond to you?

- When the co-worker returned, did he or she comment on how you handled the work? Were the comments positive? Negative?

Q. In most jobs, when things get very busy, employees are sometimes asked to work overtime. Please think back to a time when you had to work overtime without being given advance notice.

- Was this forced overtime, or could you decline it if you chose to?

- Did working the overtime interfere with personal plans you had made for after work? If so, how did you feel about it?

Q. Suppose you have spent a great deal of time planning a project and your supervisor tells you to set that project aside and begin work on a new project. How would you respond?

- Why would you react in that way?

- Would you communicate your feelings to your supervisor? If so, in what way?

- How do you think your supervisor would respond?

Q. A supplier has just informed you that he will be about three weeks late with the supplies that were promised. How would you respond?

- Why would you respond in that way?

- What could you do to work around the missing supplies?

- What steps would you take to prevent such a problem from occurring in the future?

Candidate Observations

- Does the candidate demonstrate a willingness and ability to adapt to new working conditions?

- Is the candidate able to cope with unexpected problems in the work situation in a positive and effective manner?

Skill in Relating to Others

Attribute: Skills in listening to others and dealing with conflict, and ability to develop cooperative relationships.

Q. As a manager you will need to develop excellent interpersonal skills to facilitate interacting with a variety of persons all with different needs and personalities. Please describe what you consider to be your strongest skills in relating to others.

- Why do you consider these to be your strongest skills?

- How did you develop these skills?

- Can you recall an incident when these skills helped you in an awkward work situation? What were the circumstances? What was the outcome?

Q. Tell me about a situation on your previous job when you had to resolve a serious conflict between two co-workers.

- How did you gather the facts (that is, each person's view of the situation)?

- Did you have a personal relationship/friendship with either of the workers involved in the dispute? If so, how did this affect your response to the situation?

- How long did it take to resolve the conflict?

- In the end, were both parties satisfied with the outcome?

- Can you think of any way the conflict could be avoided in the future?

- What did you learn from the experience?

Q. As managers, we sometimes have to deliver bad news to an employee. For instance, we may have to tell the employee that his or her performance is inadequate. Tell me about a time when you had to deliver bad news to a subordinate.

- How did you approach the worker?

- Where did you discuss the matter with the employee (on the plant floor, in a private office)?

- How serious was the problem before the employee was notified?

- How did the employee react?

- Looking back, would you handle the situation in the same way, or would you do things differently? In what way?

Q. Tell me about any specialized courses you have had, or training seminars you have attended, that focused on interpersonal skills.

- When did you receive this training?

- Was the training offered to you by your company, or did you take it on your own outside of work?

- What part of the training did you find most valuable?

- Describe an instance in which you were able to use this training either at work or in your personal life.

Q. Suppose a subordinate offers a suggestion about a way to improve some aspect of the work process, but you are certain the improvement won't work well. How would you respond to the worker?

- Why would you respond in that way?

- How do you think the worker would feel?

- Do you think the worker would offer any suggestions in the future?

Q. Suppose, as a manager, you were to take charge of a work team that has a history of being uncooperative with each other and with management. What steps would you take to help this group develop into a cooperative, cohesive work team?

- Of these steps, which do you think are most important? Why?

- How would you overcome resistance?

- If this method didn't work, what other steps could you try?

Candidate Observations

- Does the candidate have experience in resolving conflict among group members?

- Is the candidate sensitive to the feelings of co-workers and subordinates?

- Did the candidate demonstrate an ability to develop and encourage cooperative relationships among team members?

Skill in Coaching Others

Attribute: Skill in coaching and supporting workers in a way that enhances the worker's ability to attain his or her personal best.

Q. As mangers, one of our most important responsibilities is coaching workers so that they can perform at their highest potential. Looking back on your last job, tell me about what steps you took to help the poorest worker improve his or her performance.

- How did you identify the worker's problem areas?

- How did you determine the causes of the worker's poor performance?

- How did the worker react to your intervention (welcomed the help, resisted it, or resented it)?

- Did the worker's performance improve? If yes, to what extent? How long did it take to see an improvement?

- Looking back, would you have done things differently? In what ways?

Q. Some employees lack confidence and fear that they can't successfully complete a given assignment. Tell me about a time when you gave an employee an assignment that the employee felt was too difficult but which you believed was within the employee's abilities.

- How did the employee react?

- What did you do to encourage the employee that he or she could do the work?

- How did you monitor the employee's progress?

- What was the outcome? Did the employee accomplish the task?

Q. No matter how ambitious a team of workers may be, inevitably there will come a time when motivation and interest in a project starts to fade. Tell me about a time when you were instrumental in boosting your work team's interest and motivation and, as a result, brought about a successful project completion.

- How did you accomplish this?

- At the time you did this, were you in a leadership position within the group?

- Did you personally feel unmotivated toward the project? If so, how did you boost your own motivation? Why?

- Did you meet resistance from some team members? If so, how did you overcome the resistance?

- What was the final outcome? Was the project finished on schedule? Were the results of the project better/worse, or about what had been initially expected?

- What did you learn from this situation?

- What would you do differently?

Q. Suppose one of your employees makes frequent and careless mistakes in his or her work. What steps would you take to help this employee improve his or her work and reduce the number of mistakes he or she makes?

- Of these steps, which do you think would be most effective? Why?

- If the employee resisted your efforts, what would you do?

Q. Suppose, after observing an employee for a period of time, you conclude that the employee is lacking the necessary skills to perform the work in your unit. How would you approach the problem?

- Why would you take those steps?

- Would your approach mostly benefit the organization or the employee, or would it be beneficial to both?

- How do you think the employee would react to your decision? How do you think your supervisor would feel about your decision?

- Can you think of any alternative approaches? What might they be?

Q. Please describe any coaching or teaching roles you have had outside of work (such as, Little League coach, scout leader).

- When was this?

- In what ways has the experience helped you as a manager at work?

- What have you learned from the experience?

Candidate Observations

- Does the candidate recognize the importance of the manager's role as coach?

- Does the candidate demonstrate an ability to function as coach in a way that enables the subordinate to enhance his or her performance?

- Has the candidate had any outside experience as a coach or teacher?

Skill in Oral Communication

Attribute: Skill in oral communication.

Q. One important role of a manager is to represent his or her work team at management meetings. In such meetings he or she will frequently be called upon to give presentations regarding the team's progress on projects. Tell me about the most successful presentation you have made in the past.

- Was this presentation at work or in some other setting (school, professional or social organization)?

- When was the presentation given?

- How did you prepare for the presentation?

- What made this presentation particularly good (topic, presentation style)?

Q. Now tell me about the presentation you are least proud of.

- What went wrong?

- Why did this happen?

- What could you have done to prevent the problem?

- What did you learn from the experience?

Q. Despite our best intentions, employees sometimes don't clearly understand the verbal instructions we give, and often they don't tell us that our directions are unclear. Tell me about a time when an employee misunderstood your instructions and a serious problem arose due to the misunderstanding.

- What was the nature of the problem?

- Was the fault yours or the employee's?

- What part of the message was unclear?

- How did you find out that the employee misunderstood you?

- How was the problem corrected?

- What steps did you take to ensure that such a problem doesn't arise in the future?

- What could have been done to prevent the misunderstanding?

Q. It is not always easy to express some ideas. Tell me about the most frustrating time you had trying to get across a particular concept.

- Who were you trying to relay the information to (subordinate, co-worker, someone outside of work)?

- Why do you think this was a particularly difficult concept to convey (was the content difficult, the listener inept)?

- How did you finally get the information across?

- How did you determine that the listener understood you?

Q. Suppose an employee with a hearing impairment frequently misunderstands your verbal instructions. What could you do to enhance communication between the two of you?

- Why would you take that approach?

- Can you think of an alternative approach?

- What would you do if the employee resisted these efforts?

- How would you ensure that the employee clearly understood your instructions in the future?

Q. Imagine that I am a new employee and it is your job to instruct me on how to perform a [give example]. Please describe this procedure for me.

- [Interviewer then follows up with appropriate questions about how the task described should be performed.]

Q. Please describe any formal or informal training courses or seminars you have attended that focused on oral communication skills.

- Where did you receive this training?

- When did you receive this training?

- What part of the course has been most beneficial to you on your job? In what way?

Candidate Considerations

- Does the candidate have varied experience in giving oral presentations?

- Does the candidate demonstrate an understanding of the importance of providing employees with clear verbal instructions?

- Did the candidate explain the [example] task in a way that the interviewer could clearly understand how to perform the task, or were the instructions unclear?

- Did the candidate demonstrate an ability to patiently address misunderstandings and a willingness to work at clarifying them?

Skill in Empowering Others

Attribute: Skill in empowering others by helping others assume responsibility and make decisions

Q. What does empowering employees mean to you?

- Why is it important to an organization that employees be empowered?

- In what ways do employees benefit from empowerment?

Q. Thinking back on your last job, what steps did you take to encourage employees to take responsibility for certain aspects of the work?

- How did the employees react?

- How did other supervisors react?

- Was there resistance? If so, how did you overcome it?

- Were the results positive? Negative? In what ways?

Q. Tell me about a situation in which an employee was given responsibility for a task that he or she failed to complete.

- How did you respond?

- What did you do to prevent this from happening in the future?

- Was there anything you could have done to prevent this failure from occurring? If so, what could you have done?

Q. Suppose you have an employee who resists your efforts to give him or her some responsibility for the work. What could you do to help the employee accept responsibility?

- Why would you take that action?

- If the employee continued to resist your efforts, would you try another tactic? If so, what would that be?

Q. Suppose an employee indicated a desire for more independence in work than you feel he or she is capable of handling. How would you respond to the employee?

- Why would you respond in that way?

- How do you think the employee would react to your decision?

- Under what circumstances do you think you might increase the employee's responsibility in the future?

Q. Please describe any training courses or seminars you have attended that focused on empowering employees.

- When did you take this course?

- Where was the course given?

- What did you learn in this course that helped you on the job?

Candidate Observations

- Does the candidate demonstrate a clear understanding of the meaning and importance of empowerment?

- Does the candidate have varied experience in empowering employees and in handling related problems?

- Does the candidate demonstrate a sensitivity to the unique capabilities and needs of individual employees?

Skill in Involving Others

Attribute: Skill in involving others in the work process through employee input and participation

Q. We value the opinions and suggestions of our employees. Looking back on your last job, tell me about a time when you actively sought your employees' suggestions on a particular project.

- How did the employees react to this request?

- What suggestion did you find to be most helpful?

- What was the least useful suggestion you received?

- How did you provide the employees with feedback for their suggestions?

- Overall, were the results of the project better or worse because of input from employees?

- What did you learn from the experience?

Q. Looking back on your last job, tell me about a time when you had difficulty getting employees to offer suggestions or opinions about a project.

- Why do you think the employees were reluctant to get involved?

- What did you do to encourage them to participate?

- Were these actions successful?

Q. Think back to a situation in which you acted on an employee's suggestion and the results were disastrous.

- What happened?

- How did you respond to the employee?

- How did your supervisor react?

- What could have been done to prevent the incident?

- What would you do differently today?

- What did you learn from the experience?

Q. As the new manager of a work team, suppose after a short period of observation that you notice that a few of your employees seem to be withdrawn and rarely participate in group discussions and decision making. What steps would you take to encourage these employees to join in?

- Why would you approach the situation in that way?
- What if that approach didn't work: would you try another? If so, what would the alternative approach be?

Candidate Observations

- Does the candidate demonstrate an ability to encourage reluctant employees to participate?
- Does the candidate actively seek involvement from others?

Conscientiousness

Attribute: Performs work tasks in a thorough, responsible, and hard-working manner.

Q. In almost every job there are busy times and there are slow times. Thinking back on your most recent slow time, describe what you did during a typical work day.

- Were these jobs or tasks different from those you would normally do?
- Was your pace more relaxed or about the same as normal?
- Were your activities different from those of your coworkers during this time?
- What gains did you make during this time, if any?

Q. From time to time, everybody takes a shortcut in doing their work. Tell me about a time when you took a shortcut that resulted in a serious problem.

- How did you correct the problem?
- Did your supervisor know that the shortcut was the cause of the problem?
- How did your supervisor react?
- What did you learn from the experience?

Q. Tell me about a time when, by being very thorough, you caught an error which could have been very serious if it had gone undetected.

- What were the circumstances?

- How did you detect the error?

- Was the error your own, or someone else's?

- Did you correct the error, or did you bring it to the attention of the supervisor?

- Has this event changed the way in which you or your coworkers work?

Q. Describe a situation in which, had you put forth more effort, the results of a project would have been better.

- Did you realize more effort was needed while the project was under way? If so, what prevented you from putting forth the extra effort?

- What would you do differently in the future?

- How did your supervisor react?

- What did you learn from this experience?

Q. Suppose that, as a project deadline approaches, you realize that the only way you can finish the project on time is to set aside all your other work. How would you handle the situation?

- What alternatives might you have?

- What would you tell your supervisor?

- What steps could you take to prevent this from occurring in the future?

Candidate Observations

- Does the candidate take advantage of slow times to catch up on work or prepare for busy times?

- Does the candidate recognize past mistakes and learn from them (shortcuts, less-than-expected results due to too little effort)?

Teamwork Orientation

Attribute: Has experience working as a member of a team and actively participates in an effort to accomplish the group's goals.

Q. Most of the work in this organization is accomplished by teams of workers. Please describe the most recent project you have worked on as a part of a team.

- Was the project successful?

- What was your main contribution as a team member?

- What did you like best about being a member of the team?

- What did you like least about being a member of the team?

- In your opinion, would the project results have been better if the work had been performed by individuals? If so, why?

Q. Not all teams function well together. Tell me about a time when a team you were involved with had problems getting its work done.

- What was the nature of the problem?

- How was the problem resolved?

- What part did you take in resolving the problem?

- How could the problem have been avoided?

Q. Tell me about a time when you had a personal conflict with another member of your work team.

- How did the conflict arise?

- How did you deal with the conflict?

- How did the other team members react?

- What would you do differently in the future?

- What did you learn from the experience?

Q. Tell me about the most challenging problem you solved as a member of a work team.

- As a group, how did you come up with solutions to the problem?

- How did you test out the solutions?

- What did the group do when there was disagreement among group members?

- What contribution did you make to the group effort that made you feel the most proud?

Q. Suppose a member of your work team doesn't pull his or her weight. How would you address the problem?

- Why would you address the problem in that way?

- Can you think of any alternative solutions?

- Is there a point at which you would bring the problem to the attention of the supervisor? If so, at what point?

Q. Please describe any specialized training you have had in group dynamics, group problem solving, or small group relations.

- When did you have this training?

- What was the training setting?

- Give an example of how this training has helped you on the job.

Candidate Observations

- Does the candidate have varied experience working as a member of a team?

- Does the candidate demonstrate an ability to solve problems in a group setting?

Openness to Learning

Attribute: Is open to learning, development, and retraining.

Q. Please describe what you do to stay abreast of new developments in your field.

- Of these activities, which do you accomplish while at work, and which, if any, do you engage in outside of work?

- Which of these activities are most valuable to you?

- Of these activities, which do you like doing the least? Why?

Q. It seems that just about everyone is short on time. If you had the extra time, would you be interested in taking a class or attending a seminar and, if so, what would the topic be?

- Do you already know something about this topic?

- What is it about this topic that you find interesting?

- Do you have a second choice for a topic? If so, what is the second topic?

Q. Tell me about the last training course or class you have attended.

- What type of course was this (college, work related, personal enrichment)?

- What did you gain from the course?

- Do you feel the course was worth the time and effort you put into it? In what way?

Q. What is the next training course you intend to take?

- What type of course will this be (college, work related, personal enrichment)?

- When do you expect to take the course?

- What do you expect to gain from the course?

Creative Thinking

Attribute: Is imaginative and broad-minded.

Q. Sometimes traditional work methods don't solve some of the unusual problems that can arise at work. Tell me about the most innovative solution you had for solving a problem at work.

- How did you come up with this idea?

- How did your supervisor react to your idea?

- How did your co-workers react?

- Did you meet with any resistance?

- Did implementation of the idea go smoothly, or did you have to make adjustments? If so, in what way?

- Were you recognized or rewarded for this effort? If so, how?

- What did you learn from the experience?

Q. Now tell me about a time when you tried an innovative solution to a problem and the results were unsuccessful.

- What went wrong?

- What could you have done differently?

- How did your supervisor react?

- What did you learn from the experience?

Q. Suppose an employee offers an unusual method of performing a certain task. How would you evaluate the feasibility of implementing this method?

- Why would you respond in that way?

- How do you think the employee would feel toward your response?

- How do you think your supervisor would react to your decision?

Q. Suppose that a particular problem crops up frequently during the course of daily operations and the cause is nearly always the same. However, this time when the problem occurs, a new employee points out an underlying cause to the problem which has not been considered before. How would you respond to this new information?

- Why would you respond in that way?

- How would you investigate the new information?

Candidate Considerations

- Does the candidate demonstrate an open-minded approach to decision making and problem solving?

- Does the candidate seek out novel approaches to work problems?

Skill in Written Communication

Attribute: Is skilled in preparing clear and concise written communications.

Q. As a manager, there will be many occasions when it will be necessary for you to prepare written reports detailing your work unit's progress on projects. Thinking back to your previous job, tell me about the best-written work report you have done.

- When was this report written (for example, was it recently)?
- What made this an exceptionally good report (topic, content)?
- What did your supervisor say about the report?

Q. Describe any course you have had either in school or at work that has helped you to improve your writing skills.

- When did you take this course?
- Where was this course given (college, at work)?
- What did you learn that helped you the most?
- What was the least helpful aspect of the course?

Q. At one time or another, almost all of us have had a report returned to us for corrections or revisions. Tell me about a time when your supervisor returned one of your reports to you for corrections.

- What was the nature of the report?
- What kind of errors were there?
- Did you agree with your supervisor's comments about the report? If not, why not?
- What steps did you take to improve the report?
- What did you learn from the experience?

Q. Describe any articles or reports you have written which have been published or distributed outside of your normal work area (such as published in journals, company newsletter).

- What was the topic of the report?
- When was it written?
- What type of feedback did you get about the report?

Index